*American Architecture 1607–1976*

*Marcus Whiffen*
*and Frederick Koeper*

# AMERICAN ARCHITECTURE
# 1607–1976

The MIT Press
Cambridge, Massachusetts

This book was set in VIP Aldus and VIP Palatino Bold Italic by DEKR Corporation and printed and bound by Halliday Lithograph in the United States of America.

Library of Congress Cataloging in Publication Data

Whiffen, Marcus.
  American architecture, 1607–1976.

  Bibliography:  p.
  Includes index.
  1.  Architecture—United States.  I.  Koeper, Frederick, joint author.  II.  Title.
NA705.W473      720′.973      80-23251
ISBN 0-262-23105-0

*To Inge*

# Contents

# *Foreword*

The American architecture of the title of this book is architecture in that part of the North American continent which before the admission of Hawaii and Alaska to the Union constituted the geographical entity of the United States. Thus the adjective *American* is applied in a purely geographical sense to what was created—most obviously in colonial times, but no less in more recent—by men of many diverse national origins and cultures.

Can *American*, applied to architecture, have another sense? That is to say, does American architecture, as the product of the special conditions of a geographical area and the needs and beliefs and ideals of its inhabitants, have qualities that distinguish it from other architectures of the western world, so that we might remark, for instance, that such-and-such a building is "very American"? The pursuit of national characteristics in the arts has led some of the best scholars and critics on to perilous quicksands of generalization. Yet the question is one that the reader may fairly expect some thoughts on, if not a definitive answer to.

The fact that for the greater part of its history American architecture has been dependent on external sources, generally European, for both tradition and innovation should make it easier to detect the specifically American elements in it, if there are any. It is not easy. The church architecture of Spanish New Mexico was unique, and so was the eighteenth-century domestic architecture of the French Mississippi Valley. But both were regional developments and therefore provide no clues to Americanness. British colonial architecture, however, does have a characteristic that may fairly be called American. The wooden houses of seventeenth-century New England are perceptibly more spacious, with higher rooms, than their counterparts in the mother country. The same is true of the eighteenth-century houses of the South. None of them is really large by the English standards of the age; many of them are almost noble in scale. Singleton Moorehead of the Williamsburg restoration used to show visiting architects an elevation of the George Wythe House, a typical "double pile" built about 1750, and ask them to sketch a man at the front door. The men depicted were never less than seven feet tall. Is it permissible to see here the beginning of that enlargement of scale which by the early twentieth century had made the centers of New York and Chicago virtually different in kind from any city in Europe? The early New England house was more spacious because of the abundance of timber, no doubt. But that is no argument against the connection, for it must have been the vast forests of the new continent that implanted in the minds of the first settlers that faith in the limitlessness of natural resources which until very recently was an integral and conspicuous part of the American mentality, and to which the optimism that inspired the unprecedented scale of American cities was in great part due.

A clean-cut clarity of external form, without wings, porches, or other excrescences, is another characteristic of the colonial house which recurs often enough—for example, in the temple-form buildings of the Greek Revival, in the "neo-formalist" buildings of the 1950s and 1960s, and in an extreme degree in certain buildings discussed in the last chapter of this book—to encourage one to risk the attachment of the adjective American to it. Certainly Frank Lloyd Wright recognized it as an American characteristic when he set out to "eliminate the box" and give America an architecture embodying his own conception of space. Or was it an *American* conception of space, hitherto unformulated in architectural terms, which he revealed to his countrymen? One American critic has written: "The conception of space as flowing with a ground line, wherein the architectural shelter is only a more defined and more complex part of a great continuous whole, is as foreign to European thought as their conception of space as an isolated volume is to ours."[1] If this contention is true—and there are many twentieth-century buildings that could be cited in evidence, as well as the importance of the road as an image and metaphor in American literature—the difference described may surely be accounted for by the sheer size of America and the seeming endlessness of its landscapes, which even today are unimaginable by Europeans who have not experienced them.

Empiricism and pragmatism are often named as typically American attitudes of mind. Empirical considerations must play a part in the design of any building; nevertheless a good case can be made for the view that American architects have been more empirically-minded than their European colleagues. At the highest level Wright, in his insistence on the integration of house and site, was an empiricist, however he might try to idealize his approach to design as organicism; by contrast, Le Corbusier was undismayed when an Indian client sold the working drawings for a house and it was built in another place, for he always designed his Indian houses, he said, for the sun and prevailing winds of India and not for individual sites. However, it is in the history of the structural system that made possible that entirely American creation, the skyscraper, that evidence of the prevalence of empiricism, with its limitations, may most easily be seen. The metal frame was introduced in Chicago by Jenney, an engineer by training. It was accepted gladly by the architects of high buildings as a means of lightening them—that is, as an empirical device. Not one of these architects gave it any thought as an architectural form with its own esthetic; the greatest, Sullivan, in his finest buildings concealed it within an envelope that obeyed the classical rules of composition. It was left to architects in Europe to recognize its spatial implications, and it was a European, Mies van der Rohe, who made it the most subtle modulator of architectural design since the Greek and Roman orders and who employed it as such in a number of masterpieces in the city of its youth.

The reader of the following pages will doubtless arrive at generalizations of his own, perhaps more valid than the authors'. He will find that, as is necessary in a book of this scope if it is to be more than a chronicle, the treatment of the subject is a compromise between the chronological and the thematic; different aspects of a period are sometimes dealt with in separate chapters and there are some considerable overlappings of time. The reader will also find that in order to avoid overloading the text with dates, those of the birth and death of all architects mentioned in it who built in America are, when known, given in the index, while to save him from disappointments of a kind so often experienced by lovers of architecture visiting new places the fact that a building no longer exists is indicated there too. (Such disappointments cannot be prevented altogether; although the rage for destruction may have abated as a result of recent legislation and changed attitudes, important buildings disappear every week.) If the reader gains pleasure or profit from the book, he should be grateful, as are the authors, to all those whose help has made it a better book than it would have been without it, especially Cynthia F. Cobb, who drew all the plans in part I except those reproduced from architects' originals; Diane Gingold, who searched for photographs in the Library of Congress; William H. Pierson, Jr., who was most generous with his excellent photographs; Julian Silva, who read part II in manuscript and made suggestions relating to matters of style; and Robert L. Sweeney, who helped in matters relating to twentieth-century architects in general and Frank Lloyd Wright in particular.

# I    *1607–1860*

*Marcus Whiffen*

"The Towne itself by the care and providence of Sir Thomas Gates is reduced into a handsome forme, and hath in it two faire rowes of howses, all of framed timber, two stories, and an upper Garret, or Corne loft high." The town was Jamestown, the year 1615. There could be no better illustration of the general rule that the prime object of settlers in a new land is to reproduce as nearly as possible the living conditions of their old, to build themselves homes away from home, than that the first permanent British settlement in America should have had row houses, of the form (as archaeology has confirmed) of the English urban unit-house, about twice as deep as it was broad and with rooms back and front on each floor. The type had been developed in medieval towns where space was restricted—that is, for conditions that could only be produced artificially on the edge of the vast American continent. As one writer has remarked, "in English minds Jamestown was to be a city of continuous and adjacent habitations, like Oxford and Chipping Camden."[1] And, one might add, London. Early in the eighteenth century, the Reverend Hugh Jones, who had been professor of mathematics at William and Mary, noted: "The habits, life, customs, computations, etc. of the Virginians are much the same as about London, which they esteem their home." No doubt it had been so from the early days of the colony.

Row houses were specified in Lord Baltimore's instructions for laying out St. Mary's City, capital of Maryland, in 1634, but few were built. In the seventeenth century all but a handful of Americans lived in free-standing dwellings. At first these neither stood very high nor were constructed of such materials as to stand very long. Several primitive types were employed in the early days of settlement. The three commonest seem to have been, first, the cabin, with walls of wattle and daub (woven osier withies coated with mud) and a thatched roof whose ridgepole was supported by cratchets (forked posts); second, the English wigwam, with a framework of poles bent over into hoop form and thatched—the thatch and a door and a wooden chimney distinguishing it from the Indian wigwam with its smoke hole and covering of mats or bark skins; and third, the dugout. The use and manner of construction of the last were described by a New England settler: "They burrow themselves in the Earth for their first shelter under some Hill side, casting the Earth aloft upon Timber; they make a smoaky fire against the Earth at its highest side. . . . yet in these poor *Wigwames* they sing Psalms, pray, and praise their God till they can provide them houses." (Wigwam is here used as a generic term for any primitive dwelling.)

Even if the English wigwam owed its form as well as its name to the Indians—a moot point—all the techniques employed in it were known in rural England, where in the seventeenth century houses of various primitive types were still home to countrymen in remote districts. In any case settlers of all classes were soon able to move up to better things. Our authority for the New England dugout recorded the improvement in the Massachusetts Bay Colony in 1654: "The Lord hath been pleased to turn all the wigwams, huts, and hovels the English dwelt in at their first coming into orderly, fair and well built houses."

*Building with Wood*

Not every settler might have been ready to recognize the direct participation of the Almighty in the provision of housing; none could deny that He had been most munificent in providing the new continent with the traditional building material of England, wood. The great majority of the "well built houses" of British America, in the South as well as in New England, were timber-framed in the seventeenth century and for long after. Most Americans preferred frame houses to those of masonry. Thomas Jefferson, toward the end of the eighteenth century, complained of "the unhappy prejudice . . . that houses of brick or stone" were "less wholesome than those of wood," while as late as the mid-nineteenth century the prejudice found expression on certain Texas plantations where the slave quarters were built of the admirable local limestone and the great house was built of timber laboriously hauled overland from the port of Galveston.

The traditional English house frame, as used in America for two and a half centuries, was a work of art rather than science. Although its parts—sills, posts, studs, joists, girts, summers, and plates—were graded in size or scantling according to their functions, the stability of the whole derived in the final analysis from the carpenter's skill in cutting and fitting the joints—mortice and tenon, tusk and tenon, dovetail lap, fastened with wooden pegs or treenails—and to a degree from the sheer weight of material rather than from adherence to structural principles. The use of diagonal bracing was minimal, being limited usually to a pair of braces to each corner post. In seventeenth-century New England the walls of frame houses were sometimes covered with plaster, sometimes with flush siding, more often with wooden shingles; before the end of the century clapboards, made by splitting rather than sawing the log, were in general use. In the South sawn boards, which had the advantage of greater length and breadth, were the rule, split boards being employed only for service buildings. (All boards nailed to walls with an overlap, split or sawn, were called clapboards.)

On roofs thatch was soon superseded by shingles, which became the commonest roof covering, north and south. Their use represented a return to earlier English practice, for shingles had been a common roof covering in the Middle Ages until the rising price of wood led to the substitution of earthen tiles and stone slates. Two forms of roof were in general use, the steep-pitched **A** roof and the gambrel, which has two slopes on each side. Roof frames were broadly divisible into two classes, those having framed principals, or trusses, and those which had common rafters only. They were much more varied than house frames. In trussed roofs not only was there the choice between the king-post truss (with a single vertical post from the tie beam to the ridge), the queen-post truss (with two posts), and the simple truss without any post at all but with a collar or wind beam; there were also different ways of relating the purlins (the horizontal members joining the trusses) to the rafters and distributing the diagonal braces which stiffened the frame longitudinally. In making his choices the colonial carpenter might be influenced by individual preference or regional practice—regional here being understood to refer to England as well as to America. For example, the unusual position of the braces in the roof of the Fairbanks House (1637) the oldest wooden house in America, was standard practice in that part of East Anglia from which the Dedham carpenters came. The only feature of the colonial roof frame that can be described as un-English is a negative one, namely, the omission of the ridgepole. It was an omission that followed logically, or at least commonsensically, from the abandonment of thatch, which needs a ridgepole to hang from.

*Regional Differences*        When we turn from the construction of the seventeenth-century house in the British colonies to its plan and general design, it becomes more difficult to generalize; significant differences between New England and the South force themselves upon the attention. What can be said of both regions is that when a house had one room only, as many of the early houses did, that room was always called the hall, and when it had two the second was nearly always called the parlor. The hall was the original all-purpose room of the early medieval English house, retained as the essential nucleus in all elaborations of plan. In houses in the country its long axis lay parallel with the front of the house and it was entered near one end, the "lower" end, through one of its long sides; the chimney stood at the other, "upper" end. The parlor was described by a seventeenth-century English author as "a fair lower Room designed for the Entertainment of company"—which did not prevent it containing a bed, in England or America. The term, of monastic provenance, had come into use in the fourteenth century in the Midlands and the North; in southern England, where the two-room house became common rather earlier, the second room had been called the chamber since the twelfth century. South-of-England usage was occasionally followed in the colonies, as inventories show, but where there is no indication to the contrary it may be assumed that a chamber was a bedroom on the upper floor.

In the location of the parlor New England and the South differed radically. In New England the parlor adjoined the upper end of the hall, with which it shared a massive axial chimney; in the South it was placed at the lower end and had its own chimney. Both arrangements had English precedents. The New England plan originated in Essex and East Anglia as a product of the housing revolution which brought about so great an improvement in rural living conditions in the reign of Elizabeth I. In England there remain transitional examples in which entrance is still directly into the hall after the medieval fashion; the placing of the door in the center of the front opposite the chimney made for convenience, providing as it did easy access from outside to the hall, parlor, and stairs; it also facilitated the achievement of external symmetry, which by the seventeenth century had come to be valued even in relatively modest houses. The gable-end chimneys of the South, with their tapered offsets, were probably introduced by builders from the West Midlands, for such chimneys were characteristics of the farmhouses of that region. External symmetry was no problem in the southern type, since the door at the lower end of the hall naturally fell in the middle of the front. (Nonetheless, approximate symmetry was often considered good enough.) In early houses, such as the Adam Thoroughgood House near Norfolk, Virginia, the stair was in the hall, opposite the front door (1). A major improvement was effected when a partition was built across the lower end of the hall and the stair placed in the passage so formed. This resulted in the hall-passage-parlor plan of innumerable houses in the South built in colonial times and well into the nineteenth century.

In the early days plans were not as standardized by region as they became later; central-chimney houses were built in the South and, if more rarely, end-chimney houses in New England. It was, no doubt, a matter of the survival of the fittest, with climate as the chief determinant. In the northeastern winters the chimney of the New England house could warm two rooms on each floor—three on the

*1
Adam Thoroughgood
House, Princess Anne
County, Virginia. 1636.
View from southwest.*

first floor when a kitchen lean-to was added to the basic plan—while the passage through the middle of the Southern house created, as Hugh Jones observed in 1724, "an air-draught in summer." That is to say, the key to the success of the one plan was central heating; of the other, central cooling.

The buildings that stand today do not give a true picture of seventeenth-century housing in either New England or in the South, for it is always the better houses that tend to survive. One thinks of the two-storied Capen and Boardman houses as "typical of New England," and in one sense they are; yet such houses were certainly outnumbered by those of one or one and a half stories. Then brick is a material with greater powers of survival than wood, and in the South nearly all the seventeenth-century houses that have survived are of brick, although most Southern houses were of wood throughout the colonial period. (It is true that there were always more brick houses in the South than in New England.)

North and south, seventeenth-century houses were only one room deep under the main roof; if there was a second range of rooms at the back it was sheltered by a lean-to or shed roof, resulting in what in New England came to be known as the salt box house (2, 3). (The

2
*Boardman House, Saugus,
Massachusetts. Circa
1686. West end.*

3
*Boardman House, Saugus,
Massachusetts. Plan
of first floor.*

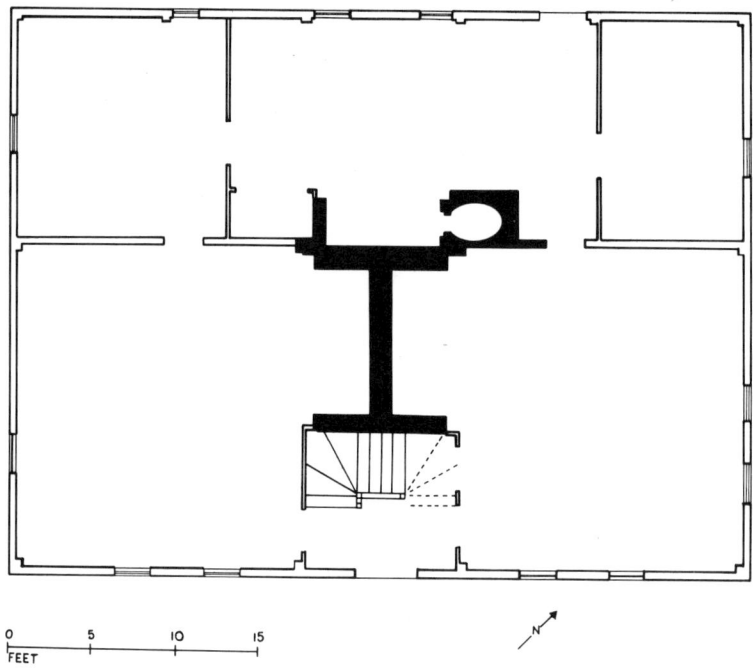

0    5    10    15
FEET

N

three known exceptions to the rule, two in New England and one in the South, will be mentioned presently.) North and south, they present themselves, compositionally, as arrangements of rectangles and triangles. Much of their character derived from their steep-pitched roofs, especially when, as in the John Ward House at Salem, Massachusetts, there were cross gables (4). In general, the upper parts of the New England house were more complex and had a greater visual impact than the ground story. A feature that often contributed to this was the framed overhang or jetty, in which the girts projected a foot or more beyond the wall below to carry the second-floor posts and wall frame. It is a feature about whose origin and purpose there has been much dispute. It may have been devised to avoid weakening the girts by making mortices in them from three directions at one point to receive the tenons of another girt and the first- and second-floor posts; in town houses it could be used to "steal" space over the street, whether or not this was its first func-

*4*
*John Ward House, Salem, Massachusetts. 1684 (west half) and later. View from southwest.*

tion. But in many cases the reason for its use must have been esthetic. That this was so is suggested by the random way in which jetties were disposed—sometimes on all four sides of a house, sometimes on two or three, sometimes on one only—and above all by the fact that they were rarely used after taste changed in the eighteenth century. The same is true of the hewn overhang, in which a much slighter projection of the upper story was produced by cutting away the lower part of the two-story posts and carving the transition between the upper and lower parts into the semblance of a bracket.

*Some Notable Houses*

In the Southern house chimney offsets and dormer windows went some way toward supplying the complexity achieved in New England with cross gables and jetties. In the seventeenth century Southern architecture was more varied than that of New England, and a number of houses that depart in one way or another from the ubiquitous hall-and-parlor and hall-passage-parlor types still survive (or survived long enough to be recorded) or are known from excavation. The so-called Governor's Castle at St. Mary's City, Maryland, built in 1634–39, was the most unusual. A brick structure of two stories, exactly square on plan, it had eight rooms on the ground floor grouped with a military symmetry; it is possible to regard it as the first American example of a "double-pile" house, though its plan has an arbitrary quality which gives it more in common with the architectural "conceits" of the sixteenth century than with the standard double-pile house of the eighteenth. Another two-story house of considerable size by American standards was Sir William Berkeley's Green Spring, near Jamestown, built around 1646. This was a long shallow house with a central chimney between the hall and parlor. A sketch made by the architect Latrobe in 1796 shows that it had a porch with a shaped gable of the kind to be seen in Bacon's Castle.

Bacon's Castle was built around 1655 by one Arthur Allen, who had arrived from England in 1649, and takes its name from Nathaniel Bacon of the 1676 Rebellion (5, 6). It is a house that might have been built in England at any time during the first four decades of the century. The shaped gable was a feature which reached England from the Low Countries just before 1600; the rows of chimney stacks, set diagonally, had a longer history going back to a time in the sixteenth century when chimneys were still relatively rare and a display of them denoted wealth and superior social status. The placing of the stairs in a tower, which balances the two-story porch and turns the plan into a cross, was a medieval arrangement that persisted down to the reign of James I; their form, that of the open-well staircase, did not appear in England until that reign.

5
*Bacon's Castle, Surry County, Virginia. Circa 1655. From west.*

6
*Bacon's Castle, Surry County, Virginia. Plan of first floor.*

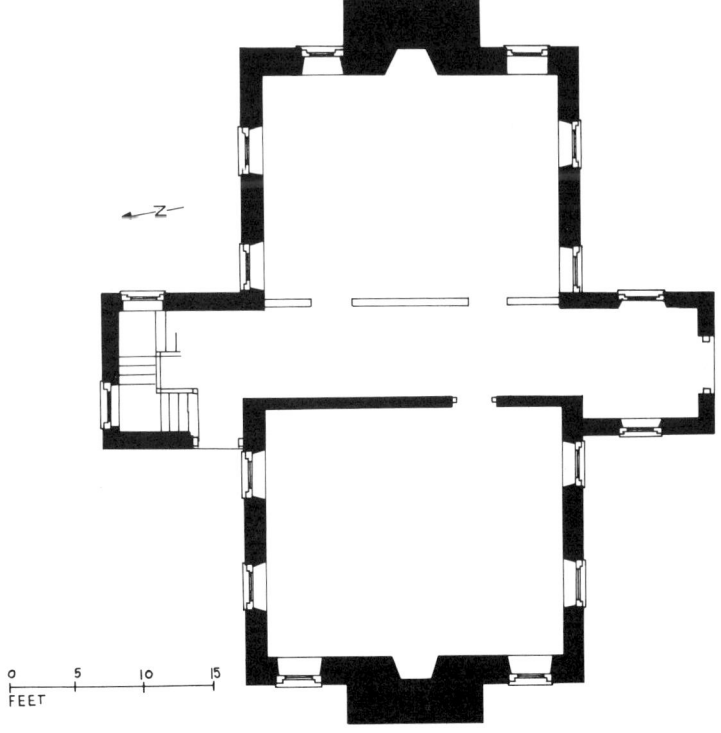

Two other seventeenth-century houses still standing in Virginia have porches with chambers above: Foster's Castle and Christ's Cross, both in New Kent County and built around 1690. They are both of brick, as was Malvern Hall in Henrico County, but the finest seventeenth-century house in the South, after Bacon's Castle, to have survived into the twentieth century was of wood. Bond Castle, in Calvert County, Maryland, was built sometime in the last quarter of the century. It had a two-story porch on either front with jettied sides and gables; the stairs were in the central passage. In its final form Bond Castle had a second parlor or chamber at one end and a kitchen at the other. This is a late example of the kitchen being incorporated in the house itself; in the eighteenth century the outhouse kitchen became the rule—a return to medieval practice encouraged by slave-owning.

With the exception of the Governor's Castle at St. Mary's, classifiable only as a sport, these houses in Virginia and Maryland are all late examples of an English tradition of house design that was at least as old as the century. In New England, the 1670s saw the building of three brick houses, which, in that they were two rooms deep under the main roof and thus "double piles," were closer to contemporary developments in the mother country. The Peter Sergeant House in Boston, completed by 1679, was large but, with its shaped gables and diamond chimneys, distinctly old-fashioned. The Peter Tufts House at Medford, which was under construction in 1675, is, with its gambrel roof, end chimneys in the thickness of the wall, and two rooms on either side of the central passage on each floor, far more prophetic of the shape of things to come, or more precisely of the shape of countless eighteenth-century houses from Maine to South Carolina.

The Boston house of the rich merchant John Foster, which in the eighteenth century came into the possession of Governor Thomas Hutchinson, was a much grander affair—very grand indeed for its time and place. Built in 1689–92, it had Ionic pilasters, of Portland stone, rising through its three stories on the street front—the first giant order in the English colonies. The discontinuance of the frieze and architrave between the pilasters to accommodate the third-story windows was a device frequently employed in the English Baroque of the early eighteenth century, but in all other respects the house represented a type of classicism owing much to Holland which had flourished in England for fifty years. The garlanded pilaster capitals, which must have been carved in England, can be paralleled in numerous buildings of the middle third of the seventeenth century in England and Holland; the cantilevered balcony was a feature more common in Holland than in England. Until 1765, when it was hacked down by a mob protesting the Stamp Act, a cupola intensified the Dutch character of the building.

In Philadelphia the largest seventeenth-century house was of H-form plan. Owned by the merchant Samuel Carpenter, on account of the rarity in America of the material used for its roof it came to be known as the Slate Roof House. It was designed and built, around 1690, by James Portues, a house carpenter who, like many colonial craftsmen, came from England as an indentured servant and set up on his own when he had satisfied the terms of his contract. With hipped roofs, Flemish-bond brickwork, and a pedimented doorway, the Slate Roof House showed a close adherence to London building practices in a city which was to continue to adhere to them more closely than any other in America.

*Public Buildings in the English Colonies*

For a monumental public architecture there was no call; nor would the means have been available if there had been. Most of the public buildings of the English colonies in the seventeenth century had a decidedly domestic air; many were to all appearance simply bigger though not necessarily better houses and few had any features not to be found in houses too. This is no matter for surprise, for nearly all—the Anglican churches of the South are the chief exceptions—are descended from English domestic ancestors.

A building which, with its dual function, bridged the gap between the domestic and the public was the New England garrison house. This served as a private dwelling in times of peace and as a fort and place of refuge for as many of the community as it would hold during Indian attacks. Outwardly there was little to distinguish garrison houses from other houses. Some of them, however, were built of logs sawn square and dovetailed at the corners, a technique introduced by Scottish settlers; the McIntire Garrison House at Scotland, Maine, is a two-story example from about 1707 (7, 8). A rarer type of fortified dwelling, which resembles the bawn or "strong house" required by law in the English settlements in Ireland, is represented by the stone-built Henry Whitefield House at Guilford, Connecticut, of which the oldest part was built in 1639–40.

The essential public building in every New England community was the meeting house. The earliest New England meeting houses were outwardly indistinguishable from dwellings (9). However, a distinctive solution to the architectural problem, which was to provide for secular meetings as well as religious worship with a building that should be both the symbolic and the physical center of the town, came into use around the middle of the century: a square structure

7
*McIntire Garrison House,
Scotland, Maine. Circa
1707. From southwest.*

8
*McIntire Garrison House,
Scotland, Maine. Plan of
first floor.*

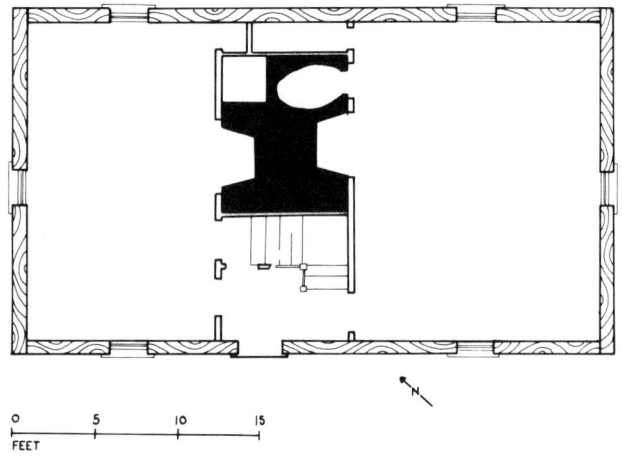

9
*Second Meeting House,
Sudbury, Massachusetts.
1653. Conjectural restora-
tion by Marion C.
Donnelly.*

10
*Old Ship Meeting House,
Hingham, Massachustts.
1681. Conjectural restora-
tion by Marion C.
Donnelly.*

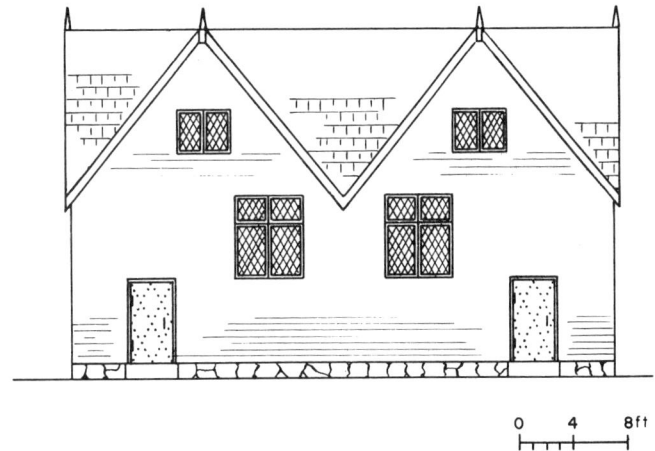

0   4   8ft

0   4   8ft

*11*
*Old Brick Church (St. Luke's), Isle of Wight County, Virginia. 1632 and (top stage of tower) after 1657. View from southwest.*

*12*
*Old Brick Church, Isle of Wight County, Virginia. Plan.*

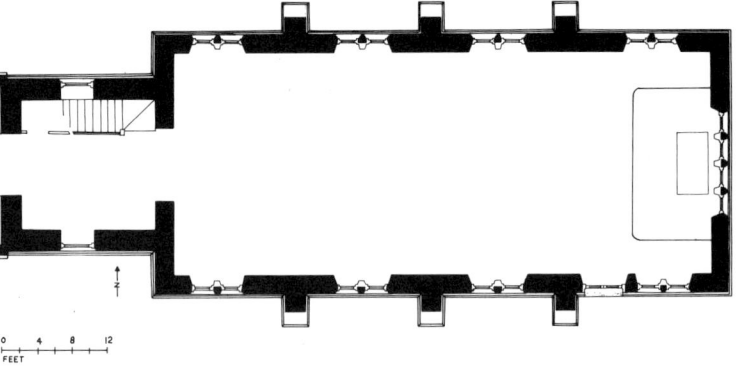

with a high hipped roof surmounted by a platform and belfry, its interior a single room with fixed benches and more often than not one or more galleries. The type was an adaptation of the English market hall—an adaptation, not an exact copy, for the English market hall was normally of two stories, with the ground story open on all four sides to the street or square to provide a covered space for the display and sale of produce and wares. (The first Boston Town House, built in 1657–58, was a substantial example on this side of the Atlantic.) In the meeting house there was no function for the open ground story and it was therefore omitted—much as in the Early Christian basilica of Western Christendom the galleries of the Roman civil basilica were omitted for want of a function. The English market hall was itself an adaptation of a type of house, built in England from Anglo-Saxon times to the fifteenth century in both town and country, with the living quarters on the second floor above a ground-floor storage cellar; in the market hall the walls of the cellar were omitted.

The only surviving seventeenth-century meeting house in New England is the Old Ship Meeting House at Hingham, Massachusetts, so called because its roof structure resembles an inverted ship's hull (10). It was built in 1681, enlarged in 1729 and again in 1755, when it also received a new belfry and porches; these additions, together with a restoration in 1930, have resulted in a building that cannot be regarded as typical. In the South, the architectural relics of the seventeenth-century Church of England are not much less rare; those still standing above ground amount to one church and a church tower in Virginia and one church in Maryland. All are of brick; not a single example of the churches of wooden frame construction, which constituted the great majority, has survived in the South from the entire colonial period. The most important is Newport Parish Church, or the Old Brick Church, near Smithfield, Virginia (11, 12).

The Old Brick Church is a remarkable building to have been begun a mere quarter of a century after the settlement of Jamestown, twenty miles upstream. It could easily be a parish church in an English county where brick was used for want of a suitable local stone. Here we have, in fact, the home-away-from-home ideal most completely realized in ecclesiastical terms. In England very few churches had been built since the Reformation; the country was amply provided with medieval churches and these were made over to accommodate the new liturgy. Gothic was therefore still the natural style for a church, and was to continue to be so in English eyes until Sir Christopher Wren invented classical paradigms for Anglican architecture in response to the need created by the Great Fire of

London in 1666. With its buttresses, pointed arches, and tracery, the Old Brick Church is essentially Gothic, an example of that survival which in England was to overlap the conscious revival of the medieval style. As for the crow-stepped gable, that was a feature which had reached England from Holland in the second half of the fifteenth century—well before the end of the Gothic era—and by this time was so thoroughly assimilated into English architecture that the builder of the church probably never thought of it as Dutch; in England a similar use of it is to be seen in the parish church of Woodham Walter, Essex, which was built in 1563. Yet the Old Brick Church is not without classical touches too: in the tower entrance with its round arch and triangular pediment, in the uppermost stage of the tower, which was built after 1657, and in the quoins that were added to the lower stages to the tower at the same time. An all-pervading naivety softens the contrast.

Buttresses, five a side, were also features of the first brick church of Bruton Parish, built at Middle Plantation (later Williamsburg) in 1683. A crude copy of a sketch made by a Swiss traveler in 1702 shows that it had a shaped gable of Anglo-Flemish type at the west end. In Dorchester County, Maryland, Trinity Church, probably of about the same date, has an apse, uncommon in English church architecture of its period. St. Mary's Chapel in St. Mary's City, built half a century earlier in 1634–38, was the first Roman Catholic church built by Englishmen in the New World. It had a Latin-cross plan and (as the finding of a mullion brick on the site has established) casement windows, but nothing is known of its general appearance. None of these churches had towers; besides the Old Brick Church, the only seventeenth-century churches in the South with towers were the first Chuckatuck church in Nansemond County, Virginia, and the first brick church at Jamestown, built in 1639–44, to which a tower was added in the very last year of the century. As for the frame churches, these were simple oblong buildings, about twice as long as they were broad, with the longer axis running east and west in conformity with Anglican practice.

Some of the most ambitious buildings of the colonial period served the needs of higher education. The first building for Harvard, the Old College, was built in 1638–42—but not very well, for in 1655 the then president described it as being "in a very ruinous condition" and it was demolished in 1678. It was wood-framed, with an E plan, and doubtless looked much like an English manor house of the later sixteenth century. Its replacement was the New College, or Harvard Hall, built in 1674–77. The external appearance of this is known from a print of 1726 by William Burgis. It was of brick and had a

gambrel roof with dormers and cross gables; the doors were flanked
by ball-topped pilasters in molded brick and there were some other
would-be classical features. If it stood in England, one would assign
it to the first rather than the second half of the seventeenth century.
Of the appearance of the Indian College at Harvard, built in 1654–
56 and demolished in 1698, nothing is known. That of Stoughton
Hall, built in 1698–99 and demolished in 1781, is well recorded in
the Burgis print. It was as classical as the Hutchinson House, but its
fenestration with windows of two different widths (the narrower
lighting the studies partitioned off from the keeping rooms) and
three different widths of wall between them, gave its facade a quasi
Mannerist variety.

The stylistic character of the only seventeenth-century collegiate
building in the South, the first building of the College of William
and Mary, is hard to determine, since the only record we have of its
outward appearance is a copy of a sketch by the Swiss traveler who
sketched the Bruton Parish Church of 1683. It was begun in 1695 at
Middle Plantation, which in 1699 was renamed Williamsburg and
became the capital of Virginia in succession to Jamestown, and finished in 1700. In 1705 it burned, though most of the walls survived
the fire to be incorporated in the rebuilding, to Governor Alexander
Spotswood's design, in 1710–16. It was to have been a square of 138
feet on plan, with a central court as in the colleges of Oxford and
Cambridge but much smaller in proportion to the total area. Only
the east range and the hall, which would have formed the center of
the north range, were built. The east range was a full story higher
than that of its Spotswood successor and had no central projection;
it did have a second-floor balcony in the middle of the front. So
much is certain.

What is not certain is that this first building of William and Mary
was designed by Wren, despite the categorical statement in Hugh
Jones's book of 1724 that it was "first modelled by Sir *Christopher
Wren*, adapted to the Nature of the Country by the Gentlemen
there." Telling against the attribution is the propagandist nature of
Jones's book, on which he was working when Wren's great funeral
in St. Paul's Cathedral could have suggested his name as one to
conjure with, and the absence of any evidence that Thomas Hadley,
who came from England to be "surveyor" of the building, had
worked for Wren. For it, there are the considerations that the College
was a royal foundation, for which Wren might have been asked to
produce a design as Surveyor-General of the King's Works, and that
Virginia was a part of the diocese of the Bishop of London, whose
cathedral was even then being rebuilt to Wren's design.

13
*Capitol, Williamsburg, Virginia. 1701–15. View from north. From the so-called Bodleian Plate, a copper plate engraved in 1737 or soon after.*

Government buildings occupied little space in the seventeenth-century scene. Their character was thoroughly domestic. The first State House at Jamestown (ca. 1635), like many of the larger Elizabethan town houses in England, was a unit-house multiplied, in this case by three, with gables towards the street; the State House of 1676 at St. Mary's City had a cross-form plan with the porch balanced by a stair tower, like Bacon's Castle. State houses were, after all, simply houses for affairs of state. The first that could not have been taken for a house was in fact called by another name by the act of the Virginia Assembly that ordered its construction. This was the Capitol at Williamsburg, one of the only two buildings—the other was its successor of 1751–53—to be called capitols in the colonial period (13). The design was accepted in the last year of the century and the building went up in 1701–1705. It had two wings, one containing the House of Burgesses and clerk's office on the first floor with committee rooms above, the other the General Court and secretary's office with the Council Chamber and clerk's office above; the wings, which terminated to the south in semicircular tribunes, were linked by an arcaded loggia or "piazza" with a conference room above, and over the center rose a tall cupola of hexagonal plan.[2] It was an admirably functional design; the architect, whoever he was, had successfully freed himself from the house concept. Its sash windows were still quite a novelty even in England; the New York City Hall of 1699–1700, not dissimilar in many respects, still had casements. Yet the detail, the vocabulary of form, was domestic. And the classical orders, whose grandiloquence has so often in history been felt to be a sine qua non of governmental architecture, nowhere appeared. In fact they were not to appear as a major motif in the external design of any governmental building in the British colonies for another half-century.

*Dutch Colonial*

Both geography and the debt that English architecture owed to the Low Countries suggest that we turn to Dutch colonial architecture next. At once we meet a terminological inexactitude, for what we call Dutch colonial architecture has a much longer history than the Dutch colony of New Netherland, which was founded on paper with the chartering of the Dutch West India Company in Amsterdam in 1621 and practically with the building of a palisaded blockhouse and thirty bark-covered houses at New Amsterdam in 1626 and which ceased to exist when Peter Stuyvesant surrendered New Amsterdam to Colonel Richard Nicolls in 1664. Neither the change of rule under which New Netherland became New York and New Jersey nor the events that led to New York and New Jersey becoming independent states affected the development of the Dutch tradition of domestic architecture; nor was there any major change internal to that development such as occurred in British colonial architecture around 1700, and which in that case makes the separate treatment of the seventeenth and eighteenth centuries more than a matter of convenience.

*14
Stadthuys (later City
Tavern), New Amster-
dam. 1641–42. From a
lithograph by George
Hayward after a sketch
by Danckers.*

After very simple beginnings—besides the bark-covered houses there were "hovels and holes"—the Dutch of New Amsterdam lost

little time building a town which must have seemed to its inhabitants as truly a home away from home as any in any colony anywhere. A lithograph from a sketch by Danckers shows how like its parent city New Amsterdam must have been (14). In 1679, when the sketch was made, the building in the center had for a quarter of a century served as the *Stadthuys* or townhouse; it was built in 1641–42 as the City Tavern, in which capacity it was much frequented by the British sailing between New England and Virginia. It had crow-stepped gables, like all the other buildings depicted except one, which had a hipped roof—another item in the invoice of Dutch contributions to English architecture. The *Stadthuys* was of stone; it may be assumed that the other buildings were of brick, which the Dutch preferred to all other materials and in the use of which their skill was unsurpassed.

Not one example of the standard Dutch town house, tall and narrow with the entrance in the gable end toward the street, has survived in New York or in Albany. Of the type of house represented by the *Stadthuys* the largest extant example—though owing to Dutch bourgeois carefulness not really a large building to be the manor house of the vast estate of Rensselaerswyck, formerly the patroonship of a director of the West India Company—is Crailo at Rensselaer, which was built about 1704. With its walls laid up in cross bond and its straight-sided gables finished with *muisetanden* (mouse-teeth), Crailo shows Dutch brickwork at its most characteristic. Other houses of the type are the Bries House at East Greenbush (1723) and the Leendert Bronck House at West Coxsackie (ca. 1738). The Dutch made less of chimneys than the English did and the end chimneys of such houses always go up inside the walls.

In northern New Jersey and southern New York, including Long Island, the preponderant type of house was quite different. Low and broad, of one or one and a half stories under a gently sloping roof which projected at least two feet beyond the walls to the front and rear, it was built of stone or wood or a combination of the two but never, apparently, of brick. The type is not found in Holland, and a theory once advanced that it was brought from Flanders by Flemish Protestant emigrants to New Netherland was not well founded. Whatever its origin, its development can be followed in existing or recorded examples. In the seventeenth century the roof was of two slopes only, with a flare given to the eaves by furring extra pieces to the rafters. Around 1700 a distinctive gambrel roof, with short upper slopes of about half the pitch of the lower, which retained their flared eaves, came into use. Then in the last quarter of the eighteenth century the *stoep* or raised platform before the front door

15
*Dyckman House, New
York City. Circa 1783.
Southwest view.*

16
*Dyckman House, New
York City. Plan of princi-
pal floor.*

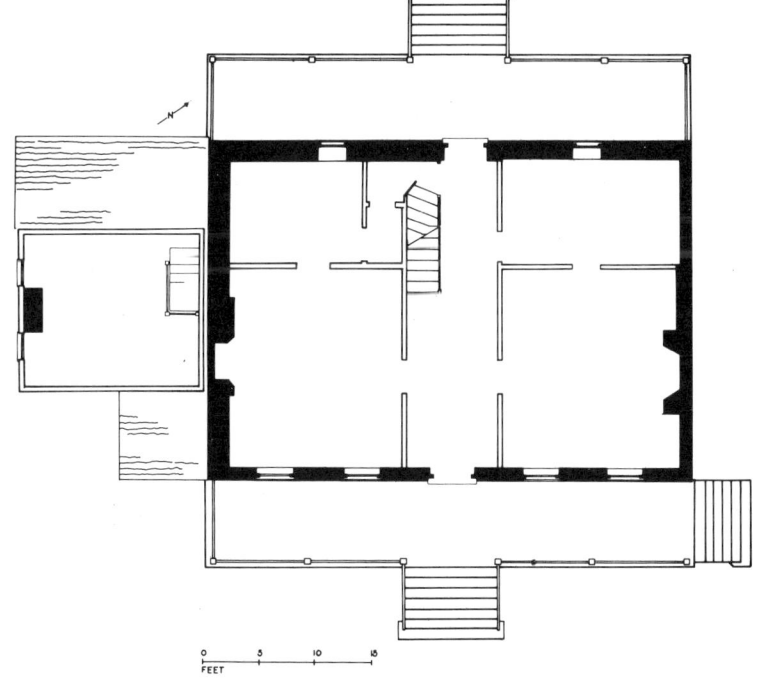

might be extended the full length of the house and posts added under the eaves, producing the equivalent of the English piazza or French *galerie* (15, 16).

Ecclesiastical architecture made a slow start in New Netherland. New Amsterdam itself had no regular church until 1642, when the need was filled by a building of stone, 72 feet by 52 feet on plan, paid for partly by subscription and partly with West India Company funds; the contractors were two Englishmen from Stamford, Connecticut. In the second half of the seventeenth century a number of octagonal churches were built; like John Wesley later, the Calvinists thought the octagon good for preaching. They were small, and were surrounded by tall candle-snuffer roofs. In the eighteenth century the Dutch in New Netherland reverted to the rectangular church plan. With its hipped roof and central cupola, the church built in 1715 at Albany looked much like a New England meeting house.

*New Sweden and the Germans in Pennsylvania*

Politically and economically, the colony of New Sweden on the Delaware River, which was chartered in 1636 and annexed by New Netherland seventeen years later, was the least successful of the attempts by European powers to stake their claims to a share of the American continent. And the only buildings of any size commissioned by Swedish communities that survive from the seventeenth century, the "Old Swedes" churches at Wilmington (1698–99) and Philadelphia (1698–1700), were both built by the same Philadelphia craftsmen, all born and trained in England. Yet the Swedes brought with them something that was to be of the greatest value as the course of empire took its way westward—the log cabin. In New England, garrison houses, as we have seen, were sometimes built of horizontal sawn logs, a Scottish technique. The construction of walls with round logs, notched at the corners and with projecting ends, was unknown in Britain, Holland, and France and never seen in America until the coming of the Swedes. On the frontier the log cabin so constructed was an ideal building, as it needed no nails and not much more skill with an axe than would normally be acquired in clearing a forest site. For two centuries, wherever wood was available, it was the frontiersman's first permanent dwelling.

The Germans, who settled in Pennsylvania in great number in the eighteenth century, were another people who had built with hewn logs in their homeland and continued to do so in America. Although concealed by clapboards, this is the method of construction of the *Saron* or Sister House, built in 1743 by a monastic community of the Seventh Day Baptists at Ephrata. The *Saron* and the adjoining *Saal* or Prayer House of 1740 are astonishing examples of the sur-

17
*The Cloister (Klosters),*
*Ephrata, Pennsylvania.*
*Left, the* Saal, *or house of*
*prayer, 1740; right, the*
Saaron, *or sisters' house,*
*1742–43.*

vival of medieval building forms into the mid-eighteenth century; the Cloister, as it is called, reminds one of the buildings in Dürer's engravings (17). Unlike the *Saron,* the *Saal* is a frame structure of oak with an infilling of stones and clay and a covering of clapboards. In other German buildings in Pennsylvania frame and infilling were left exposed to the weather as what in England would be called half-timber work—*fachwerkbau,* to give it its German name. Also a medieval technique, *fachwerkbau* was employed in German farm-houses in Wisconsin as late as the 1850s.

**The French in the**
**Mississippi Valley**

The French in their earliest buildings in North America employed a kind of construction with logs set upright in the ground. This was called *en pieux* in New France and *poteaux en terre* in the Mississippi valley settlements. It differed from English palisade construction (rarely used for houses) in that the logs were hewn flat on two sides, to form the inner and outer surfaces of the wall, and set a few inches apart, the spaces between them being filled with a mixture of grass and clay (*bouzillage*) or stones and clay (*pierrotage*). An improvement was made when the logs were set on a sill instead of in the earth. This, *poteaux sur sole,* is the construction used in the oldest house surviving in the Midwest, now called Cahokia Courthouse, which was built about 1737 (18).

Whether *poteaux* construction was known in France is uncertain. The type of house represented by Cahokia Courthouse was not; it is a striking exception to the home-away-from-home rule. The dominant feature from which it derives its special character is the hipped roof (shingled at Cahokia, though originally it was probably thatched), which changes pitch to spread out over the veranda or *galerie* surrounding the whole house. Often the *galerie* had a raised floor and a railing, like the Dutch *stoep.* When the main floor is raised on a brick ground story and the *galerie* on brick piers, we have arrived at the Louisiana plantation house—though this should not be understood as an account of the actual historical development, for it is possible that the Cahokia type, so to call it, was a simplification of the plantation house. The oldest surviving plantation house in Louisiana is Parlange, at New Roads, built about 1750 (19, 20). Few buildings have ever been better adapted to the climate and physical conditions of a region than this, with the main rooms insulated by the capacious roof from the heat of the sun above and by the brick ground story from the damp of the earth below, the French windows providing maximum ventilation and the *galerie* an amplitude of cool and dry outdoor space.[3] No wonder such houses continued to be built, with only minor changes of stylistic detail, down to the middle of the nineteenth century.

In New Orleans (founded in 1718) the commonest kind of construction at first was *colombage sur sole.* Of medieval origin, this comprised massive posts with their lower ends tenoned into the sill

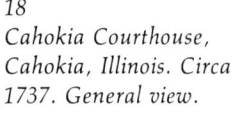

18
*Cahokia Courthouse,*
*Cahokia, Illinois. Circa*
*1737. General view.*

19
*Parlange, Pointe Coupée
Parish, Louisiana. Circa
1750. View from the
south.*

20
*Parlange, Pointe Coupée
Parish, Louisiana. Plan of
principal floor.*

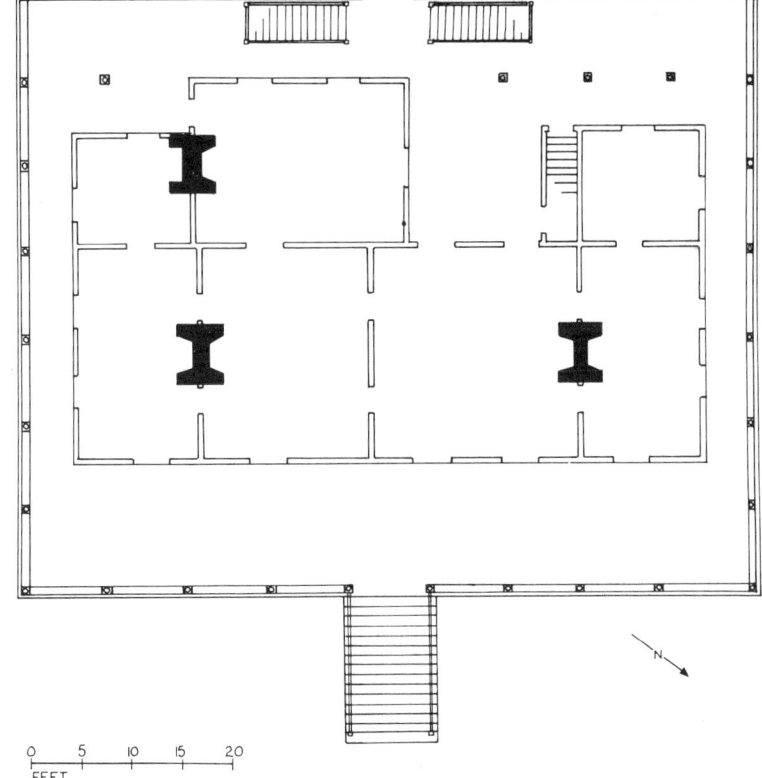

0    5    10    15    20
FEET

21
*St. Louis Cathedral, New Orleans, Louisiana. Gilberto Guillemard, 1789–94. Measured drawing of facade by Benjamin Henry Latrobe.*

(for the first story) or the girt (for the second) and their upper into the girt or plate, with diagonal braces, more often than not forming crosses, between them; the braces were also tenoned at both ends into the horizontal pieces and not, as in the English frame, at one end into posts. When there was an infilling of bricks, this was known as *briqueté entre poteaux* construction. Walls so built were faced with boards or plastered, or sometimes in New Orleans and its neighborhood left exposed to the weather (much to their detriment).

The first parish church of St. Louis was built to the design of the engineer-in-chief of Louisiana, Adrien de Pauger, in 1724–27. It was of cruciform plan, with a deep presbytery terminating in a half-octagon, and of *briqueté entre poteaux,* plastered on the exterior; its facade was pedimented, with panelled walls, rusticated quoins, and a circular window over the arched doorway.

De Pauger died before his church was finished and was succeeded as engineer-in-chief by Ignace François Broutin, who in 1727 designed the first building, of *briqueté entre poteaux* again, for the convent of Ursuline nuns who arrived in New Orleans that year. In 1729 Pierre Baron, a naturalist who had been sent to Louisiana by the French Academy, was appointed to the office. Baron completed the Ursuline Convent, with some changes in the design, and in 1730

22
*Cabildo, New Orleans,
Louisiana. Gilberto
Guillemard, 1795–1801.
Front facing Jackson
Square.*

built the first major brick building in New Orleans, the prison, which was a neat exercise in the Louis XV style. In 1732 he returned to France, and Broutin became engineer-in-chief again. In 1745 Broutin designed the second Ursuline Convent, to replace the building he had designed less than twenty years before, for whose timbers the humidity had already proved too much. Built of brick, the second Ursuline Convent is the only public building in New Orleans of the period of French rule to survive. The Ursulines were teachers; the order was founded in the sixteenth century to teach girls, whom the Jesuits, greatest of the teaching orders, did not teach. They were a poor order, and their buildings were plain. The Ursuline Convent at New Orleans has much in common with that at Bayeux, but even more with the Cistercian Abbey of Auberive, which had a three-bay pedimented center with the same curved roofs to the dormers as Broutin's original design.[4]

The cession of New Orleans and Louisiana west of the Mississippi to Spain in 1764 under the Treaty of San Ildefonso had little effect on the architecture of the region. The Spanish governor's house at Baton Rouge was a simple if spacious example of the Cahokia Courthouse type, and the three buildings that went up on the northwest side of the Place d'Armes (now Jackson Square) in New Orleans at the end of the century were as French as the surname of their architect, Gilberto Guillemard, for all that he had spent nearly twenty years in the military service of Spain when he designed the first of them. The ground was cleared for this monumental group by two fires. The first, in 1788, destroyed De Pauger's church, the Casa Curial or Rectory, and the Cabildo or Council House (built in 1769–70 with a *galerie* across the street front), besides damaging other public buildings in the vicinity; the second, in 1794, destroyed buildings that had been repaired since the first but spared the new church for its dedication two weeks later.

The rebuilding of St. Louis began in 1789, the whole cost being borne by a commissioner of the Cabildo already famous for his benefactions to the city, Don Andres Almonester y Roxas. The new church had a broad two-story facade with a pedimented center and a tower, octagonal from the ground up, at either end. In 1820 Benjamin Henry Latrobe added a third tower immediately behind the center of the facade. It was the collapse of this in 1850 that led to the replacement of Guillemard's building, the best record of which is an elevation by Latrobe (21). Guillemard's other two buildings, the Cabildo and the Casa Curial (now the Presbytère), still stand (22). Both were begun in 1795; the Cabildo was finished in 1801, its twin not until 1815. Almonester, the donor of the cathedral, undertook the building of the Casa Curial at his own expense and also financed the construction of the Cabildo. Either building could be an *hôtel de ville* in the French provinces; the finest example of the type, which Guillemard conceivably had in mind, is the Hôtel de Ville at Nancy, designed by Héré de Corny in 1750.[5]

**Old World Traditions and the Mercantile Impulse**

For all their differences, the buildings of the English, Dutch, Swedish, German, and French colonists in North America had two things in common, one of which affected their character individually, while the other, by providing a milieu that favored certain building types over others, affected the architectural scene as a whole. First, they were built by and for people for whom home was Europe, so that to be fully understood they must be seen in relation to the European architectural traditions of their builders. Second, they were built in colonies which were founded—whatever personal motives may have impelled individual settlers—for mercantile purposes. Because of the different aims, methods, and history of Spanish colonization in the New World, neither statement would be true of the buildings to be considered in our next chapter.

*A New World Tradition*

Spanish colonial architecture had a history going back more than a century, to the founding, in 1496, of Santo Domingo on the island of Hispaniola, when the earliest Spanish colonial building still standing in the United States was begun—and more than eighty years in Mexico, whence the colonists who extended the dominion of Spain into the regions north of the present border came. At first, in the Caribbean, it had been an unmodified transplant from Europe, brought by designers and builders who came directly from the Peninsula. In Mexico, however, variants and transmutations of the Spanish styles appeared almost as soon as they were introduced. This was due not so much to the employment of Indian labor, although that was certainly a factor, as to the sheer volume of building, particularly church building, and the creation of the ethnically mixed *mestizo* class who "inevitably responded to a different range of aesthetic stimuli than did the Spanish-born or the *criollo*."[1] An unsurpassed richness and inventiveness in sculptural decoration constituted the great strength of the architecture that resulted; an extreme conservatism (not to say timidity) in planning and construction was its general weakness.

In this chapter, then, we shall be concerned with buildings which with some important exceptions were the products of an architectural tradition that had already developed non-European characteristics, even though all the major changes of style that punctuated its history were due to waves of influence from the Old World. One of the most notable of the exceptions is a work of military architecture. Others of quite another kind are in New Mexico, where special conditions resulted in the creation of a distinctive regional style.

*New Mexico*

Nothing could be less like the first State House at Jamestown with its serried gables than the Palace of the Governors at Santa Fe, built in 1610–14 and still in great part surviving (23). Originally forming the side of the *presidio* or fortified enclosure, which measured more than 400 feet from east to west and more than 800 feet from north to south, it was built, as no British colonial building was, by Indian labor, and incorporates, as no British colonial building does, both European and Indian techniques. Adobe, of which the walls are constructed, was a material with which the Indians were thoroughly familiar; but before the Spaniards came they had used it in mass and never, as here, in bricks. (The sun-dried adobe bricks of Spanish New Mexico were very different from the burnt clay bricks of the British colonies, measuring about ten by five by eighteen inches and weighing fifty to sixty pounds each.) The flat roof, with its projecting beams or *vigas* and covering of earth, is of the type used by the

Indians in their own pueblos. The porch or *portal* facing the town square, on the other hand, is purely Spanish; the capitals of the wooden posts, resembling back-to-back brackets and therefore called bracket capitals (*zapatas* in Spanish), were a feature which the Moors took to Spain and which is found nowhere else in Europe.[2] Originally each end of the range toward the square was carried up to form a tower, the eastern one containing a chapel and the western a magazine.

This balancing of structures for the worship of God and the storage of gunpowder and weapons may be seen as symbolic of the aims and methods of Spain in America generally. In New Mexico, however, colonization was much more the work of missionaries, who were Friars of the Regular Observance of St. Francis, than of the military. The achievements of these Franciscans, who were nearly all Europeans by birth, are astonishing by any standards. As George Kubler has put it, "aside from the task of diverting a massive population from its ancient beliefs, these men executed ambitious building projects for which they themselves were the architects, contractors, foremen, and building-supply agents."

What was always one of the largest as well as the most dramatically sited of the New Mexico missions still stands structurally whole, though a victim of misguided "improvements" in recent years. This is the mission at Acoma, the pueblo on an isolated mesa, with its church dedicated to San Estevan (24, 25). The plan of the complex is unusual in that the *convento* or monastery lies to the north of the church, rather than the south, and the friar's house, which is surmounted by a covered *mirador* or viewing platform, forms one of the outer corners of the *convento* instead of standing next to the church.[3] In front of the church a walled enclosure, the *atrio,* served

24
*San Estevan, Acoma,*
*New Mexico. Between*
*1629 and 1642. Southeast*
*view.*

25
*San Estevan, Acoma,*
*New Mexico. Plan of*
*church and* convento.

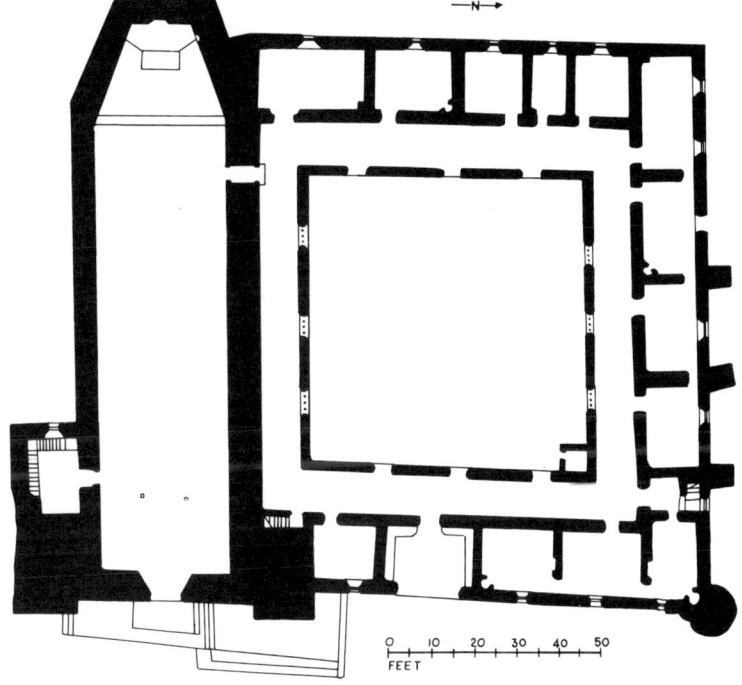

as a burial ground and could also be used for outdoor worship. The *atrio* is an ubiquitous feature of religious architecture in Spanish America. But unlike any outside New Mexico, the *atrio* at Acoma lies to the east of the church, for the church is entered through the east facade and has a western sanctuary.

This reverse orientation, or occidentation, is a matter to which we shall return. The facade of San Estevan is of the two-towered type whose history in Europe goes back to the end of the first millennium; some have seen its origins in a type of church facade with an arched central entrance flanked by vertical features, which may by courtesy be called towers, that appeared five centuries earlier in the East, where the motif was familiar as that of the palace gateway and thus symbolic of royalty. The facade of San Estevan with its battered walls and bare surfaces and rectangular openings is quite unlike any medieval two-towered facade in Europe; if one seems to see in it some resemblance to the pylon of an Egyptian temple the fancy is not an altogether empty one, for the pylon was also a royal palace symbol and the batter of its walls is due to the imitation in stone of an adobe prototype.

To enter the church at Acoma is to receive an impression of spaciousness greater than what might be expected from its actual dimensions: 128 feet by 30 feet on plan and 30 feet in height, so that the volume is practically a quadruple cube. How miraculous such a space must have seemed to the Indians, who had never known anything larger than a *kiva*! And their wonder would have been increased by a special lighting effect. Today San Estevan has only three windows, two in the south wall and one above the choir loft in the east.[4] In the bright light of New Mexico they are enough for all practical purposes. However, the church originally had another window between the roof of the nave and that of the sanctuary, which was two or three feet higher than the nave. The effect of this transverse clerestory was to flood the sanctuary and the altar with light—natural light, but to the Indian worshipper in the nave, who could not see its source and who was not accustomed to windows, surely supernatural.[5]

The use of the transverse clerestory accounts for the occidentation of San Estevan and for the extreme rarity of eastern sanctuaries in New Mexico.[6] Services were usually held in the morning; churches were therefore planned with the sanctuary to the west or north to give the altar maximum illumination from the morning sun through the transverse clerestory. As for its origin, the feature was apparently peculiar to New Mexico. Whoever invented it—presumably one of the missionary friars—had a real understanding of the principles of

26
*Santo Tomás, Trampas,
New Mexico. Circa 1760.
Southwest view before
addition of wooden bell
turrets in 1967.*

the Baroque—and a precocious one, seeing that Bernini's S. Andrea al Quirinale, the first Roman church in which the high altar was illuminated from a hidden source, was not begun until 1658. In comparison with the Old Brick Church at Smithfield, built in the same decade, San Estevan may seem unsophisticated in structure and crude in finish. Yet it is a building that is of its age in a sense in which the still Gothic church in Virginia is not.

Two plan types were employed in the colonial churches of New Mexico. Of the single–cell type extant examples include, beside Acoma, San Miguel, Santa Fe (after 1640), San José, Laguna (ca. 1700), Santa Ana in the pueblo of the same name (1734), and the Santuario of Chimayo (early nineteenth century). The other type has a transept between the sanctuary and the nave. Examples of this standing in good condition are Santo Tomás, Trampas (ca. 1760), and San Francisco, Ranchos de Taos (ca. 1780) (26, 27, 28). These are both of the second half of the eighteenth century, but the plan appeared early in the seventeenth, as is evidenced by the remains of Nuestra Señora de los Angeles de Porciuncula, Pecos (before 1625), and the substantial ruins of the stone-built churches of San Gregorio, Abó (ca. 1630), and La Concepcion, Quarai (before 1633). It derived from the Gesù in Rome, built as the head church of the Jesuit order between 1568 and 1577, to which the architect Vignola gave a new kind of plan, especially suitable for preaching, by compressing the transept arms to serve as large side chapels, lit, like the sanctuary, by windows in the drum of the dome over the crossing. In the

27
*San Francisco, Ranchos de*
*Taos, New Mexico. Circa*
*1780. East view.*

28
*San Francisco, Ranchos de*
*Taos, New Mexico. Plan.*

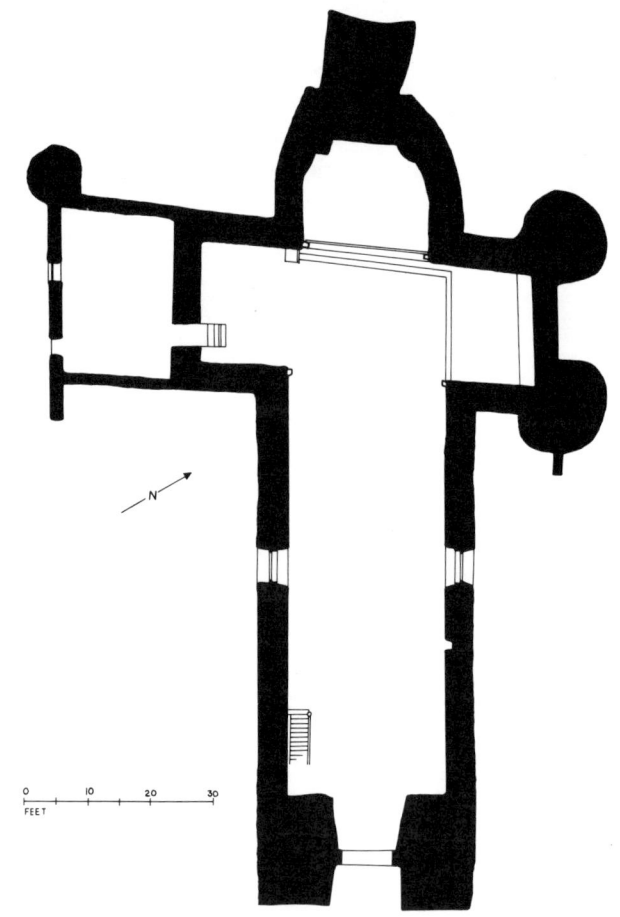

29
*San José, Laguna, New Mexico. Circa 1700. Facade with* espadaña.

30
*San José, Laguna, New Mexico. Interior, looking west.*

seventeenth and eighteenth centuries the Gesù was the most influential church in the Catholic world. In Mexico many hundreds of parish churches are versions of it, simplified as a rule by omitting the side chapels but retaining the dome over the transept crossing. In New Mexico it was simplified further by omitting the dome and substituting a transverse clerestory for the windows in its drum.

A variant of the two-towered facade as seen at Acoma and Ranchos de Taos (and formerly at Santa Cruz and in the parish church of Santa Fe) has a balcony stretching from one tower to the other at the level of the choir loft. The balcony may have been used in conjunction with the *atrio* for outdoor worship. If a sketch of the abandoned church at Pecos made in 1846 shows the original facade, as it probably does, the balconied facade was introduced before 1625; an example from the late seventeenth century is at Zuni, where the church, now in ruins, was built about 1660, while eighteenth-century examples include San Felipe (ca. 1706) and Trampas (ca. 1760). The simplest and commonest type of facade has neither towers nor balcony; it consists of a plain wall pierced by the doorway and the choir-loft window and carried up above the roof as an *espadaña*. Such is the facade of San José, Laguna, built about 1700 (29). The interior of this church is notable for the Indian murals—Indian in style and iconography as well as execution—in the nave, contrasting with, and yet as an expression of pueblo culture complementing, the purely Spanish *retablo* and decorations in the sanctuary (30).[7]

The church architecture of New Mexico changed hardly at all during the two and a half centuries of Spanish and Mexican rule, and when a flood destroyed the church of Santo Domingo Pueblo in 1886 it was rebuilt without a single feature it might not have had in the seventeenth century. The early friars set out to build churches which should be functional liturgically and Christian and Catholic in their symbolism, employing only structural principles and techniques already known to their Indian converts or easily learnt by them. The results often possess certain qualities, attractive to a century that values primitivism in art, which it would be an act of unnecessary self-denial not to enjoy because they are due to accident rather than intention.

*Florida*

There is nothing regional about the design of the Castillo de San Marcos at St. Augustine, the most important architectural relic of Spanish rule in Florida (31, 32). Here, in contrast to the mission churches of New Mexico, is a building which is not only purely European but also international in style—international as only military architecture was when it was begun in 1672. Substantially

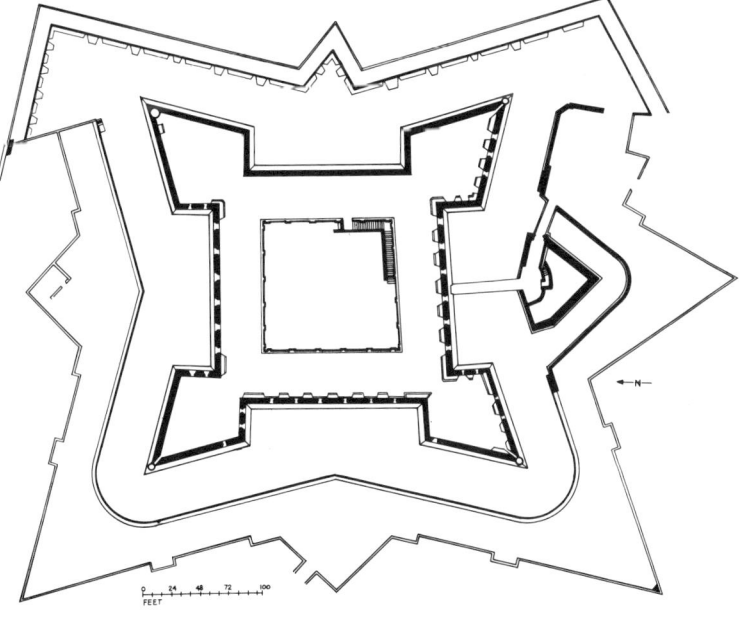

31
Castillo de San Marcos
(Fort Marion), St. Augus-
tine, Florida. Ignazio
Daza, 1672–87. Curtain,
bustion, and cavalier.

32
Castillo de San Marcos,
St. Augustine, Florida.
Plan.

finished by 1687, the Castillo de San Marcos represents a type of fort whose prototype was built at Nettuno in Italy in 1501–1502 to the design of the brothers Antonio and Giuliano da Sangallo. Military architects had been confronted with the problems presented by cannon fire since the second quarter of the fourteenth century; the great innovation of the Sangalli in what has been called "the military equivalent of Bramante's Tempietto in Rome"[8] was the substitution of triangular bastions, no higher than the outer walls or curtains, for the round towers of traditional fortress design.

On plan the Castillo de San Marcos is a square of about 200 feet, with bastions projecting about 90 feet from each corner. Its parapet is pierced for sixty-four guns, which were hauled from the inner court of parade to the firing platform or *terreplein* up a ramp (now converted to stairs). Entrance was by drawbridge over the moat and a doorway with a portcullis in the south curtain; on the outermost corner of the northeast bastion stands a round viewing tower, or cavalier.

The designer of the Castillo de San Marcos was Ignacio Daza of Havana. His greatest contemporary in the field of military architecture was the Frenchman Sebastien le Prestre de Vauban, and Vauban's influence is paramount at St. Augustine. However, the design of the bastions, which have acute outer angles and their shorter walls, or flanks, at right angles to the curtains, does not follow Vauban's practice, which was to make the outer angles of the bastions obtuse and return their flanks at right angles to the faces, as their longer walls were called. The batter or slope of the face of the ramparts, with the 25-foot-high walls thinning from 12 feet at the base to 7 feet at the top, is close enough to the batter of one-sixth of the total height employed by Vauban.

Daza's fort withstood three British sieges, in 1702, 1728, and 1740. Its success was due in large part to the material of which it is built, the *coquina* or shell-limestone quarried on Anastasia Island nearby. In forts of stone or brick, casualties among the defenders were often caused by flying pieces of masonry shattered by cannon balls, and by the seventeenth century this had led to the building of ramparts of solid earth, with stone or brick used only for their outer facing and for parapets and buttresses. But *coquina* was no ordinary stone. Nathaniel Johnson, governor of South Carolina, bore witness to its special qualities in a report to the British Board of Trade in 1720. The castle, he wrote, was built of a stone which looked like free stone but was much better for fortifications. "It will not splinter," he explained, "but gives way to cannon balls as though you would stick a knife into cheese."

Although built later, in 1736, the Fuerte de Matanzas, the ruins of which stand in the marshes fifteen miles south of St. Augustine, was essentially medieval in plan, with a keep. A third example of Spanish military architecture in Florida is the Fuerte de San Carlos in Pensacola, rebuilt in its present semi-circular form, of brick, in 1783, the year in which Florida was returned to Spain after twenty years of British rule. As for ecclesiastical architecture in Florida, the facade of the Cathedral of San Agustin, built in 1793–98 to the design of the engineer Diaz Berrio, with a correctly detailed Doric doorway and a tall gable wall or *espadaña*, pierced for bells, was retained and restored when the church was rebuilt and enlarged after a fire in 1887. Of the forty or so missions founded in Florida by the Franciscans beginning in 1593 the architectural remains are negligible.

**Texas and Arizona**

In Texas the Franciscans founded their first mission, near Nacogdoches, in 1690. It was followed by five more in east Texas, but trouble with the Indians and the French soon led to their abandonment. Activity was renewed under the leadership of the dynamic Fray Antonio Margil in 1716. By 1731 a dozen missions had been established. Today there are three eighteenth-century mission churches standing in Texas, all in or near San Antonio, while ninety miles to the southeast, at Goliad, stands the chapel of the Presidio la Bahia, which was established in 1749 to protect the mission of Espiritu Santo de Zuñiga.[9]

These four buildings must be seen in the context of Mexican eighteenth-century church architecture. The earliest, Nuestra Senora de la Purisima Concepcion de Acuna, was begun by 1743 and dedicated by 1755 (33, 34). With its Gesù-derived Latin-cross plan, barrel-vaulted nave, and two-towered facade, this church could have been built almost anywhere in Mexico in the early eighteenth or, for that matter, the seventeenth century; the merlon-like features on the parapets, at the corners of the towers and around the drum under the dome, are reminiscent of the sixteenth. The drum is circular in plan—unexpectedly, for octagonal drums were the rule all over Mexico between the sixteenth century and the advent of Neo-classicism, even when the domes resting on them were circular. In northern Mexico arches and windows were often polygonal rather than circular; the most influential model in this respect was the Basilica of Guadalupe north of Mexico City, built between 1695 and 1709. The main doorway of the Concepcion, with its half-octagon arch, is an example of the fashion, as is also the octagonal window

33
*Nuestra Señora de la Purisima Concepcion de Acuna, San Antonio, Texas. 1743–55. Facade and towers.*

34
*Nuestra Señora de la Purisima Concepcion de Acuna, San Antonio, Texas. Plan.*

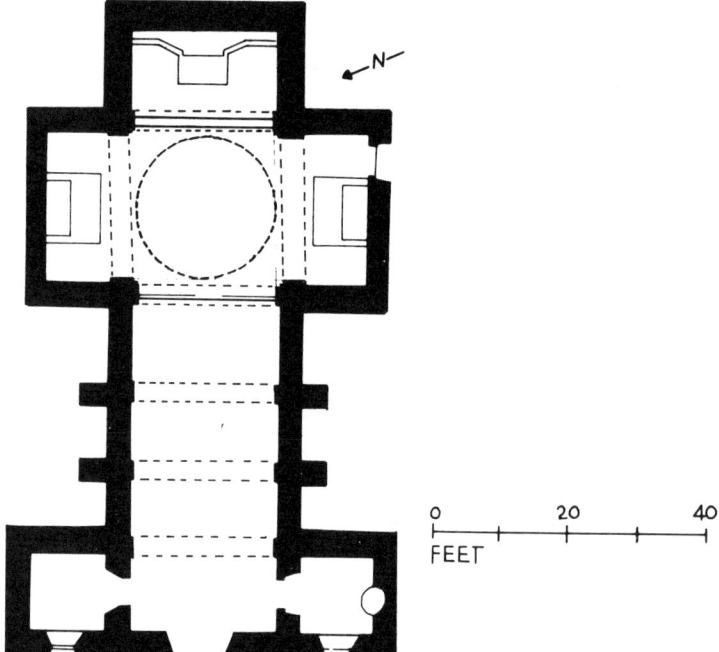

in the facade of the Presidio la Bahia chapel, which was built sometime after 1765.

The church of the mission of San Antonio de Valero, better known
as the Alamo, was begun in 1744 and still under construction in
1777. Here it is the centerpiece of the facade, the *portada*, that claims
attention (35). It was never finished; clearly a second order with
columns flanking the upper niches was intended. It represents a
regional style of Baroque that flourished in the far north of Mexico
in the second quarter of the eighteenth century, for it is modelled
on the lateral *portada* of Durango, the cathedral of the diocese that
included Texas. The imitation is not too skillful; the square blocks
between the columns and the entablature are a solecism, resulting
no doubt from a misreading of the architrave in the prototype, and
the raising of the heads of the niches above the level of the crown
of the central arch is another questionable departure.

In San José y San Miguel de Aguayo we encounter something
altogether different (36). The mission, founded by Margil in 1720,
was established on its present site about 1739. The present church
was built in 1768–77; it is of limestone with sandstone trim and has
an octagonal dome between the groin-vaulted nave and the sanctuary, which is barrel-vaulted, but no transept. The facade is flanked
by two square towers; only one of them received its belfry stage,
which has something of the clumsiness of the Alamo *portada*. There
is nothing clumsy about the *portada* of San José. This and the
window of the baptistery on the south side of the church are said to
have been carved by one Pedro Huizar. The designer of these two
features, whether Huizar or another, was fluent in the idiom of the
last, near-Rococo phase of the Mexican Ultra-Baroque. Characteristic
motifs of the style are the shell-like ornament or *rocaille*, the mixtilinear arch and window, and the niche pilaster. All are employed
in San José with a skill that invites comparison with the masterpieces
of the style in central Mexico.[10]

Niche-pilasters such as flank the doorway of San José, which are
the result of a desire to turn the seemingly if not actually structural
pilaster into a purely decorative feature, are essentially Rococo, even
though they were never used in France, where the style originated.
In Mexico they first appeared in conjunction with a distortion of the
classical column which was used by the architects of the Ultra-
Baroque so much that it has been suggested that the period from
about 1730 to about 1770 might be called the *estípite* age. The *estípite*
may be roughly but adequately defined as a stack of square balusters
with a capital on top. Like so many features of Spanish Baroque it
is of sixteenth-century, Mannerist origin; its lineage may be traced

35
San Antonio de Valero
(The Alamo), San Anto-
nio, Texas. 1744–after
1777. Facade.

36
San José y San Miguel de
Aguayo, San Antonio,
Texas. Pedro Huizar,
1768–77. Facade.

back to the downward-tapering pilasters of Michelangelo's Laurentian Library in Florence through the fantastic elaborations of that theme in the engravings of the German Wendel Dieterling. After 1770 the *estípite* yielded to the niche-pilaster as the dominant motif in Mexican facades and *retablos*.

That the *estípite* should be absent from San José yet still be the main decorative motif of the later San Xavier del Bac, near Tucson, Arizona, shows how remoteness could delay stylistic change (37, 38, 39). (Tucson is about a thousand miles further than San Antonio from Mexico City.) This church was begun in 1775 and the main fabric was completed by 1783; the facade and the elaborate interior, with three *retablos* and much painting and other carved plasterwork, were not completed until 1797. The facade would hardly have passed muster in central Mexico even in 1775. The meager *estípites* are deployed across it at wide intervals, as if Lorenzo Rodriguez had never demonstrated in the *sagrario* of Mexico Cathedral the special rhythm that the combination of *estípites* and niche-pilasters could impart to a facade. Inside the church the iconographically comprehensive *retablos* are more sophisticated, while the structure itself is both logically developed as a design and notably well built of brick. The plan once again is of the modified Gesù type. A hemispherical dome is set on an octagonal drum over the crossing and there are oval saucer domes over the sanctuary, transept chapels, and nave; a round-domed sacristy is neatly fitted into the angle between the right transept and the sanctuary. The design is attributed to Ignacio Gaona, who is said to have been a Spaniard and to have had a brother who was his assistant.

Bac was one of the northernmost of the twenty-four missions founded by the Jesuit Eusebio Kino between 1687 and about 1700 in Sonora and Arizona—Pimeria Alta, as the whole area was then called. After 1767, when the Jesuits were expelled from Mexico, these missions were placed in the charge of the Franciscans, who rebuilt most of their churches before Mexican independence ended government support. San Xavier is a more ambitious building than any erected by the Franciscans in Sonora and, despite its shortcomings, much more literate in design than the only other mission church in Arizona of which there are more than slight remains, San José de Tumacácori. This was begun in 1806. Its facade, with a *portada* of a two-story type going back to the sixteenth century, shows that whoever was responsible for it knew that the Baroque was over, while in breaking so many of the rules of classical design it suggests that he knew little else.

37
San Xavier del Bac, near
Tucson, Arizona. Ignacio
Gaona, 1775–97. South-
west view.

38
San Xavier del Bac, near
Tucson, Arizona. Plan.

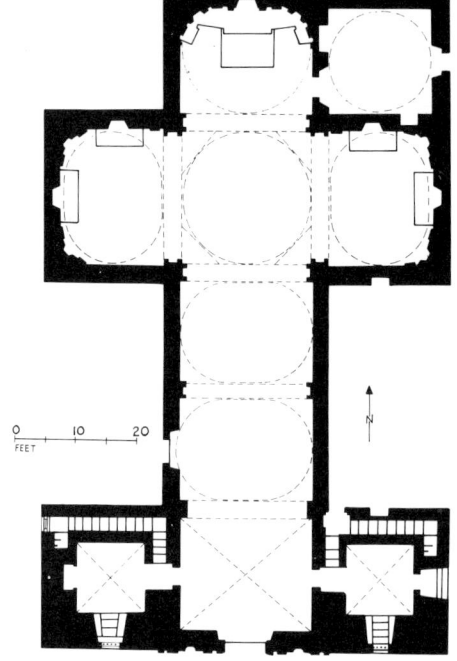

39
*San Xavier del Bac, near Tucson, Arizona. Interior, looking north.*

*California*

The colonization of California—Alta California, as it was called to distinguish it from the peninsula to the south—was motivated by the fear of Russia expanding her American territory southward from Alaska. It began in 1769, with the establishment of the first *presidio* and the first mission at San Diego. The *padre presidente* to whom the religious side of colonization was entrusted was the heroic Franciscan Fray Junipero Serra. By his death in 1784 he had founded nine missions; his successor Fray Fermin de Lasuén founded nine more by 1803, and by 1823 there was a chain of twenty-one missions and two *asistencias* stretching from San Diego to Sonoma. Three more *presidios* were established, at Monterey, San Francisco, and Santa Barbara.

Of the Californian *presidios* practically nothing remains. Of the missions the remains are substantial and extensive, the more extensive because—in contrast to the New Mexico missions, where the mission buildings consisted of the church and the *convento*, which housed one or rarely two friars and their domestics—they had to house the great numbers of Indian converts who worked on the agricultural and stock-raising estates of which they were the centers.

As in all the mission fields, the first buildings were simple in the extreme. The chapel of San Juan Capistrano, completed in 1777 and the only church of Serra's time still standing, was typical. Ninety feet long but only seventeen feet wide, it has a sanctuary raised three steps above the nave floor and a choir loft at the opposite end; it is built of adobe with a wooden roof which was originally thatched. (Manufacture of the red roofing tiles that became a regional feature began in 1786). All the other extant churches date from the 1790s or later.

There are no *estípites* in California; this is a Neo-Classical architecture in its flat wall surfaces and clarity of form, albeit that in only one major structure, the facade of the church of the mission of Santa Barbara, is an ancient classical motif employed at full scale. A spirit of compromise is apparent even in the ornate facade of the Capilla Real at Monterey—not a mission church but the chapel of the *presidio*—which dates from 1794. There are still some touches of the Baroque, in the shell heads of the niches, the shell above the relief of the Virgin of Guadalupe, and the breaking of the curved and scrolled gable to embrace the Virgin's aedicule. The total effect, however, is dry and linear, with none of the plasticity of the Ultra-Baroque.

The earliest of the major mission churches standing today is San Carlos Borromeo at Carmel, begun in 1793 (40). The master mason, who was in all probability the designer too, was Manuel Estevan

*San Carlos Borromeo,*
*Carmel, California. Ma-*
*nuel Estevan Ruiz, 1793.*
*Facade.*

Ruiz. It would seem that Ruiz, if he was the designer, knew the work of Francisco Antonio Guerrero y Torres, who (in Kubler's phrase) "broke the spell" of the *estípite* in Mexico City. In the facade the combination of classical doorway and stellar *claraboya* is reminiscent of Guerrero's Pocito Chapel of 1779; the extraordinary interior, with a barrel vault of boards supported by parabolic arches of stone and the upper part of the walls and the Doric pilaster order bent inwards to meet the curve of the arches, shows—even though the forms are quite different—the same experimental approach to stone-cutting, daring indeed when the labor force was Indian and had to be trained on the job, as the *patio* of Guerrero's Valparaíso House (now the Banco de Mexico) of 1769. The ovoid dome crowning the south tower is of Muslim derivation; the ogee molding above the south door and the doorway to the mortuary chapel, with its mixtilinear arch flanked by composite piers supporting a Doric entablature, recall the Gothic Plateresque of Spain. The Muslim, Gothic, and Plateresque traditions all made their contributions to Spanish Baroque architecture in the Old World and the New; here they have survived the Baroque age to mitigate the austerities of Neo-classicism.

In 1812 an earthquake damaged the vault of San Carlos Borromeo and in the following year it was taken down; what one sees today is the result of a rebuilding in the 1930s.[11] The same earthquake brought down a large part of the second church of the mission of San Juan Capistrano, killing forty Indian worshippers. This church was begun in 1797, the year in which the main structure of San Carlos was finished, and dedicated in 1806; the architect was Isidoro Aguilar of Culiacán. The sanctuary still stands, with enough of the walls, arches, and internal order to permit a paper restoration of the

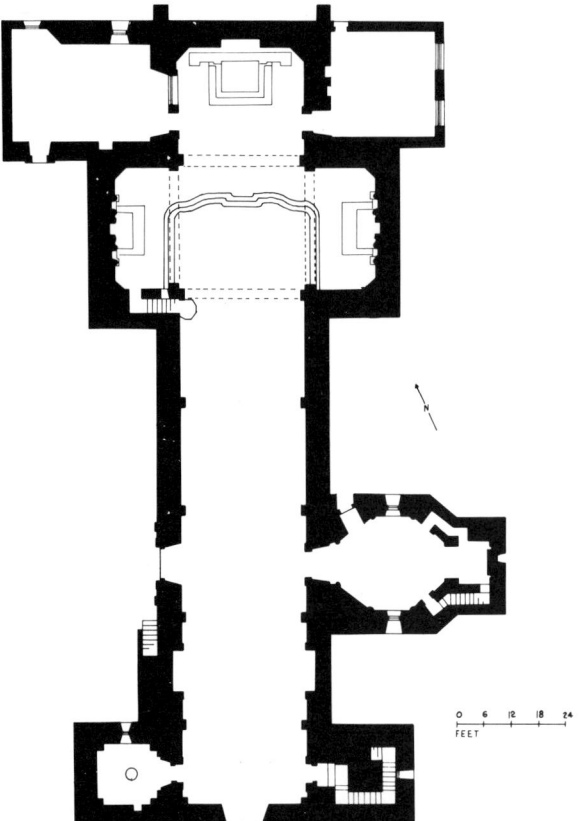

41
*San Luis Rey de Francia,
near Oceanside, Califor-
nia. Antonio Peyri, 1811–
15. Church from
southeast.*

42
*San Luis Rey de Francia,
near Oceanside, Califor-
nia. Plan.*

0  6  12  18  24
FEET

43
*Santa Barbara, Santa
Barbara, California. An-
tonio Ripoll, 1815–20.
Facade.*

body of the church, although the exact form of the tower must remain in doubt. It was the largest of the Spanish churches in California—180 feet long, with a nave 30 feet wide and 60 feet high—and the first of cruciform plan. The nave and crossing were vaulted with domes, and the transept arms, like the sanctuary, with groin vaults. The entire structure was of sandstone, quarried six miles away.

After the earthquake of 1812 no more high vaults were built in California, and masonry domes were confined to towers, baptisteries, and mortuary chapels. Thus the dome over the crossing of San Luis Rey de Francia, built to the design of Fray Antonio Peyrí in 1811–15 as the second cruciform church in the colony (and the last, as it turned out), is of wood, while the octagonal mortuary chapel is covered with an octagonal dome of brick (41, 42); the nave is wooden-roofed, though clearly designed for a vault. The facade of San Luis Rey is carried up above the roof of the church as an *espadaña* of mixtilinear profile. The resemblance of this feature to the shaped gables of Bacon's Castle may not be purely coincidental; that is, it may have reached Spain from the Low Countries. Yet it is unnecessary to suppose that it travelled to California from anywhere but Mexico. Many Baroque facades in Mexico have *espadañas* of similar outline, which tend to go unnoticed behind the incrustation of ornament and decorative features. In San Luis Rey, as also in San Diego de Alcalá (1808–13), with the stripping away of all Baroque ornament and the centering of the facades on *portadas* of Neo-Classical severity, the *espadañas* themselves have become the only decorative feature

The rebuilding of the church of Santa Barbara in 1815–20 was made necessary by the complete destruction of its predecessor by the 1812 earthquake (43). The architect was Padre Antonio Ripoll, who in designing the facade consulted a Spanish edition of Vitruvius in a copy still preserved in the mission library. One of the plates shows a tetrastyle temple portico with a fret interlace on the frieze, and this Ripoll took as his model, increasing the number of columns to six, attenuating their shafts, and standing them on high pedestals. The result is hardly Vitruvian; the splitting of the columns into two groups of three to accommodate the doorway is naive, and Ionic capitals were beyond the technical skill of the Indian stonemasons. On aesthetic grounds one may well prefer the masculine and unaffected towers. But Ripoll's temple-form facade brought the story of ecclesiastical architecture in Spanish California to an end with a brave Neo-Classical gesture.

Within a year of the completion of Santa Barbara the Mexican revolution set in motion forces that led to increased activity in domestic building in Alta California, resulting in the single-storied but spacious *casas de campo* and *casas de pueblo* of the later twenties and the thirties. In 1835–37 the Bostonian Thomas Larkin, United State consul in Monterey, built the first two-story house, initiating a peaceful pentration by American architectural fashions a decade before the transfer of rule. Not only did the second story catch on; so did the two-storied porches, which were perhaps suggested to Larkin by his experience of the piazzas of houses in North Carolina during ten years he spent in that state. The result was what has come to be called the Monterey Style, the products of whose revival in the 1930s far outnumber the nineteenth-century examples.

*A Time of Change*

In British America the period 1700–76 saw many times as much building as the seventeenth century did. And architecture underwent a fundamental change. At the opening of the period the form and appearance of buildings were determined by that complex of practices and predilections, transmitted from one generation to the next by personal example and word of mouth, which we call tradition; by its end tradition had yielded to taste, which as the eighteenth century understood the term was the product of the combination of cultivated sensibility and special knowledge. In America the special knowledge could be acquired only from books, and it was the stream of books on architecture which began to issue from the London booksellers' shops soon after the accession of George I and reached flood force in the 1730s that did more than anything else to bring the change about.[1] It took time; the new books were rarely used—probably rarely seen—before 1730, and the dominance of taste, evidenced by the taking of designs for whole buildings from them, was not absolute until mid-century. Nonetheless, there were three important developments in the first thirty years of the century: the establishment of the double pile as the standard type for houses of any pretension, a change in the treatment of domestic interiors, and the introduction of a new type of church.

*The Double-Pile House*

The earliest known use of the term double pile occurs in the notebooks of the amateur architect Sir Roger Pratt, which were compiled in the third quarter of the seventeenth century. The earliest known double-pile house was Coleshill, Berkshire, built to Pratt's design circa 1650; the next seems to have been Thorpe Hall, Northamptonshire, which was built in 1654–56 to the design of Peter Mills, a London bricklayer. Like the Foster-Hutchinson House in Boston, Thorpe Hall shows the influence of the published designs of Philip Vingboons, and the type generally owed much to Holland. Certainly there was more than a little that was Dutch about the first double pile in Virginia, the Governor's Palace at Williamsburg, with its tall proportions, cantilevered balcony, steep hipped roof, and two-story cupola (44). The act of the Assembly that authorized its construction in 1706 made no mention of a plan but specified the internal length and breadth, the number of stories, the materials (brick, with slate for the roof), and the use of sash windows. It also provided "that in all other respects the said house be built and finished according to the discretion of the overseer"—or the supervising architect, as we would say today—and went on to appoint to that position Henry Cary, who until its completion a few months before had been overseer of the capitol in which the Assembly sat. Cary completed the main structure within three years, but the house was not fully finished for another twelve, during six of which the work was under the direct supervision of Alexander Spotswood, lieutenant governor of Virginia from 1710 to 1722. Spotswood was responsible for "many alterations and decorations," as an early writer puts it. The most significant of the alterations was the creation of a parlor out of the upper end of what had been built as a great hall of medieval pattern. This gave the entrance side of the house a classical symmetry of plan corresponding with the symmetry of the facade. The decorations included a formal garden laid out in the Anglo-Dutch style which was still current in England, though soon to make way for something quite different.

The stairs of the Governor's Palace at Williamsburg occupied one of the rear corners of the building. In what came to be the commonest double-pile plan, they were in a central passage. This is the arrangement in the McPhedris-Warner House at Portsmouth, New Hampshire, built in 1718–23, which is the grandest double pile surviving from the early eighteenth century in New England (45). The same arrangement is found in Brafferton Hall, which was built in 1723 as the Indian school of the College of William and Mary and would appear to be the second double pile in Virginia, and in the matching President's House of 1732 (46, 47). With nothing more than transom windows to admit daylight at first-floor level, poor lighting of the passage was a built-in problem. One solution was to widen the passage to accommodate a full-size window to one side of the door. This was done in two large Virginian houses, Westover and Nomini Hall, both begun about 1730 (48). The result was a plan whose asymmetry was not very classical but which may have been well suited to the habits and customs of those living in the house, since it was in effect simply a doubling of the hall-passage-parlor plan Virginians knew so well.

Externally these houses and the many others like them are rectangular blocks of a basic simplicity, with proportions that were often determined geometrically. By their time, jetties, cross gables, and projecting porches were things of the past. Ornament is confined to variations in the color and texture of the brickwork, as when glazed bricks are used for headers and rubbed bricks for quoins, window arches, and string courses. Nor is there really very much classical detail—an eaves cornice certainly, perhaps a pediment over the front door, or more rarely a tabernacle frame, complete with pilasters, to give consequence to it. In contrast to this external plainness the interior of the house was much more elaborately finished than before. In seventeenth-century rooms the walls were plastered and white-

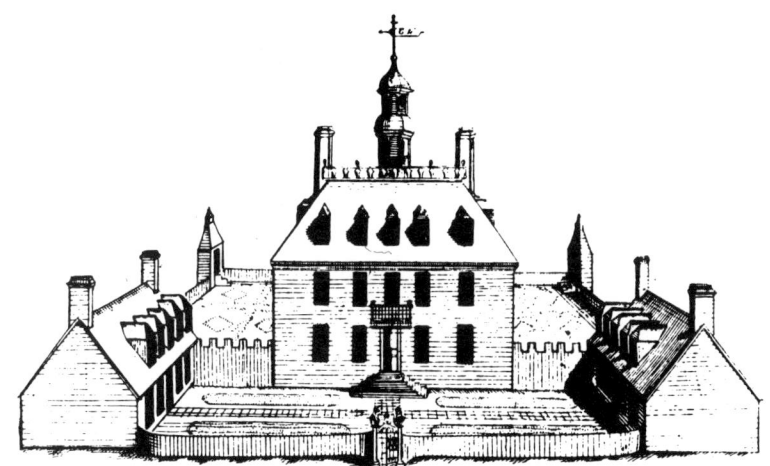

44
*Governor's Palace, Wil-*
*liamsburg, Virginia.*
*1706–20. View from*
*south. From the Bodleian*
*Plate.*

45
*McPhedris-Warner*
*House, Portsmouth, New*
*Hampshire. 1718–23.*
*Street front.*

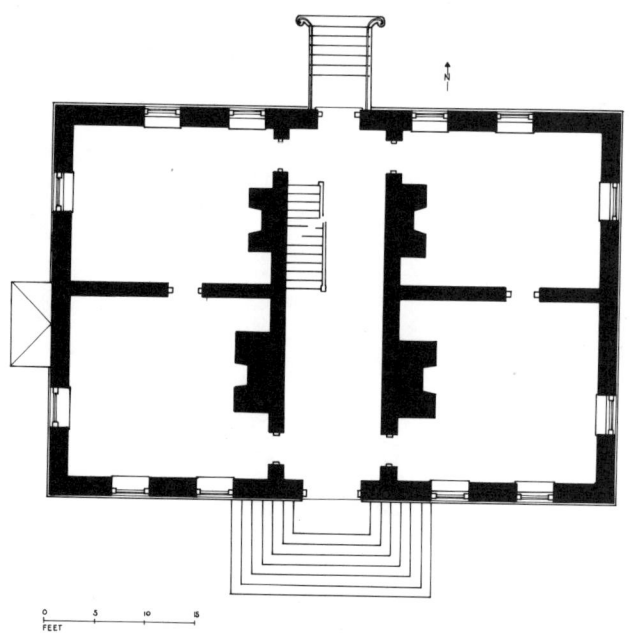

46
*College of William and
Mary, Williamsburg, Vir-
ginia. Left, Brafferton
Hall, 1723; center, Main
Building, Alexander
Spotswood, 1709–15;
right, President's House,
1732. View from east.
From the Bodleian Plate.*

47
*President's House, College
of William and Mary,
Williamsburg, Virginia.
Plan of first floor.*

48
*Westover, Charles City
County, Virginia. Circa
1730–35. View from
northwest.*

washed, beams and joists and the massive lintels over fireplaces were left exposed, doors and wainscot were of vertical boarding. Around 1700 wood panelling—no novelty in England, of course—came into use. At first—in the Samuel Wentworth House at Portsmouth, New Hampshire, for instance, and in Morattico, Richmond County, Virginia—it was used as a means of articulating the wall surfaces, with little or no suggestion of structure or strictly architectural effect. Later the full architectural treatment with pilasters and a complete entablature made its appearance; Stratford, in Westmoreland County, Virginia, begun in 1725, contains one of the earliest examples. Of an intermediate sort of treatment that became popular—without pilasters but with pedimented doorcases and an entablature scaled as if there were pilasters rising from the dado—an early example is to be seen in the drawing room of Graeme Park at Horsham, Pennsylvania, begun in 1721. Panelling was usually of pine, and pine was always painted; in the eighteenth century only walnut and mahogany, used mostly for doors, stairs, and stairrails, were not painted.

If one had to single out one feature that immediately distinguished eighteenth-century buildings from their seventeenth-century predecessors, it would be the sash window. As we have seen, the first building of the College of William and Mary at Williamsburg, completed in 1700, and the Virginia capitol there, completed in 1705, had sash windows. That they were already being used in houses in the colonies is attested by a letter written in 1701 by a Boston merchant to his London agent, in which they are called "the newest fashion." They were, it seems, an English invention to which the Dutch contributed the weight-and-pulley device to hold the sash at the required height as an improvement over the notch and catch that performed the function in the earliest examples. The importance of the sash window as an element of design was that the grid of sash bars provided a new and easily read measure of scale. (It was one that could be employed to produce illusionistic effects—as in Westover, where the slightly smaller size of the second-story windows, which are identical in design with those below them, increases the apparent height of the house.) To the end of the colonial period window frames and sashes were set close to the outer face of the wall, in contrast to the practice in London, where an Act of Parliament of 1709 required that all window and door frames be set back at least four inches behind it.

Sash windows, eaves cornices, dormers, these were the three leading features common to houses and public buildings in the early eighteenth century. The second Town House at Boston, built in 1712–13 to replace the wooden building which burned in 1711, had all three; so did the second building of the College of William and Mary, built after the burning of the first in 1705 (46). Not much is known about the former, but of the second building of William and Mary there were enough records of various kinds, including a plan by Thomas Jefferson, to ensure an accurate restoration in 1928–31. It was built in 1709–15 to the design of Governor Spotswood, who reused the walls of the original building but reduced the height of the east front from three full stories above the half-basement to two and added a pedimented entrance pavilion. This last feature made the building, for all its domesticity of detail, rather more monumental in character than either of the two other major college buildings of the decade in which it was completed. These were the first buildings of Yale College, built of wood in 1717–18, and Harvard's Massachusetts Hall, built of brick in 1718–20. The Yale building, like the William and Mary building, contained a hall, chapel, and library as well as students' chambers and studies; Massachusetts Hall contained chambers and studies only. Both were elongated double piles of three full stories; Yale had three doorways in each front and a central cupola, while Massachusetts Hall, which followed the example of Stoughton Hall and formed an open-sided quadrangle with it and Harvard Hall, has two doorways in each front with no central feature of any kind. Both had sash windows, eaves cornices, and dormers.

Dormers were not called for in houses of worship, but eaves cornices and sash windows were soon adopted by the Congregationalists of New England. The Old Brick Meeting House in Boston, built in 1713, had both, as well as round windows, like those in the tribunes of the Williamsburg capitol, and classical pilasters applied to its two-story porch. With a squarish plan, the entrance in the middle of one of the long sides, and a hipped roof with central cupola, this was a meeting house of seventeenth-century form in eighteenth-century dress. As time went on, Congregational meeting houses grew more churchlike. But rectangular sash windows were the rule until after the end of the colonial period; Congregationalists generally eschewed the type of window that came into use in Anglican churches in the colonies early in the eighteenth century and may be regarded as the ecclesiastical counterpart of the secular sash, the round-arched, or compass window, as it was called. Its use was due to the example of Sir Christopher Wren, who, in the fifty-one churches that he designed to replace those destroyed in the Great Fire of London in 1666, established a new style, an Anglican Baroque, for Church of England architecture.

*The Influence of Wren*

The Wren church did not cross the Atlantic at once. The first Trinity Church in New York City was begun in 1698, when all Wren's London churches had been in use for twelve years or more and all but a handful had received their steeples, but it still had traceried windows and a Gothic spire. A quarter of a century was to pass before the first American church with a steeple of the Wren type was completed— in the year of Wren's death. In the meantime, however, the basic vocabulary of forms employed by Wren in his churches, including the compass window, had reached the colonies with the English-trained carpenters and bricklayers who contracted to build churches (as other buildings) according to simple specifications of size and materials, which might or might not be accompanied by rudimentary plans. Some of the results are still to be seen, though often obscured by later additions and alterations, in about thirty country churches scattered through the South from Maryland to South Carolina, with more than twice as many in Virginia as in all the rest of the area. To keep to examples begun before 1730, St. James's, Goose Creek, near Charleston, South Carolina, built about 1713, is notable for its West Indian character[2] and the completeness of its furnishings, which include a pompous reredos of painted stucco with composite pilasters and the royal arms in the pediment (49); Merchants' Hope Church in Prince George County and Ware Church in Gloucester County, both built about 1715, are Virginian representatives of the oblong A-roofed type at its smallest and simplest

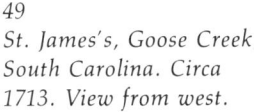

*49*
*St. James's, Goose Creek, South Carolina. Circa 1713. View from west.*

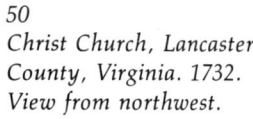
*Christit Church, Lancaster County, Virginia. 1732. View from northwest.*

and at its most spacious and highly finished respectively; Old Wye Church at Wye Mills, dating from 1717, in which the compass windows are flanked by residual buttresses of medieval form, may stand for the same type in Maryland; Vauter's Church in Essex County, Virginia, was built in 1719 and given a T plan (common in Virginia, where it was possibly due to Scottish precedent) by the addition of a "wing" twelve years later. These were all, one may be sure, the work of builder-architects.

The second brick church of Bruton Parish at Williamsburg, built in 1711–15 to replace the building of 1683, was designed by Governor Spotswood at the request of the Assembly of the colony, which was to share its cost with the parish. Spotswood, like Wren, was a mathematician. He produced a Latin-cross plan with dimensions derived from an equilateral triangle with sides of 75 feet, which was to be the total length of the building; the altitude of such a triangle is 66 feet, which, most conveniently for the staking out of the building before construction, is the length of a surveyor's chain. As for the Latin-cross plan, that was convenient because the parish was to pay for the nave and sanctuary and the colony for the transept or wings. The church of the capital, Bruton fathered no less than seven Virginian churches with cruciform plans (very rarely used in England since the Reformation). The handsomest of its progeny, and one of the handsomest of all colonial churches, is Christ Church, Lancaster County, built in 1732 (50); those with the strongest resemblance to their parent are St. John's, Hampton (1728), Mattapony (ca. 1732), and St. Paul's, Norfolk (1739).

None of the foregoing churches in the South had steeples originally, though one was added to Bruton Parish Church in 1769–70. Wren's London churches had to have steeples, and this faced him with the problem of how to translate a feature which in the phrase of another architect of Anglican churches, James Gibbs, was "of Gothic extraction" into the form-language of classical architecture

51
*St. Philip's, Charleston,*
*South Carolina. 1711–23.*
*View from north. Draw-*
*ing by Thomas Birch.*

without diminishing its symbolically charged verticality. He solved it in a fascinating variety of ways, with the result that every parish had its own distinctive landmark, visible and recognizable from the Thames or from the heights to the north of the city. In designing his steeples Wren drew on many sources, Baroque and ancient, but in only one did he follow a particular continental model; the steeple of St. Magnus the Martyr, near London Bridge, is a restrained, Anglican version of that of St. Charles Borromeo in Antwerp (built about 1620.)

The first eighteenth-century colonial church to have a steeple, the second St. Philip's, Charleston, was also, according to a well-informed traveller, the Rev. Charles Woodmason, writing in 1766, "built on the Model of the Jesuit Church at Antwerp", though it is easier to see its steeple as a stubby version of the steeple of St. Magnus's (51). St. Philip's was begun in 1711 but not opened for service until 1723; it was destroyed by fire in 1835. In the eighteenth century it was enormously admired; Woodmason wrote that it was "allowed to be the most elegant Religious Edifice in British America." Built of brick and plastered, it had a nave of five bays, 100 feet long and 60 feet broad, with a single tier of round-arched windows alternating with pilasters. The interior was galleried, with Corinthian pilasters, applied to the piers of the arcades, carrying a full entablature which ran unbroken from end to end. From the entablature a plaster barrel vault rose over the central space, while the ceilings over the aisles were flat. The octagonal tower rose out of a sixth bay, to which were attached three tetrastyle Tuscan porticoes, facing north, west, and south—the first porticoes with free-standing columns in the English colonies. None of Wren's churches (except St. Paul's) had porticoes. But Wren had recommended their use in a letter written when he was consulted in connection with plans to build more churches in London, authorized by an Act of Parliament in the very year in which St. Philip's was begun. His views would

52
*Old North Church (Christ Church), Boston, Massachusetts. William Price, 1723; spire, 1741, rebuilt 1807. Steeple from west.*

53
*Old North Church, Bos-
ton, Massachusetts. Inte-
rior, looking east.*

almost certainly have been known to the Society for the Propagation of the Gospel, which helped to raise funds for St. Philip's, if not to its unidentified designer, and the church represented an application of Wren's principles even if it was not an imitation of any one of his churches.

Such an imitation was begun in the year in which St. Philip's was opened for worship: Christ Church, or Old North Church, in Boston (52, 53). In the letter referred to, Wren expressed doubt as to the possibility of building a church "so capacious . . . as to hold above 2,000 persons, and all to hear the service and both to hear distinctly and see the preacher," and then went on to name St. James's, Westminster, known today as St. James's, Piccadilly, as the building in which he had come closest to realizing this ideal. "In this church I mention," he writes, "though very broad, and the middle nave arched up, yet there are no walls of a second order, but the whole roof rests upon pillars, as do also the galleries; I think it may be found beautiful and convenient, and as such, the cheapest of any form I could invent." Was there any connection between Wren's recommendation of St. James's, Piccadilly, and its adoption as the model for Old North Church, Boston? If there was, it may well have been through the Society for the Propagation of the Gospel, which raised funds for Old North too. Perhaps the Society even supplied information and visual materials for the use of the cabinetmaker and dealer in books and engravings, William Price, who made the design. In any case, although the "middle nave" is less "arched up," while square pillars take the place of the columns rising from the gallery fronts in Wren's church and a semicircular apse has been added, in all essentials the interior of Old North is an imitation of St. James's. The tower also follows St. James's very closely, with stringcourses dividing it into the same four stories and the same combination of arched and round windows; the wooden spire, which was not built until 1741, is a taller version of that of another Wren church, St. Lawrence Jewry.

Old North was scarcely finished when another copy of St. James's, Piccadilly, was built in Rhode Island, this time of wood. Trinity Church, Newport, was designed and built by Richard Munday, a carpenter, in 1725–26; its spire is a duplicate of the Boston one, and like it was built in 1741. But the sincerest flattery of Old North came from the Congregationalists of Boston, when the Old South Meeting House was built in 1729–30 to the design of Robert Twelves (54). Although Old South has the traditional nearly square meeting house plan, its external treatment, to the top of its brick tower, is virtually identical with that of the Anglican building. The spire, which was

54
*Old South Meeting
House, Boston, Massa-
chusetts. Robert Twelves,
1729–30. From a photo-
graph of circa 1890.*

often imitated in New England later in the century, is different but nonetheless of Wren type; its lowest stage and its silhouette are reminiscent of the spire of St. Mary-le-Bow.

*Palladianism,*
*Pure and Less Pure*

Neither St. James's, Piccadilly, nor St. Lawrence Jewry was to be found in any book. The direction of a new movement in English architectural publishing was set in 1715 by two books: the first volume of *Vitruvius Britannicus,* a collection of all that seemed best in British classical architecture to its Scottish architect compiler, Colen Campbell, and *The Architecture of A. Palladio* by the Venetian architect Giacomo Leoni, which purported to be an English edition of Andrea Palladio's *Quattro Libri dell' Architettura,* first published in Venice in 1570. Both in their different ways were designed to promote what we now call Anglo-Palladianism, which was soon to gain a dominance in the English architectural scene that lasted some forty years and to whose adherents Wren's Anglican Baroque was something to be left behind as quickly as possible.

As we have already noted, in America designs for whole buildings were not taken from books until the middle of the century. Before that, books were resorted to for plans on the one hand and for ornamental features and detail on the other. Not all were English; the plan of Stratford—a house which was altogether exceptional in the colonies for the suggestion in the treatment of its chimneys of the Baroque style of Sir John Vanbrugh—looks as if it came from a plate in Sebastiano Serlio's *Architettura,* which architects in Britain began to find useful soon after its publication in the sixteenth century (55, 56). The coeval Rosewell, in Gloucester County, Virginia, appears to have been the first American building whose plan was derived from *Vitruvius Britannicus,* combining features of Buckingham House, London (John Talman, 1705), and Roehampton House, Surrey (Thomas Archer, 1710–11).

Neither Stratford nor Rosewell was Palladian in any real sense. The Ionic doorcase of Whitehall, the house near Newport, Rhode Island, which George Berkeley (then Dean of Derry, later Bishop of Cloyne) remodelled and enlarged and occupied in 1728–31, was perhaps the first Anglo-Palladian feature in America (57). Anglo-Palladian rather than Palladian, for Berkeley took the design not from the *Quattro Libri* or Leoni's edition of it but from *The Designs of Inigo Jones* by William Kent, published in 1727 (the year before he came to Rhode Island). Inigo Jones was revered by the English Palladians no less than Palladio himself, and imitated nearly as often. By working in a style that owed a great deal to Palladio in the early seventeenth century he had given their movement an English ances-

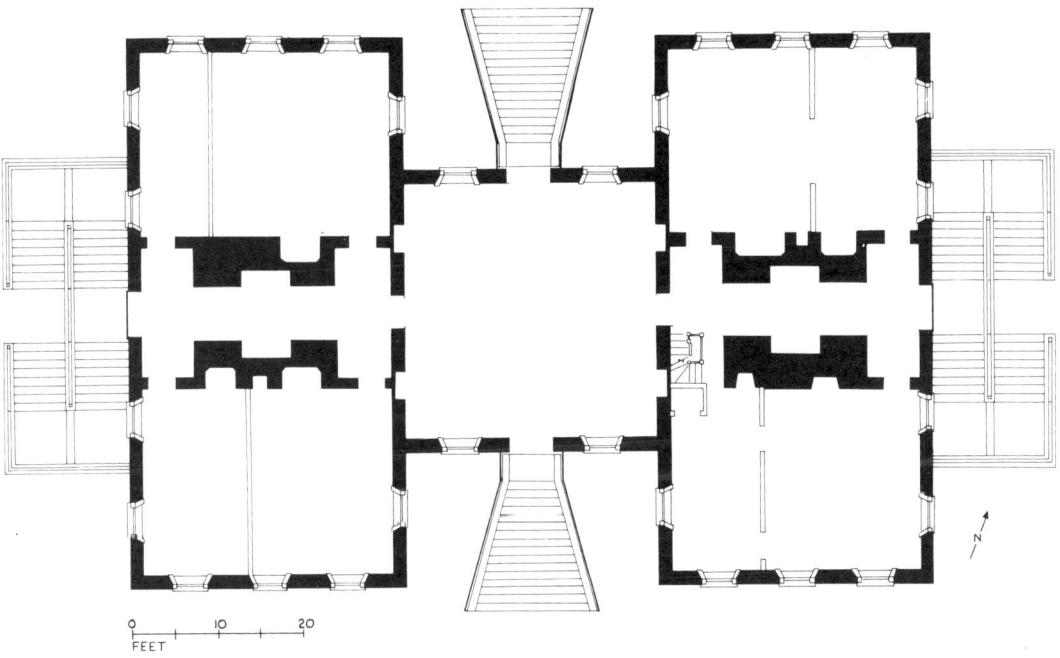

55
Stratford Hall, West-
moreland County, Vir-
ginia. Circa 1725–30.
View from south.

56
Stratford Hall, West-
moreland County, Vir-
ginia. Plan of principal
floor.

try. This was a matter of much consequence because the Anglo-Palladian program was strongly nationalist; England was to have a national architecture, free from the associations with popery and absolute monarchy that tainted the Baroque of continental Europe. One may be sure that it was not simply the requirements of scansion that caused Alexander Pope to name the British architect first in his exhortation to the leader of the movement, Lord Burlington:

*"Jones and Palladio to themselves restore,*
*And be whate'er Vitruvius was before."*

All three of the names in Pope's couplet, it will be noted, appeared in the titles of the three books by members of the Anglo-Palladian movement mentioned above. But Palladio's name on a title page was no guarantee that the contents would have met with the master's approval. Leoni had deliberately altered Palladio's designs to suit his own taste, and his "corrected" versions were republished in the mid-thirties by Edward Hoppus and Benjamin Cole in a volume shamelessly entitled *Andrea Palladio's Architecture . . . Carefully Revis'd and Redelineated.*[3] The fact of the matter was that Palladio's name sold books. Among those who recognized this was the author of *Palladio Londinensis: or, The London Art of Building,* the Colchester carpenter William Salmon. *Palladio Londinensis* was first published in 1734 and reached its seventh edition in 1759. It was of all the many books of its class—the builder's handbook—the one most used in America. Its contents comprise some geometry and instructions for drawing the classical orders, together with much useful information about business and structural matters, based on contemporary London practice, and a few designs for doorways and windows and chimneypieces. There is really nothing Palladian about the latter; Salmon was publishing stock designs—"corrected," to be sure—of the sort that had been common property in the masons' yards for twenty or thirty years. Two of his doorway designs, executed (presumably in London) in Portland stone, were used at Westover (58). Their builders' Baroque, so to call it, contrasts tellingly with the Palladianism (or Jonesianism) of Berkeley's doorway in Rhode Island.

Two buildings which illustrate the coexistence in the 1730s of the old and the new, respectively, are the Hancock House, Boston, built in 1737–40, and Drayton Hall, in South Carolina near Charleston, which was built in 1738–42. Each represented the ultimate in domestic magnificence for its time and place. The Hancock House was built by Joshua Blanchard, who had been the mason of Old South Meeting House. Of granite with sandstone dressings, it had a standard double-pile plan with four rooms to a floor, the main stairs in

57
Whitehall, Newport,
Rhode Island. George
Berkeley, 1728. Doorway.

58
Westover, Charles City
County, Virginia. Circa
1730–35. Doorway in
south front.

a wide central passage, and a service stair between the rooms on one side of it. The exterior, with an elaborate pedimented frontispiece of two orders against a rusticated background, was exceptionally rich in effect for the colonies but would not have been surprising in England thirty years earlier; the balcony over the front door, with the massive brackets supporting it, was a product of the old Anglo-Dutch architectural alliance.

In South Carolina domestic architecture had been less homogeneous than in the other southern colonies. The oldest existing house, Medway, which is now buried under later accretions, was built in 1686 by a Dutch settler with the stepped gables of his native land; Middleburg, built in 1699 for a Huguenot settler and now the oldest surviving wooden house in South Carolina, showed the Barbadian influence already noted at Goose Creek; Mulberry, built in 1714, has the odd conceit of four all but detached corner pavilions capped with curvilinear roofs and may have been some Huguenot builder's interpretation of a French château, though the first owner was an Englishman and the body of the house is a double pile with a great hall of English descent (59); the Brick House on Edisto Island, built about 1725, was another double pile with a great hall, its exterior enriched with stucco quoins and other ornamental features reminiscent of French work of the early seventeenth century. Exeter, begun in 1726 or soon after, had an H plan closely resembling one published by Stephen Primatt in *The City and Country Purchaser and Builder*

59
*Mulberry, St. John's Parish, South Carolina.*
*1714. General view.*

60
*Drayton Hall, Charleston, South Carolina. 1738–42.*
*View from southeast.*

61
*Drayton Hall, Charleston,*
*South Carolina. Hall.*

62
*Drayton Hall, Charleston,*
*South Carolina. Plan of*
*principal floor.*

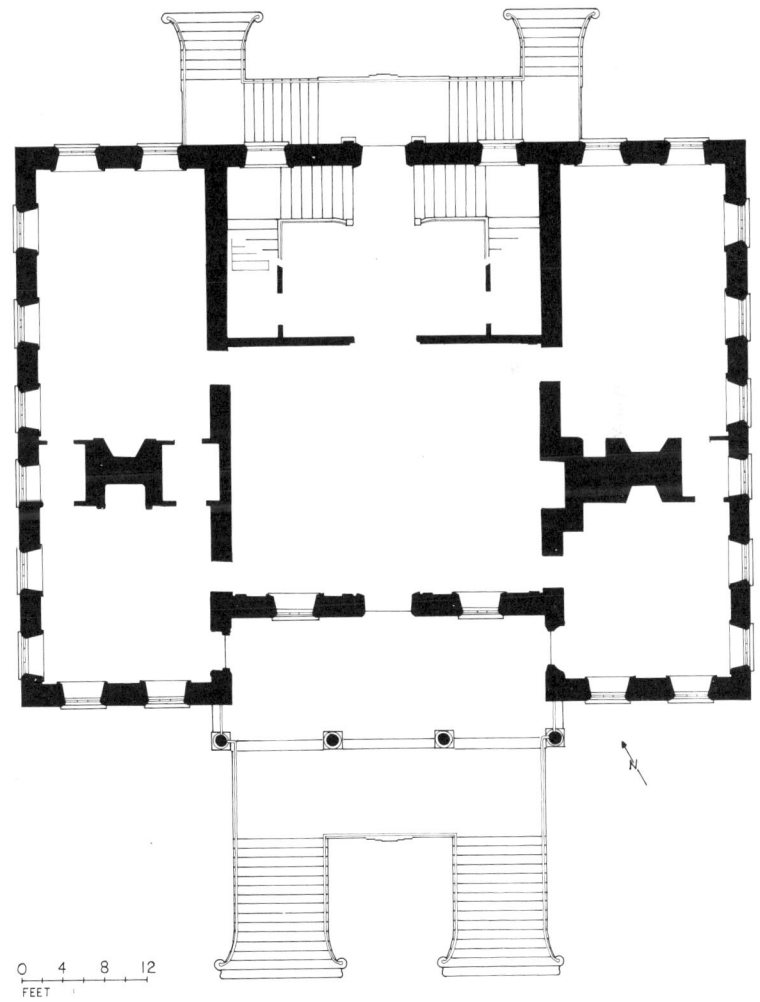

0  4  8  12
FEET

in 1667; Crowfield and Fenwick Hall, built in 1730, were hip-roofed double piles of the usual Southern kind, both with great halls. Yet in all this variety there was nothing that could be regarded as an anticipation of Drayton Hall (60, 61, 62).

Drayton Hall was the first Anglo-Palladian house in America. Until research turns up the name of an architect or builder that can be attached to it, the credit for this must go to John Drayton, the member of the King's Council for whom it was built. Its most Palladian and least English feature is the portico on the entrance front—least English because two-story porticoes were rarely built in England, where the climate prevented any kind of portico from being more than a showpiece. It is modelled on the portico on the garden front of Palladio's Villa Pisani at Montagnana; the columns, more widely spaced than Palladio would have allowed, are of Portland stone and were imported from England. The English side of Anglo-Palladianism is represented in the entrance hall, which is panelled in wood with pilasters and a full Doric entablature, by a chimneypiece based on a plate in Kent's *Designs of Inigo Jones* and also—in a most striking and indeed unique manner—by the double stairs that occupy their own hall behind the garden front. These are modelled on the stairs of Coleshill, which in the eighteenth century was believed to be a work of Inigo Jones, although the architect was actually Sir Roger Pratt.[4] They are the least Palladian feature of the house. Palladio had never, in his country houses, placed a grand staircase on the main axis, and Pratt owed the idea to the Dutch.

No public building completed before 1750 is comparable to Drayton Hall. The style of the Pennsylvania State House, now Independence Hall, which was built (except for the tower, to which we shall come later) in 1731–36, has been described by Sir John Summerson as "a Palladianism totally lacking in scholarship and virtuous only by a combination of chance and instinct." One of the two master builders who contracted for its construction, the carpenter Edward Woolley, supplied the design; he was paid five pounds for drawing the plans and elevations. Another carpenter-architect, Richard Munday, whom we met in connection with Trinity Church in Newport, Rhode Island, designed and built the state house (Old Colony House) there, in 1739–41 (63). It is a jolly affair in its Dutch way, with a balconied frontispiece more than a little like that of the Hancock House in Boston. Faneuil Hall, the market house presented to Boston by Peter Faneuil and built in 1740–42 to the design of the painter John Smibert, who had come to America with Berkeley, was more up-to-date. In what Summerson has called a "somewhat naively learned design," Smibert applied a Doric pilaster order to both stories of his

63
*Old Colony House, New
port, Rhode Island. Rich-
ard Munday, 1739–41.
View from southeast.*

64
*Christ Church, Philadelphia, Pennsylvania. Begun 1727; spire, Robert Smith, 1750–54. View from south.*

building, and this would appear to be the first time that a full-scale
order was used externally for any public building except a church in
the colonies.

The first colonial church to have an applied order was, as we saw,
St. Philip's, Charleston. The second was Christ Church, Philadelphia,
which has Doric pilasters framing two tiers of windows on either side
of the nave (64). Christ Church was begun in 1727, but work proceeded slowly enough through the 1730s for someone concerned to
get hold of a copy of *A Book of Architecture* (1728) by James Gibbs,
as the interior order, with the entablature reduced to a square block
over each column, and the Palladian or Venetian window at the east
end show (65). In the second half of the century *A Book of Architecture* was to be the most influential work of its kind, which was a
very different kind from Salmon's *Palladio Londinensis,* in America—so far as church architecture was concerned, in the whole Eng-
lish-speaking world. It is not known for certain who was responsible
for this first American use of it in Philadelphia. A physician, John
Kearsley, used to be named as the architect of Christ Church. He
certainly superintended its erection on behalf of the parish, and when
he died a newspaper said that he was "well acquainted with the
principles of architecture, a monument of which we have in *Christ
Church."* He was also one of the committee of three which superintended the building of the State House. Yet it is more likely that
the design of Christ Church was the work of some member of the
powerful Carpenters' Company of Philadelphia, which had been
founded in the 1720s—tradition says 1724—and dominated the
building scene in that city.

*Taste Triumphant*

In 1760 James Bridges, architect, offered to rebuild St. Nicholas's Church, Bristol, for the modest sum of £1,250, in accordance with what he described as "a plan I saw executed, when on my travels through the Province of Pensilvania, in America." Had his offer been accepted—in the event, St. Nicholas's was rebuilt to another, less economical, design by him—Bristol would have had the only eighteenth-century building of any consequence in England modelled on an American prototype. Which Pennsylvanian church Bridges had in mind is not a matter of importance; what is remarkable is that in 1760 an architect as sophisticated as he was could propose to imitate any American building in Bristol, then in point of size the second city in England and in point of architectural sophistication the third (after London and Bath). Fifteen years before it could not have happened; in 1760 it could because around the turn of the century taste had succeeded tradition as the main shaping force in colonial architecture.

Drayton Hall was not without its naiveties. The first American building that could have earned unqualified approval from the English *cognoscenti* of the age was the templelike Redwood Library at Newport, Rhode Island, built in 1749–50 (66). Here for the first time in the colonies appeared that ingredient in Anglo-Palladianism which was the special contribution of Lord Burlington, the Neo-Classical. A plate in Edward Hoppus' edition of Palladio (1736), inspired by a building in Burlington's own garden, was the main source of the design. The wooden siding of the walls was worked to give the illusion of chamfered stone rustication. This contrivance, however distasteful it may be to those brought up to believe that design should express the nature of materials, would have seemed a happy one to those who had read Burlington's protegé Isaac Ware on boarded walls: "These are of a very inferior kind, and only fit for meaner purposes," and who agreed with him that it was "the honour of the architect that the form triumph over the materials."

*Peter Harrison*

The Redwood Library was designed by Peter Harrison, the most talented colonial architect of whom we have any real knowledge. Born in York in 1716, Harrison landed in Newport for the first time in 1739, as a member of the crew of a merchant vessel commanded by his brother Joseph; before the end of the year he was given a command of his own. His seagoing career lasted for nine years, after which he settled down near Newport to farm his wife's land and help manage the affairs of his business partnership with his brother, trading in luxury goods with England, South Carolina, and the West Indies. In 1766 he was appointed Collector of Customs at New

66
*Redwood Library, Newport, Rhode Island. Peter Harrison, 1749–50. Portico.*

Haven, where he lived until his death of a stroke, after suffering much persecution as a loyalist and a government official, in 1775.

With occasional exceptions—he was paid forty-five pounds for "drawing the plan" of Christ Church, Cambridge—Harrison's designs were supplied gratis, while he had no financial interest in the construction of the buildings he designed. The only other amateur architect we have met with more than one building to his name has been Alexander Spotswood, and it is interesting to compare the qualifications of the two men for the practice of architectural design. Spotswood's rested, in the view of his contemporaries, on his mathematical ability, Harrison's on his skill as a draftsman (which he employed in cartography some years before he turned to architecture) and on his book-learned familiarity with what was admired and to be imitated; at his death he owned the largest collection of books on architecture recorded in the colonies, numbering twenty-seven titles. The degree of control exercised by Spotswood and Harrison over the detail of their buildings differed too. Spotswood's "platt or draught" that was laid before the vestry of Bruton Parish in 1711 is unlikely to have been more than a plan with a single elevation; matters of detail would be left to the master craftsmen. The set of six drawings that Harrison sent to the building committee for King's Chapel, Boston, in 1749 included plans, elevations, and a section, while for Christ Church, Cambridge, in 1760 he supplied designs for the pulpit and organ loft as well as plans and elevations for the building itself.

King's Chapel must be accounted Harrison's masterpiece, even though the steeple was never completed and its granite-walled exterior is bleaker than it would have been had the building committee been able to afford the shipping and working of the Bath stone offered by Ralph Allen for the columns and other classical features and ornaments. The interior is modelled on St. Martin-in-the-Fields, the church with which the Roman Catholic (and Roman-trained) Gibbs had set a new standard for Anglican architecture (67). As in St. Martin's, there is a Venetian window at the east end and Corinthian columns carry isolated blocks of entablature. Here, however, the blocks of entablature are not square but oblong, and each is carried by two columns instead of a single one. It is a change which shows that Harrison had a feeling for the structural origins of the classical elements of design. For an entablature is a stylized representation of a beam spanning the space between free-standing supports and the visible parts of a roof above it; when reduced, as Gibbs (and Brunelleschi before him) reduced it, to a square block with four identical faces, it loses all structural meaning.

In the exterior design of King's Chapel Harrison solved a problem that had proved too much for Gibbs: how to combine a steeple and a portico. In St. Martin-in-the-Fields the tower rises out of the body of the church behind the portico, with the result that it seems to be riding the roof. Harrison brought his tower forward so that it shares only its east wall with the nave, and he emphasized the separateness of tower and nave by giving the latter a hipped roof instead of the gabled roof usual in churches of the time. Instead of a pediment, which would have conflicted with the hipped roof, he gave the portico a balustrade—and with it a resemblance, certainly intentional, to Inigo Jones's west portico of St. Paul's, destroyed in the Great Fire of 1666, which he knew from his copy of Kent's book. Thus even in imitating a work of Gibbs that was in no sense Palladian, Harrison paid a tribute to the great seventeenth-century forerunner of Anglo-Palladianism.[1]

Harrison's other public buildings were the Synagogue (1759–63) and the Brick Market (1761–72) in Newport and Christ Church, Cambridge (1760–61). The Touro Synagogue, as it is now called, was the first public synagogue in colonial America. Here Harrison turned for detail to Gibbs—this time, to his *Rules for Drawing the Several Parts of Architecture* (1732)—and to Kent's *Designs of Inigo Jones*. But the model for the building as a whole was the Bevis Marks Synagogue of the Spanish and Portuguese Jews in London, dedicated in 1701, whose builders had worked for Wren and adopted the plan of James's, Piccadilly.

67
*King's Chapel, Boston, Massachusetts. Peter Harrison, 1749–54. Interior looking east.*

68
*Brick Market, Newport, Rhode Island. Peter Harrison, 1761–72. View from northwest.*

*Christ Church, Cam-
bridge, Massachusetts.
Peter Harrison, 1760–61.
Interior, looking west.*

For the Brick Market Harrison adopted, and adapted, the elevation
of the New Gallery of Somerset House, London, as shown in *Vitruvius Britannicus,* where Campbell notes that it was "taken from a
Design of Inigo Jones, but conducted by another hand"—that is,
Jones's pupil, John Webb (68). Besides omitting the rustication of
the arcaded ground story and the balustrades under the second-floor
windows and changing the order from Corinthian to Ionic—modifi-
cations justifiable on grounds of economy—he substituted corner
pilasters, with two faces, for the single-faced end pilasters of his
model. This change, called for by the wrapping of the Somerset
House facade around a freestanding building, gives a sense of structure to the pilasters and is analogous to the coupling of the columns
in King's Chapel. The Brick Market stands near the foot of the street
of which Munday's Colony House forms the head. Nowhere can the
difference between the architecture of tradition and the architecture
of taste be better seen.

Christ Church, Cambridge, like the Redwood Library, is of wood
simulating stone, although funds ran out before the walls could be
rough-cast to complete the illusion. The building is Doric outside,
with a full entablature under the eaves, and Ionic within; details are
from Gibbs (69). For the supports of the coved ceiling over the nave
Harrison abandoned the logic of his coupled columns in King's Chapel
and employed single columns with square entablature blocks. The
result justifies him, for not only do the repeated units of the order
define the nave and aisles when seen in series but each tells individually as a decorative yet stately object in the luminous interior.

*Church Design
and James Gibbs*

In Anglican church architecture in the colonies the third quarter of the eighteenth century was the age of Gibbs, for all that Gibbs himself died near the beginning of it, in 1754. In 1750–54 a steeple with a spire modelled on St. Martin-in-the-Fields was added to the already Gibbsian nave of Christ Church, Philadelphia (64); the builder, and designer too in all probability, was the carpenter Robert Smith, the most successful of all the Philadelphia builder-architects of the time. In 1752–61 St. Michael's, Charleston, was built with a Doric portico and a disproportionately tall steeple—fifty-six feet taller than the church is long—which is unmistakably Gibbsian even though it does not follow any particular one of Gibbs's designs; of masonry to the top of the second octagon, this steeple is one of the most daring structures of the colonial period (70, 71). The interior is not Gibbsian at all; a galleried hall with a tray ceiling unsupported by columns, it most resembles St. Alphege's, Greenwich, of which Nicholas Hawksmoor was the architect. The designer of St. Michael's has not been identified; he may well have been its builder, Samuel Cardy. In 1764–66 St. Paul's Chapel, New York City, was built to the design of Thomas McBean with an interior which was the closest to St. Martin's to date; the steeple—St. Martin's with an extra octagonal stage—was added thirty years later.

Country churches still showed regional characteristics, usually in conjunction with academic or at least bookish features that distinguished them from similar buildings of the first half of the century. Thus in Virginia cruciform plans were adopted for Abingdon Church, Gloucester County, and Aquia Church in Stafford County, both begun in 1751, while Abingdon (a Latin cross) has pedimental gables and Aquia (a Greek cross) a rusticated doorway of a type much used by Gibbs. In South Carolina, Pompion Hill Chapel was built in 1763 to the same plan as St. James's, Goose Creek, with entrances in the middle of the north and south sides and the same roof, hipped above the wind beams, but with the addition of an apsidal chancel (outwardly rectangular) and a Venetian east window; St. Stephen's, Santee, was built in 1767 to the same plan with a ceiling imitating St. Michael's, Charleston. However, the South Carolinian partiality for porticoes did produce two country churches that were quite out of the ordinary. The earlier, Prince William's Church at Sheldon, was built in 1751 in the form of a Roman temple, with a tetrastyle portico to the west and half-columns around the nave, all of brick. Nothing as classical had been built for Anglican worship since Inigo Jones's St. Paul's, Covent Garden. Woodmason thought it "far more elegant than St. Michael's" and noted that it was "by many esteem'd a more beautiful building than St. Philip's." The other porticoed

70
*St. Michael's, Charleston,
South Carolina. Samuel
Cardy (?), 1752–61. View
from north.*

71
*St. Michael's, Charleston,
South Carolina. Plan.*

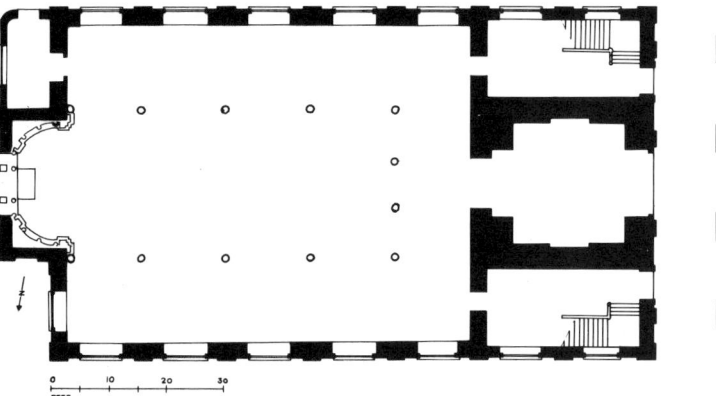

country church in South Carolina, St. James's, Santee, was built in 1768; it has matching Tuscan porticoes to north and south.

In New England, where Anglican churches were few and far between, the frame building of Old Trinity at Brooklyn, Connecticut, built in 1770–71, merits a mention. It was designed and in large part paid for by Godfrey Malbone, who had moved to Brooklyn from Newport in 1766 to manage his father's estate there and who objected to the prospect of being taxed for a new Congregational church. His models were the Synagogue and Trinity Church in Newport, the former for the general design of the interior, the latter for its detail. The hipped roof and compass windows of Old Trinity contrast with the gable roof and square-headed windows of the Brooklyn meeting house, in competition with which it was built. The latter differs from it also in having a steeple modelled on the steeple of Old South in Boston, which was a favorite model with the Congregationalists when they built steeples (which in the colonial period was seldom); the most elegant version is the steeple of the Farmington meeting house, built in 1771. Early in the previous decade the other Boston steeple, that of Old North, had been imitated at Wethersfield, Connecticut, whose brick meeting house, built in 1761–64, was considered the finest in New England outside Boston.

The Congregationalists had no use for Gibbs. Whether this was because they were conservative in architectural matters—as they certainly were—or because they regarded Gibbs's style as specifically Anglican is an open question. Surprisingly enough, the most thoroughly and uncritically Gibbsian of all the churches in the British colonies was built, on the eve of the Revolution, for the Baptists. This is the First Baptist Meeting House at Providence, Rhode Island, which went up to the design of Joseph Brown in 1774–75 (72). Brown was another amateur architect—like Harrison a merchant, like Spotswood a student of mathematics. However, mathematics was not to serve Brown in designing the First Baptist Meeting House as it served Spotswood in designing Bruton Parish Church. What did serve him, from beginning to end, was *A Book of Architecture*. The interior, originally square, follows St. Peter's, Vere Street; the porch is a more open version of the porch of the same church. For the steeple Brown turned to plate 30 in Gibbs's book, where he found three alternative designs for the steeple of St. Martin-in-the-Fields. He chose the middle one, which was executed line for line by the master carpenter James Sumner of Boston. That the steeple of a Baptist meeting house should follow a design made for an Anglican church by a Catholic architect is clear proof that considerations of

72
*First Baptist Meeting House, Providence, Rhode Island. Joseph Brown, 1774–75. View from southwest.*

taste took precedence over all others by this time. The whole building
is of wood; the spire, white today, was originally painted to simulate
various marbles.

**Public Buildings
1750–1776**

Among secular public buildings of the third quarter of the century
Harrison's Brick Market at Newport was exceptional in representing
the academic side of Anglo-Palladianism; the style of most of them
was that carpenter's classic, Palladian only by courtesy, of which
Independence Hall was an extensive earlier example. Nor was Dutch
influence a thing of the past, at least at the opening of the period;
the cupola crowning the tower added to Independence Hall by Ed-
mund Woolley in 1750–53 bore a marked resemblance to a design
by Pieter Post.[2] The capitol at Williamsburg as rebuilt in 1751–53
after a fire in 1747 had a two-story portico, Doric below and Ionic
above, which essayed Palladian propriety—without much success,
according to Thomas Jefferson.[3] The South Carolina State House,
built in 1752–56 and burnt in 1788, seems to have been a much
more literate design; the general scheme of its facade—it had a
pedimented center, with Ionic pilasters above and arches below (a
common Palladian formula), flanked by Venetian windows—was repeated in the Exchange and Custom House of 1767–72. Both of these
Charleston buildings have been attributed to William Rigby Naylor,
who was the son-in-law of Samuel Cardy, the builder of St. Michael's. The Maryland State House as rebuilt in the seventies had
the special distinction of being the first domed state house in America. It was designed in 1772 by Joseph Horatio Anderson, who
claimed to have been "regularly bread to those Sciences architectural
design and construction & the only one upon the Continant." Yet
in 1784 his dome, which was of octagonal plan and pointed contour,
was found to have been built "contrary to all rules of architecture,"
and in the next three years Joseph Clark, a rich merchant and
occasional architect, replaced it with the existing much taller
structure.

Anderson made his claim to architectural expertise in a letter
written in 1770 from Philadelphia to the corporation of Rhode Island
College (now Brown University); he had read in the papers that the
college was about to build and tendered his services "as Architect
& Superintendant for that purpose." Although there is no positive
evidence that his offer was accepted, University Hall at Brown, built
in 1770–71, may be attributed to him. An elongated double pile of
four stories, with three entrances a side, a pedimented pavilion in
the center, and a cupola, it represents one of the two main types of
college building in the eighteenth century, the other colonial ex-

amples being Spotswood's William and Mary, Nassau Hall at Princeton (1754–56), and Hollis Hall at Harvard (1762–63), while the
original building of Dartmouth College (1784–91) was a post-Revo-
lution one. The alternative type, which lacks any emphatic central
feature, reappeared early in the second half of the century in Connecticut Hall at Yale (1750–52), which is virtually a duplicate of
Harvard's Massachusetts Hall built thirty years earlier. The first
building of King's College (Columbia University), erected in 1760,
was a hybrid, with no less than four pedimented pavilions—one for
each entrance—but no central feature below the cupola. New Harvard
Hall, built in 1764–66 to replace the burnt building of 1677, had a
pediment on each front and a very large cupola; the chapel, which
occupied the western part of the first floor, was distinguished by
compass windows. As Morrison has said, it was the first major
Harvard building to attempt a nondomestic effect.

Before 1750 public buildings in the colonies were ecclesiastical,
governmental, or educational; the third quarter of the century saw
the beginning of that multiplication of building types which is one
of the developments that make its last quarter the beginning of the
modern era in architecture as in so much else. The first hospital in
the colonies, the Pennsylvania Hospital, was founded in 1751 and,
thanks to Benjamin Franklin's interest and his invention of the device
of matching funds, opened its doors in 1755. The building was
designed, and its erection supervised, by Samuel Rhoads, carpenter,
member of the American Philosophical Society, and one of the man-
agers of the hospital. The five-part design was a translation of Beth-
lem Hospital (Bedlam), London, designed by Robert Hooke in 1674,
into carpenter's classic. Only the east wing was completed in 1755;
the west wing followed in 1786, while the center was not completed
(in another style) until 1805. The long wards accommodated men on
the first floor and women on the second; in the basement were cells
for the insane, who could be observed by the public outside the
building across a small moat like those in modern zoos.

The insane were to have been relegated to the basement again in
the New York Hospital, built in 1773–75, but the building burned
before any could be admitted. By then, the first American hospital
built exclusively for the insane was already in use. This was the
Public Hospital at Williamsburg, Virginia, built in 1770–73 "for the
Reception of Persons who are so unhappy as to be deprived of their
reason." It was a plain two-story affair, with a pedimented pavilion
in the middle of each front; access to the cells (twelve to a floor) was
from central corridors. The designer, but not in this case the builder,
was Robert Smith of Philadelphia, whom we know as the builder of

the spire of Christ Church in that city and who followed that up with designing and supervising the construction of Nassau Hall at Princeton. In addition to these, Smith had designed a building for Pennsylvania College and churches in Philadelphia for the Presbyterians and the Lutherans. He was also, it is said, master carpenter for the Philadelphia Bettering House, a building of curious plan which combined the functions of an almshouse and a workhouse. In 1768 he designed the Hall of the Carpenters' Company of Philadelphia, a cruciform structure with four pediments and a central cupola, which was built in 1770–73. Historical associations have made Carpenters' Hall the best known of all Smith's buildings, but his biggest commission was Walnut Street Prison in Philadelphia, which he designed and built in 1773–74. This had a street range 184 feet long and 32 feet wide, with a tall cupola and the pedimented center of which Smith was so fond, and two wings of the same width running back 90 feet to form a squat U on plan. Technically, it was notable for its fireproof construction, with the floors supported by groined brick vaults. It would doubtless have had a more important place in the history of prison design if it had not been planned six years before John Howard's Act of Parliament of 1779 recommended the "separate system," or solitary confinement, as a means of prison reform.[4]

*The Golden Age of the Colonial House*

The hallmark of Palladianism in domestic architecture is the temple portico with a single giant order employed as the central feature of a facade. In the American colonies it made its first appearance in the Pinckney House, Charleston, which was begun in 1746. With the portico flattened against the front and having pilasters instead of columns, this house was reminiscent of that pre-Burlingtonian Palladianism of Dutch origin which had arrived in England in the 1660s. By all accounts one of the grandest houses in the colonies, the Pinckney House was a casualty of the Civil War.

The finest New England house of the later 1740s was Shirley Place at Roxbury, Massachusetts (73). It was built for Governor William Shirley soon after his purchase of the land on which it stood in 1746. Unlike the Pinckney House, which was of brick, Shirley Place was a frame structure, faced with rusticated boards. The latter have suggested to some the hand of Peter Harrison, and the possibility that he was the architect is strengthened by the fact that Mrs. Harrison and Mrs. Shirley were related. Certainly the design was as bookish as any of Harrison's. The plan followed closely that of Wilbury House in Wiltshire, which was designed and built for himself between 1710 and 1725 by William Benson (Sir Christopher Wren's successor as Surveyor-General of the King's Works), as published by Colen Campbell in the first volume of *Vitruvius Britannicus* (74). The Wilbury plan was itself based on Palladio's Villa Poiana at Poiana Maggiore, and so far as its plan went Shirley Place was without question the most purely Palladian house in America to its date. Baroque rather than Palladian, though, were the giant Doric pilasters supporting isolated sections of entablature on each elevation. (An Ionic version of this motif was already to be seen in New England in the Foster-Hutchinson House.) It is the coupling of eight of the ten pilasters on the east or entrance front—on the west front, which had a large Venetian window in the center, there were only four pilasters—that perhaps affords a clue to the specific source of inspiration. For the entrance front of Castle Howard in Yorkshire, Sir John Vanbrugh's first masterpiece, has coupled Doric pilasters with a discontinuous entablature, while behind it rises a cupola which may well have been the model for Shirley Place's "ornate and somewhat gargantuan cupola," as Morrison has called it. These resemblances constitute additional circumstantial evidence in favor of the attribution of Shirley Place to the Yorkshireman Harrison, who must have seen Castle Howard in his youth and may even have renewed an admiration for it on his last visit to England in 1747.

The use of architectural books increased greatly after the mid-century, as did also the number of books available. Eighteen titles appear in colonial records up to the end of 1750; by the end of 1760 the total had nearly tripled, to fifty-one. The impact of books on domestic design in the 1750s is well seen in three Virginian houses: Carter's Grove, Gunston Hall, and Mount Airy. Carter's Grove, near Williamsburg, was built in 1750–53. As a plantation account book shows, Carter Burwell, the owner, contracted separately with local craftsmen for the building of his house, while for the finishing of the interior he brought a joiner and woodcarver, Richard Bayliss, from England, paying his and his family's passage money. Externally, Carter's Grove is a typical double pile, not unlike Westover. Its plan, however, is perfectly symmetrical and is set out according to a geometrical system of squares and root-two rectangles (75). Instead of Westover's off-center passage, there is an oblong entrance hall with its longer axis parallel to the front of the house and a square stair hall centered behind it. The design of the woodwork in the hall, with its Ionic pilasters, and in the west parlor, where the order is Doric, came from Salmon's *Palladio Londinensis,* a copy of which Carter Burwell purchased from a Williamsburg bookseller while his house was going up (76).

Gunston Hall, in Fairfax County, is another house of traditional form with elaborate woodwork by a craftsman brought from England

73
*Shirley Place, Roxbury,
Massachusetts. 1746. Ele-
vation of entrance front,
restored by W. W.
Cordingley.*

74
*Shirley Place, Roxbury,
Massachusetts. Plan of
first floor by W. W.
Cordingley.*

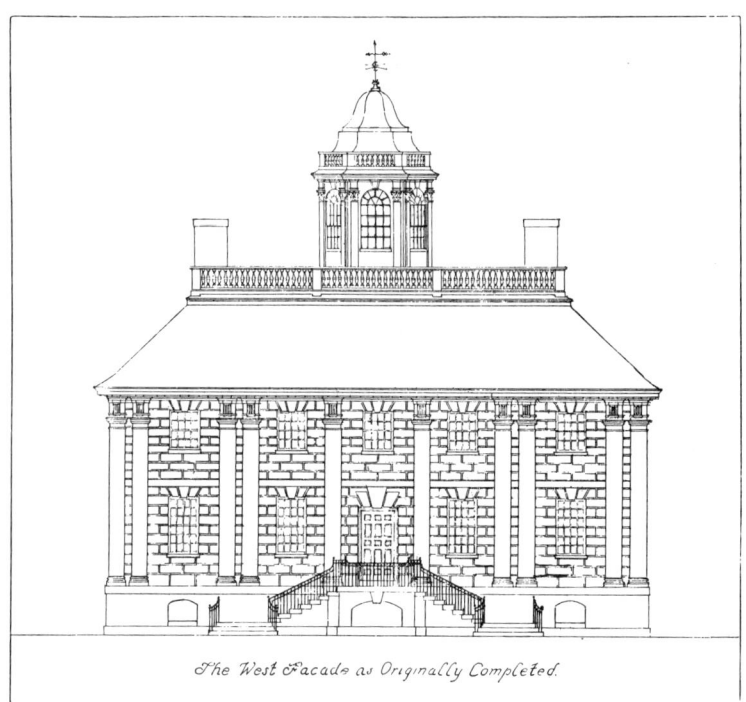

*The West Facade as Originally Completed.*

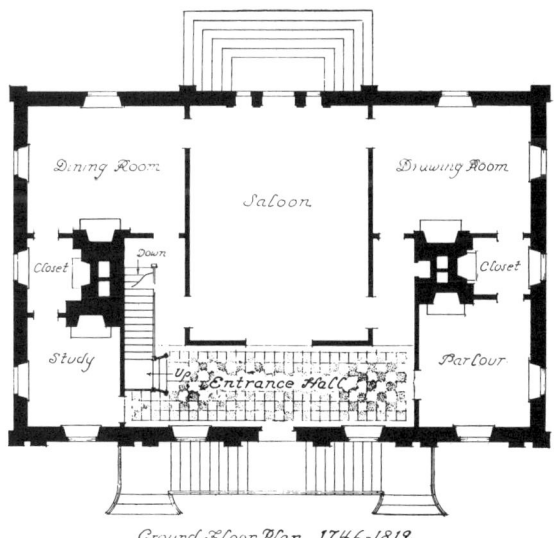

*Ground Floor Plan 1746-1819.*

75
*Carter's Grove, James
City County, Virginia.
1750–53. Plan of first
floor.*

76
*Carter's Grove, James
City County, Virginia.
Entrance hall and stairs.*

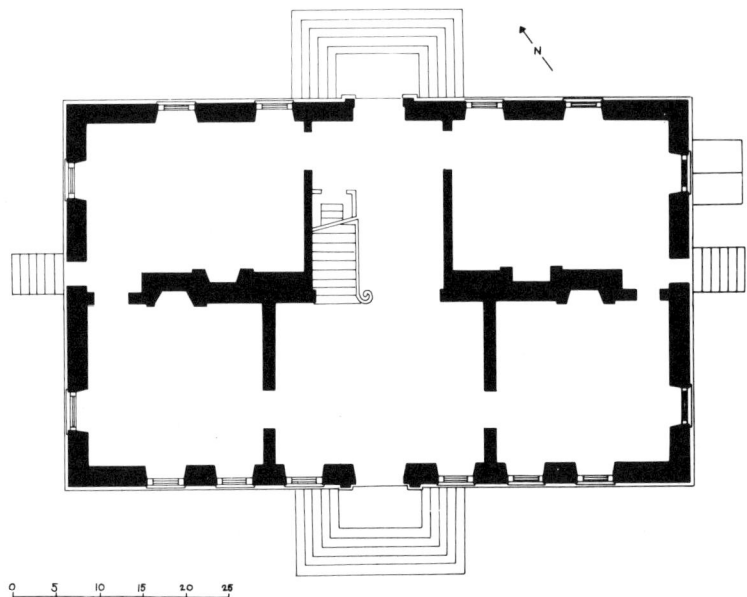

O   5   10   15   20   25
FEET

to execute it. Built in 1755–59 for George Mason, author of the Virginia Bill of Rights, Gunston Hall is a story-and-a-half double pile. The two porches, as well as the interior woodwork, are the work of William Buckland. Born at Oxford in 1734, Buckland was apprenticed at the age of fourteen to an uncle, a London joiner; in 1755, having served his articles, he bound himself as an indentured servant to George Mason's brother Thomson, then in London on a visit, convenanting to "well and truly serve the said Thomson Mason, his Executors or Assigns in the Plantation of Virginia beyond the Seas, for the Space of Four Years, next ensuing his Arrival in the said Plantation, in the Employment of a Carpenter & Joiner." His assignment to George Mason for the finishing of Gunston Hall gave the young joiner a chance to demonstrate his taste and skill of which he availed himself to the full. The landward porch is a novel adaptation of the so-called Palladian motif, while the porch toward the gardens and the Potomac River is of the half-octagon plan that architects in England were beginning to adopt as a relief from Palladian rectangularity and combines a Doric order with a touch of Gothic—or Gothic Rococo—in its ogee arches. Nothing like either of them had been seen in the colonies before, and the same may be said of the dining room, where the doors, windows, and overmantel have frames with scalloped cresting on the cornice which made it the first colonial example of "the Chinese taste," or Chinoiserie. The drawing room, on the other hand, is purely classical. It has a modillion ceiling cornice, and its door, windows, and two niches for the display of china are set in tabernacle frames with fluted pilasters and moulding enrichments of great delicacy (77). The books used here were *The British Architect* and *A Collection of Designs in Architecture* by Abraham Swan, *The Builder's Companion* by William Pain, and *A Collection of Ornamental Designs, Applicable to Furniture Frames, and the Decoration of Rooms* by Thomas Chippendale. The first and last of these Buckland could have brought with him from London—Chippendale's book appeared the year before he left—but the other two were not published until 1757 and 1758, respectively. Evidently Mason was determined that his house should be finished in the very latest taste. For the drawing room he imported from England a marble mantel in the Neo-Classical Style that took its name from the Scottish architect Robert Adam and was to dominate the architectural scene in America after the Revolution.

Buckland also had a hand in the interiors of Mount Airy, Richmond County (78).[5] This house, together with several others in Virginia, has been attributed to John Ariss, who in 1751 advertised in the *Maryland Gazette* that he would undertake "Buildings of all

77
Gunston Hall, Fairfax
County, Virginia. Wil-
liam Buckland, 1755–59.
Drawing room.

78
Mount Airy, Richmond
County, Virginia. 1758–
62. South front.

Sorts and Dimensions . . . either of the Ancient or Modern Order of Gibbs' Architect," giving an address in Westmoreland County, Virginia. But there is no reason to suppose that Ariss was the only builder in Virginia to own a copy of *A Book of Architecture*, from which the plan and elevations of Mount Airy, which was begun in 1758, were taken—the plan from a design that Gibbs had made for the poet Matthew Prior, and the elevations from "A Design for a Gentleman in Dorsetshire" (three plates further on). Gibbs's shade must have been gratified. In his introduction he had stated that it was the opinion of "several Persons of Quality and others" that "such a Work as this would be of use to such Gentlemen as might be concerned in Building, especially in the remote parts of the Country, where little or no assistance for Design can be procured."

The Dutch Palladian type of house, with pilasters applied to a pedimented central pavilion, continued to be built in the late colonial decades. The Vassall-Longfellow House at Cambridge, Massachusetts (79), and Nanzatico in King George County, Virginia, are examples in New England and the South, respectively. In the mid-sixties the only two colonial houses to have giant porticoes with free-standing columns went up, in Maryland and New York City. The former, Whitehall, in Anne Arundel County, was begun in 1764 for Governor Horatio Sharpe, and the three-room central block was completed the next year. After Sharpe's retirement in 1769 wings were added to convert what had been built as a pavilion for the entertainment of boating parties from Annapolis into a house for year-round occupation. The central room is admirable equally for its stately proportions and its exquisite woodwork, which includes Baroque masks in the ceiling cove of a virtuosity unsurpassed in colonial America; it is likely, though not proved, that the carver was William Buckland again (80). The New York house with a prostyle portico is the Roger Morris Mansion, built in 1765. Whereas Whitehall was thoroughly Palladian, the portico of the Roger Morris Mansion showed, with its slender and widely spaced columns, the new freedom from the rules of proportion claimed by Robert Adam and his followers. But the finest house of the colonial period in New York was the stone-built Apthorpe House of circa 1767. This had a deeply recessed porch with engaged Ionic columns and a pediment; the full entablature was carried around the house and there were four pilasters at each end, where the roof was of pedimental form; there were pediments over the first-floor windows, while the doorway within the porch followed the Palladian motif. No other house in the colonies made such a display of confident Latinity.

79
*Vassall-Longfellow
House, Cambridge, Mas-
sachusetts. 1759. Entrance
front.*

80
*Whitehall, Anne Arundel
County, Maryland. 1764–
65. Central hall.*

*Miles Brewton House,*
*Charleston, South Caro-*
*lina. Ezra Waite, 1765–*
*69. Street front.*

The Miles Brewton House at Charleston, South Carolina, built in
1765–69 (81), and Shirley in Charles City County, Virginia, circa
1769, have two-storied porticoes. At Shirley the present columns
and steps are early nineteenth-century replacements; in all probability the original upper columns were Ionic, as in Drayton Hall, the
Miles Brewton House, and the Palladian prototypes. Both the Miles
Brewton House and Shirley have rich interiors. The Miles Brewton
House was finished by Ezra Waite, "civil architect, Housebuilder in
general and Carver from London." The drawing room, with its coved
ceiling, tabernacle frames, and pedimented chimneypiece, reminded
Fiske Kimball of Inigo Jones's Double Cube Room at Wilton; the
gallery of Colen Campbell's Mereworth Castle, itself inspired by
Jones, affords even closer parallels. Inside Shirley the grand feature
is the flying stair, which rises in a hall taking up more than a quarter
of the ground floor.

The Wentworth-Gardner House at Portsmouth, New Hampshire,
shows that much skilled craftsmanship could still be lavished on the
straight-fronted, hip-roofed double pile in the sixties. But houses of
any consequence more commonly had a pedimented pavilion projecting from the center of the front. Mount Airy seems to have been
the first colonial example; it was closely followed—in design, as well
as in time—by Mannsfield (ca. 1760), near Fredericksburg. Both
houses had flanking buildings, "dependencies" in Southern parlance,
connected to the main block by quadrant passages with solid walls;
at New Bern, North Carolina, quadrant colonnades reached out to
embrace Governor William Tryon's guests. (The conceit is Palladio's,
used by him of his design for the Villa Trissino at Meledo.) Tryon

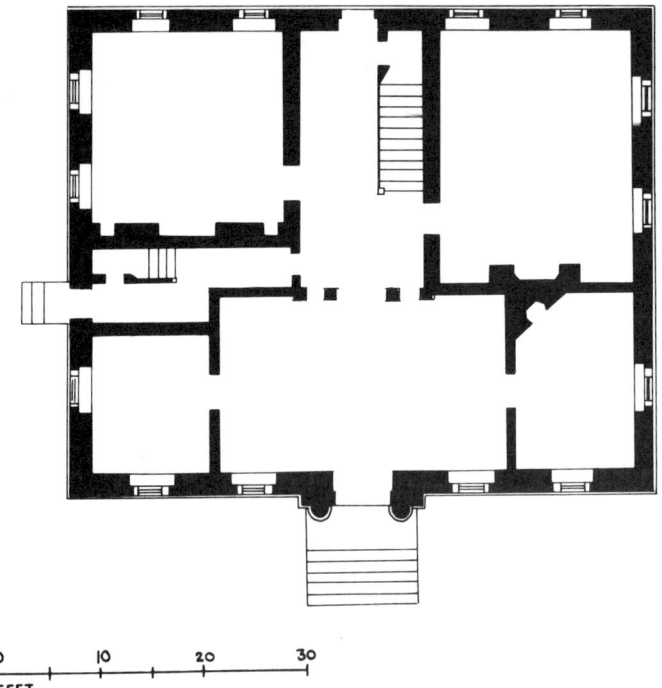

82
Cliveden, Germantown,
Pennsylvania. Benjamin
Chew, 1763–64. Entrance
front.

83
Cliveden, Germantown,
Pennsylvania. Plan of
first floor.

brought his architect, John Hawks, from England; Hawks had worked under Stiff Leadbetter on Lord Harcourt's house in Oxfordshire, Nuneham Park (1760), with which the New Bern Palace had points in common. Blandfield, in Essex County, Virginia, built circa 1770, differs from Mount Airy and Mannsfield in being of brick instead of stone and in having the dependencies connected with the main block by straight passages.

In their Virginian plainness the elevations of Blandfield are very different from those of the two finest Pennsylvanian examples of the pedimented-center type of house, Mount Pleasant and Cliveden, with their livelier, more Baroque effect and display of pattern-book features. Mount Pleasant, in Fairmount Park, Philadelphia, was begun in 1761 for an immigrant sea captain, John MacPherson; the name of its architect is not known. Cliveden, in Germantown, was begun two years later for Benjamin Chew, attorney general of Pennsylvania (82). Chew was his own architect. Surviving drawings from his hand show that he toyed with the idea of a three-story house modelled on Kew Palace, which had been built for Frederick Prince of Wales to William Kent's designs in the 1730s; the plan of Cliveden as built surely must have been suggested by Colen Campbell's "New Design for Tobiah Jenkyns Esq." in the second volume of *Vitruvius Britannicus* (83). The columnar screen between the entrance hall and stair is an unusual and stately feature which was employed also by William Buckland in the Chase-Lloyd House at Annapolis, Maryland, in 1771; Buckland combined it with the stateliest of all types of stair, the Imperial stair, in which a central flight ascends to a landing at half-story level and parallel side flights return on either side to reach the upper floor (84).

The Chase-Lloyd House is of three stories and distinctly urban character. The Hammond-Harwood House, Annapolis, completed to Buckland's design in 1774, is a country house in town (85). A five-part composition with half-octagon fronts to the outer pavilions or dependencies, this house has a good claim to be considered the culminating work of domestic architecture in the colonies as well as the crowning achievement of Buckland's career. Gibbs was the principal source, and in this it differs from the last group of houses, also cinquepartite, that remains to be mentioned in this chapter. All are in Virginia; the earliest, Belle Isle, Lancaster County, was built about 1760, while Battersea, Dinwiddie County, and Brandon, in Prince George County, went up between 1765 and 1770 (86). Robert Morris's *Select Architecture*, published in 1757, was clearly the book referred to in each case. (It was a book much used by Thomas Jefferson—to whom Brandon has been attributed.) While the

84
Chase-Lloyd House,
Annapolis, Maryland.
William Buckland, 1771.
Stairs.

85
Hammond-Harwood
House, Annapolis, Mary-
land. William Buckland,
1773–74. Street front.

86
Brandon, Prince George
County, Virginia. 1765–
70. View from south.

Hammond-Harwood House is strongly centripetal, owing to the pediment spanning three of the five bays of the central block, these Virginian houses show in an extreme degree what Vincent Scully has seen as an "American instinct . . . toward horizontal expansion and dispersion."

**The Domestic Interior**

In interior design the general tendency was toward lightness and delicacy. Rooms were sometimes given the full classical treatment, with floor-to-ceiling panelling, tabernacle frames and complete entablatures, down to the end of the colonial period—at Shirley, for example, in the early seventies. But a simpler treatment, encouraged by the introduction of wallpaper, was becoming common; in this, panelling was confined to a dado, the entablature beneath the ceiling was reduced to a cornice, and doors were framed by architraves supporting a frieze and cornice at most. In both kinds of room the richest feature was the chimneypiece, in the ornamentation of which two main styles may be distinguished. Kent's *Designs of Inigo Jones* was the source for the chimneypiece in Governor Wentworth's council chamber in the Wentworth-Gardner House circa 1760, as it had been for that in the entrance hall of John Drayton's house near Charleston twenty years before; the result, as Kimball recognized, is the most elaborate of all the chimneypieces carved in the colonies. But the Baroque massiveness of Jones-Kent ornament was by then beginning to look a little old-fashioned, and designs for chimneypieces of the same type enlivened and lightened with Rococo ornament had already crossed the Atlantic in copies of *The British Architect* by Abraham Swan. Buckland, as we have seen, used Swan's book (which in 1775 became the first book on architecture to be

*87*
*Mount Vernon, Fairfax County, Virginia. 1757–87. Dining room, with chimneypiece and ceiling of 1775.*

published in America) in the later fifties at Gunston Hall. There he eschewed any hint of *rocaille*, but in the Hammond-Harwood and Brice houses in Annapolis he used it, albeit in a restrained manner, in chimneypieces derived from plates in the same book. Two other notable chimneypieces taken from Swan, in both cases almost line for line, are in the "mahogany room" of the Lee House at Marblehead, Massachusetts, dating from 1768, and in the dining room of Washington's Mount Vernon, from 1775 (87).

In 1776 the imported mantel in the drawing room at Gunston was still the only Adam Style chimneypiece in America. Of plaster ceilings in the style there was a small handful. Kenmore, at Fredericksburg, Virginia, had three, put up in the early seventies; two of them are knowledgeable translations of designs in *The City and Country Builder's and Workman's Treasury* by Batty Langley, which was first published in 1740, into the more delicate forms popularized by the great Scottish architect. At Mount Vernon there was the west parlor ceiling of circa 1770, a timid and underscaled affair, and there was the fine one of 1775 in the dining room. In England it would have been unimaginable that a room should have been given an Adamesque ceiling and a Rococo chimneypiece in the same year. The Mount Vernon dining room shows how dependent the colonial building owner was on the sources and resources, books and craftsmen, that chance made available.[6]

In the long run the most important developments in European architecture in the second and third quarters of the eighteenth century were those which led to the overthrow of the Renaissance-Baroque tradition by Neo-Classicism. Three epoch-making structures were the Assembly Room at York (1730–32), in which Lord Burlington recreated, with minimal concessions to contemporary needs, what the Romans called an Egyptian hall, the facade of St.-Sulpice, Paris (begun in 1733), in which G. N. Servandoni "broke with all the accepted rules of church design" to follow principles of composition that were to be those of Neo-Classicism, and the church of Ste.-Geneviève, Paris (begun in 1756, secularized as Le Panthéon in 1791), in which J.-G. Soufflot restored to the column, defined by Alberti as "the principal *ornament* in all architecture," its primal structural function.

In many respects Ste.-Geneviève was a practical demonstration of the rationalist theory of the abbé M.-A. Laugier as set forth in his *Essai sur l'architecture*, which, first published in 1753, was the most influential theoretical work of the age. The other books that did most to forward the Neo-Classical cause were the products of the great flowering of classical archaeology in the 1750s and 1760s, depicting ancient Greek architecture and the architecture of the Eastern Roman Empire. It soon became evident that the rules that had controlled classical design since the Renaissance had been derived from too few buildings within a too limited geographical range. Even those prescribing the proportions of the orders were called in doubt. "The great masters of antiquity," wrote Robert Adam, "were not so rigidly scrupulous, they varied the proportions as the general spirit of their composition required, clearly perceiving, that however necessary these rules may be to form the taste and correct the licentiousness of the scholar [that is, student] they often cramp the genius and circumscribe the ideas of the master." By 1773, when these words appeared in the preface to *Works in Architecture of Robert and James Adam*, Palladianism in Britain had made way for the Adam Style, which was the first nationally accepted Neo-Classical Style in Europe.

In America, political revolution delayed the architectural one, and the first complete building in the Adam Style was not begun until 1788. Three years before that a building with a claim to notice in any history of Western architecture was designed, in Paris, by a former governor of Virginia for that (his native) state. The building was the Virginia State Capitol, Thomas Jefferson its designer. Jefferson was born twenty years before the leading American practitioner of the Adam Style, and it is proper to consider his work before we turn to the latter, from which it differs in intention and character.

**Thomas Jefferson**

Jefferson's very first building was the south outchamber, the "honeymoon cottage," of his own Monticello. It was built in 1769; he designed the house proper, in the form in which it was finished in 1780, in 1771–72. Monticello I (so to distinguish it from the much enlarged and altered building that stands today) had a Palladian *parti*, modified by the introduction of octagonal elements suggested by Robert Morris's *Select Architecture*, with a two-storied portico on either front (88). So described it sounds ordinary enough; what made it extraordinary was the reversal of the normal Palladian scheme, in which the service wings flank an entrance court, so that the wings flanked a lawn on the other side of the house, while the slopes of the site were utilized to turn their flat roofs into terrace walks, reached from the lawn by short flights of steps; underground passages linked the wings with the main block. Such underground passages, as Jefferson knew from his reading of Pliny the Elder, were features of the ancient Roman villa, and the hilltop site which he chose for the house, to the surprise of his contemporaries, was of precisely the kind favored by the Romans for their country retreats in the Alban Hills.[1]

Two other pre-capitol designs by Jefferson must be noticed, though neither was executed. The earlier, made while Jefferson was working on the design of Monticello I, was for an octagonal chapel, presumably at Williamsburg. *Select Architecture* contained a plan for a chapel of this form which Jefferson developed in classical terms with

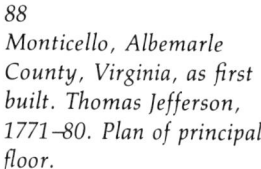

88
*Monticello, Albemarle County, Virginia, as first built. Thomas Jefferson, 1771–80. Plan of principal floor.*

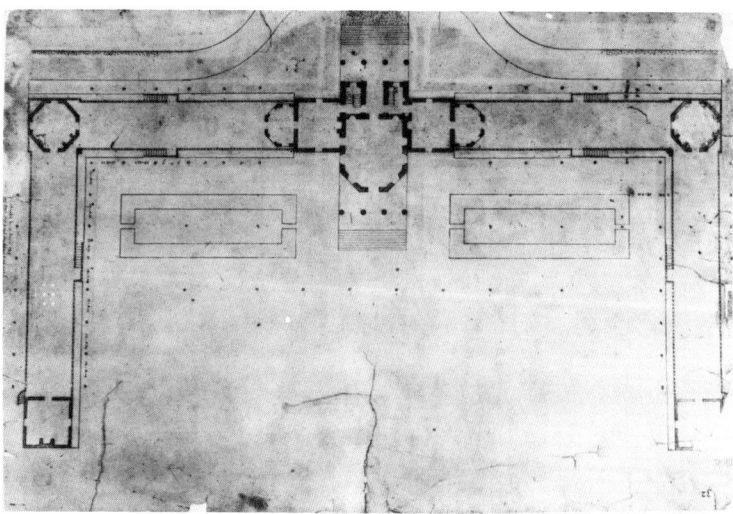

89
*Virginia State Capitol,
Richmond, Virginia.
Thomas Jefferson, 1785–
88. View from southwest.*

a peristyle of twenty-four Tuscan columns and a hemispherical Roman dome, complete with oculus. The other design, one of several for remodelling the Governor's Palace at Williamsburg, was made between Jefferson's sponsorship of a bill to move the Virginian capital to Richmond in 1779 and the destruction of the Palace by fire late in the following year; it was evidently conceived as a scheme for converting the building, of which Jefferson wrote in his *Notes on the State of Virginia* that it was "capable of being made an elegant seat," into a private dwelling. The hall is enlarged into an octagon with a projecting bay. But the features without precedent in domestic architecture in America or Europe are the two porticoes, octastyle, pedimented, and of the full width and height of the building. Had the design been executed, the old Palace would have become the first temple-form house in the history of Neo-Classicism.

The Virginia State Capitol was the first public building of temple form (89). An early design, made about 1780, resembled the design for the remodelling of the Williamsburg Palace in being amphiprostyle and octastyle. In 1785, however, when the state's Directors of Public Buildings wrote to Jefferson in Paris asking him "to consult an able Architect on a plan fit for a Capitol" and he complied by obtaining the collaboration of C.-L. Clérisseau, the simpler form of a Roman temple with a hexastyle portico at one end only was adopted. "We took as our model" Jefferson explained, "the Maison Carrée at Nîmes." The shade of the abbé Laugier must have approved of the choice. In his *Essai sur l'architecture*, after deducing from his ideal of the "cabane rustique" or primitive hut that the only essentials in any kind of architecture are the column, the entablature and the pediment, Laugier went on to praise the Maison Carrée "because everything in it is according to the true principles of architecture." And the probability that Jefferson had the *Essai* in mind is turned into a virtual certainty by his statement to the Directors of Public Buildings that his design was inspired by "the most perfect and precious remains of antiquity"—a phrase whose similarity to Laugier's characterization of the Maison Carrée as "un des plus précieux restes de la bonne antiquité" can hardly be coincidental.[2]

The final drawings for the capitol were sent to Richmond early in 1786; they were followed nearly a year later by a plaster model. Inevitably there were a number of departures from the Roman prototype. Jefferson himself explained the reason for one: the order was changed from Corinthian to Ionic "because of the difficulty of the Corinthian capitals"—an allusion to the scarcity of stonecarvers in Virginia, or anywhere in the United States, at the time. Some, such as the windows and the two-storied interior, were necessary concessions to the functional requirements of the program. Another, the omission of the half-columns along the sides of the Roman temple, may have been due to Jefferson's reading of Laugier, who thought that engaged columns should be used only as a "licence authorized by necessity" and should then be three-quarter columns at least. In execution, however, pilasters, to which Laugier objected even more strongly as "only a bad representation of columns," were added. Samuel Dobie, who supervised the completion of the building, was presumably responsible for this, for no other building by Jefferson has external pilasters.

During his four years in Europe Jefferson conceived a great admiration for French architecture, and this showed in most of the designs he made after his return to America in 1789. The remodelling of Monticello carried out in 1796–1809, giving it the appearance of a single-story house, made it both more French (for houses with only one full story were the fashion in France) and more Roman (for Roman villas were generally of one story) (90). It did not, however, destroy its overall Palladian character. The octagonal dome and drum with which it was crowned resembles the same feature on Burlington's villa at Chiswick and designs in Gibbs's and Morris's books far more closely than it resembles the dome of Pierre Rousseau's Hôtel de Salm in Paris, with which Jefferson, by his own account, was so "violently smitten" that he "used to go to the Tuileries almost daily to look at it." Moreover, while inventing his own version of the

90
Monticello, Albemarle
County, Virginia, as re-
modelled and enlarged in
1796–1809. West front.

French window, with triple-hung sash instead of casements, and
adopting other French practical conveniences, Jefferson remained
faithful to English books for architectural detail and to Palladio for
the proportions of the orders. Monticello II is a very eclectic work
of architecture which lacks the unity and consistency of Monticello
I. Yet while the critic may regret what Jefferson did to his house,
the historian will recognize Monticello II as standing proof of Frank
Lloyd Wright's contention that designing a house is like painting a
portrait—and as one of the most fascinating self-portraits in the
history of architecture. From its site to its gadgetry—wind-dial,
geared double doors, dumb waiter—it is all Jefferson.

Jefferson's admiration for Palladio, already old-fashioned by European standards when he designed Monticello I, makes even his
later work different from other varieties of Neo-Classicism. For the
Governor's House in Richmond around 1780 and for the President's
House in Washington in 1792 he produced versions of La Rotonda,
Palladio's four-porticoed villa outside Vicenza. Neither ever came
near to being built. Edgemont, although it lacks the central domed
room that earned the Villa Capra its local name, has a portico on
each of its four sides. Designed in 1797, square on plan with a part-
octagonal bay projecting into the covered space of the portico on the
garden front, Edgemont is one of Jefferson's most fetching works
even if its wooden construction contravened his principles. As at
Monticello, he made skillful use of a sloping site—here not only to
provide underground passages to the flanking pavilions but also to
conceal the basement story on the entrance side. The garden-front
portico, unlike the other three, is without steps and raised on a
triple-arched loggia (a Palladian feature), and thus becomes an outdoor room. The same functional distinction is made, again with the
aid of a sloping site, between the two porticoes of Jefferson's own

"occasional retreat," Poplar Forest. The plan of Poplar Forest, which was begun in 1806, was probably suggested by one in Kent's *Designs of Inigo Jones*. It is a transformation of the Villa Capra plan in which all the rectangles, including the square of the outer walls, are turned into octagons, while the central rotunda is turned into a square dining room, expressed externally by a platform surmounting the hipped roof; Jefferson's addiction to the octagon was never more ingeniously indulged. Jefferson's last two houses, Farmington near Louisville (the only building by him outside Virginia, begun in 1808) and Barboursville (1817), had three octagonal rooms between them— Farmington two, back to back with a hall between. Barboursville was much like Monticello II. The dome designed for it was never built, however, so that despite the high value he set on the feature Jefferson saw only two domes rise to his design, one at Monticello and the other five miles away at the University of Virginia.

In designing the University of Virginia Jefferson was creating a physical environment for a public institution of which he was the begetter, a situation in which few architects have found themselves (91, 92, 93). The revolutionary idea of building a university as an "academical village" came to him in 1804 or 1805. In 1810 he already saw it in the form of "lodges" for the professors, with classrooms

*91*
*University of Virginia, Charlottesville, Virginia. Thomas Jefferson, 1817–26. Plan.*

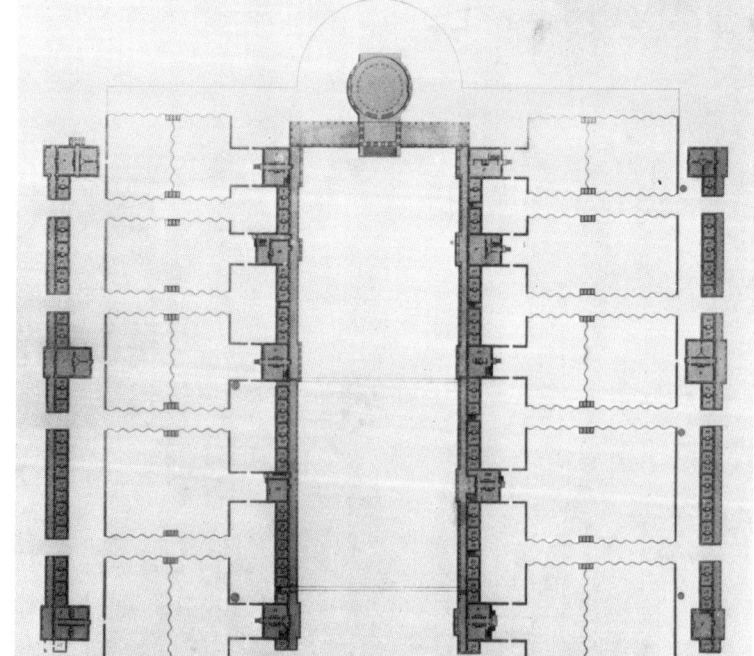

92
*University of Virginia,
Charlottesville, Virginia.
Rotunda, from west.*

93
*University of Virginia,
Charlottesville, Virginia.
Pavilions on south side of
lawn.*

on the ground floor, joined by "barracks" for students, "opening into a covered way to give dry communication between all the schools," the whole "arranged around an open square of grass or trees." In 1817, as soon as construction of the first lodge—or pavilion, as they came to be called—was authorized, he wrote for suggestions to William Thornton and Henry Latrobe. The latter responded with a design showing a domed central building, much higher than the pavilions, intended for an auditorium. Jefferson accepted the suggestion but made it a library. Another change from the original design, in which the green of the academical village, seven or eight hundred feet across, became something more like a grassy street two hundred feet wide (the "lawn"), was due to the exigencies of the site, which also necessitated terracing. And behind the ten pavilions, separated from them by gardens in which the professors were to grow their vegetables, were added more dormitories and six dining halls, or "hotels."

Just as Jefferson had taken the best preserved Roman temple of rectangular plan as his model for the Virginia State Capitol, so for the library of the University of Virginia he took the best preserved and greatest circular one, Hadrian's Pantheon. In his own terminology, one was an exemplar of cubic, the other of spherical architecture. His imitation of the Pantheon is half the height and width of the prototype. Externally, the design is verticalized by the building being raised on a terrace and by the number of columns across the front of the portico being reduced from eight to six, while the portico and the rotunda proper are tied together, as they are not in the prototype, by the entablature of the portico being continued around the rotunda. Internally, the building is of three stories, including the basement, so that the sphere is only a proportional device without any spatial reality. Jefferson had never seen the Pantheon; a more recent building which he had seen and admired, the house in the form of a broken column in the Désert de Retz near Paris, was evidently in his mind when he planned the first floor of the library with its three oval rooms and dumbbell-shaped stairhall. To each of the pavilions he gave a different form and a different order, carrying out his intention, as he described it to Thornton, that they should be "models of good taste and good architecture, and of a variety of appearance, no two alike, so as to serve as specimens for the Architectural lecturer." Today's architectural lecturer with a taste for source-hunting can have a field day at the University of Virginia, beginning with the overall layout. (Palaestra, Roman villa, or French academicism?) But in the balance of the human scaled and the monumental, of uniformity and variety, in the clarity with which the hierarchy of functions is given physical expression, and in the rightness of the relationship between the buildings and the spaces between them, Jefferson's last work of architecture has qualities that transcend such considerations.

The Virginia capitol was the forerunner of the countless temple-form buildings that sprang up all over the United States in the second quarter of the nineteenth century. During Jefferson's lifetime the influence of his architecture was limited; Jeffersonian Classicism, most typically represented by a four-square kind of house with one or more Tuscan porticoes, was in the main a Southern style. Among its practitioners were builders who had worked for Jefferson at the University of Virginia or elsewhere, and one of them, John Neilson, in collaboration with the building owner, John Hartwell Cocke (who had rejected a design by Jefferson), was responsible for the remarkable house called Bremo, in Fluvanna County, Virginia (94). Here four porticoes, three projecting and one recessed, create a spatial counterpoint around the main block, while lateral pavilions echo the pedimented portico on the entrance front, behind which is a hall in the exact form of a cube.

94
*Bremo, Fluvanna County,*
*Virginia. John Hartwell*
*Cocke and John Neilson,*
*1820. Park front.*

Monumental public buildings, Jefferson believed, were among the first needs of the new nation. They were slow in appearing. The most important of all, the United States Capitol, was the subject of an architectural competition instigated by Jefferson in 1792 but was not finished until 1830. The next two legislative buildings after the Virginia capitol to be completed were the Connecticut and Massachusetts state houses. Both were designed by Charles Bulfinch.

Like Jefferson, whom he visited in Paris while on his Grand Tour of Europe in 1785–87, Bulfinch was a gentleman-architect, an amateur in the sense of being self-taught, though after bankruptcy in 1796 he turned professional in the sense of taking fees. There any resemblance between them ends. For Jefferson architectural design was an exercise of the intellect, for Bulfinch of sensibility. Jefferson hoped, through the example of his works, to establish a better, more classical taste among his countrymen, perhaps even to help implant in them those qualities of "Roman virtue and greatness" of which (as he had read in Leoni's translation of Palladio) ancient architecture gave "a certain knowledge." Bulfinch, it is safe to assume, was never greatly concerned with any moral purpose in architecture; he was content to cater to the taste of his New England clients, which was, as in colonial times, for the latest (or what they took to be the latest) from England—where Jefferson found architecture "in the most wretched style [he] ever saw, not meaning to except America . . . nor even Virginia."

The latest in England when Bulfinch was there in the mid 1780s were the Adam Style and the works of Sir William Chambers; the innovations of Soane and the last works of Soane's master, the younger Dance, were still in the future. The Adam Style had been taken up and modified since the sixties, when the Adams' practice was at its height, by other architects, of whom one of the most talented was James Wyatt. In London there were two buildings, one by Wyatt and the other by Chambers, that no visitor could miss. Wyatt's was the Pantheon, on Oxford Street, with an interior modelled on Santa Sophia, which had been an enormously popular rendezvous for masquerades from its completion in 1772 until 1784, when it became a concert hall. Chambers's was Somerset House, the great Thames-side building for government departments and learned societies begun in 1776 and finished, but for much later wings, in 1786. It was these two buildings which Bulfinch took as his models for the Massachusetts State House, designed in the year of his return from Europe though not built until 1795–97 (95, 96). Its main front is a lightened or Adamized version of the center of the south front of Somerset House, which in a letter to the legislative committee

95
*Massachusetts State House, Boston, Massachusetts. Charles Bulfinch, 1795–97. View from southwest.*

96
*Massachusetts State House, Boston, Massachusetts. Old Representatives Hall.*

Bulfinch referred to as "a building celebrated all over Europe," while its largest interior, the Representatives Hall, follows in all essentials the Great Room in Wyatt's Pantheon, a fact not mentioned by Bulfinch to the committee, which probably would have considered the model a frivolous one. The Massachusetts State House was much admired from the first, and the fact that a central dome became an almost universal feature of American state houses and capitols is due at least as much to its example as to that of the national capitol.

The state house at Hartford, designed in 1792 and built in 1793–96, was Palladian rather than Adamesque. Externally it was a much simplified version of Liverpool Town Hall, which was built to the design of the John Woods, father and son, in 1748–55. More original, and of considerable historical importance as "the first professionally designed American theater by a native architect," was The Theatre on Federal Street, Boston, built to Bulfinch's design in 1793–94. Its facade was based on a plate in a book by one of Adam's most talented English followers, John Crunden; a tetrastyle portico of the Corinthian order projected from the front on a high basement story which formed a *porte-cochère*. The interior departed radically from English practice with a domed auditorium of three-quarter-circle plan and cantilevered boxes. The model was the Grand Théâtre at Bordeaux by Victor Louis, which Bulfinch had seen on his travels and called "the most superb in France."

Earlier than any of these buildings, and in fact Bulfinch's first executed design, was the Hollis Street Church in Boston, built in 1787–88. For its plan Bulfinch went back to Wren's St. Stephen Walbrook. It was the first church in what had been British America to have a central dome, while its entrance front, with a Doric portico flanked by two towers with cupolas, was without precedent in American or in English architecture, though soon to be imitated in the First Presbyterian Church, Baltimore (1789–95). Bulfinch was the architect of eight churches and meeting houses in all. In planning his first two meeting houses (at Pittsfield and Taunton, both designed in 1789) he took the biggest step toward the abolition of all architectural distinctions between the two building types by placing the main entrances at the end instead of in the middle of the long sides. His finest buildings for worship were New South Church, Boston (1814), and the First Church of Lancaster (1816) (97, 98). New South, built of Chelmsford granite, had a tall steeple and a tetrastyle Doric portico attached to, and dominating, an octagonal nave. The marked difference in style between the spire and the body of the church was due to the conservatism of the building committee, which preferred this purely Gibbsian design to a Neo-Classical version of

97
*New South Church, Bos-
ton, Massachusetts.
Charles Bulfinch, 1814.
Portico and steeple.*

*98*
*Meeting House, Lancas-*
*ter, Massachusetts.*
*Charles Bulfinch, 1816.*
*View from southwest.*

the spire of Old North also submitted by the architect.[3] No such disharmony mars the Lancaster meeting house, with its delicately detailed Adam Style cupola. Architectural quality, even more than the red brick of which it is constructed, sets this building apart from the contemporary carpenter-built New England meeting house, often pretty enough in its way, of which the Unitarian Church at Wayland, designed in 1814 by Andrews Palmer, is a good example (99). It is no less different from the many churches that still followed in the tradition of St. Martin-in-the-Fields, such as the Center Church at New Haven (1812–14) by Asher Benjamin and the Independent Presbyterian Church at Savannah (1817–19) by John Holden Greene.

Early in 1818 Bulfinch was appointed architect of the Capitol in Washington. New England was much the loser by his departure, seeing only two more buildings of any importance, one in Massachusetts and the other in Maine, go up to his design. The first was Massachusetts General Hospital, built in 1818–23. In 1816 Bulfinch visited the middle states to study hospital design, and the central section of the Pennsylvania Hospital, designed by David Evans, Jr., and added to Samuel Rhoads's building in 1794–1809, supplied the prototype of the clinical amphitheatre, the Ether Dome,[4] of Massachusetts General. Stylistically the two buildings are utterly different; Evans's is the Adam Style at its showiest, while Bulfinch's has all the simplicity of his later manner.

Bulfinch's last building was the Maine State House at Augusta, built in 1829–32. From several designs the legislators chose one "representing the Boston state house reduced." In a letter to the governor, Bulfinch wrote that while he had preserved the general outline of his earlier building he had tried to prevent the design being "a servile copy" and had "aimed at giving it an air of simplicity, which, while I hope it will appear reconcilable to good taste, will render it easy to execute in your material"—which was again granite. Among the changes was the substitution of a Tuscan portico, complete with pediment, for the Corinthian colonnade of the Massachusetts State House, and of a circular cupola with an Ionic peristyle for the Wren-like lantern on the dome of the latter. That Bulfinch should have described the cupola to the Governor as "a copy of the Temple of Vesta at Rome" shows his awareness of the spirit of the times, which by 1829 set much store by the close imitation of specific ancient buildings; that it should have borne only a vague resemblance to the nominal model shows how his approach to antiquity differed from that of the architects who in the near future were to respond to the need for towers with molding-for-molding reproductions of the Monument of Lysicrates.

99
*Unitarian Church, Way-*
*land, Massachusetts.*
*Andrews Palmer, 1814.*
*View from west.*

*The Adam Style House*

In domestic architecture the Adam Style brought in a new kind of plan, with rooms of different and contrasted shapes instead of the squares and rectangles of Palladianism. (Adam himself described the change as "a remarkable improvement in the form, convenience, arrangement, and relief of apartments.") It was a kind of plan that was Neo-Classical programmatically in its derivation from the Roman *thermae* or public baths and aesthetically in the clarity of definition of the individual spaces, to which respect for the integrity of the wall-plane (however richly ornamented that might be) made an indispensable contribution.

The first American house with this kind of a plan, and the first complete building in the Adam Style in America, was The Woodlands in West Philadelphia (100, 101). Its owner, William Hamilton, had recently returned from England when in 1788 he set about re-modelling a house built by his father some thirty-five years before. Perhaps he brought the plan with him; in any case it is remarkable in incorporating a specimen of almost every room form in the Adam repertory: square, oblong, circular, octagonal, oblong with semicircular apses at either end, and oval. The last of these, the oval, was virtually unknown in domestic architecture in Britain before Adam. In France, however, it had been established as an admired form for a grand room by the example of Le Vau's château of Vaux-le-Vicomte in the seventeenth century, and one thing Adam had in common with Jefferson was an admiration for French domestic architecture.

Externally, too, The Woodlands is a remarkably comprehensive Adam Style design. On the entrance front six Ionic pilasters, with the outer pairs coupled, support a pediment with paterae on the frieze. The cornice is continued around the house to join the full entablature of the portico on the other front, which has six widely spaced Doric columns attenuated to Ionic proportions. The door on this front has a semi-elliptical fanlight, and on either side of the portico is a Venetian window recessed within an arch; semicircular windows light the basement.

Within months at most of Hamilton's beginning work on The Woodlands, the banker William Bingham was building the first American town house in the style, in Philadelphia. Modelled on Manchester House in London, it was by all accounts of a sumptuousness never before seen in the city of brotherly love; Bulfinch, after visiting it in 1789, wrote that it was "in a stile which would be esteemed splendid even in the most luxurious parts of Europe," and six years later he copied its street front in his first house for Harrison Gray Otis in Boston. Adamesque features in the Otis House that do not appear in The Woodlands were delicate wrought-iron balconies,

*100*
*The Woodlands, Philadel-*
*phia, Pennsylvania.*
*1788–89. Entrance front.*

*101*
*The Woodlands, Philadel-*
*phia, Pennsylvania. Plan*
*of first floor.*

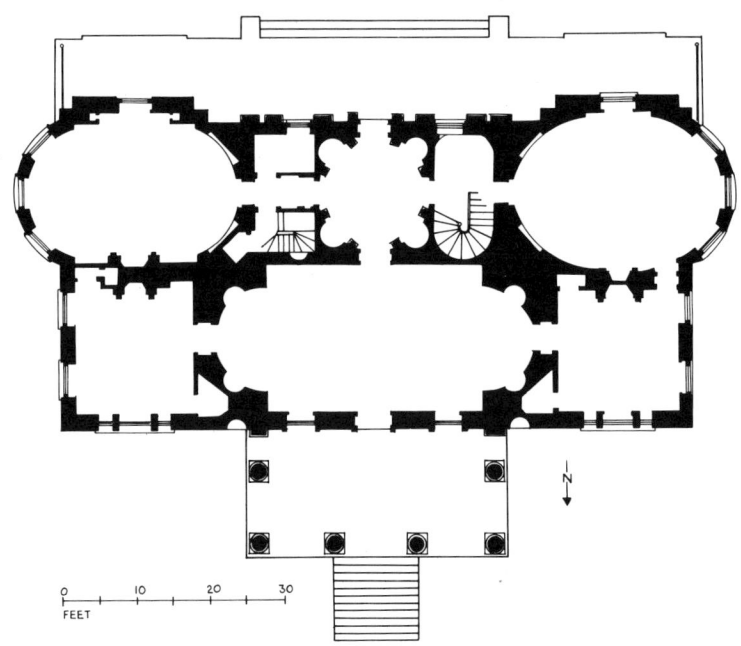

spiderweblike leading in the semicircular window on the top floor, and small panels bearing reliefs set into the wall above the second-floor windows. Neither The Woodlands nor the Bingham House had a roof balustrade, as many of the later houses in the style did—including the President's House in Philadelphia, whose construction with public funds was authorized by the Pennsylvania legislature in the hope of attracting the federal government to the city in 1791.

It was in the year 1791 that Bulfinch designed his first three houses. The most innovative was the house for the Boston merchant Joseph Barrell at Somerville. On the garden front of Pleasant Hill, as it was called, a central pavilion, formed by the projection of an oval salon on the ground floor and a loggia with Corinthian columns above it, rose half a story above the rest of the house. The bowed center became a common feature in domestic architecture. Within the decade Bulfinch used the projecting oval again in the Knox Mansion at Thomaston, Maine (1794), and the Mason House, Boston (1799); Samuel McIntire used it in the Lyman House at Waltham, Massachusetts (1793), and the Derby Mansion at Salem (1795), and unidentified architects in Gore Place, Waltham (1797), Lemon Hill, Philadelphia, and Montebello, Baltimore (1799) (102, 103). In 1796 Bulfinch substituted the circle for the oval in the Swan House at Dorchester, Massachusetts, and David Manigault made the same substitution in his own house at Charleston, South Carolina, completed in 1797. Whether based on the oval or the circle—or the octagon, as in the Nathaniel Russell House at Charleston, finished to the design of Russell Warren by 1809 the bowed center resulted in what Adam had called "a greater movement . . . in the outside composition."

In porticoes the wide spacing and attenuation of the columns noted in The Woodlands were typical of the American Adamesque; in *The American Builder's Companion* (1806) Asher Benjamin showed columns with shafts lengthened two diameters beyond normal practice, and builder-architects sometimes carried the process to the point of caricature. The next domestic portico after The Woodlands which can be dated with certainty was that of the more-than-half-Palladian presidential mansion in New York (from 1791 to 1797 the official residence of the governors of New York State), which was completed to the design of John McComb, Jr., in 1790. In 1791 Hampton Plantation House at McClellanville, South Carolina, received the addition of a portico copied from the one added to David Garrick's villa at Hampton on the Thames, to Adam's design, fifteen or twenty years before. Homewood, Baltimore, designed by its owner, Charles Carroll, Jr., in 1801, was the earliest of a group of porticoed houses

102
*Gore Place, Waltham,
Massachusetts. 1797.
South front.*

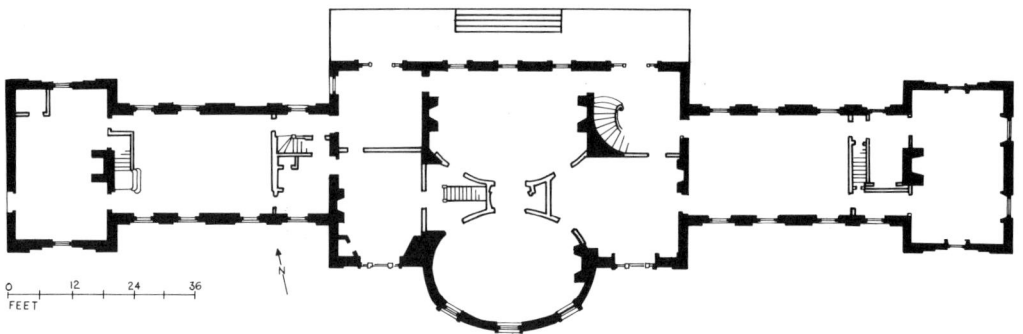

103
*Gore Place, Waltham,
Massachusetts. Plan of
first floor.*

104
*Homewood, Baltimore, Maryland. Charles Carroll, Jr., 1801–03. Entrance front.*

105
*Gardner-Pingree House (Essex Institute), Salem, Massachusetts. Samuel McIntire, 1804–05. Street front.*

of which it would be hard to find the like in Britain—long and low, composed of three of five parts of only one full story, with the central block rising slightly higher than the rest (104). Others are Ridgeway at St. Matthews, Kentucky (ca. 1805), Rose Hill in Lexington (1818), and the Baum-Taft House in Cincinnati (ca. 1820).

Columnar porches, as distinct from porticoes, were much used. Often they were semicircular on plan, like that of the Gardner House (now the Essex Institute) in Salem, Massachusetts, which was built in 1804–05 to the design of Samuel McIntire (105). For facade orders pilasters were the rule, and Ionic and Corinthian about equally used. All the main facade treatments employing a pilaster order were used by Bulfinch. The Morton House at Roxbury, Massachusetts (1796), had two pairs of coupled pilasters rising through its two stories to support a pediment. The Mason House had very slender pilasters rising through three stories at each end of its bowed front; a design for the Elias Hasket Derby Mansion at Salem shows a two-story front with an astylar ground story and pilasters deployed across the second. Commonest of all was the combination of an astylar ground story and two upper stories with a pilaster order, as in Bulfinch's own house in Boston (1793), the houses by him in Franklin Place, Boston (1794), the Ezekiel Hersey Derby House at Salem (ca. 1800), and his second house for Harrison Gray Otis in Boston (1800–02). This had been the standard treatment of the London house front, when an order was used, since the middle of the seventeenth century; in the Adamesque variations on the theme the pilasters were often, as in all the examples named except the Franklin Place houses, omitted from the central bays.

Another feature of the London scene that was naturalized in the early years of independence was the row of contiguous houses sharing party walls; the economics of building succeeded where in the seventeenth century government fiat had failed. The most ambitious project of the kind was begun in 1793 in Boston, to Bulfinch's design. Tontine Crescent, as it was called from the method by which the architect hoped to finance it, was doubtless inspired by the Adelphi, the great Thames-side development of the Adam brothers next to Somerset House. It was planned as two segmental rows of sixteen houses facing each other to form an ellipse; only one row was built. The houses were of the standard London plan, three bays wide with front and back rooms and a side passage for entry and stairs; the row was given a monumental treatment with a pedimented building in the middle and a pilaster order applied to the last two houses at either end, which stood slightly forward from the rest. The central building was pierced by a carriageway. Its upper stories with their Ionic columns were reminiscent of the Society of Arts building in the Adelphi and, housing as they did a library and the office of the Massachusetts Historical Society, not dissimilar in function.

*"The Decoration of the Inside"*

"The massive entablature, the ponderous compartment ceiling, the tabernacle frame, almost the only species of ornament hitherto known, in this country, are now universally exploded, and in their place, we have adopted a beautiful variety of light mouldings, gracefully formed, delicately enriched and arranged with propriety and skill." Thus Robert Adam on the "almost total change" in "the decoration of the inside" that his example brought about in domestic architecture in Britain in the 1760s. In general terms the change can be described as the substitution of decorative forms derived from Roman domestic architecture for architectonic forms derived from the Roman temple. There were precedents: grotesques, as one common kind of Roman decoration was called, had been employed by Raphael and others in Italy in the sixteenth century and more recently in England by William Kent. What was new was that Adam used them and other Roman motifs consistently in the service of a philosophy of design that placed sensibility and visual effect above "the rules."

By the time it was established in America the style of decoration introduced by Adam had itself undergone a change. In 1785 Horace Walpole, after a visit to the future king George IV's Carlton House, which had just been completed to the design of Henry Holland, wrote: "How sick one will be of Mr. Adam's gingerbread and sippets of embroidery after this chaste palace!" Holland's style owed more to the publications of certain mid-eighteenth-century French architects than to Adam, but the new taste for chastity affected the Adam Style and there was a general reaction against what came to be regarded as excesses in the work of its originator. The Adamesque interior in America is apt to be almost overwhelmingly chaste; typically the decoration is sparse and walls and ceiling are an unrelieved bridal white. Nor is the detail often such as to invite or hold close attention; there were enough craftsmen who could follow or adapt designs from the builders' guides (most often those by the English William Pain and the American Asher Benjamin), but only the carver-architect Samuel McIntire, in whose houses at Salem the inevitable paterae and chains of husks are combined with naturalistic ornaments, stands out as an interior designer with any real artistic personality.

106
*Nathaniel Russell House,
Charleston, South Caro-
lina. Russell Warren, be-
fore 1809. Entrance hall.*

In nothing did the Adam Style house differ more from its colonial predecessor than in the design of the stair. Colonial stairs rise in straight flights; corners are turned with landings; balusters and rails are full-bodied if not massive. The Adam stair is much lighter in appearance, with the balusters attenuated or reduced to plain sticks; and on plan it is nearly always partly, and sometimes wholly, curvilinear. Both circle and oval were employed. Among the earlier examples, the main stair in the David Manigault House at Charleston is fully circular, while in Bulfinch's Thomas Russell House at Charlestown, Massachusetts (1793–96) it was a complete oval on plan; in the Ezekiel Derby House at Salem it was semicircular; in the Nathaniel Russell House, at Charleston, Warren combined circle and oval at different levels (106). Whatever their geometrical form, such stairs, which are as ingenious in construction as they are graceful in effect, were the chief means of imparting movement to the interior of the house. They are also the feature of the Adam Style with the strongest appeal to twentieth-century taste.

*Enter the Professional
Architect*

With the possible but unproved exceptions of The Woodlands and Gore Place, all the American buildings mentioned in the last chapter were designed by native Americans who had had nothing that could be called professional training in architecture for the good reason that in their youth there had been no professional architects in America to train them. We come now to the work of the immigrants active during the same period, most of whom had had some technical training—in engineering if not in architecture—and some of whom had already practiced architecture on the other side of the Atlantic, and to the early designs of the first Americans to be professionally trained, by one of those immigrants, as architects.

The immigrants' work was not always up-to-date. James Hoban, who arrived from Ireland in 1785, remained faithful to the Irish Palladianism of the third quarter of the century in both the President's House in Washington and the First Bank of the United States in Philadelphia; the latter, designed in 1795, is closely modelled on the Royal Exchange in Dublin (Thomas Cooley, architect) on which Hoban had worked. Nor is their work always distinguishable from that of the American-born; in his Park Street Church in Boston, designed in 1809, Peter Banner, an Englishman whose name first appeared in the New York city directory in 1795, adopted the attenuated manner of the New England builder-architects so wholeheartedly that he may fairly be said to have gone native. Yet without the immigrants' contribution American architecture of the Federal period, for all Jefferson's originality, would be little more than an interesting backwater outside the main stream of architectural history.

The first of them to arrive was the engineer Pierre Charles L'Enfant, who came from France to join Washington's army in 1777. Eleven years later it fell to him to remodel the old New York City Hall to serve, as Federal Hall, for Washington's inauguration and the first session of Congress. In the Louis XVI style with a liberal application of American and republican emblems, Federal Hall was an architectural declaration of independence that was admired enough by both the public and the president to ensure L'Enfant's appointment as planner of the new capital city on the Potomac. His only other architectural work of note was a large and strange house in Philadelphia for Robert Morris, begun in 1794 and demolished while still a shell in 1800; also Louis XVI in style, it had a French mansard roof—the earliest in America outside New Orleans by some sixty-five years.

Of the immigrants who left their mark on American architecture in the Federal period the most gifted—in the order of their arrival—

were Etienne Sulpice Hallet (ca. 1782), William Thornton (1787), Joseph François Mangin (1794), George Hadfield (1795), Benjamin Henry Latrobe (1796), Maximilien Godefroy (1805), Joseph Jacques Ramée (1811), and William Jay (1817). Four of them were involved in the central public work of the age, the building of the national Capitol.

*The United States Capitol*

The competition, suggested by Jefferson, for designs for a Capitol and a President's House "to be erected in the city of Washington & territory of Columbia" was announced in the newspapers in March 1792. When the designs came in, Hoban's for the President's House was quickly approved, being preferred to one submitted anonymously by Jefferson. For the Capitol, ten designs were received, most of them from builder-architects who, however competent they may have been in domestic work, were clearly out of their depth when it came to a monumental building which should symbolize the achievements and aspirations of the new nation. Among the more accomplished was Samuel McIntire's, with elevations put together from two plates in Gibbs's *Book of Architecture*; it would have made a fine English country house, but America had been ruled from English country houses long enough. Less domestic, in spite of the model that inspired it, was the Gargantuan version of Palladio's Villa Capra with which Samuel Dobie, who had supervised the completion of the Virginia Capitol, weighed in.

The Commissioners for Federal Buildings found none of the designs entirely satisfactory, but favored the one by Etienne Hallet. They showed it to the president, whose approval of it, tempered by financial prudence—"if it were not too expensive, it would, in my judgment, be a noble and desirable structure"—seemed to Hallet to have settled the question, and he proceeded to revise it to meet the commissioners' requirements in the matter of "the distribution of parts." Then in October, three months after the competition had closed, Dr. William Thornton, the winner in 1789 of the first American architectural competition, for a building for the Philadelphia Library Company, asked to be allowed to submit drawings in accordance with the terms of the original advertisement. The request was granted, and early in 1793 Thornton submitted a design which, in Jefferson's words, "captivated the eyes and the judgment of all." Most importantly, it captivated the eyes and judgment of Jefferson himself and of Washington, with the result that in March the commissioners adopted it.

The choice of Thornton's design was attended by a major practical disadvantage. Hallet, who had come from France in connection with an abortive scheme to found an academy of the arts on French lines, was an experienced architect and presumably would have been capable of supervising the execution of his own design. Thornton, born in the West Indies and educated in Europe, was the complete amateur without technical knowledge of construction or experience in the supervision of building operations. Many of the troubles that were to plague the long building history of the Capitol were due to the necessity of appointing other architects to supervise the execution of a design to which they were officially but not personally committed.

First Hoban was appointed superintendent of the Capitol and the President's House while Hallet, who had been retained by the commissioners to revise Thornton's plan, was made assistant superintendent for architectural matters. This arrangement was terminated in less than a year, when Hallet was dismissed for exceeding his authority. Next, in the fall of 1794, the young English architect George Hadfield was made superintendent on the recommendation of the painter John Trumbull, who was then secretary to the American minister in England; he held the position until the spring of 1798. James Hoban, still busy with the President's House, was then put in charge as Surveyor of the Public Buildings, an office abolished in 1802 and revived in 1803 to be given by Jefferson to Benjamin Henry Latrobe, who held it until the end of Jefferson's second term in 1811. Between 1811 and 1814 little was done; in 1814 British troops burned the Capitol, which then consisted of two wings without a center, and also the President's House, which owes its soubriquet to the white paint applied to conceal the effects of the fire. In 1815 Latrobe was recalled for the work of repair and reconstruction; he resigned in 1817 and was succeeded by Bulfinch, under whom the center and dome were built by the end of 1822 and the building was completed in 1827 (107, 108). Bulfinch followed Latrobe's design for the most part. The biggest changes he made were due to Congress's insistance on more committee rooms and on a higher dome. One member of the cabinet wanted a dome of Gothic form.

Thornton had no specific model for the Capitol. A design made by William Kent in the 1730s for new Houses of Parliament in London has a circular dome of Pantheon type rising behind an octastyle portico on a rusticated basement, like Thornton's earliest known design for the east front, but it is unlikely that he knew Kent's drawings. In any case his elevations are less Anglo-Palladian than Louis XVI, while his plan also showed French influence if, as is probable, the semicircular Senate Chamber was suggested by the School of Medicine in Paris (designed in 1771 by Jacques Gondouin). His Hall of Representatives was elliptical; one of Latrobe's first

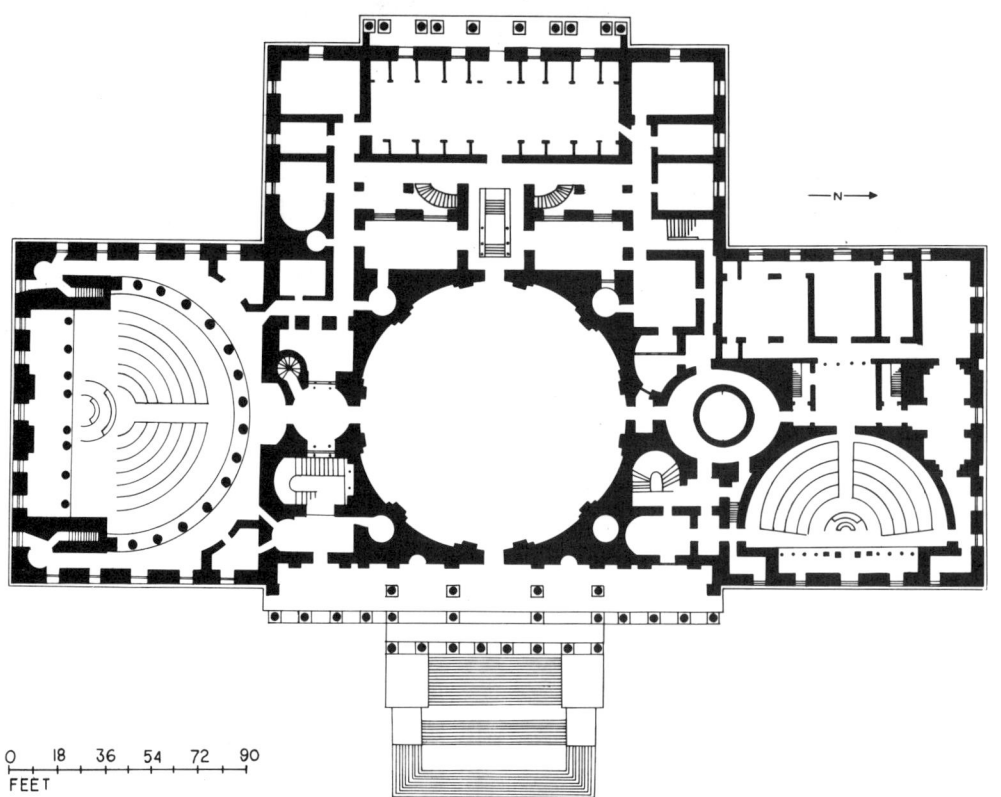

107
*United States Capitol,
Washington, District of
Columbia. William
Thornton, Benjamin
Henry Latrobe, and
Charles Bulfinch, 1793–
1830. View from east in
1847. From a daguerreo-
type by John Plumbe, Jr.*

108
*United States Capitol,
Washington, District of
Columbia. Plan of princi-
pal floor.*

109
*United States Capitol,
Washington, District of
Columbia, Senate Ro-
tunda, with columns of
tobacco order.*

proposals in 1803—by then there was another French precedent in the Room of the Five Hundred (later the Chamber of Deputies), built to the design of J. P. Gisors in 1795–97—was to change it into a semicircle, as he actually did in the rebuilding after 1814.

In a letter to Jefferson, Latrobe wrote: "My principles of good taste are rigid in Grecian architecture. I am a bigoted Greek in the condemnation of the Roman architecture of Baalbec, Palmyra, and Spalatro." He was never able to express his admiration for Greek architecture on the outside of the Capitol, although he made a design for the west front in which the entrance was through a propylaeum with a Greek Doric portico. Inside he was able to give his Grecianism full play and used a wide range of Greek orders: in the basement under the Supreme Court and in the central Crypt versions of Paestum Doric, in the Senate Chamber and Lobby a fifth-century Ionic, in the Hall of Representatives the Corinthian of the Monument of Lysicrates, in its vestibule and at the entrance to the Library that of the Tower of the Winds. For the vestibule and stairs and small rotunda in the north wing he invented two new orders representing two staples of agrarian America, the capitals of the one being carved with ears of corn, of the other with flowers and leaves of the tobacco (109). Members admired the corn cob capitals, as they were inaccurately but alliteratively called, more than anything else Latrobe ever did for them.

While the interior of the United States Capitol as completed in 1827 was Latrobe's, the exterior was the work of three architects. The elevations with pilasters were by Thornton; the east portico was by Latrobe (who was responsible for moving the main entrance, which was in the west front in Thornton's original design); the dome and the west terrace and colonnade were by Bulfinch. As major public buildings not infrequently do, the Capitol looked old-fashioned by the time it was finished. Not only were Thornton's elevations of Louis XVI character, but in the grouping of the columns on the west front Bulfinch went back to his model for the Massachusetts State House, Somerset House. Yet the intrinsic quality of the building considered as a whole was such that it would be a severe critic who did not concede that history proved Jefferson right in at least the first part of his prediction in a letter to Latrobe: "I think the work when finished will be a durable and honorable monument of our infant republic, and will bear favorable comparisons with the remains of the same kind of the ancient republics of Greece and Rome."

*William Thornton and*
*Benjamin Henry Latrobe*

After his connection with the Capitol was severed, Hallet disappeared from the architectural scene, although he was still in America when he died in 1825. Nor are the later works of Thornton, who died in 1826, numerous. They include, however, two of the finest houses of the Federal period, the Octagon House in Washington and Tudor Place in Georgetown (110, 111). The Octagon, built in 1799–1800, is fitted into its corner site with a plan in which circular, triangular, and oblong components are ingeniously combined; the half-cylinder swelling out from the front and the splayed side walls impart movement, in the Adam sense of the term, to the house as seen from the street, while its detail, outside and in, is also Adamesque. Tudor Place, completed in 1816, is reminiscent of Wyatt rather than Adam. The first-floor windows on the south front resemble those used by Wyatt in Bowden, Wiltshire (1786), and like them echo in two dimensions a columnar central feature crowned by a low dome. But whereas in Bowden the wall behind the columns is convex, in Tudor Place it curves back to complete the circle under the dome.

Hadfield, who also died in 1826, had a disappointing career for one who in youth had shown much promise.[1] The two buildings for which he is best remembered fall within the scope of the next chapter. And so we may now turn to the extra-Capitoline work, so to call it, of his exact contemporary—they were both born in 1764—Latrobe.

Benjamin Henry Latrobe was the son of the head of a Moravian school in Yorkshire; his mother was American. After receiving most of his general education in Germany and his architectural training in the office of Samuel Pepys Cockerell, he set up in private practice

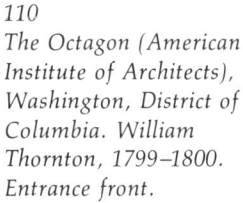

*110*
*The Octagon (American Institute of Architects), Washington, District of Columbia. William Thornton, 1799–1800. Entrance front.*

111
*Tudor Place, Georgetown, District of Columbia. William Thornton, 1816. Garden front.*

in London in 1791. In 1795 he went bankrupt and decided to emigrate; he landed at Norfolk, Virginia, early in 1796. He came with good introductions and was soon visiting Mount Vernon as Washington's guest.

In the course of his American career Latrobe had dealings with many of the famous (and some of the infamous) of the early days of the republic, while canals and waterworks, dockyards and steamboats, as well as buildings of all kinds, engaged his powers of invention. As a professional architect in a country in which professionalism was a new and somewhat suspect concept, he suffered frustration at every turn. Yet in the sixty or so buildings which he designed between his arrival in America and his death in 1820 (in New Orleans, from yellow fever), he set new standards for American architecture. Only fifteen of those buildings stand today.

Latrobe's first public commission in America was the Virginia Penitentiary at Richmond. In 1785 Jefferson, in Paris, came across a plan for an octagonal prison published by the architect P. G. Bugniet in the *Mercure de France* twenty years before, and sent the engraving home to Virginia together with a design of his own based upon it. Twelve years later, in 1797, the idea thus implanted came to fruition when the state of Virginia decided to build a new prison. A competition was held, and won by Latrobe. In the quarter-century since Robert Smith had built the Walnut Street Prison in Philadelphia, two major events affecting prison design had occurred. The first had been the passage of the British Act of Parliament of 1779 which initiated the "separate system"—miscalled solitary confinement—recommended by the prison reformer John Howard; in the Richmond prison Latrobe provided solitary cells for men and for women but modified the Howard system by also providing communal cells for from three to seven "reformed prisoners." The other event affecting prison design had been the publication in 1791 of Jeremy Bentham's *Panopticon, or the Inspection House*, which recommended the building of circular prisons in which all the prisoners' activities could be supervised both visually and audially (through speaking tubes) by guards in the center; at Richmond Latrobe placed the men's cells and workrooms in a semicircular range of building, commanded by the governor's house, behind a rectangular section comprising three courtyards, the women's cells and workroom, the infirmary, certain service rooms, and the reception building. The elevations, of random masonry on the entrance front and brick elsewhere, were of a severity consonant with the building's function (112).

The Virginia Penitentiary may fairly be called the first modern prison in America. By the end of the century Latrobe had two more firsts to his credit: in Sedgeley, Philadelphia, built in 1799, the first

112
*Virginia Penitentiary, Richmond, Virginia. Benjamin Henry Latrobe, 1797. Entrance front, from a sketch by the architect.*

Gothic Revival house in America, and in the Bank of Pennsylvania in the same city, built in 1798–1800, the first use of a Greek order in America. The Bank of Pennsylvania was by far the more important building (113, 114). Built of Schuylkill marble, in general form it resembled a temple with a portico at each end, like Jefferson's early design for the Virginia Capitol, and a rotunda in the center. But there was no attempt to create the illusion of a temple; Latrobe expressed the rotunda externally with a lantern of a type borrowed from Soane's Bank of England set on a forty-five foot dome, stepped on the outside, emerging from a square block which not only rose above the main cornice but also projected slightly on either flank of the building. All the external detail was Greek, the Ionic columns of the porticoes being a simplified version of those of the north portico of the Erechtheum at Athens. Inside, for the first time in the history of what had been British America, masonry vaulting was employed for architectural effect, as well as for practical reasons.[2]

Philadelphians did not have to wait long to see the first Greek Ionic columns in America joined by the first Greek Doric ones. These stood in the porches of the Pump House in Central Square, which was built (like the bank, of Schuylkill marble) to Latrobe's design in 1799–1801 to house the steam pump of the Philadelphia waterworks. Some have seen in this building the influence of one of the customs houses or barrières by Ledoux which were built at the gates of Paris in 1784–89. But the Pump House was crowned with a low dome while the cylindrical tower of the Barrière de la Villette is flat-roofed, and this difference, together with the wall arches in which its windows were recessed, suggests that a belvedere tower in Soane's *Sketches in Architecture* (1793) gave Latrobe his first idea. In any case the final result had neither the calculated heaviness of Ledoux's design nor the mannered elegance of Soane's.

Latrobe has been called the American Soane. Certainly their roles in history were quite similar. They were the greatest architects of their generation in their respective countries, and each did more than any of his compatriots for the recognition and advancement of architecture as a profession. (It was Latrobe who introduced in America the practice by which an architect's fee is established as a percentage of the cost of the building—not without much difficulty, and rarely obtaining the five percent then customary in Europe.) But their personal styles were as different as their personalities. This comes out very clearly when one examines Latrobe's surviving masterpiece, St. Mary's Roman Catholic Cathedral in Baltimore (115, 116, 117).

113
Bank of Pennsylvania,
Philadelphia, Pennsylva-
nia. Benjamin Henry
Latrobe, 1798–1800. From
a drawing by the
architect.

114
Bank of Pennsylvania,
Philadelphia, Pennsylva-
nia. Plan.

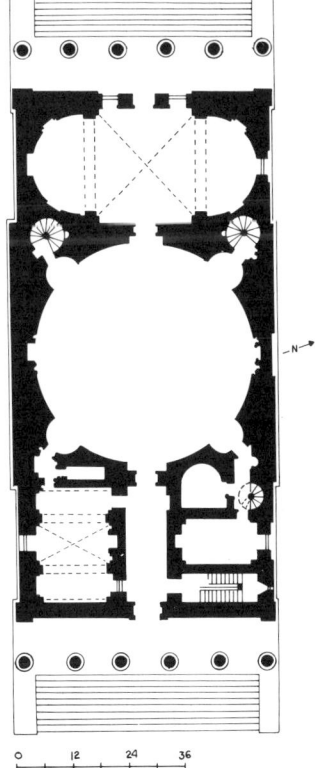

115
St. Mary's Cathedral,
Baltimore, Maryland.
Benjamin Henry Latrobe,
1814 18; belfry domes,
1832; portico, John H. B.
Latrobe, 1863. View from
southwest.

116
St. Mary's Cathedral,
Baltimore, Maryland.
Plan. The choir was added
in 1890 in conformity
with Latrobe's original
design.

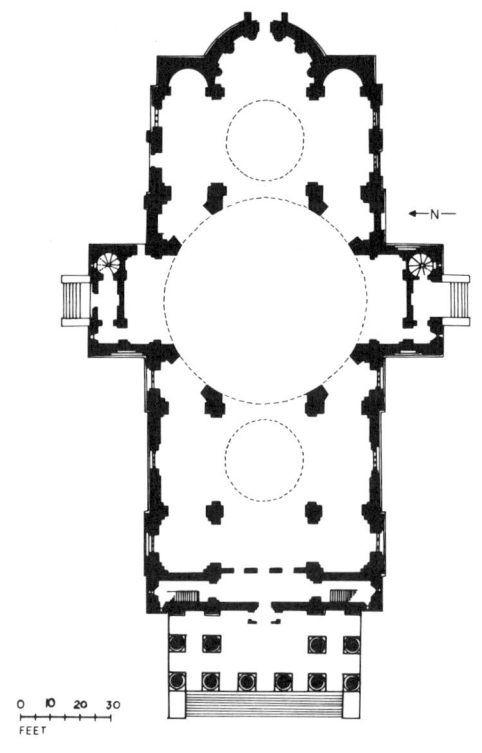

0  10  20  30
FEET

117
*St. Mary's Cathedral,
Baltimore, Maryland. In-
terior, looking southeast
across rotunda.*

For Baltimore Cathedral Latrobe submitted two designs, one classical and one Gothic; the bishop and diocese chose the classical. Construction began in 1806, but the design eventually executed (the seventh, according to the architect) was not made until 1808.[3] The first design is reminiscent of Soufflot's Panthéon. In making the seventh Latrobe looked further back in time. It was hardly possible that any English-trained architect designing a cathedral on a Latin-cross plan with a dome spanning the full width of the nave and aisles (a requirement of the client) should forget St. Paul's Cathedral. Latrobe did more than remember it; Baltimore Cathedral is a condensed translation of St. Paul's into Neo-Classical terms, with quotations from Wren's rejected Great Model design for the same building. The most important of the latter is the ring of eight piers with segmental inner faces and straight outer ones, forming a circle, from which the dome can rise without the aid of (un-Roman) pendentives, inside an octagon, which is expressed externally in a plinth beneath the dome. As in both the Great Model and St. Paul's as built, there are two different intervals between the piers. In the Great Model Wren used semicircular arches for both spans, with the result that their crowns are at different heights; in St. Paul's as built he used two segmental arches across the narrower spans, extending the face-moldings of the upper ones into semicircles to match the arches across the wider spans. Latrobe used both semicircular and segmental arches but reversed Wren's arrangement, making the wider arches segmental and the narrower ones semicircular, with only one arch spanning each of the narrower intervals between the piers. This combination of wide segmental arches flanked by narrower and lower segmental ones is a leitmotiv of Soane's Bank of England. Yet Baltimore Cathedral is no more Soanesque than the Philadelphia Pump House was. Above all, it is quite without that "sense of deflation, as if all *mass* had been exhausted from the design" which (in Summerson's words) characterizes Soane's personal style.

The difference between Baltimore Cathedral and the churches of the colonial period is one of kind. Their interiors, whether their architect's inspiration was from Wren or Gibbs, are essentially—however they may be subdivided horizontally by colonnades or vertically by galleries—single volumes of space, comprehended at a glance. At Baltimore the visitor passes through a succession of spatial units, each defined by the surfaces, flat or concave, of the actual masonry structure, until he reaches the circular space under the dome, the full extent of which cannot be seen from the entrance. There physical movement is succeeded by ocular, the eye circling with the cornice or leaping with the arches from pier to pier. The dome above is low and sheltering, as may be thought appropriate in a dome covering a church's main congregational space.

After Baltimore Cathedral Latrobe's finest church was the much smaller St. John's, Washington, which he designed in 1815. In its original Greek-cross form, this was as lucid an exercise in Neo-Classical geometry as could be found. A cupola here gives the worshipers beneath the domical ceiling of the central square a sense of vertical release as well as light—a potentiality of domed structures which Latrobe exploited to the full in the same year in designing the Baltimore Exchange, a work in which he was associated with Maximilien Godefroy. The central hall of the Exchange was 53 feet square on plan; two of its sides opened into barrel-vaulted spaces crossed at second-floor level by balconies, supported by Greek Ionic columns, while the other two had wall arches matching the face arches of the vaults; between the four arches pendentives carried a circular gallery, level with the roof of the rest of the building, offering views not only down to the floor of the hall 50 feet below but also out over the city through huge arched windows in a high drum (cylindrical inside, octagonal without), which was surmounted by a hemispherical dome; the crown of the dome, built like the rest of the structure of brick, was 115 feet above the floor. Nothing like it had been seen in America before, and Latrobe's management of the statics, with the weight of the drum distributed in such a way as to provide maximum abutment where it was needed for the gallery pendentives, was impeccable.

Latrobe's inventiveness was nowhere more evident than in his houses. Varied though they were in plan, compactness was a quality of them all, while they showed a concern for privacy—in the invariable presence of discreetly placed service stairs, for example—which is documented in the architect's letters. Nor were mechanical aids to domestic convenience overlooked. Both Adena at Chilicothe (1805) and the Van Ness House in Washington (Latrobe's largest house, built in 1814–17) had rotating servers in their dining room walls; as early as 1799 a design for John Tayloe (who built Thornton's Octagon instead) included a water closet on the second floor, and by placing tub and toilet in the same room in the Markoe House, Philadelphia (1808), Latrobe initiated a practice which was to give the term *bathroom* its special American meaning. Outside, Latrobe's houses were plain to the point of severity, being designed entirely in terms of the architectural basics of circle and square, cube and cylinder, mass and void. Inside, he employed all the room shapes that were the legacy of Robert Adam to Neo-Classicism, though in Adena (where the impossibility of supervision due to remoteness may have been a reason) and in the Van Ness House (where it could not have been) he used rectangles almost exclusively—the stair well of the Van Ness House is the exception—in *partis* much resembling the colonial double-pile house. There was always a high space rising through the upper floor. In the Pennock House, Norfolk (1796), this takes the form of a stair hall entered directly by the front door and lit by windows in both stories. But more often than not the two-story space is top-lit through a glazed lantern, as in Clifton, near Richmond (1808) and in the Tayloe House design, in which a domed rotunda with a gallery at upper floor level affords direct access to all the rooms on both floors. Top-lit domed rotundas without galleries were the central features of the Pope House, Lexington (1811), and Brentwood, near Washington (1818). The one in Brentwood, instead of being a hall of passage, was the chief reception room—and the grandest domestic example in Latrobe's *oeuvre* of a feature which he had first used in the Bank of Pennsylvania, his own favorite among all his designs.

Latrobe's last design was for a bank, the State Bank of Louisiana (118, 119). While he was working on it he must often have thought of another, much more important bank which he had failed to win in competition two years before, and which was even then being built to the design of one of his former pupils, William Strickland. But that is a matter which must wait for consideration later. Due for our attention now are four immigrant architects, three French and one English, who were never lucky or unlucky enough to be involved in the building of the Capitol.

*J. F. Mangin and John McComb*

The architectural competition for New York City Hall in 1802 produced twenty-six designs. Among them was one by Latrobe incorporating the central rotunda and other features of the Bank of Pennsylvania but with Corinthian porticoes instead of Ionic. To judge from the architect's perspective, it would have been something of an architectural understatement. It is easy to see why the city fathers preferred the much more decorative design by Mangin and McComb (120).

Joseph François Mangin came from a family of architects. He was in New York by 1794, when he was recommended to Washington as an engineering consultant for the fortifications; his earliest known work of architecture was the Park Street Theater, designed in collaboration with his brother Charles, which opened in 1795. John McComb, Jr., has been mentioned already as the architect of the New York presidential mansion, subsequently Government House.

118
*State Bank of Louisiana,
New Orleans, Louisiana.
Benjamin Henry Latrobe,
1820. Street view. The
parapet and dormers are
later additions.*

119
*State Bank of Louisiana,
New Orleans, Louisiana.
Plan of first floor.*

0   5   10   15   20
FEET

120
New York City Hall, New
York. Joseph François
Mangin and John Mc-
Comb, Jr., 1802–11. Gen-
eral exterior.

121
New York City Hall, New York. Stair rotunda.

He and his father before him were among the most successful builder-architects in New York. Trained as masons and bricklayers, they often undertook the execution of their own designs; on other occasions—as in the case of the presidential mansion—they supplied designs which were executed by others.

The drawings submitted in the New York City Hall competition by Mangin and McComb were the work of the former, who must also have been responsible for the design of facades. The horizontal rustication, the windows with swags in panels above them, the projecting portico without a pediment, the openness of the facade above the portico, the sculpture in front of the cupola, and the cupola itself in its original form are French.

The plan, one suspects, was McComb's. The *parti* is Palladian and the grandest interior feature, the stair rotunda, clearly came from James Paine's Wardour Castle (1770–76) via that architect's *Plans, Elevations and Sections of Noblemen and Gentlemen's Houses* (121). Construction was supervised by McComb alone, who was also responsible for the detailed design of the interior. He made good use of his copy of Adam's *Works*; not only is the ornament exceptionally sophisticated but columns are used to create spaces within spaces and change the apparent shape of rooms, as often in Adam's work but rarely in his American followers'. He also redesigned the cupola, Neo-Classicizing it and its relation to the building below; in Mangin's competition design the skyline of the central section of the building was distinctly Rococo.

*Maximilien Godefroy*

There is nothing Rococo about any of the designs of Maximilien Godefroy; their stylistic affiliations are with the Neo-Classical architecture of post-Revolutionary France. Godefroy arrived in America in 1805, after a term of imprisonment on suspicion of being an enemy of the Napoleonic regime. Before the end of the year he joined the faculty of St. Mary's College, Baltimore; by the following March he had designed a new chapel for the college, thus beginning a new career as an architect—in France he had been a civil engineer, apparently concerned more with canal works than with building construction—at the age of forty.

St. Mary's Chapel is Gothic; it has a place in the history of the Gothic Revival and will be treated of under that head. In 1810 the reputation it brought Godefroy led to an invitation to submit a design for the monument to George Washington that the Maryland legislature had authorized. He submitted two, one a rotunda and the other a triumphal arch, but the Commission went to Robert Mills.

In 1815 he designed the monument erected to commemorate the Battle of Baltimore.

The Battle Monument may be described in general terms as a column standing on a high pedestal with griffins on the four corners and supporting a statue (here a personification of Baltimore). Omit the griffins (symbols of immortality whose eagles' heads made them seem specially American) and that could be a description of any one of scores of commemorative columns. What was new about the Battle Monument came from Godefroy's treatment of its two largest components, the pedestal and the column. The pedestal, as befits what is a cenotaph to the thirty-nine Baltimoreans who died in the battle as well as a monument to the victory, is in the form of a tomb. Its battered sides, tapered doorways, and cavetto cornice ornamented with winged solar disks make it an early example of Egyptian Revivalism. The column is what Godefroy himself described as fascial. This is to say, it is a representation of the ancient Roman lictor's fasces, which had come to symbolize republican unity, stylized and enormously enlarged but immediately recognizable and thus an architectural equivalent of those colossal statues of which the Neo-Classical age produced so many.

It was shortly before he laid the cornerstone of the Battle Monument that Godefroy was invited by Latrobe to collaborate in a design for the Baltimore Exchange. While the plan and the domed exchange room (already described) were Latrobe's, we have Latrobe's word for it that the main front "in its general effect" was Godefroy's. The collaboration was short-lived; before 1816 was out Latrobe was sole architect for the Baltimore Exchange. Meanwhile, Godefroy had been called to Richmond to improve the environs of the capitol. This planning commission led to two architectural ones, the more important being the revision of a design by Mills for a new Richmond courthouse. By making the building two-storied throughout instead of only in the center and setting an unpedimented Roman Doric portico with giant columns against either front he both monumentalized and Frenchified it.

Godefroy's last American building, the Unitarian Church in Baltimore (1817–18), has been called "a monument which might well have risen in the Paris of the 1790s, had the French Deists been addicted to building churches" (122).[4] The description is apt so far as the general form of the building is concerned, although in designing it Godefroy used a work that did not appear until the end of the 1790s, namely *Palais, maisons, et autres édifices modernes, dessinés à Rome* by the architects Percier and Fontaine. This was the first

122
*Unitarian Church, Baltimore, Maryland. Maximilien Godefroy, 1817–18. Facade. The Angel of Truth in the pediment, replaced by a modern copy in 1960, is by Antonio Capellano.*

major French publication of Italian Renaissance architecture, and the Unitarian Chapel, while quintessentially Neo-Classical in its composition of basic geometrical shapes, was the first nineteenth-century building in America in which Renaissance forms and detail were used, a single swallow more than thirty years ahead of the Renaissance Revival summer. Among the features owed to Percier and Fontaine are the doorways within the porch; an account of the building published soon after its dedication and probably written by Godefroy himself describes them as imitations of the doors of the Vatican with archivolts after the style of the Farnese Palace. The arcaded porch or loggia was an Italianate feature that had been a favorite with French architects since the 1780s. A building in which it was combined with a pediment and which Godefroy could have known was the Théâtre des Jeunes Artistes by J.-N. Sobre. In this, the pediment stretched across the whole facade and the porch was an opening in an otherwise unbroken wall; in the Unitarian Chapel the pediment surmounts a central section breaking forward from the main mass and square piers flank the outer columns of the porch so as to make it a distinct portico. The difference shows Godefroy's regard for character, or *caractère*, as defined by the eighteenth-century French theorists he had read in the course of his architectural self-education.

The central space inside the Unitarian Church was a square, fifty-three feet and six inches on a side, under a hemispherical Pantheon-type dome which rose from a circle produced by four pendentives between four wide arches (123).[5] The spaces under the arches turned the plan into a short-armed cross, the arm toward the entrance containing the organ loft and the one opposite it being rounded off as an apse. Again Renaissance detail appeared—in the impost moldings under the arches, for example—while Greek architecture was represented by columns of the Tower of the Winds order under the organ loft.

Godefroy left America, never to return, in 1819.[6] The American
career of Joseph Jacques Ramée was little more than a third as long.
Born, like Latrobe, in 1764, in 1792 Ramée found himself under the
necessity of fleeing France and went to Hamburg, where he established a flourishing practice in landscape gardening and interior decoration as well as architecture. In 1811 the financier David Parish
persuaded him to join him on his estate in northern New York.
There Ramée designed a variety of buildings in the towns of Parish-
ville and Rossie and landscaped the grounds of the Ogden mansion
nearby. In 1813 Parish introduced him to Eliphalet Nott, president
of Union College near Schenectady. Chartered in 1795, Union was
one of the four largest colleges in the country and quite the most
progressive.

The first building of Union College, by Philip Hooker of Albany,
was an altogether conventional specimen of American collegiate architecture, of three stories with a central pedimented pavilion and a
tall cupola. For the new site above the existing campus on which
Nott had decided to build Ramée designed an entirely new kind of
college complex (124). The focal structure was a Pantheon-like rotunda standing on the chord of a range of building, partly of one
story and partly of three, resembling an omega on plan; in front of
the rotunda there was a wide lawn flanked by buildings like back-to-
back Ls and with its fourth side left open toward the country; the
surroundings were to be landscaped in the English manner. Only
two of the buildings, those flanking the lawn, were ever built to
Ramée's design; stylistically they are rather conservative. Nevertheless, Union has a place in the history of collegiate architecture alongside the University of Virginia. And although Jefferson's concept of
an academical village antedated Ramée's plan by eight or nine years,
knowledge of the latter may well have inspired Latrobe's suggestion
to Jefferson that gave the University of Virginia its rotunda. Ramée's
other American works included designs for a commemorative arch
to George Washington in Baltimore and for the Baltimore Exchange.
The failure of the latter to win acceptance was evidently the cause
of his return to France in 1816 after only five years in America.

William Jay was another architect whose stay in America was
brief. In less than seven years he gave Savannah, Georgia, where he
landed in 1817 at the age of 23 after serving his articles in the office
of D. R. Roper in London, a handful of the most original Neo-
Classical buildings on this side of the Atlantic. The austere geometry
of the Scarborough House (1818) is reminiscent of Ledoux; behind
its porch lies what has been called "one of the grandest spacial
compositions in American domestic architecture," an atriumlike hall,

124
*Union College, Schenec-*
*tady, New York. Joseph*
*Jacques Ramée, 1813.*
*Plan of buildings and*
*landscaping.*

125
Scarborough House, Savannah, Georgia. William Jay, 1818. Porch.

two stories high, with four Doric columns supporting a mezzanine. The porch columns of the Scarborough House are unfluted but support a complete Doric entablature (125); in Jay's Branch Bank of the United States (1820) the Doric columns were fluted but the entablature was devoid of triglyphs and the other customary details of the order. In the Telfair House (ca. 1820) the geometry of the subtly proportioned facade is relieved by a porch in the Corinthian of the Monument of Lysicrates; in the Bullock-Habersham House (1820) the same Athenian model was imitated in a circular porch, which led to a rectangular hall from whose floor a free-standing stair spiraled up inside a ring of six more Lysicratean columns.

Jay was as energetic as he was inventive. Practicing in Charleston as well as Savannah, he was a member of the Board of Public Works in South Carolina and a founder member of the South Carolina Academy of Arts. His return to England as a result of the financial depression suffered by the South in 1822 was a serious loss to American architecture.

*Latrobe's Pupils*

Latrobe's contribution to American architecture was not limited to his own buildings or confined to the span of his own short life. Many of the most important buildings that went up between his death and the Civil War were designed by architects trained in his office, the first American office in which young men were accepted with the status of pupil-assistants. Foremost among them were Robert Mills and William Strickland. The bulk of their work belongs to the period 1820–1850, when they were among the half-dozen most successful architects in the country, but their earlier designs are not without importance and should not be omitted from any account of Neo-Classicism during the Federal period.

Robert Mills was a native of Charleston, South Carolina, where he was born in 1781. After a brief spell as a draftsman with Hoban he was taken up by Jefferson and spent two years at Monticello. In 1803 he entered Latrobe's office, where he remained five years.[7] In 1808 he designed the circular Sansom Street Baptist Church in Philadelphia, with a wooden roof modelled on that of the Halle au Blés in Paris, a structure greatly admired by Jefferson. His first public commission after he left Latrobe was Washington Hall, Philadelphia. Designed in 1809 but not completed until 1816, this also was remarkable for its roof, which covered a hall that could hold nearly 6,000 people without intermediate supports; its facade, with a columnar screen in a domed niche, was inspired by Ledoux's Hôtel Guimard in Paris. Assisted by the understanding of construction that was one of Latrobe's greatest gifts to his pupils, in his early career

126
*Monumental Church,
Richmond, Virginia. Rob-
ert Mills, 1812. General
Exterior.*

Mills was something of a specialist in large auditoria, secular and ecclesiastical. The ecclesiastical ones included the Octagon Unitarian Church, Philadelphia (completed in 1813), the Monumental Church, Richmond (designed in 1812), which also is octagonal, and the First Baptist Chruch, Baltimore (1817–18), an Ionic Pantheon. The Monumental Church, the only survivor of these three, was the one into which Mills put most of himself (126). The simplifications of classical detail are perhaps more odd than original. But then Mills, for all his solid ability, was not the most original of architects. Nor did he have the sensibility of Latrobe's other star pupil, William Strickland.

Mills's junior by seven years, at fifteen Strickland was apprenticed to Latrobe by his father, a carpenter who worked on the Bank of Pennsylvania; the apprenticeship was terminated by Latrobe less than two years later when the boy absented himself without leave. In 1808, when he was twenty, Strickland designed the Masonic Hall, Philadelphia, which was completed in 1811 and destroyed by fire eight years later; Gothic, it had a wooden steeple, 180 feet high. He had few architectural commissions in the next ten years and supported himself for the most part by surveying, engraving, and scene painting. Strickland's day came in September, 1818, when he was proclaimed winner of the competition for the Bank of the United States in Philadelphia—his old master Latrobe taking the second premium. His design, which was executed in 1819–24, ushered in a new age in American architecture.

# The Greek Revival

On May 13, 1818, *The Philadelphia Gazette and Daily Advertiser* carried an advertisement by the Board of Directors of the Bank of the United States inviting "architects of science and experience" to submit designs for a banking house to be erected on a site between Chestnut and Library streets. "The ground plan will include an area of about ten or eleven thousand square feet. . . . The building will be faced with marble, and have a portico on each front, resting upon a basement or platform of such altitude as will combine convenience of ascent with due proportion and effect. In this edifice, the Directors are desirous of exhibiting a chaste imitation of Grecian Architecture, in its simplest and least expensive form."

Clearly the Directors, in specifying a portico on each front, were thinking of Latrobe's Bank of Pennsylvania, designed twenty years before, while in desiring that the building should be Grecian "in its simplest and least expensive form" they were virtually stipulating that the order should be Doric. And the designs that they received from Latrobe and from his former pupil Strickland were both Doric and both *criticisms* (rather than imitations) of the earlier bank. But the criticisms were based on different premises. In Latrobe's design a high attic concealing a dome over the central banking hall supplies a secondary mass which would have given the building a much greater sense of weight than the Bank of Pennsylvania had. The architect seems to be saying that his earlier bank was not monumental enough; in any event, the changes are esthetically motivated. In Strickland's design, on the other hand, the barrel-vaulted banking hall was denied any but the most perfunctory expression on the exterior, and the pediments were joined by an unbroken roof to preserve the temple form of the whole, the implication being that his former master's bank was not Greek enough. Strickland's criteria, that is to say, were historical. So were those of the bank's directors, who found his design more "classic" (meaning more like a Greek temple) than Latrobe's. As a result, the Second Bank of the United States (from 1844 to 1932 the Customs House) became the first building of the Greek Revival that was to dominate the architectural scene in America for more than thirty years (127, 128, 129).

In theory, revivalism puts learning before sensibility and values deference to authority more highly than originality. The English Gothic Revival architect Augustus Welby Pugin wrote of himself in 1843: "Mr. Pugin, we believe, never claimed the least merit on the score of originality . . . but simply to revive . . . the glorious but till lately despised work of the Middle Ages." Yet the architectural revivals of the nineteenth century were saved from producing mere copies and became true styles because in practice the need for a

*127*
*Second Bank of the
United States (later Cus-
toms House), Philadel-
phia, Pennsylvania.
William Strickland, 1818–
24. South portico.*

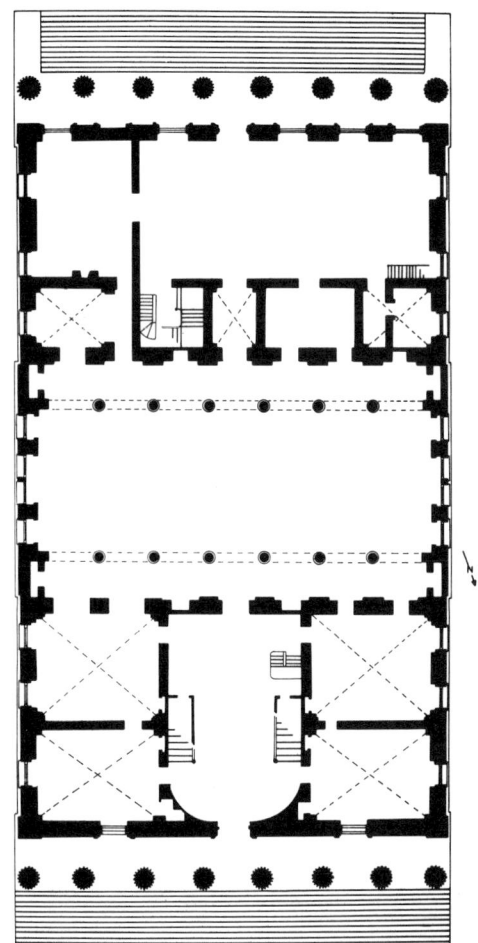

128
Second Bank of the
United States, Philadel-
phia, Pennsylvania. Plan
of first floor.

129
Second Bank of the
United States, Philadel-
phia, Pennsylvania.
Banking room.

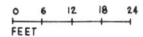

degree of adaptation to modern requirements was always recognized and, however self-denying an architect's intentions, a personal sense of form has a way of asserting itself. Ignorance might also play a part. Strickland modeled the porticoes of the Second Bank of the United States on the Parthenon, reducing them to three-fifths the scale of the prototype. But those slight departures from the rectilinear and the vertical which go under the name of refinements and which give the temple an organic quality that it otherwise would not have are altogether absent from the bank—simply because Strickland did not know of them.[1] Consequently the Second Bank of the United States could never be mistaken for a real Greek temple from any viewpoint.

*Capitols and Customs Houses*

The Second Bank of the United State is amphiprostyle but not peripteral. As Strickland pointed out, lateral colonnades would have obscured the windows. It was Ithiel Town who solved the problem of how to preserve the trabeated system (at least in appearance) on the flanks of a temple-form building without denying light to its interior in his design for the Connecticut State House, which went up in 1827–31 within a stone's throw of his Gothic Trinity Church in New Haven. The order was again that of the Parthenon, although the porticoes were hexastyle only; along the side walls in the original design—though not in the executed one—were series of prominent antae, forming what may most handily be called pilastrades.

The pilastrade was a feature of both the state capitols designed by Town and Alexander Jackson Davis, his partner for the fifteen years 1829–44 (when their New York office was the biggest and busiest in the country). In other respects they differed significantly. The Indiana State Capitol, designed in 1831, had a dome and lantern rising from a high drum on an octagonal plinth midway between its octastyle porticoes. In the North Carolina Capitol, designed in 1833, the temple form has been abandoned for a cruciform plan and the porticoes stand on high rusticated basements; the dome rises directly from an octagonal plinth—as it also did in the Vermont State House, designed in 1832 by Ammi B. Young.

The placing of Roman domes upon buildings otherwise Greek did not escape criticism. In 1835 *The American Monthly Magazine* attacked Town and Davis's design of 1833 for the New York Customs House on the ground that its dome was "an excrescence, which, however elegant in itself, is utterly monstrous when added to a model of the present Grecian architecture." Again the criteria were historical; the dome was an expression of the largest space within and its lowering under the roof by the architect who supervised

130
Customs House (later
Sub-Treasury, now Fed-
eral Hall National Memo-
rial), New York City.
Town and Davis and
James Frazee, 1833–42.
South portico.

131
Customs House, New
York City. Plan.

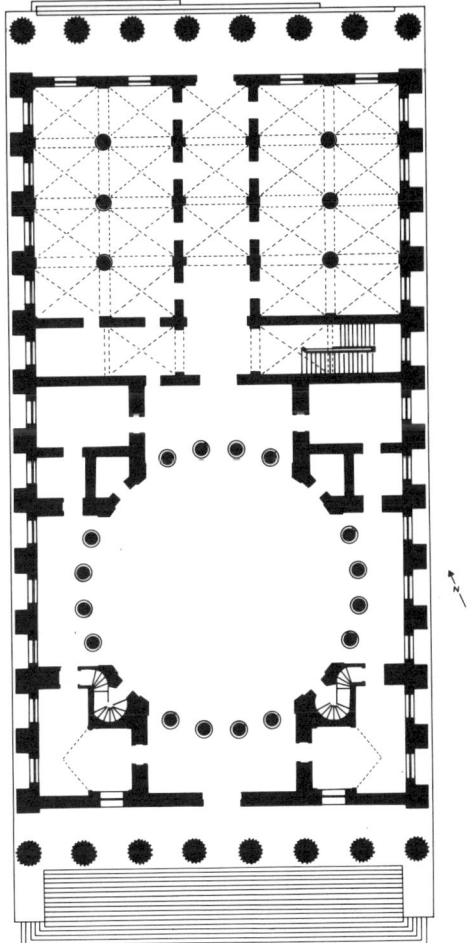

0  6  12  18  24
FEET

*132*
*Ohio State Capitol, Columbus, Ohio. Thomas Cole, 1838–61. View from southwest.*

construction, John Frazee, only intensified the conflict between interior and exterior that the use of the temple form made inevitable (130, 131). A low dome crowned the Boston Customs House, built in 1837–47 to Young's design. Young eschewed the pilastrades of Town and Davis and used half-columns instead, thereby giving the Boston building a massiveness and a richness of light and shade that save it from being visually crushed by the skyscraper for which since 1915 it has served as a pedestal. The Ohio State Capitol at Columbus has as its central feature a tall drum, sans dome (132). The complex history of this, perhaps the finest of the pre-Civil War capitols, began in 1838 with a competition of which Henry Walter of Cincinnati was declared the winner, with Martin E. Thompson, an associate of Town and Davis, taking the second premium and Thomas Cole, the landscape painter, the third. After asking Town and Davis to synthesize the three prize-winning designs, the commissioners for the building finally settled on Cole's, which was executed, with a few changes, in the next twenty-four years. The unbroken rectangle of the plan, the simplicity of the pilastraded elevations, and the unfluted columns of the recessed porticoes recall the Neo-Classicism of an earlier age.

The instructions to the architects competing for the Ohio capitol suggested the use of the Greek Doric order, though "not with a view of governing exclusively in the choice." This was an expression of a widely held preference, for Doric was the rule for Greek Revival capitols; besides those already mentioned, the Arkansas State Capitol (Gideon Shryock, 1833, with modification by George Weigart), the Illinois State Capitol (John Rague, 1837), and the Iowa State Capitol (Rague, 1840), were Doric. Of the two most notable exceptions one appeared at the beginning and the other near the end of the revival. The first was the Ionic temple at Frankfort, Kentucky, designed in 1825—and so antedating Town's Connecticut State House—by Gideon Shryock of Lexington, whose builder-architect father had apprenticed him to Strickland for a year; it has a hexastyle portico of the order of the Temple of Athena Polias at Priene and a domed lantern lighting a double circular stair, leading to the legislative chambers on the second floor, which must have been inspired by the stair in New York City Hall. The other was the Tennessee State Capitol, built in 1845–59, in which Strickland made a great display of the Ionic of the Erechtheum in an octastyle portico at either end and an unpedimented hexastyle one on either flank, while catering to the mid-century taste for height which was among the causes of the demise of the Greek Revival with a square tower surmounted by a version of the Monument of Lysicrates (133, 134).

*Porticoed Churches*

For the first churches of the Greek Revival we must return to Philadelphia. Even before the Second Bank of the United States was finished two of temple form, both with hexastyle Ionic porticoes facing the street, had risen in that city: the first Presbyterian Church, in which the order was taken from the Temple on the Ilissus, and St. Andrew's Episcopal Church (now St. George's Greek Orthodox), with the delicately enriched Ionic of the Temple of Dionysus at Teos done in wood. They were designed, in 1820 and 1822, respectively, by John Haviland, a young English architect who had come to America from Russia in 1816 at the urging of John Quincy Adams. Most often remembered for his prisons (to be discussed later), Haviland was a prolific architect and a protean one even within the limitations of the Greek Revival; in Philadelphia his archaeologically imitative Ionic portico of St. Andrew's was followed in 1824 by the radically simplified Doric one of his Pennsylvania Institution for the Deaf and Dumb (now the Philadelphia College of Art), and that in 1825 by the Franklin Institute (now the Atwater Kent Museum), in which he employed the order of the Monument of Thrasyllus with four massive antae to give monumentality and a powerful sense of structure to a street front of little more than domestic scale.

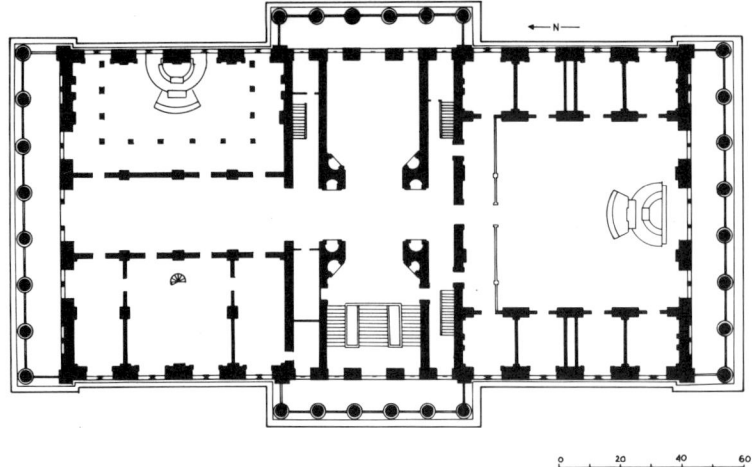

Haviland's *The Builder's Assistant*, published in Philadelphia in 1818, was the first American book to give the Greek orders; nine years later Asher Benjamin followed suit in the sixth edition of *The American Builder's Companion*. Moderately priced handbooks, substituting for the expensive volumes of Stuart and Revett's *Antiquities of Athens*—and also supplementing them, with examples of the application of Greek forms to modern functions—did for the builder-architects of the Greek Revival what the handbooks of William Salmon and others had done for their colonial predecessors a hundred years before. Among the most used were those of Minard Lafever, whose first, *The Young Builder's General Instructor*, appeared in 1829. It was Lafever who designed, in 1834, the ecclesiastical counterpart of the Second Bank of the United States. The First Reformed Dutch Church in Brooklyn was amphiprostyle and octastyle, like the bank, but the order was Ionic, after the Temple on the Ilissus; as in the bank, the side walls were plain; however, Lafever went one better than Strickland—or perhaps, counting the columns, one should say two better—by providing a vestibule or pronaos, distyle in antis, within the front portico.

Lafever's Dutch Church in Brooklyn had no steeple of any kind. In this it was exceptional; enthusiasm for Greek architecture rarely absolved an architect designing a church from the obligation of providing such a feature, "of Gothic extraction" though it was. The Greek Revival architect's problem was the problem that had been Wren's a century and a half before, with the added difficulty that it was now thought desirable to imitate specific prototypes as closely as possible. There were two Greek structures that could serve as such for church steeples, namely the cylindrical Monument of Lysicrates, of the fourth century B.C., and the octagonal Tower of the Winds, of the first. The Monument of Lysicrates was the more frequent choice. Among the churches on which it found a place—it was not, as we have seen already and shall see again, confined to churches—was the French Protestant Episcopal Church in New York (1832–34) by Town and Davis. But freely composed Greek versions of the Wren-Gibbs type of steeple were a common solution, and the St. Martin-in-the-Fields formula continued to be followed; a graceful example of the latter in New England is the Congregational Church at Madison, Connecticut (1838), and a showy one in the South is St. Paul's, Richmond, Virginia, completed to the design of Thomas S. Stewart of Philadelphia in 1845 (135). The interior of St. Paul's, Richmond, with its colonnaded apse, is an exception to the rule that Greek Revival church interiors are featureless and boxlike. Another, earlier exception is the interior of Old St. Louis Cathedral at St.

135
*St. Paul's, Richmond,
Virginia. Thomas S.
Stewart, 1845. Steeple
and portico.*

136
*Unitarian Church,*
*Quincy, Massachusetts.*
*Alexander Parris, 1828.*
*Steeple and portico.*

Louis, Missouri, which was completed in 1834 to the design of George Morton and Joseph C. Laveille. The facade and steeple of Old St. Louis Cathedral are also remarkably fine, with more of Latrobe and Wren than of the Greek Revival about them. Perhaps the finest facade and steeple combination in a strict (though simplified) Greek idiom is that of the Unitarian Church at Quincy, Massachusetts, built of the local granite in 1828 to the design of Alexander Parris, whose St. Paul's, Boston (1819), was the first Greek Revival church in New England (136).

*Courthouses and Colleges*

A building type whose Greek Revival examples may often be mistaken for churches at first glance, or even second, is the courthouse. The earliest courthouse of temple form was a modest affair designed in 1821 for Buckingham County, Virginia; it was not Greek but Roman, with a Tuscan portico, and the architect was Thomas Jefferson. It had no cupola, but most Greek Revival courthouses did. Sometimes they have what can only be described as steeples. The Hustings Courthouse at Petersburg, Virginia, built to the design of Calvin Pollard in 1838–40, has one that might well belong to a church, but for the statue of Justice on its summit; the order of the Tower of the Winds is used both in its first stage and in the portico, but H. W. Inwood's St. Pancras Church, London, must have been the immediate progenitor, while the clock stage comes from St. Anne's, Soho, by Latrobe's master, S. P. Cockerell (137).

It is said that the handsome Ionic courthouse at Dayton, Ohio, built in 1848–50, was the result of the revision by its architect, Howard Daniels, of a fully peripteral scheme proposed by a local amateur. The only full peripteral temple of the American Greek Revival actually built was not a temple of justice but a temple of learning, the Center Building of Girard College, Philadelphia (138).

The history of Girard College began with a competition held in 1832–33 for a school for orphans to be built in accordance with the terms of the will of the banker Stephen Girard. It was won by Thomas Ustick Walter, not long out of Strickland's office, with a simple Doric design. But the chairman of the trustees was Nicholas Biddle, another banker, who had traveled in Greece and believed that "the two great truths in the world" were "the Bible and Grecian architecture," and he had grander ideas which led him to persuade Walter to make a new and much more costly design, the City Councils to accept it, and his fellow trustees to divert funds intended by Girard for other purposes to its execution. The result was the colossal Corinthian temple, containing twelve classrooms on three

*137*
*Hustings Courthouse, Pe-*
*tersburg, Virginia. Calvin*
*Pollard, 1838–40. Tower*
*and portico.*

138
*Girard College, Philadel-*
*phia, Pennsylvania.*
*Thomas Ustick Walter,*
*1833–48. Founder's Hall.*

floors and two stair halls, that was completed at the cost of over a million and a half dollars in 1848. It is still impressive for its scale as well as the beautiful execution of its detail; its "incorrect" proportions—for a Greek temple it is too short for its width—are due to the architect having to follow the dimensions on plan specified in Girard's will, which also specified the fireproof brick vaulting whose design shows Walter's mastery of masonry construction.

Although no other college or university had a Girard fortune at its disposal, the number of buildings for higher education that went up in the Grecian years was large. In mood they ranged from the austerity of the stern Doric library (later Manning Hall) at Brown University, designed by James Bucklin in 1833, to the cheerfulness of the unlearned mixture of Greek and Roman which has been on parade, so to speak, in Jeffersonian red and white, at Washington and Lee since 1842. An earlier group that, like Washington and Lee, owes much to its landscape setting is at Amherst, where plain dormitories flanking a chapel with a tetrastyle Paestum portico were built in 1821–27 to the design of Isaac Damon.

***Buildings for Bureaucracy and Commerce***

The architect who left the biggest mark on the government buildings of Washington, where the Greek Revival made its debut in the Ionic-porticoed City Hall (now District of Columbia Courthouse), designed by George Hadfield in 1820, was Robert Mills. The former pupil of Latrobe spent the twenties in his native Charleston, where he designed various buildings for the South Carolina Board of Public Works; the Record Office at Charleston, with its arched windows, unfluted Doric columns, plain entablature, and raking blocking course instead of a pediment, is a good example of the non-doctrinaire

Neo-Classical style of this period of his career. In 1830 Mills moved to Washington and three years later, repeating his Baltimore success of 1815, won the competition for the monument to be erected there to the first president. In 1836 he was appointed supervising architect for federal buildings, thus becoming responsible for the construction of the Treasury Building, the Patent Office (now the National Portrait Gallery), and the Post Office and Land Office (now the Tariff Commission). Although one William P. Elliot had already prepared designs for the first two, as built they are to be counted Mills's work. Both are vaulted in masonry throughout. The Treasury Building is Ionic; its immensely long colonnade is a piece of architectural rhetoric which is no less impressive for having been rather too often emulated by later architects in Washington. The National Portrait Gallery is Doric; the effect of its sixteen-column Parthenaic portico was much diminished when the steps were removed in a street-widening operation in 1936, but the cantilevered double stair behind it and the Lincoln Gallery on the third floor are still two of the finest features of their respective kinds in the city, or indeed in the country (139). The Tariff Commission is Corinthian, with long facades punctuated with columnar pavilions in the manner of Chambers's Somerset House; the recessed portico with coupled columns that answers the portico of the National Gallery across the street was designed by Walter, who succeeded Mills as supervising architect for federal buildings in 1851. Mills's Washington buildings can perhaps be best characterized in the phrase of a greater architect, Inigo Jones: "solid, proportionable according to the rules, masculine and unaffected"— all admirable qualities in the office buildings of a republic.

A commercial building that challenged comparison with anything built for the federal government was the Merchants' Exchange in New York, designed by Isaiah Rogers in 1836 (and so exactly contemporaneous with the Treasury Building). It too had an Ionic colonnade on a high podium; its exterior was of Quincy granite and the floors were carried by brick vaulting; the exchange room was a brick-domed rotunda eighty feet in diameter, with columns of a Corinthian order of Rogers's own invention set in antis in four recesses opening out of it. Its stern monumentality was in strong contrast to the elegance of the Merchants' Exchange in Philadelphia, designed by Strickland four years earlier, with its Lysicratean lantern rising from a hemitholos of the same order. The Boston Merchants' Exchange (completed in 1842), in which Rogers employed the temple portico formula but substituted antae for columns, was both monumental and rich. A New Englander who before opening his own office spent four years with Solomon Willard, Rogers would have a

139
*Patent Office (National
Portrait Gallery), Wash-
ington, District of Colum-
bia. Robert Mills, 1836.
Stairs.*

good claim to be regarded as the greatest commercial architect of his time even without his hotels (of which more shortly).

From among market buildings the Quincy Market in Boston, begun in 1825 to the design of Alexander Parris, may be singled out for mention on account of both its functional plan and its construction of large blocks of Quincy granite—stone skeleton construction, so to call it. Of the shopping arcade, which had appeared in France (where it is called a *passage*) around 1790, America had two examples before the twenties were out. The first was the Philadelphia Arcade, designed by John Haviland and built in 1827, the second the Providence Arcade, designed by Russell Warren and James Bucklin and completed in 1829 (140). The street fronts of the Philadelphia Arcade were opened up with arches, like the Burlington Arcade in London (1818–19); at Providence the glass-roofed interior is visible from the street through screens of Ionic columns.

The hotel is a building type that falls somewhere between the commercial and the domestic. The first American hotel to be so called was the City Hotel in New York, built in 1794–96; architecturally it was not distinctive. Much more of a hotel by nature though not in name was the seven-story Exchange Coffee House in Boston, designed by Asher Benjamin, built in 1806–09, and burnt in 1818. But it was Tremont House, Boston, built in 1828–32 to the design of Isaiah Rogers, that deserved the appellation, first given to it by Talbot Hamlin, of the first modern hotel in America (141, 142); with its spacious Doric porch, its circular lobby with the reception office opening off it, its seventy-by-thirty-foot dining room with a peristyle of fourteen Ionic columns, its sumptuous public rooms and its commodious private ones (from singles to suites), and not least its plumbing (with a row of eight water closets on the first floor and baths below them in the basement), it set a new standard. Its fame made Rogers the leading hotel architect of the next three-and-a-half decades. In 1834 he was commissioned to design Astor House, New York, with more than 300 rooms against the 170 in Tremont House and with plumbing carried through all three stories; among his many later hotels were the (second) St. Charles Hotel in New Orleans, Burnet House in Cincinnati, Galt House in Louisville, and Maxwell House in Nashville. There is some doubt as to whether the Charleston Hotel, opened in 1839, is his. In any case its Corinthian colonnade is a worthy fellow to the Ionic one of the New York Merchants' Exchange.

140
*Providence Arcade, Provi-*
*dence, Rhode Island. Rus-*
*sell Warren and James*
*Bucklin, 1828–29.*
*Interior.*

141
Tremont House, Boston,
Massachusetts. Isaiah
Rogers, 1828–32. Tre-
mont Street front.

142
Tremont House, Boston,
Massachusetts. Plan of
first floor.

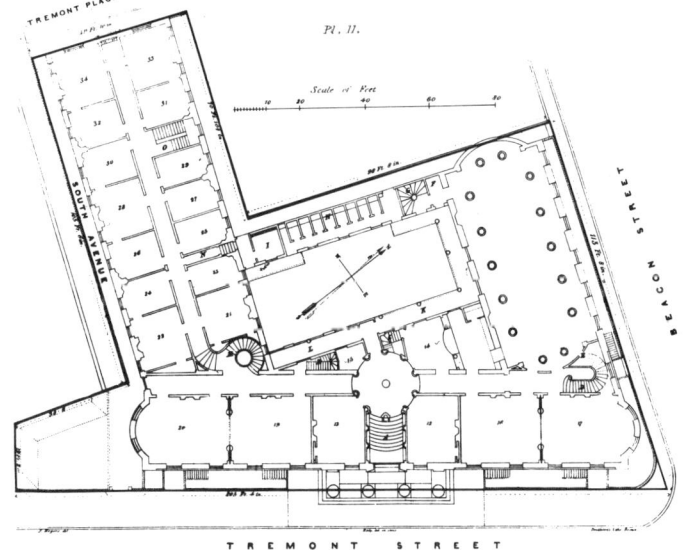

*Houses Great and Small*

The first temple house of the Greek Revival appeared in 1820 when George Hadfield transformed the Lee Mansion at Arlington, Virginia, by adding a porticoed center which overwhelmed the earlier structure (143); in choosing the order, Paestum Doric with unfluted columns, he had an eye to the effect of the house on its hill as seen across the Potomac from Washington. Five years later the Bowers House at Northampton, Massachusetts, was built to the design of Ithiel Town as an Ionic temple with low wings, their roofs at right angles to the roof of the two-storied center, which the wings seemed to penetrate—a scheme that became very common in the thirties, when it was popularized by Lafever's *Modern Builder's Guide*. Then in 1828–30 Town's partner Davis built the Russell House at Middletown, Connecticut, with a hexastyle Corinthian portico and no wings or other projections to compromise the temple form.

In the third and fourth decades of the century domestic temples went up everywhere. Among the grander ones, two that demand notice are Andalusia in Pennsylvania, where in 1833 T. U. Walter helped Nicholas Biddle bear witness to the great truth of Grecian architecture by wrapping the order of the Temple of Hephaestus at Athens around three sides of the house, and Berry Hill in Virginia, built in 1835–40, with an octastyle portico after the Parthenon which is approached between two porticoed dependencies. Size and quality were not necessarily commensurate, however, and many of the

*143*
*Lee Mansion, Arlington, Virginia. George Hadfield, 1820. Portico.*

144
*Judge Wilson House, Ann
Arbor, Michigan. 1843.
General view.*

145
*Judge Wilson House, Ann
Arbor, Michigan. Plan of
first floor, with additions
removed.*

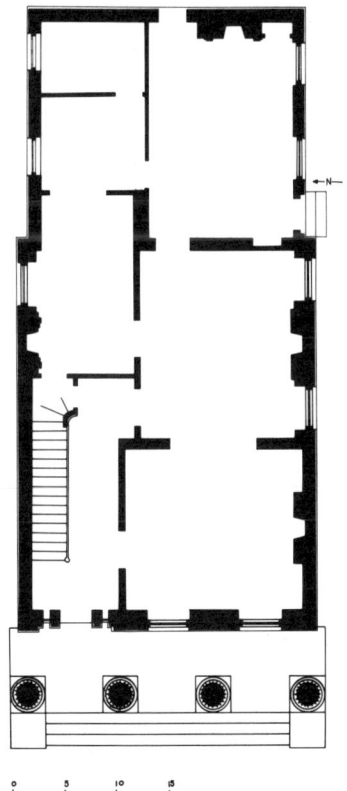

146
Uncle Sam Plantation, St.
James Parish, Louisiana.
Circa 1850. South front.

147
Uncle Sam Plantation, St.
James Parish, Louisiana.
Plan of first floor.

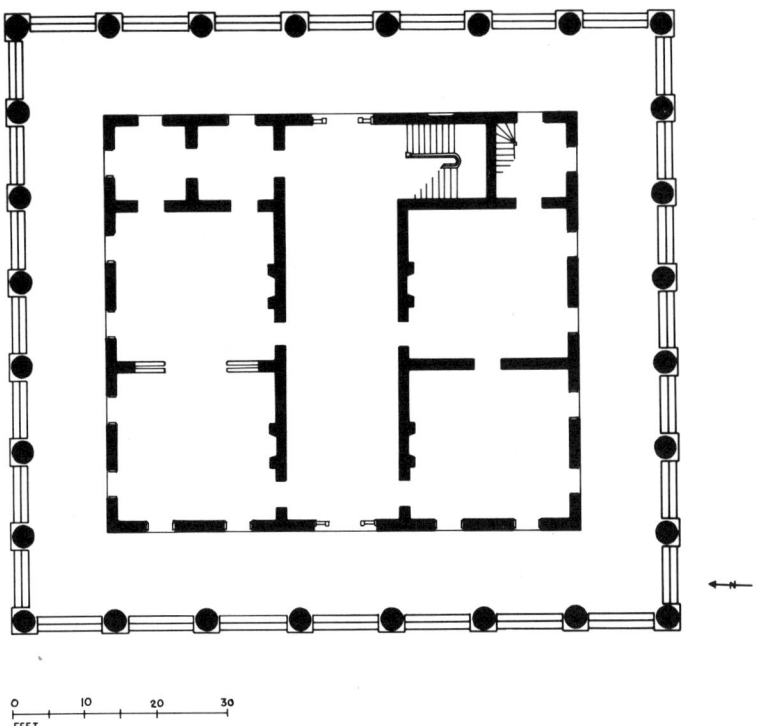

0    10    20    30
FEET

smaller temple houses, designed by builders of local fame only with the aid of their Benjamins and their Lafevers, deserve as much notice as the great show places (144, 145).

Characteristic and conspicious though they were, temple-form houses never constituted an absolute majority. More often Greek forms were used to dress up houses of traditional plan, with the long axis parallel to the front; a portico might be applied to the center of the front in the Palladian manner, or an order might be used without any pretense that it belonged to any part of a temple. The result could be original, as it is in the house that Hitchcock singles out for illustration in his international survey of nineteenth-century architecture: Elmhyrst at Newport, Rhode Island, which was designed by Russell Warren about 1833. Then there were the many houses in which a colonnaded porch ran the length of the front, and those in Louisiana and the Deep South for which Hitchcock coined the term "peripteral mode," with giant columns on all four sides (146). The peripteral mode was the result of classicizing the French colonial plantation house with its *galeries*; the earliest examples predated the Greek Revival, and as late as 1832 Oak Alley in St. James Parish was designed (by George Swainey) with Tuscan columns and Adam-esque fanlights and dormers. Greenwood, in West Feliciana Parish, begun in 1830, would appear to have been the first Grecian plantation house in Louisiana. In many cases the designers of these houses are obscure or unknown. However, Ashland, in Ascension Parish, which was built in 1841 and with its square piers in the place of columns is one of the most impressive of them, is attributed to James Gallier, Sr., Irish by birth and English by training, whose work in New Orleans, where he arrived in 1835, includes the City Hall (1845–50). In the larger Greek Revival houses of this period a great interior space for formal entertainment was a general requirement that was often met by providing sliding doors between the dining room and the parlor, as was first done in New York city houses in the 1820s (147).

Externally, the city house of the period was distinguished from its Federal predecessor by the insistence on the principle of trabeation shown in its design; the oblong overdoor light took the place of the fanlight and window lintels were often emphasized by one means or another; the front might be crowned by a full entablature, often with windows in the frieze. If there was a porch, it might consist of two columns supporting a section of entablature; or antae, perhaps decorated with a form of the Greek fret, might be used instead of columns; patterns for both treatments were available in the books of Benjamin and Lafever. Attempts at giving row houses a monumental effect were few; the most ambitious was Lafayette Terrace, New

York, formerly attributed to A. J. Davis, which was built in 1832–33, of Westchester marble, with a Corinthian colonnade screening the two upper stories as in the Charleston Hotel.

*The Egyptian Episode*

From time to time an architect would forsake the acanthus for the lotus, the vertical wall for the battered, and produce a design which paid homage to a civilization that was already more than two thousand years old when the Parthenon was built. The tangible results were not numerous—they totalled about eighty—but they were often substantial and sometimes very substantial indeed.

The first architect to propose the use of Egyptian forms in America was, as might be expected, Latrobe; this was in a design for the Library of Congress in the Capitol made in 1808. Seven years later, as we saw, they were used by Godefroy in the Battle Monument in Baltimore. In 1825 the many-talented Willard (who had worked as a sculptor on Godefroy's Unitarian Church) began the construction, with granite from his own quarries at Quincy, of the first of the colossal obelisks, commemorating another battle, on Bunker Hill at Charlestown, Massachusetts. In 1833 Mills won the competition for the monument to George Washington in the federal city with an obelisk which, denuded of the Doric peristyle that concealed its base in the winning design, was to rise—though not until 1884—to the unprecedented height of 555 feet.

While the solidity and permanence of Egyptian architecture recommended its imitation for commemorative functions generally, the funerary purpose of so many of its remaining monuments made it seem especially appropriate in cemeteries, with results that range from the simple granite portals provided by Rogers for the Old Granary Burying Ground in Boston and the Touro Cemetery in Newport in 1840 and 1843 to the elaborate columnar gateway of the Grove Street Cemetery in New Haven, designed in 1845 by Henry Austin. As for churches, the only two in which Egyptian forms preponderate are the Whalers' Church at Sag Harbor, Long Island, which was built, probably to Lafever's design, in 1843–44, and the First Presbyterian Church at Nashville, by Strickland, built in 1848–51. But some Greek Revival churches—St. Paul's Richmond, for example—have Egyptian touches, while in the First Baptist Church at Essex, Connecticut (ca. 1845), battered walls are combined with an Adam Style cupola. In Philadelphia two Egyptian synagogues were built: the Mikveh Israel Synagogue on Cherry Street to Strickland's design early in the revival in 1822 and the Beth Israel Synagogue on Crown Street toward its end in 1849.

148
*New York City Halls of Justice and House of Detention (The Tombs), New York City. John Haviland, 1835–38. Portico on Centre Street front.*

Egyptian forms were employed in a number of other types of building. Sometimes the choice seems reasonably apt, as in the case of the Medical College of Virginia at Richmond, designed in 1844 by Stewart, the architect of St. Paul's Church nearby, in which it was doubtless suggested by the traditional view of Egypt as the cradle of medicine. It is less easy to account for the Egyptian railroad station at New Bedford, Massachusetts, designed in 1840 by Russell Warren. Nor is the popularity of the style for prisons and courthouses easily explained.[2] The first two Egyptian prisons, both designed in 1832, were the Moyamensing Debtors' Prison, in Philadelphia, by Walter, and the New Jersey State Penitentiary, Trenton, by Haviland. In 1835 Haviland designed the New York City Halls of Justice and House of Detention, better known as The Tombs, which was unquestionably the most important work of the revival (148). Completed in 1838, the prison in The Tombs was planned on no less progressive lines than the Eastern State Penitentiary in Philadelphia to accommodate, like that earlier prison by Haviland (to be treated in our next chapter), the separate system as opposed to the "silent system," then in use in Auburn and Sing-Sing, under which prisoners worked together but were forbidden to talk or communicate with each other in any way; it was not as influential, however. In 1836 Haviland designed an Egyptian courthouse for Essex County, New Jersey, at Newark. His last Egyptian design, made in 1838, was a building for the Pennsylvania Fire Insurance Company in Philadelphia; it was John Rague, architect of the Illinois and Iowa capitols, who ten years later designed, in the City Jail of Dubuque, Iowa, the last building of any importance in which Egyptian forms were employed to go up before the Civil War.

The Egyptian Revival was never more than a part of, or an episode in, the Greek Revival. The frequency with which Egyptian and Greek forms were combined, if nothing else, shows that architects regarded Egyptian as a kind of proto-Greek rather than as an alternative style. The alternatives to Greek were supplied by later periods of history.

*Situational Esthetics*

However sonorously Robert Adam might declare that "the buildings of the Ancients are in Architecture what the works of nature are with respect to the other arts . . . the models which we should imitate and the standards by which we ought to judge," his insistence on the architect's right to break "the rules," together with his emphasis on the "novelty and variety" (both *relative* qualities) of his own designs, opened the door to a kind of situational esthetics that could be used to justify the imitation of other buildings of the past than those of the Ancients. The recognition of an alternative kind of beauty to the classical in the Picturesque supplied further justification, while the growing historical consciousness and the associationist theory of Archibald Alison revolutionized the way in which people looked at architecture—including classical architecture, so that while to the eighteenth-century man of taste the Greek Doric column was ugly because it was "ill proportioned," to his nineteenth-century counterpart it was beautiful because it was Greek.

*The Gothic Revival and the Picturesque*

In England Gothic architecture had been esteemed for its associations long before Alison published his *Essays on the Nature and Principles of Taste* in 1790, and it was imitated for the sake of them, and for the relief from Palladianism it afforded, in the first phase of the Gothic Revival, the Gothic Rococo, of which Horace Walpole's Strawberry Hill, built piecemeal between 1749 and 1776, is the most famous product. Walpole called Gothic "picturesque" in 1760, but the second phase of the revival, Picturesque Gothic, was not initiated until Payne Knight, the leading theorist of the Picturesque movement—or *point of view*, as it is termed in the subtitle of Christopher Hussey's classic study of the subject—designed Downton Castle for himself in 1774 as the first house in Europe to be built in one campaign to an asymmetrical plan to harmonize with its landscape setting, in obedience to his rule that "houses should be irregular where all the accompaniments are irregular." Knight was followed, at a distance, by James Wyatt, who in Lee Priory (designed in 1782) and in the prodigious Fonthill Abbey (designed in 1795) employed an ecclesiastical vocabulary of forms in place of the military one employed at Downton—and preferred by the greatest of all the masters of the Picturesque, John Nash. The last masterpiece of Picturesque Gothic in England, the Houses of Parliament, was designed by Charles Barry in 1835; soon after that, owing in large part to the writings of Barry's collaborator Pugin, the Gothic Revival entered another phase.

The Picturesque was slow to cross the Atlantic. Although Haviland discussed its principles in *The Builder's Assistant*, published in 1818, neither he nor anyone else applied them in America until the thirties. The first buildings of the Gothic Revival in America (as in England) were classical in general conception and Gothic, or "Gothick," only in detail. The first of all—assuming that its predecessor of 1698 represented the survival rather than a revival of Gothic—was the second Trinity Church, New York, built in 1788–89. It was followed ten years later by Sedgeley, near Philadelphia, by Latrobe. The first Gothic Revival house in America, this was altogether classical in its symmetry and massing, with four corner pavilions linked by verandas; the architect himself was not pleased with it and such records as there are suggest that it was a rather peculiar affair. The last adjective might well occur to anyone confronted for the first time with another early Gothic Revival building already mentioned in these pages as Godefroy's first work of architecture: St. Mary's Chapel, Baltimore, designed in 1806 (149). Here again the proportions are classical—if any single medieval building influenced Godefroy, it was Nôtre-Dame de Paris, the most classical of the great Gothic cathedrals—while the second story of the facade is merely a screen wall, as in a Roman Baroque church, though stabilized by flying buttresses. Yet the way Godefroy has used arches of identical form in four different sizes shows that he had grasped an important principle of Gothic architecture antithetic to the rules of classicism, and the more one studies St. Mary's Chapel the clearer it becomes that its design merits an adjective which can be applied to few indeed of the buildings of the early Gothic Revival, in America or England— thoughtful.

Had Latrobe's Gothic design for Baltimore Cathedral been executed it would certainly have been the finest Gothic church of the first quarter of the century in America, if no more "correct" than most of the rest; forced by the lack of books to design "from memory" Latrobe used his sensibility to greater effect in it than in any of his later Gothic designs. These were three in number: the Bank of Philadelphia (1807), Christ Church, Washington (1808), and St. Paul's, Alexandria (1816). The bank was a brick box with a pointed arch over the entrance and other token Gothic detail outside and a fan vault, of plaster, over the banking hall inside; the Washington church has the distinction of containing the earliest iron columns in American architecture, supporting the roof; the one in Alexandria, which was botched by the builder, cannot be said to be distinguished for anything in particular. More attractive than any of these was the Federal Street Church in Boston, designed in 1809 by Bulfinch—his one Gothic building and the first Gothic Revival church in New England. Its steeple, with pinnacles on the four corners of the tower

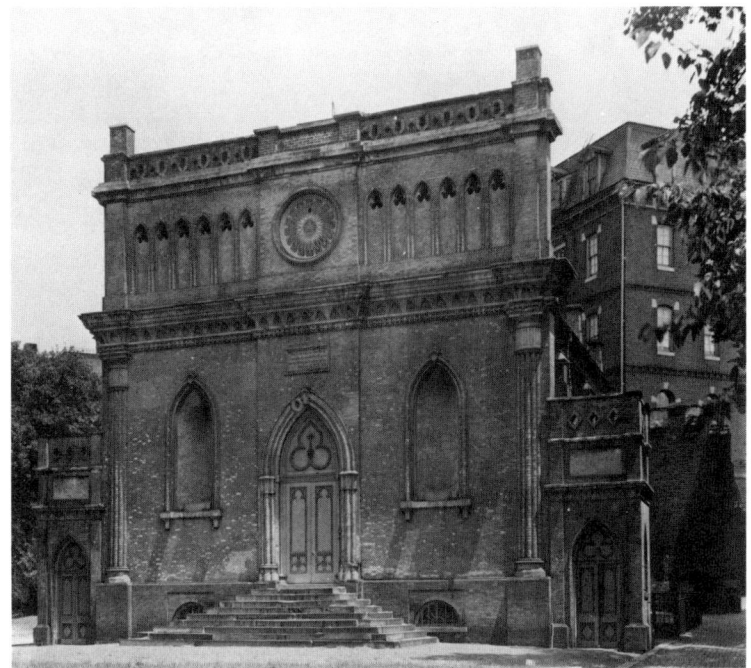

and a needle spire growing out of two octagonal stages with gablets and pointed arches, was a translation into Gothick (rather than a retranslation into Gothic) of the Wren-type steeple, such as that of Old North; the galleried interior, with slender clustered columns between the nave and aisles and ogee arches framing the tables of the Commandments behind the pulpit, was of a purely eighteenth-century character.

The year 1809 saw both of the architects of New York City Hall designing Gothic churches in that city—Mangin St. Patrick's, Mott Street, and McComb the Presbyterian Church on Wall Street. Both buildings have gone, as has also Town's Trinity Church, New Haven (1814), but the second Gothic Revival church in New England, dating from 1810, survives. St. John's Cathedral, Providence, was designed by John Holden Greene, who combined pointed windows with, in the porch and front, a "Gothic order" of the kind that had been offered first in the mid-eighteenth-century books of Batty Langley and later by William Pain. It all seems very anachronistic until one remembers how few books on Gothic architecture were then available, and that the first serious study of Gothic detail, Thomas Rickman's *Attempt to Discriminate the Styles of English Architecture*, did not appear until 1817.

Gothic was rarely employed for secular purposes before 1830. The design for Columbia College, New York, made in 1814 by James

BIRDS EYE VIEW OF THE NEW STATE PENITENTIARY, NOW ERECTING NEAR PHILADELPHIA

150
*Eastern State Peniten-*
*tiary, Philadelphia, Penn-*
*sylvania. John Haviland,*
*1823–29. From an en-*
*graving by C. G. Childs.*

Renwick, Sr., may be mentioned, though nothing came of it, as the first Gothic collegiate design; the first Gothic Revival building for higher education was Kenyon College at Gambier, Ohio, begun in 1827, and the first of architectural distinction New York University, built in 1833–35 by Town and Davis. In the 1820s enthusiasm for the Grecian led to a decline in the number of Gothic church designs, though in 1822 Strickland himself returned to Gothic—it will be recalled that his first design, the Philadelphia Masonic Hall, was Gothic—for St. Stephen's, Philadelphia, a plain structure to which he gave presence with a high screen-wall facade flanked by octagonal towers. In 1827–30 the Georgia Capitol at Milledgeville (built 1805–07) was gothicized. But the most important Gothic building of the twenties—and arguably the most important American building of that decade—was the Eastern State Penitentiary in Philadelphia, built in 1823–29 to John Haviland's design (150). A stone wall with a tower at each corner enclosed a square of 650 feet, which was entered through the crenellated governor's house, complete with portcullis, in the middle of one side. Seven cellblocks for separate confinement, each cell with a tiny exercise yard attached, radiated from a round center building. "The first American building to have real influence abroad," as Hitchcock has pointed out, the Eastern State Penitentiary established the superiority of the radial prison over the panopticon—of which the Western State Penitentiary at Pittsburgh, designed by Strickland in 1820, was a contemporary example—in the eyes of penologists both in America and in Europe.

In 1832 Alexander Jackson Davis designed a large Gothic country house near Baltimore for a client, Robert Gilmor, who had recently visited Sir Walter Scott, whose books did so much to promote Romantic medievalism in America. The plan of Glen Ellen was essentially classical, with two axes crossing in a rotunda and only slight adjustments in the interests of "irregularity." The octagonal tower at one corner which gave its outline an overall asymmetry was hardly massive enough to prevail over the individual symmetries of the elevations, and there was still much of the Gothic Rococo in the small-scale intricacy of the detail. For all that, Glen Ellen must be accounted the first major work of Picturesque Gothic in America. Davis went on to design many more Gothic houses, large and small, in which he developed a complete mastery of the compositional principles of the Picturesque. The finest is Lyndhurst, at Tarrytown, New York, which he designed for General William Paulding and his son in 1838, when it was called Knoll, and greatly enlarged for another owner, George Merritt, in 1865–67 (151, 152). In both the plan and the elevations the symmetry of the parts is absorbed by the irregularity of the whole, while the detail is distinguished from that of Glen Ellen by its authenticity as well as its greater solidity, having been taken from Pugin's *Examples of Gothic Architecture*. Of Davis's smaller houses the Delamater Cottage at Rhinebeck, New York (1844), and the Rotch House at New Bedford, Massachusetts (1848), may be named. Both are symmetrical and have high central gables, ornamental bargeboards ("gingerbread"), spacious verandas, and Gothic detail of the least learned sort. Davis supplied his friend Andrew Jackson Downing—horticulturalist, landscape gardener, architectural theorist, and popularizer of the Picturesque—with designs for his immensely successful and influential books; one for a house of this type in *Cottage Residences*, where it is described as "A Cottage in the English or Rural Gothic Style," may well be the most frequently adopted house design ever published.

Many other architects designed Gothic houses in the twenty-five years before the Civil War; Richard Upjohn, John McMurtry, and James Renwick, Jr., are among the better known names. Upjohn at least showed himself the equal of Davis in the genre when in 1839 he designed Kingscote, at Newport, Rhode Island, the first of the summer houses or "cottages" that were to give that resort of the very rich its unique character (153, 154, 155). But Davis was the dominant figure and the greatest influence in the Picturesque Gothic episode. Most of its unattributed products could be labelled "school of Davis," and it comes as no surprise to learn that the architect in 1847–50 of the Gothic capitol at Baton Rouge, Louisiana, James Harrison Dakin, was trained in the Town and Davis office.

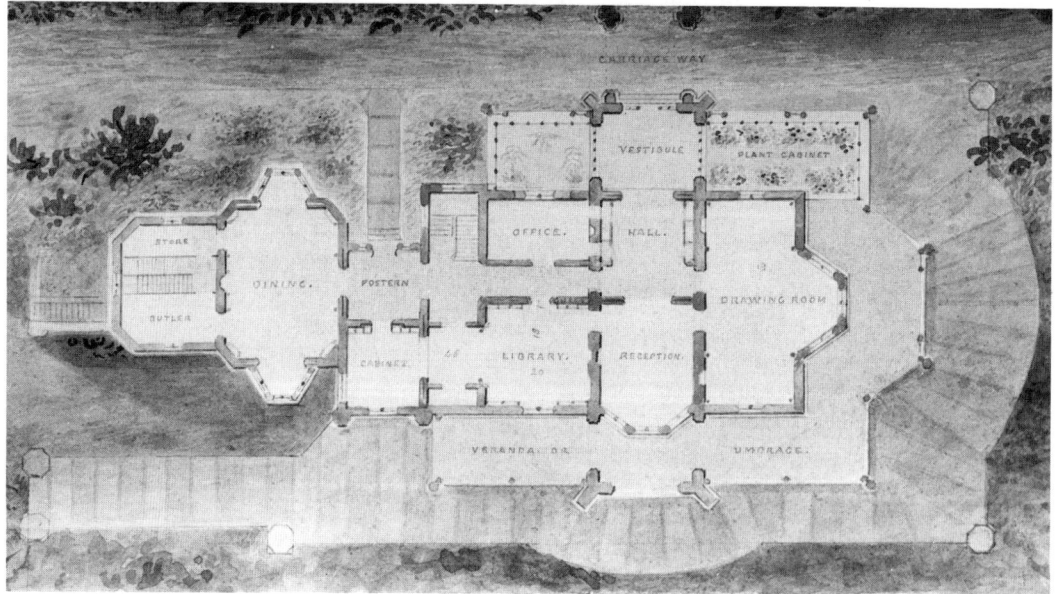

151
Lyndhurst, Tarrytown,
New York. Alexander
Jackson Davis, 1838 and
1865–67. East front.

152
Lyndhurst, Tarrytown,
New York. Plan of first
floor. Everything to the
left (north) of the stair,
together with the porte-
cochère on the east front,
was built in 1865–67.

153
Kingscote, Newport,
Rhode Island. Richard
Upjohn, 1839–41. En-
trance front from
southwest. (Addition to
left by Stanford White,
1880–81.)

154
Kingscote, Newport,
Rhode Island. Original
plan of first floor.

155
Kingscote, Newport,
Rhode Island. Hall.

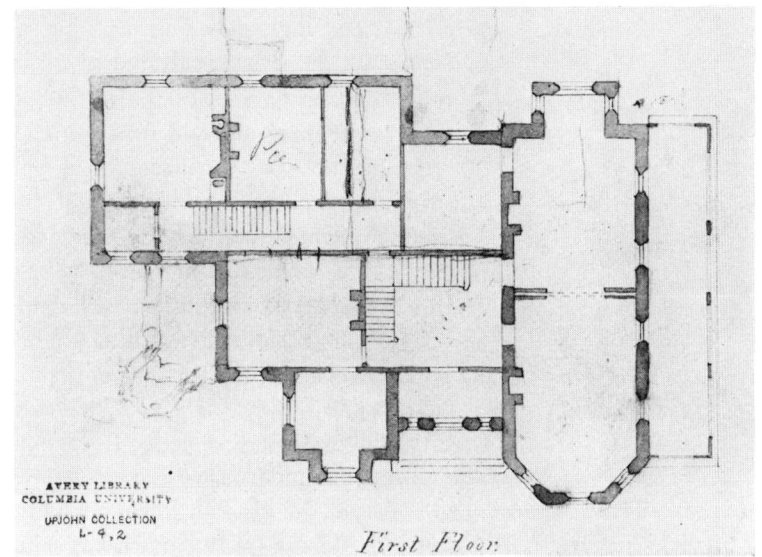

First Floor.

*The Italian Villa Style*    In 1837 the Scottish-born architect John Notman designed a house at Burlington, New Jersey, for the Rt. Rev. George Washington Doane, Bishop of New Jersey, of a type that was new to America, although it had been well established in England for a couple of decades. The Italian villa, as it was called, was the result of the discovery, around 1800, of the Picturesque qualities of the "vernacular" or anonymous architecture of the Italian countryside; John Nash was the architect of the first English example in 1802. Downing, who published Bishop Doane's house in his book on landscape gardening in 1841 and designs for Italian villas in both of his later books, thought that "as a rural style" the Italian was "inferior to pointed and high-roofed modes" but nevertheless "remarkable for expressing the elegant culture and variety of accomplishment of the retired citizen or man of the world"; the English architect Francis Goodwin pointed out that it permitted "many freedoms which in a more finished and consistent style would not unjustly incur censure"; the American architect Samuel Sloan wrote that "the irregular outline" demanded by the Picturesque was "formed without difficulty," the "predominant figure" being the rectangle, of which many were "introduced and so disposed as to break in upon each other." It is not surprising that with all these advantages the Italian Villa Style soon became the rival in domestic design of the so much trickier Gothic, and was even on occasion—as when Upjohn designed Utica City Hall in 1852—employed for public buildings.

Notman, Upjohn, Davis, and Austin were the leading practitioners of the style. For another Italian villa by Notman, Prospect at Princeton, New Jersey (1849), much larger than Bishop Doane's, may be named. Upjohn's first, and perhaps finest, was the Edward King House at Newport, Rhode Island, built in 1845–47, in the plan of which irregularity is achieved without sacrifice of axial discipline (156, 157). Homewood Villa, Baltimore (1851), is a mirror-image copy of the King House. In the E. B. Litchfield House at Brooklyn (1855) Upjohn moved the tower from its customary corner position to the center of the entrance front over a vestibule to the hall, which ran back the whole depth of the house with stairs at the far end, supported the arches of the loggia with columns instead of piers, and gave the second story an emphatically Renaissance character, with classical architraves framing the windows and triangular pediments surmounting several of them. Davis's chief works in the style came in the fifties, although he had exhibited an Italian villa design in 1835. His Haskell House at Belleville (1851), Munn House at Utica (1854), and E. C. Litchfield House at Brooklyn (1854) shared the motif of a three-story octagonal tower with a more slender square

*156*
*Edward King House,*
*Newport, Rhode Island.*
*Richard Upjohn, 1845–47.*
*Entrance front.*

*157*
*Edward King House,*
*Newport, Rhode Island.*
*Plan of first floor.*

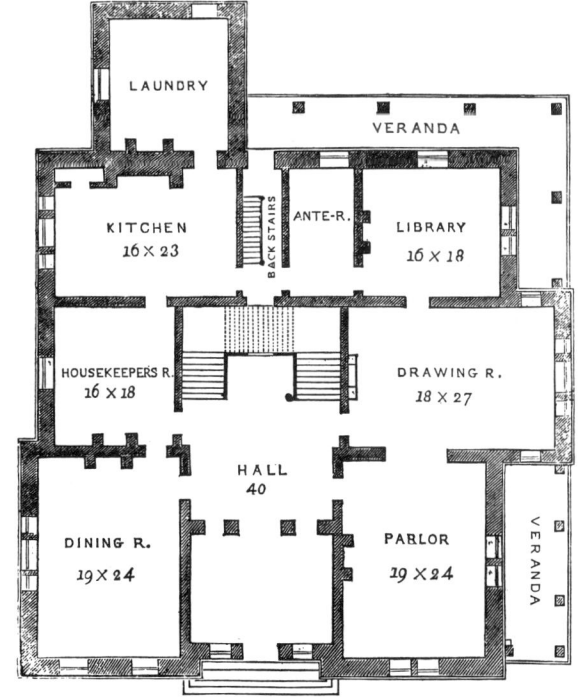

158
Morse-Libby House, Portland, Maine. Attributed to Henry Austin, 1859–63. Street front.

tower of four stories attached; in most Italian villas the only polygonal elements were bay windows, though Henry A. Sykes combined two octagons with singularly happy effect in the observatory and "cabinet" (natural history museum) of Amherst College (1847–48). Henry Austin's Norton House at New Haven, designed in 1849, shows the style at its plainest; the walls are smooth planes, the windows are simple apertures, and there are no quoins to soften the geometry of the component parts. When he came to design the Morse-Libby House at Portland ten years later Austin showed that his taste had changed with the times (158).[1] Richness, not simplicity, was now the ideal, and height and verticality were sought in contrast to the opposite qualities of the Greek Revival buildings that had dominated the scene for so long. Hence the rusticated quoins of the Morse-Libby House, the Baroque plasticity of its window pediments and the ornamental brackets supporting them, the great projection of its eaves, and its tall proportions. In all but its lack of certain forms and mannerisms with which postwar architects were to show their devotion to "reality," it is a High Victorian design.

While Bishop Doane's villa at Burlington was going up, the first church of the architect he was nine years later to commission to design his church there was rising 500 miles to the north. The church was St. John's, Bangor, Maine; the architect was an English cabinetmaker and joiner who had landed in New York at the age of twenty-seven in 1829, Richard Upjohn, whom we now meet in his most important historical role,[2] as initiator in America of that development in ecclesiastical architecture which, because of the emphasis placed by its theorists on the moral qualities they perceived in Gothic, may be called Ethical Gothic—or alternatively, from the name given to their studies by a group of Cambridge undergraduates whom a common interest in medieval churches brought together in 1836, Ecclesiological Gothic. Not that St. John's, Bangor, would have satisfied the ecclesiologists; for although its detail was much more convincing, archaeologically, than that of any previous Gothic Revival church in America, its nave was lined with galleries (which they hated), it had no chancel (a feature they insisted on), and—worst of all—the whole thing was of wood. But a lithographed view of it, according to a credible story, was the cause of Upjohn being asked, in 1839, to superintend repairs to Trinity Church, New York, and subsequently to design a new church, the third on the site, which stands to this day (159).

As finished in 1846 Upjohn's Trinity was externally a smaller and somewhat simplified version of an ideal church of which Pugin, the most aggressive theorist of Ethical Gothic, had published a perspective in his *True Principles of Pointed or Christian Architecture* in 1841. Inside, there were no galleries, and there was a raised chancel of two full bays—a feature which, as Upjohn's biographer puts it, "to many smacked of popery," and which the architect, as a devout Episcopalian imbued with ecclesiological ideas, had to fight hard for. Neither Pugin nor the ecclesiologists of the Cambridge Camden Society could have approved of the plaster vaults, but they were ordered by the building committee in place of the timber roofs intended by Upjohn; as for the style of the whole, although by the time the building was completed Perpendicular had been rejected by Pugin and the ecclesiologists in favor of Decorated or "Middle Pointed," it had been acceptable when Upjohn made the design. All in all, with its noble proportions and consistent detail Trinity was a fine exemplar for the new movement.

New York was not without churches in the ecclesiologists' favorite style for long. In 1843 James Renwick, Jr., then only twenty-five, designed Grace Church in Decorated, and in 1844 Upjohn followed suit with the Church of the Holy Communion. In other respects the

159
*Trinity Church, New York City. Richard Upjohn, 1839–46. View from southeast.*

two buildings had little in common, for the Church of the Holy Communion was as simple as Grace Church is highly wrought. Both had transepts, but while the steeple of Grace Church stands axially at the end of the nave, like that of Trinity, the tower of the Church of the Holy Communion stood beside it. The latter arrangement, repeated more often than not in Upjohn's later churches, is certainly the more picturesque—but only incidentally, for ecclesiological theory was functional, stressing liturgical requirements and symbolism, rather than esthetic, while Pugin had stated in *True Principles* that it was a great defect when a building was *"designed to be picturesque"*—the italics are his—and, again in italics, that *"the picturesque effect of the ancient buildings results from the ingenious methods by which the old builders overcame local and constructive difficulties."*

Two of the largest and most elaborate of the Gothic churches of the forties were Holy Trinity, Brooklyn Heights, by Minard Lafever, and Calvary Church, New York, by Renwick. Both were built in 1844–47. As first designed Holy Trinity was Perpendicular, but Lafever went over to Decorated in the course of the work. For Calvary Renwick employed Early English or "First Pointed," as did Upjohn in the much smaller church which he designed for Bishop Doane in 1846. The latter, St. Mary's, Burlington, is of great importance in the history of the Gothic Revival in America, for here for the first time an architect developed his design from measured drawings of a medieval church (160). St. John's, Shottesbrook, in Berkshire, was the model; Upjohn introduced certain simplifications—the use of Early English was one, for Shottesbrook is Decorated—and gave St. Mary's what one comes to recognize as the stamp of his personal style. In the same year, 1846, in Philadelphia, work began on a church that followed a medieval model much more closely, with the aid of drawings provided by the Cambridge Camden Society, which had long been anxious to promote its doctrines in America (which its journal, *The Ecclesiologist*, was apt to refer to as "the colonies"). This was the church of St. James the Less (161); the model was St. Michael's, Longstanton, Cambridgeshire, built circa 1230. Although some slight alterations were made in England by the architect G. G. Place and the contractor added a vestry and an extra bay to the nave, St. James the Less was a copy of St. Michael's rather than an adaptation or an imitation in the old sense— and in ecclesiological eyes all the better for that. During its construction and furnishing the donor, Robert Ralston, corresponded with Benjamin Webb, one of the two founders of the Cambridge Camden Society. No expense was spared and in the end it cost just five times

160
St. Mary's, Burlington,
New Jersey. Richard Up-
john, 1846–48. View from
east.

161
*St. James the Less, Phila-
delphia, Pennsylvania.
G. G. Place, 1846–50. In-
terior, looking east.*

the amount of the original estimate. Its influence was considerable, one of those who felt it being Upjohn, as appears most obviously in his Calvary Church at Stonington, Connecticut (1847–49).

In 1847 the Cambridge Camden Society sent to Philadelphia drawings of All Saints, Brighton, the latest work of R. C. Carpenter, its favorite architect at the time, in response to a request by Ralston for a pattern to guide John Notman, who had been commissioned to design a large church by the vestry of St. Mark's parish. The triple roof of Carpenter's church with its deep valleys would not have survived many American winter snows; so Notman adopted St. Stephen's, Westminster, by Benjamin Ferrey, which had also been begun that year and was known to him from an illustration in the *Illustrated London News*, as his model instead. St. Mark's is a fine building, and it led to Notman being much sought after as an architect of churches; one of his most successful, Emmanuel Church at Cumberland, Maryland, built in 1850–51, was modelled, with the aid of an illustration in *The Ecclesiologist*, on another Brighton church by Carpenter, St. Paul's (162).

There was never a more English architecture in America than the Gothic Revival of the 1840s and 1850s; even the German hall church which Robert Cary Long, Jr., designed in 1841 for the German Redemptorist Fathers in Baltimore, St. Alphonsus, is clothed in English detail—as is the interior of St. Patrick's Cathedral, New York (1857–79), Renwick's version (Anglicized also in plan and proportions) of Cologne. Yet it produced one group of buildings for which there is no English analogue. In the fifties Upjohn designed a number of town churches, of which St. Paul's, Buffalo (1850–51), was the biggest (and in the architect's opinion the best), and a larger number of country churches. Many of the latter are of wood, and the frankness with which the fact is acknowledged and the boldness with which Gothic forms are modified to suit the material show that there had been a revolution in architectural thought since Ware declared that it was the honour of the architect that the form should triumph over the material (163). Pugin, more than any other one writer, had brought this revolution about. In America the new principles were championed by Downing in *The Architecture of Country Houses*, first published in 1850. "To build a house of wood so exactly in imitation of stone as to lead the spectator to suppose it stone, is a paltry artifice, at variance with all truthfulness," wrote Downing, and: "We greatly prefer the vertical to the horizontal boarding. The main timbers which enter into the frame of a wooden house and support the structure, are vertical, and hence the vertical boarding properly signifies to the eye a wooden house." Upjohn used vertical

162
*Emmanuel Church, Cumberland, Maryland. John Notman, 1850–51. View from east.*

163
*St. John Chrysostom's, Delafield, Wisconsin. Richard Upjohn, 1851–53. Church and bell tower from west.*

164
The Chalet, Newport,
Rhode Island. Leopold
Eidlitz, 1854. General
view.

boarding in his wooden churches, as Davis had a little earlier in his wooden cottages. Here we have the beginning of that American structuralism in wood which in the fifties was further developed in such buildings as that striking example of what Downing considered "the most picturesque of all dwellings built of wood," The Chalet at Newport (1854) by Leopold Eidlitz, which in the sixties and seventies occupied a central place in the architectural scene, and which in more recent decades has shown itself to have an enduring vitality (164).[3]

## Romanesque Revival

In the later 1840s, while the Gothic Revival was coming under the influence of the English ecclesiological movement, an alternative medieval style was gaining ground; in the 1850s it overtook Gothic, and most of the churches of that decade, as well as many public buildings, are round-arched. This revival of the Romanesque was different from any comparable phenomenon we have encountered in that it was not of English origin or inspiration. In England Neo-Romanesque buildings were hardly numerous enough to warrant one's speaking of a Romanesque Revival, and none of them has been shown to have been imitated on this side of the Atlantic; what was English in the products of the American Romanesque Revival—and much was—came out of archaeological publications. In Germany, however, there had been a flourishing Romanesque Revival since

about 1830, and even if this did not give the initial impetus to the
American one it certainly influenced it. Not only is there evidence
of a familiarity with the round-arched works of von Gärtner and
Schinkel in designs by the Prague-born (but Upjohn-trained) Leopold
Eidlitz but the Rhode Islander Thomas Tefft must have been referring
to something that many people knew of when in 1851 he wrote:
"The round arch school of Germany is employing much invention
and originality in their designs and we hazard but little in predicting
a favorable result." For most Americans at the time the Germans
were the cultural leaders of Europe.

Romanesque, as the mid-nineteenth century saw it, had qualities
of just the kind to recommend its use in America. An itemization of
those of one regional style by the English architect John Shaw could
be applied to Romanesque as a whole: "Lombard Architecture,"
Shaw wrote, "contains in an eminent degree the qualities now so
important. These appear to be first, economy; secondly, rapidity of
execution; thirdly, strict simplicity combined with high capability of
ornament; fourthly, durability; fifthly, beauty." One might change
the order—since he was writing to a bishop about the provision of
churches in the East End of London, Shaw naturally put economy
first—but one could but agree that Romanesque did indeed possess
those advantages. Its simplicity was particularly welcome in a country where the level of skill in stone-cutting required that direct
imitations like Notman's Gothic churches in Philadelphia and at
Cumberland be considerably simpler in detail than their English
models. Robert Dale Owen, in his *Hints on Public Architecture*
(1849), emphasized that Romanesque, or "Norman," had "fewer
members and less complication of details" than Gothic, while the
author of *Plans for Churches*, published by the Congregational
Church in 1853, went a step further in recommending what he called
"the modernized Romanesque," which was "based upon the sup-
position that the Romanesque . . . progressed as such instead of
turning into Gothic" and was "remarkable for the simplicity of its
moulding." And then, besides possessing these practical advantages,
Romanesque could be shown to be preferable to Gothic on religious
and political grounds. Thanks to a typical sophistry of the associative
sense, Protestants regarded it as free from the taint of popery—which
Gothic, in the eyes of many, never could be. As for the politics of
the style, Owen was cautious but definite: "Its entire expression is
less ostentatious, and if political character may be ascribed to Architecture, more republican."

The first building of the Romanesque Revival was the Church of
the Pilgrims, Brooklyn, which went up in 1844–46; the architect

was Upjohn. It was a plain structure, with arcaded corbel tables under the eaves as the only enrichment; the gabled facade was flanked on the left by a low tower with a concave pyramidal roof and on the right by a high one with an upper stage terminating in four gables (in the manner of the towers of the German abbey church of Corvey, for example), from which rose a spire with a curious wavy outline. It cannot have been an altogether successful design—the first historian of the revival characterized Upjohn's approach here as tentative—but it might be called a prophetic one because arcaded corbel tables, pairs of unmatched towers, and spires were to adorn scores or even hundreds of later churches. The arcaded corbel table was of course incontrovertibly Romanesque, having been employed by several regional schools in the eleventh and twelfth centuries; American architects evidently regarded it as the hallmark of the style and it would be hard to find a Romanesque design of any pretensions without it. On the other hand there was little medieval precedent for unmatched towers flanking a facade (165); whether they were a concession to economy justified by the Picturesque esthetic or a concession to the Picturesque with welcome economic consequences is a question which doubtless should in some cases be answered one way and in others the other. As for spires, they were not really Romanesque at all. But besides being time-honored components of churches and universally understood symbols they appealed to the competitive spirit—a congregation would pride itself on having the highest spire in its city or neighborhood, and many of them rose to more than 200 feet—and those who thought like the author of the Congregational Church's manual could have argued that if the Romanesque had not turned into Gothic it would have produced spires in due course.

In 1845 work began on Upjohn's second Romanesque building, the chapel of Bowdoin College at Brunswick, Maine. It is of an emphatically German character, with two matching spire-crowned towers; what appear to be aisles held classrooms, while the nave, the chapel proper, was arranged like an English college chapel with banked-up rows of seats on either side facing each other across the central space. (Romanesque Revival churches as a class had spacious but characterless preaching-hall interiors, often galleried.) Before the decade was over three more architects we have met in other connections designed Romanesque churches: James Renwick, the Church of the Puritans, New York (1846); Leopold Eidlitz, with assistance from a young Bavarian architect, Otto Blesch, St. George's on Stuyvesant Square, New York (1846); and Henry Austin the Congregational Church at Kent, Connecticut (1848). The Eidlitz and Blesch

*165*
*Old Stone Church, Cleve-*
*land, Ohio. Charles*
*Heard, circa 1855. West*
*front.*

166
*Smithsonian Institution, Washington, District of Columbia. James Renwick, Jr., 1848–49. View from west.*

building, whose two towers were surmounted by openwork spires, was purely German; the other two were at least as German as they were anything else. The stylistic terminology of the time was far from exact; any Romanesque building was liable to be called Lombard, while any that did not have the characteristics of the regional style of Lombardy was liable to be called Norman. Churches that we would call Lombard today began to appear in the fifties; the finest remaining one, which would be even finer had its campanile been built, is St. Paul's, Baltimore (1852–56), by Upjohn. As for a church that we would call Norman today, the finest is perhaps Holy Trinity, Rittenhouse Square, Philadelphia, designed by Notman in 1857, spireless—a spire was planned—though it is.

Downing included a "villa in the Norman style"—"this is not a house to please a practical, common-sense man"—in *The Architecture of Country Houses* in 1850, and in 1851 Sloan built one, Bartram Hall, near Philadelphia; but Romanesque had a rather less than moderate success as a domestic style. A select list of secular buildings of the Romanesque Revival would include Tefft's Union Station at Providence (begun in 1848), Eidlitz's City Hall at Springfield (1854–55), and St. Luke's Hospital, New York (1856) by John W. Ritch; it would be headed by the Smithsonian Institution in Washington, designed by Renwick in 1846 and built in 1848–49, to which pride of place is due as not only the first public building of the revival but also its one masterpiece (166). Admittedly, the detail of the Smithsonian is mechanical and repetitive, and for all that it is built of solid brownstone the building has a seeming fragility that reminds one of the early Gothic Revival. (Hitchcock has likened it to "an enormous garden fabrick.") Yet seen from the right distance across the leaf-strewn sward of the Mall on a mellow autumn day it could make the most hardened classicist a temporary convert to the Picturesque.

*Renaissance Revival*

Although as time went on more and more architects abandoned Greek for one or another of the styles discussed so far in this chapter for individual commissions, none of them was a real threat to the Greek Revival; only an alternative classical style, which with a Roman revival out of the question had to be (in the terminology of the time) "modern," could be that. Downing was one of the first to attack the Greek Revival, in 1842, on the grounds that "the taste for Grecian temples" tended "to destroy expression of purpose" and also for the Picturesque reason that its buildings were generally white and "no painter of landscapes, that has possessed a name, was ever guilty of displaying in his pictures a glaring white house." Then in 1844 the young Boston architect Arthur Gilman, writing anonymously in the *North American Review,* described Greek buildings as the "offspring of a remote age, an antagonistic religion, an obsolete form of government, and a widely different state of society than our own" and proposed the adoption of "the style of Bramante, of Palladio, and Michael Angelo," or the *"palazzo* style." In the next year, 1845, the first two buildings of the Renaissance Revival were begun, soon to be joined by so many more than in 1854 a writer in *Putnam's Monthly* could state: "The Grecian taste . . . has within the last few years been succeeded and almost entirely superseded, both here and in England, by the revival of the Italian style."

The Renaissance Revival was no less an English import than Palladianism had been, with the illustrated magazines now providing the chief means of transatlantic conveyance. In England Charles Barry had been the first to use the cinquecento *palazzo* formula in the Travellers' Club, built in 1829–32, which he followed up with the larger, Farnese-inspired Reform Club of 1836–40. It is therefore no surprise that one of the first two buildings of the revival in America should have been a clubhouse, the Athenaeum of Philadelphia, designed by Notman (167). To say that Notman's clubhouse will stand comparison with Barry's is to say much, but by no means too much. The heightening of the second floor or *piano nobile* (as in Peruzzi's Palazzo Massimi, one of seven Italian *palazzi* named by Gilman for "a true greatness of manner") is a telling difference, justified functionally by the placing of the library on that floor. It is easy to sense what welcome relief (in two senses) the balcony and crowning *cornicione* provided after all the flat fronts of the Adam Style and the Greek Revival.

167
*Athenaeum of Philadel-
phia, Philadelphia, Penn-
sylvania. John Notman,
1845–47. Washington
Square front.*

There is still some question about the identity of the architect of the other American *palazzo* begun in 1845; there is none at all about the impression it made. This was Stewart's Downtown Store in New York, of a more generalized Renaissance Style than the Athenaeum but much bigger and faced with gleaming Westchester marble. There were plenty of English precedents for the application of the *palazzo* formula to commercial buildings; the first had appeared in the late thirties. But Stewart's was the first commercial building to demonstrate a great practical advantage of the mode: extensibility. Greek buildings were finite forms; they could not be enlarged. *Palazzi* could be and in 1850 Stewart's was, thus starting a tradition that may be followed down to Sullivan's Carson Pirie Scott & Company store.

More than a fair share of the buildings Putnam's writer might have pointed to in 1854 were designed by Thomas Thomas, an English architect who had established his practice in New York in the thirties. He and his son, Griffith, were the most successful commercial specialists of the fifties and sixties; their works already included the large and plain Moffat Building (1847–48), the large and ornamental Lord & Taylor Store (1852–53), and the smaller Chemical Bank (1850–51) and Broadway Bank (1852–53), both of which were interesting for their architects' attempt to give vertical emphasis to narrow fronts. All these were more or less Roman or Florentine in style; the richer Venetian or Sansovinesque Style (first used in England in 1847 by Sydney Smirke in the Carlton Club) made its American *début* in Baltimore, in the Sun Building (1851). Designed by the architect R. G. Hatfield in collaboration with James Bogardus, a former engraver who in 1848 had built a factory in New York for the production of iron building components, this had two fronts entirely of iron, cast in sections and bolted together.[4] In 1854 Bogardus produced a second edition of the Sun Building for Harper Brothers in New York. In these two buildings iron was used not only for the ease with which elaborate ornament could be mass-produced (as it had been for decades) and for the very open facades that it permitted but also for its structural advantages. For behind their cast-iron fronts were complete iron frames—the columns of cast, the beams of wrought iron—that were capable of supporting themselves and the floors without the aid of the brick walls at the sides or back. They are thus early examples—very early for America—of the internal skeleton or "cage" structure. In 1855 Bogardus put up the first metal-frame structure in which the brickwork was no more than an infilling—a shot tower for the McCullough Shot & Lead Company in New York—and thus anticipated the first use of this type of construction in Chicago by nearly thirty years. It was a building

168
Haughwout Store, New
York City. J. P. Gaynor,
1857. Broadway facade.

manufactured by Bogardus's chief rival in the iron building industry, Daniel Badger, the Sansovinesque Haughwout Store in New York, that had the distinction of being the first commercial building equipped with that other essential of the modern skyscraper, the passenger elevator (168).

The impact of the Renaissance Revival on the design of public buildings was not long delayed. During Ammi B. Young's tenure of the federal post of Supervising Architect of the Office of Construction (1852–62) most new post offices and customs houses were of Renaissance character; the post office at Windsor, Vermont, and the customs house (now post office) at Georgetown, District of Columbia, are among the surviving examples (169). In the domestic field, the astylar *palazzo* mode was obviously suitable for large town houses; the first in which it was adopted seems to have been the Herman Thorne House on West Sixteenth Street, New York, built in 1846–48, which was much praised in the press at the time though no one thought fit to mention the name of its architect. In 1859 *The Builder*, the leading English architectural magazine, told its readers: "In the city of New York, avenues are springing up lined not with houses, but with palaces. . . . Neither London nor Paris, with all the accumulations of wealth of a thousand years, can show such a street as Fifth Avenue." Most of the palaces were *palazzi*.

Although the first buildings of the revival in both England and America were academic imitations of a High Renaissance type, ar-

170
*United States Capitol,*
*Washington, District of*
*Columbia. Dome. Thomas*
*Ustick Walter, 1855–65.*
*View from southeast.*

chitects were soon imitating, in the freest manner, anything dating from the early fifteenth to the late sixteenth century. Some, in their search for "modern" (as distinct from "ancient" models), moved on to the seventeenth century and even the eighteenth—as did the first American to propose a renaissance revival, Gilman, the exterior of whose Arlington Street Church in Boston (1859–61) is almost purely Gibbsian. In ecclesiastical design a one-man Wren revival was initiated by Minard Lafever as early as 1846–48 in the Church of the Holy Apostles, New York, and carried on by him in the Reformed Church on the Heights, Brooklyn (1850–51), the Reformed Protestant Dutch Church, Kingston, and the Pearl Street Congregational Church, Hartford (both 1851–52). The biggest tribute to Wren, however, was paid by Thomas Ustick Walter, when in 1855 it fell to him to design a new dome for the United States Capitol and he responded with a paraphrase in iron of the masterpiece of construction in masonry, timber, and lead that crowns the cathedral of the bishop of whose diocese a vast tract of the North American continent once formed a part (170).

# II     *1860–1976*

*Frederick Koeper*

The mid-century years saw revivalism replaced by a wholly contemporary eclecticism with the French Second Empire and the English High Victorian Gothic as the predominant styles. The interpretative license afforded by these two importations was seen in American buildings of the seventies in independent experiments, variously regarded as bold inventions or regrettable lapses in taste. Then Henry Hobson Richardson returned to historical eclecticism with his Romanesque Revival and created from this base a personal style that reintegrated architectural values and is properly regarded as proto-modern.

*The Second Empire Style*     The Second Empire Style is marked by a quality of cosmopolitan urbanity. Its first American appearance was in a New York town house on lower Fifth Avenue, the Hart M. Shiff House of 1850. The Danish-born architect, Detlef Lienau, had studied in Paris before emigrating in 1848—well before the accession of Napoleon III, whose reign (1852–70) gave the style its name. The style was popular in every Western country, England being no exception. Visitors to the Paris expositions of 1855 and 1867 saw vast building operations in that city, including major extensions to the Louvre and the impressive boulevards of Baron Haussmann, the emperor's city planner. No new avenues appeared in America, but the gridiron streets of New York accommodated Parisian-type row houses, a number of which were designed by Lienau. As an urban architectural style, Second Empire was just what America needed at a time of unprecedented urban growth. It was more appropriate for the hotels, railway stations, and government buildings that were the product of post–Civil War prosperity than any other style then current. Certainly its connotations of prestige, affluence, and authority, as well as of cosmopolitan Paris itself, together with the fact that it was notably free from the esthetic and moral entanglements that surrounded the High Victorian Gothic, appealed to practical men of commerce and government.

French buildings of the sixteenth century, half medieval, half Renaissance, such as the Louvre and the Tuileries, furnished the Second Empire Style with its two identifying features, the mansard roof and the pavilion motif. The latter is a forward break in the elevation, usually at the center and frequently at the ends as well but always symmetrically disposed, which is acknowledged by a corresponding break in the roof. These features were treated in various manners; for example, the restrained surfaces of the Shiff House contrast with the robust modelling and sculpture of the Philadelphia City Hall, which recalls Charles Garnier's Paris Opéra (1861–74), itself more Neo-Baroque than Second Empire in style.

Accomplished gothicist though he was, James Renwick yielded quickly to mid-century stylistic license, as his use of Egyptian and Romanesque motifs in the 1840s testifies. His were the first two major works in the Second Empire Style: the Corcoran (now Renwick) Gallery of Art in Washington (1859) and Vassar College in Poughkeepsie, New York (1861–65). The banker and art collector, William Corcoran, and his architect-to-be made a trip together to the Paris Exposition of 1855 and, as a belated memento four years later, the Corcoran Gallery rose in showy Parisian style. However, neither its coloration of red brick and brownstone nor its column capitals, which repeated Latrobe's invention for the United States Capitol, were French. For his new college, the brewer-philanthropist Matthew Vassar received from Renwick's hand an enormous but rather plain, four-story brick building, whose extended array of pavilion accents recalls the Tuileries Palace.

Precedent for government buildings in the French style was to be found in recent English architecture, notably the designs submitted in the 1857 competition for government offices in London that were much publicized by the English journals. The controversy between the Goths and the classicists that followed this competition, the so-called "Battle of the Styles," was settled in favor of classicism by the whim of one man, the prime minister. An American example that reflects Lord Palmerston's taste is the New York Capitol in Albany by Thomas Fuller. Described as conforming to a "Renaissance style similar to that of the Louvre in Paris," it was begun in 1867; the original scheme was later modified and completed by Leopold Eidlitz and H. H. Richardson.

The most prolific designer in the Second Empire Style—thanks to his being Supervising Architect of the Treasury from 1865 to 1875—was Alfred B. Mullett. The unmistakable prototype of many of the designs that issued from his office was Boston City Hall (1861–65) by Arthur Gilman with his partner Gridley Bryant (171). Unlike Renwick, Gilman was capable of self-criticism and never mistook fashion for architectural elegance. Boston City Hall is suave and consistent even if without the sculptural richness of the New Louvre.

The Boston City Hall motif of recurrent columns and arched windows on every floor was repeated *ad nauseam* in Mullett's courthouses and post offices, such as those in St. Louis, Philadelphia, Cincinnati, and New York. This repetitiveness, an inescapable characteristic of bureaucratic architecture, has a counterpart in the cast-iron Renaissance facades of the Haughwout Store in New York and

171
*Boston City Hall, Boston,*
*Massachusetts. Arthur*
*Gilman and Gridley*
*Bryant, 1861–65.*
*Exterior.*

172
*State, War and Navy
Building (Executive Office
Building), Washington,
District of Columbia.
Alfred B. Mullett, 1871–
87. Exterior.*

similar examples of these years. Mullett's buildings, however, were substantially built, usually of granite, with the use of iron limited to interior stairs and skylighted courts; for example, the State, War, and Navy Building in Washington, renamed the Executive Office Building (1871–87) (172). Although technically satisfactory, they are compositionally uninteresting. An exception was the New York Post Office at the tip of City Hall Park, with its crescendo of multiple breaks leading to a center pavilion capped by a bulbous dome supporting an open lantern.

The most opulent of civic monuments in the French mansard style was built not by federal or state but municipal government. Designed by John McArthur, Jr., the marble Philadelphia City Hall was begun in 1871 and completed a decade later when the style was no longer in fashion. This Brobdingnagian building illustrates the fate of Second Empire design in America: it became florid, restless, and fragmented. No longer did substantive wings link pavilion accents; the whole became a bundle of verticals. A great tower, frequent in English Gothic Revival buildings of the time but incongruous with the French sources drawn on here, rises from the hollow square of the building to mark the intersection of Market and Broad streets, the center of William Penn's 1681 city plan, and to support a statue of the seventeenth-century Quaker.

*Victorian Gothic*

The assertive, at times aggressive, character of High Victorian architecture is achieved, in part, with color. That a church striped from top to bottom in red and yellow should have inspired two young men to become architects hardly seems likely; yet such was the case. The church was All Souls' Unitarian in New York (1853–55); the architects-to-be were Russell Sturgis and Peter Bonnett Wight, both later active Ruskinians. All Souls' was designed by Jacob Wrey

Mould, an inexperienced young man recently arrived from England, where he had studied under the colorist Owen Jones.[1] The contrast between layers of yellowish Caen stone alternating with bands of dark red brick was too violent even for Leopold Eidlitz, an architect sympathetic to Mould's approach, and the public soon labelled the building the "Holy Zebra" (173). Unfortunately economy cut the height of the walls by six feet and the free-standing corner campanile was never built. Part Romanesque, part Byzantine, with its strident polychromy, a foretaste of High Victorian Gothic, and its willful dissonance, felt in the tension of horizontal banding broken by pilaster strips, Mould's church remains an avant-garde example of the mannerisms that formed the "character" of postwar buildings.

High Victorian Gothic was in large part the unintentional creation of John Ruskin, the English writer and critic, who never designed a building. The spell Ruskin cast over American architecture of the sixties and seventies is understandable when one considers the persuasiveness of his prose style and his appeal to nineteenth-century moral values. Despite his popularity in America, he refused an invitation to cross the Atlantic, saying he could not be happy in a land where there were no castles. His books, *The Seven Lamps of Architecture* of 1849 and *The Stones of Venice* of 1851–53, appeared in simultaneous, pirated American editions. These two works, his most influential on architecture, were reprinted throughout the century. Ironically the very architectural style that Ruskin's writings inspired was one he disowned as untrue to his preachings. Ruskin's own opinions were never wholly consistent, but he remained firm in his distinction between architecture and mere building, the former being adorned with "unnecessary features" of decoration. The encrustation of structure was, for Ruskin, the essential problem of architecture and the measure of its success. To his eyes the chromatic decoration of the Gothic palaces of Venice—in particular that model of all perfection, the Doge's Palace—deserved his greatest praise. That Ruskin was opposed to the adoption of Italian Gothic for northern countries did not prevent its adoption in England and, a decade later, in America.

In 1860 Ruskinian Gothic was used for the first time by Mould in his Trinity Church Parish School in New York. More noticed and praised by contemporary critics, however, was Peter B. Wight's National Academy of Design in New York (174). Wight shifted from Romanesque of his 1861–62 competition design, now lost, to Venetian Gothic in the executed building of 1863–65. The Doge's Palace was his obvious model, made more utilitarian by the inclusion of a row of street-level shops along the side. The banding of stone and

173
*All Souls' Unitarian*
*Church, New York City.*
*Jacob Wrey Mould, 1853–*
*55. Exterior.*

174
*National Academy of*
*Design, New York City.*
*Peter B. Wight, 1863–65.*
*Exterior.*

175
*Museum of Fine Arts,
Boston, Massachusetts.
John H. Sturgis and
Charles Brigham, 1870–
76. Exterior.*

176
*Nott Memorial Library
(Alumni Hall), Union
College, Schenectady,
New York. Edward T.
Potter, 1872–75. Exterior.*

brick between the pointed arches of the lower floors and the diagonal patterning of the top story were a response to Ruskin's plea for constructive truth: surface ornament integral with the building.

The proper way to achieve decorative effects in architecture became a debated issue with the growing use of cast iron and terra-cotta in the 1840s in England. Ruskin never approved of the use of cast iron, however easily and cheaply it could reproduce carved ornament; yet he approved of molded terra-cotta as a substitute for cut stone.[2] In America terra-cotta (manufactured in England) was first used in quantity in the Museum of Fine Arts in Boston (1870–76) by the local architects John H. Sturgis and Charles Brigham (175). Sturgis, who maintained an office in England and commuted across the Atlantic, emulated the terra-cotta of the Victoria and Albert (formerly South Kensington) Museum in London of 1867 as well as the design of the New Museum at Oxford by Deane and Woodward, a building in which Ruskin had a proprietary interest and which he intended to be a manifesto of the new style.

Ruskin's eloquence, high-mindedness, and equation of ethics and esthetics made Victorian Gothic a frequent choice for institutions of art and education. The classical rotunda proposed by Ramée for Union College in Schenectady, New York, at the beginning of the century became, in Edward T. Potter's hands, an Italianate baptistery, serving as the Nott Memorial Library, now Alumni Hall (1872–75). Behind its polychromed stone arcading there is a partial iron skeleton (176). In the year in which it was begun his brother, William A. Potter, designed in a less declamatory manner the Chancellor Green Library at Princeton, which was an octagon with flanking Palladian-type appendages. Much simpler than either of these was Russell Sturgis's Farnam Hall at Yale (1869), whose expanses of plain brick wall would not have interested Ruskin but would have given pleasure to the eye of William Morris.

Ruskinian Gothic found little favor among the Anglicans, although they had previously been submissive to English church fashion. In 1848 Leopold Eidlitz, schooled under the Anglican Upjohn, settled on German Romanesque for St. George's, New York, where he provided a straightforward auditorium for its evangelical rector. Later, in 1873, he designed the Ruskinian Church of the Holy Trinity, also in New York City, for the rector's son (177). Here again he emphasized the function of the church as an auditorium with a curious elliptical interior contained within a rectangle, which, incidentally, provided Eidlitz an opportunity to apply his structural ingenuity with roof trusses. The striking appearance of Holy Trinity, with walls and roofs alike covered with diagonal patterns that are

*177*
*Church of the Holy Trin-*
*ity, New York City. Leo-*
*pold Eidlitz, 1873.*
*Exterior.*

178
*Memorial Hall, Harvard
University, Cambridge,
Massachusetts. Ware and
Van Brunt, 1870–78.
Exterior.*

more assertive than tasteful, provoked its nickname, "Church of the Homely Oilcloth." Throughout his long career, during which he designed more than thirty churches, Eidlitz was faithful to medievalism; for him structure was the generator of architecture even if he was unable to curb the restless eclecticism of his designs.

Memorial Hall at Harvard University (1870–78) has a strongly ecclesiastical look, although its architects claimed that its cathedral form was accidental and resulted directly from the requirements of the 1865 competition for a theater and a dining hall, the theater forming a "choir," the dining hall a "nave," and their shared circulation area a "transept" (178). Henry Van Brunt and William R. Ware, partners from 1863 to 1888, were never disciples of Ruskin. Yet Memorial Hall, designed by Van Brunt, was praised for this very connection. "It speaks of sacrifice and example," wrote Henry James, underlining the moral and esthetic unity of the Victorian Gothic Style.[3] Curiously enough in the introduction to his translation of Viollet-le-Duc's *Entretiens*, Van Brunt took exception to Ruskin as "dictator on questions of art," criticizing Victorian Gothic as "based in literary exposition [rather than] practical knowledge."

*Frank Furness*

Far more of value came from Ruskin's writings than Van Brunt gave credit for. It was Ruskin, more than anyone, who created that larger view of architecture as a "real" experience, who set the value of immediacy on the sight and feel of actual stones, bricks, and marble, preferring the rough to the smooth and demanding that materials be "true," not painted imitations. Rejecting the "prejudices of taste" and disdaining the book-learning and the perfunctory teaching of the academies, he conceived of architecture as, first and last, a participatory pleasure of the senses.

No architect was more Ruskinian than Frank Furness, who lived most of his life and did most of his building in Philadelphia. The independent and subjective eye of Furness gave "character" to all his designs; "wild" and "fearless" were the adjectives used of them by his contemporaries. The individuality of his work makes it difficult to place; the closest parallel is found in the New York buildings of Mould and Eidlitz, which were surely known to him during his apprentice years with Richard Morris Hunt immediately before and after the Civil War. Hunt's influence appears in the Néo-Grec that is reflected in the architectonic patterning and fluted details of the facade of the Pennsylvania Academy of the Fine Arts in Philadelphia (1871–76), designed in partnership with George W. Hewitt (179). The academy is a major work of Furness's early maturity. Its orderly facade comprises three mansarded pavilions, each with its pointed-

179
*Pennsylvania Academy
of the Fine Arts, Phila-
delphia, Pennsylvania.
Frank Furness, 1871–76.
Exterior.*

arch window, changing gradually from simple to ornate as the building rises. Furness's unhesitant translation of Ruskin's "construc-
tional coloration" and his irreverent mixing of stylistic motifs are
visual shock treatment. Materials are given maximum definition:
rusticated purplish brownstone, smooth pale sandstone, cylinders of
polished granite, and sharp-edged panels of red brick sometimes set
with black brick patterns, are ruthlessly juxtaposed. The architect's
minister father gave utterance to the contemporary view: "The mo-
notony of [Quaker] streets is disappearing [as] the spirit of beauty
is beginning to brood over our city . . . ."

Furness's several banks express none of the traditional conservatism of those institutions. The Provident Life and Trust Company
(1879) was the most daring (180). Here Furness defied the limits of
a narrow facade with overscaled granite stones framing shadowed
openings and a cantilevered mass over the entrance, as precariously
stacked as a child's building blocks. The facade was tense and threat-
ening; harmony and grace were scorned. While trying to adjust to
its calculated rudeness, one could not escape its undeniable force.
Inside, the walls of a high, simple hall were sheathed in patterned
green and white tiles and the roof had skylights like those of the
Pennsylvania Academy supported by visible, polychromed girders.

180
*Provident Life and Trust
Company, Philadelphia,
Pennsylvania. Frank Fur-
ness, 1879. Exterior.*

*The Taste for the Exotic*

Nineteenth-century scholarship provided architects and their clients with an ever-increasing choice of styles. In the uninhibited postwar years, the urge to mix them was indulged to the full. Governed only by subjective taste, the result was a synthetic eclecticism beyond all rules and precedent. "Let us glory in all styles, character is the thing," exclaimed an English lecturer. Among those available, thanks to Owen Jones's book on the Alhambra, was the Saracenic or Moorish Style. For his Hudson River retreat the American painter Frederic E. Church, assisted by Calvert Vaux, created Olana (1874), a picturesque and personal combination of Moorish themes. Like other styles Moorish was used indiscriminately for disparate building types; in New York alone, it was used for the Temple Emanu-El synagogue by Eidlitz (1866–68), a cast-iron store front, the Tweedy and Co. Building by Hunt (1871–74), and a billiard room in the W. K. Vanderbilt House, also by Hunt (1879–81). Reaction from the tensions of war and a certain recklessness and spirit of speculation found in society at large conditioned architecture far more than associations for the advancement of truth in art.

*Henry Hobson Richardson*

There are few hints in the mediocre work of Richardson's early years of what was to come in his maturity, when, beginning with his competition-winning design of 1870 for the Brattle Square Church in Boston, he adopted the Romanesque. As we have seen, the Romanesque Revival in America was initiated with Upjohn's churches of a quarter of a century earlier. Their Lombard and Germanic prototypes were not what inspired Richardson; his inspiration came rather from certain Parisian churches of the sixties, from sketches of early medieval churches in English and French magazines, and also from the early Christian churches of Syria, which had recently received archaeological study. Never pedantic in his use of historical styles, he organized his designs, in silhouette, materials, and stylistic details, with the greatest freedom. His dependence on the Romanesque in the early seventies soon gave way to a firmness of plan and massing that is more Richardsonian than Romanesque; the architect came to dominate the style and not the style the architect.

In 1872 Richardson won the commission for Trinity Church in Boston, the culminating work of his early career. Larger and more imaginatively Romanesque than his Brattle Square Church, it shares the open Greek cross plan, the breadth of which is better suited to preaching than liturgy (181). The short nave and stubby transepts of Trinity Church—all three provided with balconies—abut a crossing bay that is nearly fifty feet square, which has an equally wide combined chancel and apse that is deeper than the nave. The aisles

181
*Trinity Church. Boston,
Massachusetts. H. H.
Richardson, 1873–77.
Interior.*

182
*Trinity Church, Boston,
Massachusetts. Exterior.*

are negligible, and the interior effect is that of a single great room. The space does not recall any Romanesque church ever built, nor does it convey visually the structural strength associated with medieval churches. Its roof is of timber trusses, it is not vaulted in stone—no nineteenth-century church ever was. All interior surfaces are furred out, plastered over, or otherwise sheathed in wood. This intentional concealment of the granite walls allowed applied decoration to achieve the "color church" Richardson wanted. Stirring yet not garish, the colors, primarily terra-cotta red, blue-green, and gold, remind us that we are still in the age of Ruskin. Even the four piers supporting the central tower were to have been sheathed in mosaic. John La Farge, assisted by the young Augustus Saint-Gaudens, was responsible for the murals and much of the stained glass.

The greater glory of Trinity Church is its exterior, notably the splendid massing of forms leading to the apex of the tower, freely observed on its isolated site facing Copley Square (182). With good reason it has always been admired. The competition design has been lost, but we know that Charles Follen McKim, who was in Richardson's office for two years, had a hand in the executed design. An early revision drawn by McKim shows a taller and more slender octagonal tower on a square base, somewhat Victorian Gothic in character. The present one was designed by Stanford White, McKim's replacement in the office. White followed Richardson's suggestion that the tower should be modelled on that of the Salamanca cathedral, using a photograph recently sent by La Farge from

Spain. White's tower may be a bit overdressed with detail for the more severe body of the church, but it is nonetheless a decided success. The entrance porch and the capping of the western towers of the facade were added by Richardson's successors, Shepley, Rutan and Coolidge; both features were intended by the architect, who spoke of his Trinity design as "a free rendering of the French Romanesque" (in particular that of ancient Aquitaine) and thought its central tower might be reminiscent "of the domes of Venice and Constantinople." The portal came from St. Gilles in southern France. This mixing of stylistic references to Spain, France, and the Byzantine world was a kind of eclecticism that Richardson later disavowed; however, in the eighties and beyond it became the accepted method of McKim, Mead and White and others, who relied more on intelligence than on intuition.

Although Trinity Church fixed his fame and caused congregations to seek duplicates, Richardson's forte was in secular rather than ecclesiastical work. He built only two churches after the completion of Trinity in 1877. He preferred monumental buildings, yet he accepted smaller commissions—houses, suburban railway stations, even two bridges for Boston's park system, which was laid out by his Brookline neighbor, Frederick Law Olmsted. "The things I want most to design" he once said, "are a grain elevator and the interior of a great river-steamboat."

Of Richardson's five libraries, all similar in plan, the Crane Memorial Library in Quincy, Massachusetts (1880–83), is the best (183, 184). It represents the culmination of the process of simplification seen in his work of the seventies. A picturesque silhouette is replaced by an unbroken roof-ridge, capping a rectangular plan as simple as that of a seventeenth-century colonial house. Richardson's concentration on the relation of solid to void, of wall to window, becomes the basis for a harmonious abstraction with scarcely a reference to any past style. The magnificent horizontal series of windows placed above the high-breasted wall and below the simple roof is one of Richardson's most lyrical passages. Like his English contemporary, Philip Webb, Richardson was reacting to the disordered eclecticism of the Victorian era. For both Webb and Richardson, walls, roofs, and chimneys were sacred. In the Quincy Library the random ashlar of gray granite is relieved by strips of brown granite trim. Sensuous details were shaped in this hardest of stones; for example, the sculptured lips of the corner waterspouts, which equal the best of Art Nouveau design yet to come. In all successful masonry the skill of the builder is paramount and the Norcross Brothers, Richardson's

0 5 10 15 FEET
0 1 2 3 4 5 METERS

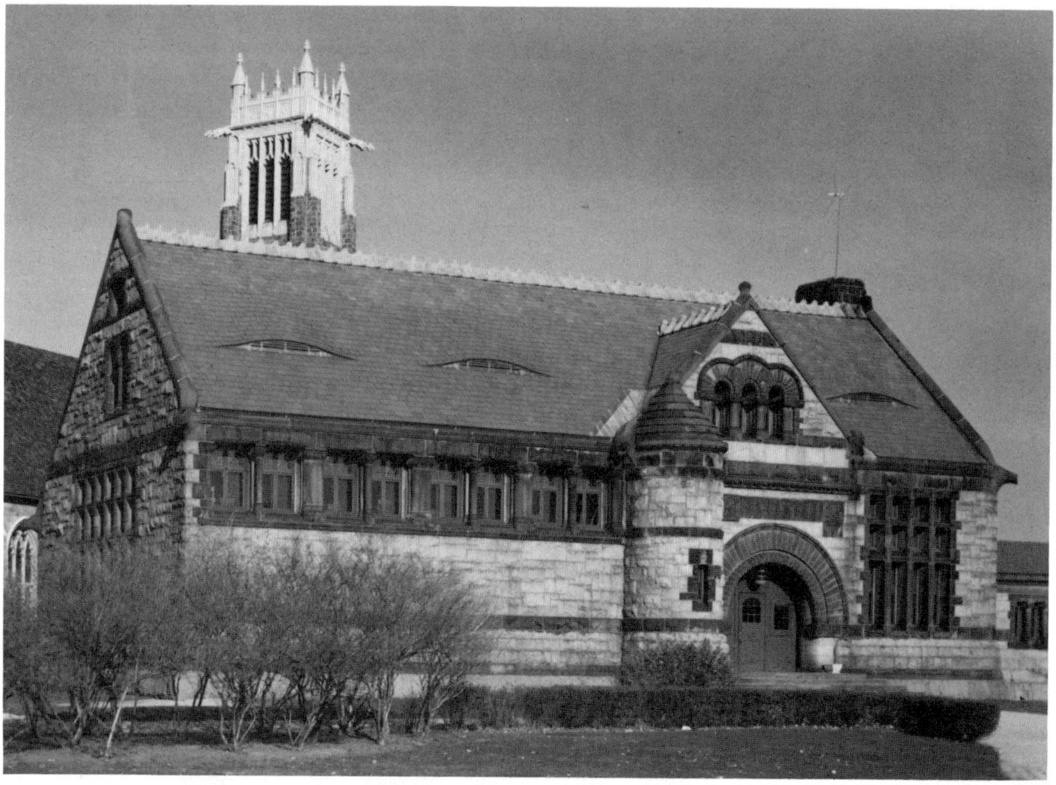

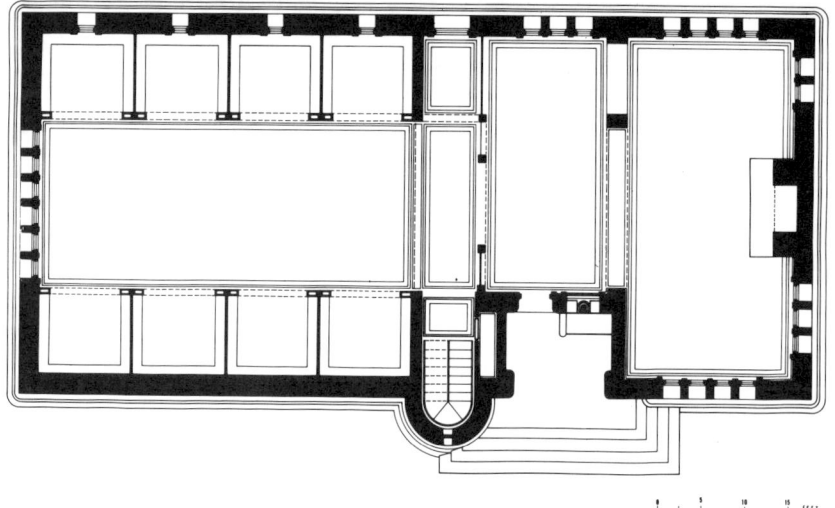

183
*Crane Memorial Library,
Quincy, Massachusetts.
H. H. Richardson, 1880–
83. Exterior.*

184
*Crane Memorial Library,
Quincy, Massachusetts.
Plan.*

185
*Sever Hall, Harvard
University, Cambridge,
Massachusetts. H. H.
Richardson, 1878–80.
Exterior.*

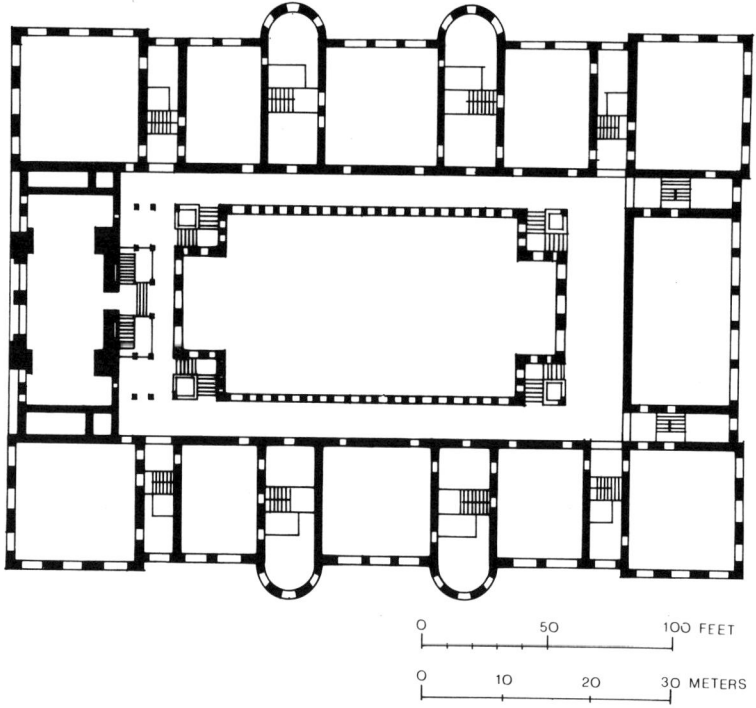

186
*Allegheny County Court
House, Pittsburgh, Penn-
sylvania. H. H. Richard-
son, 1884–88. Exterior.*

187
*Allegheny County Court
House, Pittsburgh, Penn-
sylvania. Plan.*

favorite contractors, were wonderfully skillful in realizing the effects
their architect sought. Tactile experiences were not the least part of
Richardson's "reality."

The commission to design Sever Hall in Harvard Yard, which
came to him in 1878, may have hastened Richardson on his course
toward simplicity (185). Nearby stood the utilitarian, red brick Massachusetts Hall of the early eighteenth century and Bulfinch's restrained, pale granite University Hall. Richardson followed their
rectangular plans and simple roofs and played variations on the
theme of their straightforward, symmetrical fenestration in the
richer but disciplined grouping of his classroom windows. He
achieved a design that was "neither monotonous nor restless" by
relieving the red brick plainness of the walls with molded and cut
brick panels and string-courses, handsome details whose assorted
historical origins make Sever Hall Richardson's most hybrid work.
Particularly notable are his wholly original fluted brick chimneys at
the ridge of the low-hipped roof. In her biography of the architect,
Mrs. Schuyler Van Rensselaer characterized Sever Hall as "so striking yet so serious, sensible, uneccentric, and appropriate." Her words
might apply to all of Richardson's late work.

Richardson did not live to see the completion of his two favorite
designs: the Allegheny County Courthouse and Jail in Pittsburgh
(1884–88) and the Marshall Field Wholesale Store in Chicago (1885–
87). One must not be misled by the quarry-faced gray granite walls
and lofty tower of the Pittsburgh building and fail to observe that its
logical plan and monumentality are qualities advocated by the Ecole
des Beaux-Arts, where Richardson had studied after his years as a
Harvard undergradute (186, 187). Even the strong emphasis on
corner pavilions suggests a French *hôtel de ville* scheme. The courtyard elevations, composed of unadorned masonry arcades in the
tradition of ancient Roman aqueducts, are the part of the building
one might regard as characteristically Richardsonian. But the intricate fantasy of the stairhall, the equal of any eighteenth-century
northern Italian or Bavarian Baroque example, and as fine in its
different way, is also Richardson's.

In the utilitarian commission of the Marshall Field Wholesale
Store we recognize Richardson's true destiny: to compose cubic forms
in rugged masonry, uninhibited by picturesque conventions of his
time (188). The motif of layered arcades with graduated openings in
his earlier commercial buildings, the Cheney in Hartford (1875–76)
and the Ames in Boston (1882–83), is expanded and simplified and
given an intensity and vigor unmatched in Richardson's previous
work. First conceived for brick, the design was carried out in stone,

188
*Marshall Field Wholesale
Store, Chicago, Illinois.
H. H. Richardson, 1885–
87. Exterior drawing.*

red granite for the two-story base and red sandstone above. Inside, timber framing carried plank floors, the typical construction of New England mills. Only on the first three floors were cast-iron columns used, and they were jacketed in terra-cotta, as was the practice in Chicago after the disastrous fire of 1871. Richardson was never particularly interested in new materials.

What form Richardson might have given to skyscraper construction, which was being proposed by Chicago architects in his last years of life, can only be suggested by the work of Sullivan, the architect who best understood Richardson's mind. The strength of Richardson's designs made most architects pause to reconsider the "wobbling mockeries" of their own. But when they heeded Richardson, it was less the severity of his Marshall Field Store that they regarded than the pictorial manner, which he had long since abandoned. Richardsonian Romanesque was perhaps too personal a style, too much of its own time to endure for long. Within a few years of his death, it vanished with scarcely a trace, except for what survived in the no less personal style of Sullivan.

The Richardsonian interlude is well represented in the Midwest, particularly in Chicago, St. Paul, and Minneapolis. These prosperous and ambitious "Western" cities, as they were then regarded, saw in Richardsonian Romanesque a congenial means of expression for their civic, cultural, and domestic virtues. To extend the Romanesque style to the commercial skyscraper, as Burnham and Root did in the Woman's Temple in Chicago (1892), for example, proved to be a mistake. The steel frame contradicts the structural message of the masonry-bearing wall. The architects were on better ground in their moderate-size Art Institute in Chicago (1886–87), in whose elevations logic and pictorial values are nicely balanced. The designer was John Root, whose talent almost matched his partner's ambition. Better trained than either Burnham or Root was Henry Ives Cobb, who had studied at Harvard and MIT. Although his design ability was less than Root's, his Chicago Historical Society (1892) comes closer to the essence of Richardson than the Art Institute. It is more emphatic in basic form and wall treatment, although hardly as felicitous as the work that inspired it.

The quality of Richardsonian Romanesque imitations was not necessarily commensurate with their proximity to the Brookline source. In Minneapolis an imposing replica of the Allegheny County building was built by Long and Kees, who were the devoted Richardsonians of that city. Their City Hall and Hennepin County Courthouse (1888–1905) is at once both more utilitarian and more picturesque than its prototype. The addition of numerous turrets to corner pavilions makes for a more animated roofline, but the arrangement of windows, greater in number but smaller in size, is better suited to office use. The solid shaft of Richardson's tower was here opened up with windows, unfortunately weakening the visual effect.

Another Richardson enthusiast was Leroy S. Buffington. His Pillsbury Hall (1887–89) on the University of Minnesota campus is evidence that architectural picture-making continued strong in the profession. Harvey Ellis, an itinerant draftsman employed by Buffington, was the actual designer. In designing, Ellis never paid any attention to construction, but his considerable talent in delineation—never Richardson's forte—led him to concentrate on details rather than on the simplification of plan and profile, which Richardson, however blunt and crude his sketches, never failed to do.

Within months of Richardson's death in 1886, a major commission came to his successors, Shepley, Rutan and Coolidge, who all were his young assistants. They were asked to design the new Stanford University in Palo Alto, California (189). The donor made it a troublesome assignment. The campus plan is a formal one based on two

189
*Stanford University, Palo
Alto, California. Shepley,
Rutan and Coolidge,
1887–1902. North face of
outer quad.*

concentric rectangles formed by low buildings executed in rough yellow stone with tile roofs. Extensive arcades link the classrooms and provide them shade but also obscure their form. The arcaded courtyards suggest Spanish missions; whether intentional or not, this was something of which Leland Stanford approved. The short axis of the central quadrangle is marked by a memorial church in the manner of Boston's Trinity and, opposite the church, by a triumphal arch for which the economical architects rescued Richardson's 1875 proposal for a Civil War monument. The arch was toppled in the 1906 earthquake and was never rebuilt.

**Richard Morris Hunt**

Although Richardson looms larger in the perspective of history, it was Richard Morris Hunt who, after the retirement of Upjohn and Walter, was acknowledged by his contemporaries as the dean of American architecture. For forty years, from his return from the Ecole des Beaux-Arts, where he was the first American pupil, in 1855, to his death in 1895, Hunt was a prominent figure in the architectural scene despite the fact that he contributed little to the major stylistic trends of his time. The Second Empire Style as practiced in America was too coarse for his educated taste; the morality-laden Victorian Gothic could not interest a Francophile; Romanesque was alien to his temperament. A disciplined Romantic, Hunt is most often remembered for his brilliant adaptations of Loire Valley châteaux in grand houses, located mostly in New York and Newport.

Always a busy practitioner, Hunt was also active in the profession. He assisted in the founding of the American Institute of Architects in 1857. At a time when there were no architectural schools, he established a Parisian type *atelier* within his office that included such pupil-assistants as Post, Ware, Van Brunt, and Furness.[4] Once the young Sullivan sought his advice. In 1893 he became the first Amer-

ican to be awarded the Gold Medal of the Royal Institute of British Architects.

Hunt's early work does not flaunt Parisian Second Empire fashion; instead it restates the sober Néo-Grec of Henri Labrouste, the leading practitioner of this inappropriately named reforming style. Néo-Grec was a rationalized classicism that emerged in Paris in the 1840s and was soon eclipsed by the exuberant expressions of Napoleon III's reign. Hunt's simpler versions of Néo-Grec in New York are the Tenth Street Studio Building (1857) and the Stuyvesant Apartments (1869), both typically astylar with emphasis on flat surfaces. Hunt's best Néo-Grec building is the Lenox Library (1870–75), also in New York City (190). The rational composition of its plan and the way it is expressed in the elevations are clearly derived from the lessons of J.-N.-L. Durand.[5] Its monochromatic limestone and restrained ornament were departures from contemporary American taste. Though admired, the Lenox Library was not imitated, not even by Hunt; a later generation of architects, however, acknowledged its discipline.

In his last fifteen years Hunt found his *métier* in commissions for the Vanderbilt family and others of their kind. The first of his works in the château style that had a special appeal for them, and his masterpiece, was the William K. Vanderbilt House in New York (1879–81). Hunt skirted the free eclecticism of his time and followed a more scholarly path, pointing the way for the connoisseur's architecture of McKim and others. The facades of the Vanderbilt mansion were extremely flat, of finely tooled limestone, itself a contrast to the prevailing brownstone. Small-scaled decorative carvings were discreetly placed and sensitively executed (191). Hunt's assurance with manorial late French Gothic was shown in other town houses: the William Borden House in Chicago (1884), more severe than the

191
*W. K. Vanderbilt House,*
*New York City. Richard*
*Morris Hunt, 1879–81.*
*Exterior.*

Vanderbilt mansion but with the same corbelled tourelle; the El-bridge T. Gerry House in New York (1891), in which he used the brick and limestone combination of Blois; and the double house for the Astors, Mrs. William B. and John Jacob IV, also in New York (1891), which aspires to the early Renaissance of Chambord.

At Newport, Rhode Island, Hunt helped to transform a modest summer colony into a display of seasonal palaces and manor houses for America's new aristocracy. The Breakers (1892–95) for Cornelius Vanderbilt is his most successful Newport work. Here with great flair he adapted an Italian Renaissance villa and arranged stately rooms in a disciplined cruciform plan around a central two-storied hall, suggesting a *cortile*, which served as a ballroom. From still another Vanderbilt, George W., Hunt received his most regal commission, Biltmore (1890–95), near Asheville, North Carolina. It gave him the opportunity to design, with the assistance of Olmsted, on a regional scale, combining nature and art. The expansive landscaping gives the house an appropriate detachment denied to those in Newport. Drawing heavily on the château of Blois, Biltmore stands as the grandest house in America (192).

Hunt was at heart a knowledgeable eclectic rather than a rigorous theorist. For him the value of an idea was less important than an experienced eye. His polished works and cosmopolitan spirit were a contrast to provincial practice in times when, as Van Brunt put it, "sentiment was keenly aroused but discipline was silent."

192
*Biltmore, Asheville,*
*North Carolina. Richard*
*Morris Hunt, 1890–95.*
*Exterior.*

*A New Skyline*

In 1904 Henry James returned to America after more than twenty years' absence. As he approached New York by water, the skyline he saw astonished and displeased him. "Monsters of greed" were beginning to transform Manhattan into "a huge, jagged city." In his absence the skyscraper had been born.[1]

The two cities responsible were New York and Chicago. The skeletal metal frame, essential for the construction of tall buildings, appeared first in New York in the cast-iron structures of James Bogardus and Daniel Badger in the 1840s and 1850s. The crucial refinements that turned it into "Chicago construction" were assembled by William LeBaron Jenney in his Home Insurance Company Building of the early eighties in that city. If there has to be a "first" skyscraper, it was Jenney's "unlovely" building. By 1890 the perfected metal skeleton had been adopted by New York architects and the focus shifted back to the East, where the tallest examples were to be built, culminating in Cass Gilbert's Woolworth Building (1910–13), which stands nearly 800 feet high and was for twenty years the world's tallest office building.

The post-Civil War period marked the beginning of intense commercial growth. The convenience of doing business within a small number of blocks drastically increased the value of land in lower Manhattan and the Chicago Loop. Land values and technology were interrelated: as multiple floors became technically feasible, land values rose with increased heights. When the elevator broke the height limit of approximately sixty feet, changes were immediate. Greed and the elevator produced a serrated skyline in contrast to the relatively level one produced by five-story buildings. Certainly the primary motive was profit; yet in a competitive environment the tall office building was, on occasion, designed to be a mark of prestige. An example is "Publishers' Row" overlooking Manhattan's City Hall Park, consisting of the Tribune, the New York Times, and the New York World buildings, each with its own distinctive architectural treatment. But the bottom line of profit remained the most exacting: if the office building did not pay, it did not succeed. Never before in history had the demand for profit been so explicitly related to architecture.

*Early Elevator Buildings*

The first elevator building (to use the term current for high office buildings in the seventies) was the Equitable Life Insurance Company in New York (1868–70) by Arthur Gilman and Edward Kendall. It had seven stories of offices for rent, a modest increase over the usual five but an increase that was only made viable by the elevator. Its masonry exterior was Second Empire, with stories grouped in pairs to belie its true height of 130 feet. The interior structure, partly of iron, was the work of the consulting architect George B. Post, who later, when more active on his own, was once introduced by Daniel Burnham as the father of the New York skyscraper.

When one recalls that the elevator was used for the first time commercially in the Haughwout Store, the appearance of the first elevator office building a decade later seems remarkably tardy. However, the profitable Equitable Building soon provoked more lofty rivals: Post's Western Union Building, 230 feet high, and Richard Morris Hunt's Tribune Building, 260 feet high, both built in 1873–75 (193, 194). Their dramatic heights made them skyscrapers in a sense in which the Equitable was not. Yet, like it, they were structurally conservative, relying on masonry walls and partitions supporting iron beams, a type of structure that required walls four feet thick at their base. Obviously this mass of masonry limited the usefulness of the ground floor for shops, and the deep reveals of the office windows impeded the admission of daylight. Visually the Western Union and the Tribune buildings were clumsy; both were horizontally banded with cornices and weighed down with enlarged mansard roofs to contain the upper floors, a weak disguise of their full heights. The esthetic of the Picturesque persists in a curious way in the clock towers that rise well above their rooflines. Such Victorian towers can be traced to the Gothic Revival work of A. W. N. Pugin at Scarisbrick Hall and the Houses of Parliament in London; their more distant ancestors were the towers of the late medieval town halls, guild houses, and trade halls of Italy and northern Europe, which symbolized the prosperity of the merchant class and its ascendancy over the nobility and independence of the Church. With iconographic consistency the tower motif reappeared in many nineteenth-century commercial buildings and satisfied the Victorian taste for a broken skyline.

The closest New York ever came to true skyscraper construction in the eighties was in George B. Post's New York Produce Exchange, built in 1881–84 (195). Perhaps it was the necessity of providing a large banking room that led to the use of a complete metal skeleton, with cast-iron columns supporting wrought-iron beams and joists. The exterior loads were carried by the peripheral metal columns and, to a lesser degree, by the brick piers of the facade; thus it was not quite a true skeleton-support structure. The impressive banking

193
Western Union Building,
New York City. George
B. Post, 1873–75.
Exterior.

194
*Tribune Building, New
York City. Richard Morris
Hunt, 1873–75. Exterior.*

195
*New York Produce Ex-*
*change, New York City.*
*George B. Post, 1881–84.*
*Exterior.*

room, lofty and skylighted, was identified by the four-story arcading of the Renaissance Style facade. The Produce Exchange was one of Post's most satisfying compositions. His reputation for progressive work, however, seems less well founded when we view his later World-Pulitzer Building in New York (1890), with twelve-story masonry walls carrying a vast French Baroque dome.

**Jenney and Skyscraper**
**Construction**

In these New York buildings no substantial or consistent method of fireproofing the metal was employed. Builders of the 1870s were understandably cautious about metal structures; their vulnerability was dramatized in the collapsed heaps after the great fires of 1871 in Chicago and 1872 in Boston. The solution to an urgent problem came from Chicago with John Van Osdel's Kendall Building of 1873. At the suggestion of George H. Johnston, a New York employee of Daniel Badger, who had viewed the Chicago ruins, Van Osdel used light, specially molded, hollow terra-cotta tiles to replace the brick floor arches spanning metal joists; these hollow tiles weighed only a quarter of the brick counterparts. Soon molded terra-cotta integument over all metal supports came to be standard practice. Thus with a fireproofing solution at hand, a constantly improved elevator mechanism, and the understanding of the metal skeleton, the first true skyscraper was imminent. The epoch-making step was taken, perhaps fortuitously rather than intentionally, by Jenney in Chicago.

The term "Chicago School" is now commonly used to designate the commercial architects of Chicago in the 1880s and 1890s. However, the term was not always so used. Its first appearance in 1908 referred to Frank Lloyd Wright and contemporaries of his who were, for the most part, doing domestic work. Later, historians of the skyscraper, notably Hitchcock and Giedion, applied the term to the skyscraper designers of earlier decades and this usage now prevails.

The 1880s were a momentous decade for Chicago. There was a frenzy of activity by architects of talent: Jenney, Burnham and Root, Adler and Sullivan, Beman, Holabird and Roche. The eldest of these was William LeBaron Jenney, a practical man who had studied engineering at the Ecole Centrale des Arts et Manufactures in Paris and who had been a major in the Army Corps of Engineers during the Civil War and a professor of architecture at Michigan. Chicago's demand for commercial loft space often led to stringent designs, one of which was Jenney's first Leiter Building (1879). Originally of five stories, its interior framing was of cast-iron columns and girders with timber beams and joists. What was remarkable was that its peripheral loads as well as its interior loads were carried by cast-iron columns placed immediately behind brick piers of the facade. Carrying only their own weight, these slender piers allowed very large windows, which gave the facade an amplitude of scale prophetic of the boldness of Chicago skyscrapers to come (196). Technically the building was just short of skyscraper construction, but a step ahead of Post's New York Produce Exchange.

Jenney gained immortality with his Home Insurance Company Building, built in 1883–85 (197). This was the first true skyscraper, notwithstanding certain changes made during construction and the masonry party walls required by the city. Its historical eminence was corroborated by inspection during demolition in 1931. The first two stories were of granite load-bearing masonry, from the top of the second story to the sixth floor cast-iron columns and wrought-iron girders were used as a full frame except for the party walls; from the sixth floor up the newly available Bessemer steel beams were substituted for wrought-iron ones. Banded about its exterior at every second floor were cast-iron shelf angles bolted to the structure and carrying eighty-two percent of the masonry facing. True, this curtain wall was excessively thick, while its classical pilasters and cornices were inappropriate and diminished its apparent height. Likewise, the arched windows of the top story expressed a masonry esthetic un-

196
First Leiter Building, Chi-
cago, Illinois. William
LeBaron Jenney, 1879.
Exterior.

197
*Home Insurance Company Building, Chicago, Illinois. William LeBaron Jenney, 1883–85. Exterior.*

related to the steel frame. Henceforth the skyscraper was no longer a technical problem but an esthetic one, one that caught architects unprepared. The prevailing nineteenth-century practice of eclecticism had conditioned them to think only in terms of historical models. How to design a building whose proportions had no historical precedent was a question that was finally answered in the 1920s by a German architect whose first skyscraper was not built—in Chicago—until 1950.

*Other Chicago Pioneers*

Among Chicago firms making history in the 1880s was that of Burnham and Root. Daniel H. Burnham and John Wellborn Root met as draftsmen in the Chicago office of Peter B. Wight in 1872 and formed their celebrated partnership in the following year. Their talents were perfectly complementary; Burnham was primarily the office manager and client-relations man, Root the sensitive and imaginative designer. They established their office in a building of their own design, the Rookery of 1885–86 (198). This was a hybrid example of the tall office building, with interior framing entirely of metal and richly ornamented street facades of bearing masonry. On the alley sides the architects proved more courageous, for the lower two floors were of stark metal skeleton construction carrying masonry walls above. Inside, a generous lightwell extended down to the second floor skylight over an enchanting two-story lobby, later to be remodelled by Frank Lloyd Wright (199). Root's richly inventive motifs on the two street facades range from Romanesque through classical to Hindoo. In his day Root's reputation as a facile designer rivalled that of Sullivan. His early death in January of 1891 aborted a career that promised much, including participation in the World's Columbian Exposition.[2]

Root's favorite building was the one he called Jumbo, the Monadnock Block (1889–91). With its sixteen stories of plain dark brick, it was the last of the great masonry load-bearing skyscrapers in Chicago (200, 201). Its construction was originally planned for 1885 but delayed by the shrewd Boston investor-client. In extended preliminaries Burnham and Root proposed using the new metal skeleton, but the client ruled it out, citing "risk and uncertainty in regard to its lasting strength"; the durability of iron against eventual rust was widely suspect at the time. As built, the Monadnock has an interior metal frame combined with two masonry crosswalls as wind bracing. The foundation problems presented by the spongy, compressible Chicago soil were sometimes solved with wood piles and sometimes, as in the Home Insurance Building, with massive subterranean py-

198
The Rookery, Chicago,
Illinois. Burnham and
Root, 1885–86. Exterior.

199
The Rookery, Chicago,
Illinois. Interior court
as originally built.

*200*
*Monadnock Building,*
*Chicago, Illinois. Burn-*
*ham and Root, 1889–91.*
*Exterior detail.*

*201*
*Monadnock Building,*
*Chicago, Illinois. Ground*
*floor plan.*

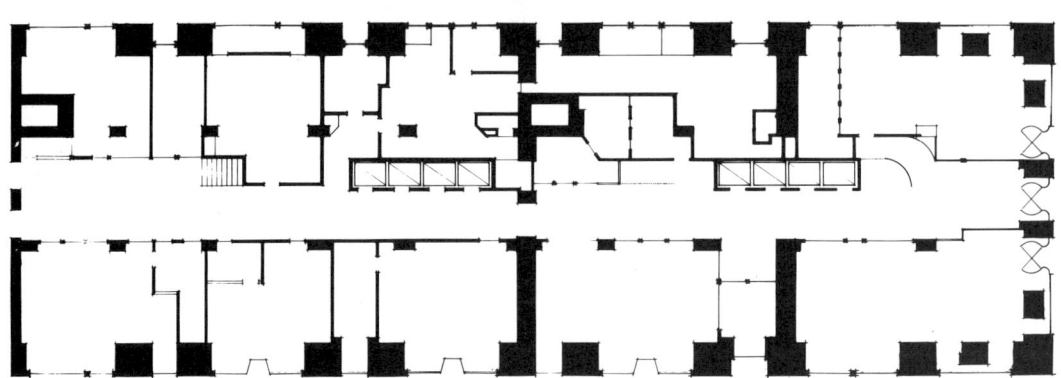

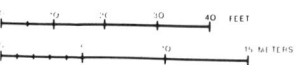

ramidal piers of layered masonry. In the Monadnock a concrete raft reinforced with a grillage of iron rails was used, extending well beyond the building line. Thus the weighty building was floated on the unstable soil.[3]

The Monadnock's most memorable aspect is its severe exterior, with slightly battered walls, delicately chamfered corners, and a subtly flaring cornice reminiscent of an Egyptian pylon. Vertical breaks occur with projecting tiers of bay windows, starting with the third floor and stopping short at the fifteenth. Had Root had his way, the simple drama of the building would have been enhanced by colored bricks, shading from yellow at the top to a dark brown below. But the client objected on the grounds that the effect would merely suggest dirt washed down. It was at his request that the Monadnock design was carried out without ornament or a dissenting line. The Monadnock Block shows how in the conflict between art and utility a decision mandated by a speculator in favor of the latter may result, paradoxically, in a handsome building.

The economy and regard for utility demanded by Chicago investors are reflected most consistently in the designs that came from the firm of Holabird and Roche. The objective clarity of their solutions drastically reduced pier and spandrel, allowing for vast areas of window. In their use of a large center pane of glass flanked by a narrower, operating sash, they originated what became known as the Chicago window. It is seen in their McClurg (now Crown) Building (1899–1900), which is as declarative of its metal skeleton as any of Mies van der Rohe's designs half a century later. Holabird and Roche's Tacoma Building (1887–89), once thought to be the first completely skeletal skyscraper, was faceted with multiple bay windows across its two facades (202). It was a precursor of an architecture to come, not of masonry with its shades and shadows but of reflecting glass walls around a skeleton frame. Tiered bay windows were cantilevered over the property line to obtain more office area—"stolen space," as Wright said—a practice now forbidden by municipal code, yet these bay windows also caught the breeze in canyoned streets and gave more light to offices within.

Similar to the Tacoma in appearance is the Reliance Building (1890–95) by Burnham and Root, the last design in their free experimental manner of the 1880s. After Root's death in 1891 the work of the firm reflected, more and more, the ideals of the Ecole des Beaux-Arts. The Reliance design was begun by Root and completed by Charles B. Atwood, who replaced him as Burnham's chief designer. The exact share of each is unclear; in any case, the result

202
Tacoma Building, Chicago, Illinois. Holabird and Roche, 1887–89. Exterior.

203
*Reliance Building, Chicago, Illinois. D. H. Burnham and Co., 1894–95. Exterior.*

is a striking finale to the Chicago School and equal to any of Sullivan's skyscrapers (203). The exterior of the Reliance Building is largely of glass, and its minimal opaque portions are sheathed in white terra-cotta embossed with Gothic detailing.[4] As in the Tacoma, vertical tiers of bay windows are cantilevered out over the property line. Originally a flat roof plane also extended itself to this outer line, forming a most effective termination, but it was later removed in obedience to municipal safety regulations. A contemporary critic, Montgomery Schuyler, saw the Reliance Building as a statement rather than a solution of the skyscraper problem. "If this is the most and best that can be done with the sky-scraper, the sky-scraper is architecturally intractable. . . ." Schuyler was uneasy with the problems of skeletal design and preferred the Monadnock to the Reliance.

*Minneapolis in the 1880s*   That Chicago had no monopoly in inventive solutions is seen in Minneapolis. There in 1888–90 the Milwaukee architect E. Townsend Mix built the memorable Guaranty Loan (later the New York Metropolitan Life) Building (204). Its twelve-story masonry-wall exterior was a rather conventional example of Richardsonian Romanesque. But inside the architect's imagination took flight, and a metal skeleton formed a skylighted interior court running the full height of the building. Its thrilling effect was heightened by ambulatory balconies, which served as accesses to the ring of office suites. These so-called corridors were cantilevered out into space, and their lightness was accentuated by floors of translucent glass, one-inch thick, set in wrought-iron frames. This spatial experience was animated by a ride in one of its open-cage elevators, an experience similar to that received today in John Portman's hotels with their atrium courts.[5]

Another Minneapolis episode relevant to our story is the claim of the local architect Leroy Buffington, who might well be called the Jules Verne of the skyscraper. He claimed to have invented the metal frame skyscraper in 1882, but he delayed his application for a patent until 1888. His scheme proposed a continuous skeleton of laminated iron plates, structurally rather inefficient, to which shelf angles were attached to carry the collars of masonry walls around each story— essentially curtain-wall construction. His specific proposal was for a twenty-eight story building, but he envisioned buildings of fifty and even one hundred stories in which his principle could be used (205). He cited Viollet-le-Duc, the rebel historian who saw in Gothic cathedrals a language of structural rationalism whose translation into iron was imperative if a modern architecture was to emerge. Buffington's case was no doubt well founded; his mistake was to wait six years to patent his idea.

205
*Proposal for a twenty-*
*eight-story building.*
*Leroy Buffington, 1888.*

*Adler and Sullivan*    It was Louis Sullivan who recognized and seized on the expressive possibilities of the skyscraper. "It must be tall," he wrote, "every inch of it tall. The force and power of altitude must be in it, the glory and pride of exhaltation must be in it. It must be every inch a proud and soaring thing, rising in sheer exhaltation that from bottom to top it is a unit without a single dissenting line . . ."

The fifteen years Sullivan spent with his partner Dankmar Adler were flourishing ones. After proving his talent as draftsman, Sullivan was invited to form the Adler and Sullivan partnership in 1881, when he was not yet twenty-five. As with Burnham and Root, complementary talents underlay their success. Adler, who took charge of clients and the office management, had a fine sense of structural matters, so that Sullivan was left to employ his imagination in the visual aspects of architecture. It is above all Sullivan's love of ornament and his originality in designing it that give a subjective stamp to all his designs. His genius escaped the bondage and anonymity of eclecticism, which he deplored. He applied Ruskin's theory of an architecture of encrustation to his own system of brilliant ornament. His earliest designs betray traces of the Gothic Revival and Frank Furness, once briefly his employer. Around 1900, in the Carson Pirie Scott & Co. store and the Gage Building, Sullivan's ornament became the most intricate and seductive in the whole history of architecture. Geometrical interlocking shapes are combined simultaneously with fanciful, curvilinear plant forms not unlike, though not derived from, the European Art Nouveau.

Adler and Sullivan's ability to execute large and complex commissions was put to the test in the Chicago Auditorium Theater and Hotel Building, built in 1887–89 (206). Adler showed his engineering skill in coping with foundation problems and devising a variable-size auditorium fitted with a remarkable acoustic shell. The entire building is of masonry-wall construction with iron framing within. For Sullivan the auditorium project recorded a swift passage from indecision to design maturity. (His earliest scheme was adorned with châteauesque turrets.) It was Richardson's newly completed Marshall Field Wholesale Store in Chicago that guided him toward a resolution. His final scheme incorporates Richardson's bold arcading and blocklike massing. The tower, which rises another seven stories above the ten-story building, is prescient of Sullivan's skyscraper designs. Both the tower and the motif of the lower block are articulated and graceful with slender arcading and recessed spandrels, giving a foretaste of Sullivan's characteristic handling of multistory elevations.[6]

Two office buildings stand out as Sullivan's finest skyscrapers: the Wainwright Building in St. Louis (1890–91) and the Guaranty (now

206
*Auditorium Theater and
Hotel Building, Chicago,
Illinois. Adler and Sulli-
van, 1887–89. Exterior.*

Prudential) Building in Buffalo (1895). In them are embodied Sullivan's whole theory of skyscraper design, which, starting in 1896, he set forth in published articles. In neither structure nor planning did they present any advance beyond current practice. What was new was the esthetic expression of the multistory repetitive bays of the steel frame. "Every problem contains and suggests its own solution," Sullivan wrote. In the Wainwright and Guaranty buildings Sullivan accented the essential verticality of the skyscraper instead of denying it or compromising it with incongruous historical styling (207, 208, 209). In recognition of the shops and entries at street level and the large suites on the second floor, reached by stairs, the first two floors are treated as a base. Above this Sullivan acknowledged the repetition of identical office floors by deliberate uniformity throughout the height and breadth of the composition, but chose to accent the vertical rather than the theoretically equally important horizontal. The topmost story, which functioned as a service floor for elevator machinery and toilets and such, was an opportunity for creating a friezelike termination to the whole composition, the final touch being a slab projection representing the roof plane. The logic of the design is plausible until one notices that extra nonstructural piers have been inserted between the structural ones, without any differentiation in form or ornament. The esthetic intent of these gratuitous piers is obvious: to multiply the vertical rhythms and to quicken the upward movement. In the Wainwright Building the verticals end with decorative capitals and are capped by the horizontal frieze of the tenth floor, which is interrupted only by small round windows; the piers are of wine-red brick and the recessed spandrels of decorative terra-cotta. In the Guaranty-Prudential Building the entire surface is animated by low-relief designs in reddish terra-cotta, and the piers are joined together at the top by arches occurring within the sixteenth-floor frieze. At street level the building is supported by stout, rounded piers with extensive glass between, so as to dramatize the openness of the ground level and give it a visual continuity with the street scene, a feature unhappily altered by remodelling.

The Wainwright and Guaranty-Prudential buildings meet the Aristotelian requirement that a work of art should have a beginning, a middle, and an end, like the classical column with its base, shaft, and capital. The so-called columnar theory of skyscraper composition, a theory not incompatible with the conventions of Beaux-Arts teaching, was widely discussed independently of Sullivan's application of it—which he would instantly deny, given his antagonism toward orthodoxy. Yet Sullivan's own education had included a year at MIT's Rogers Hall in Boston, where he admired its Beaux-Arts–

258

*207*
*Wainwright Building, St.*
*Louis, Missouri. Adler*
*and Sullivan, 1890–91.*
*Exterior*

208
*Wainwright Building, St.
Louis, Missouri. Plan of a
typical floor.*

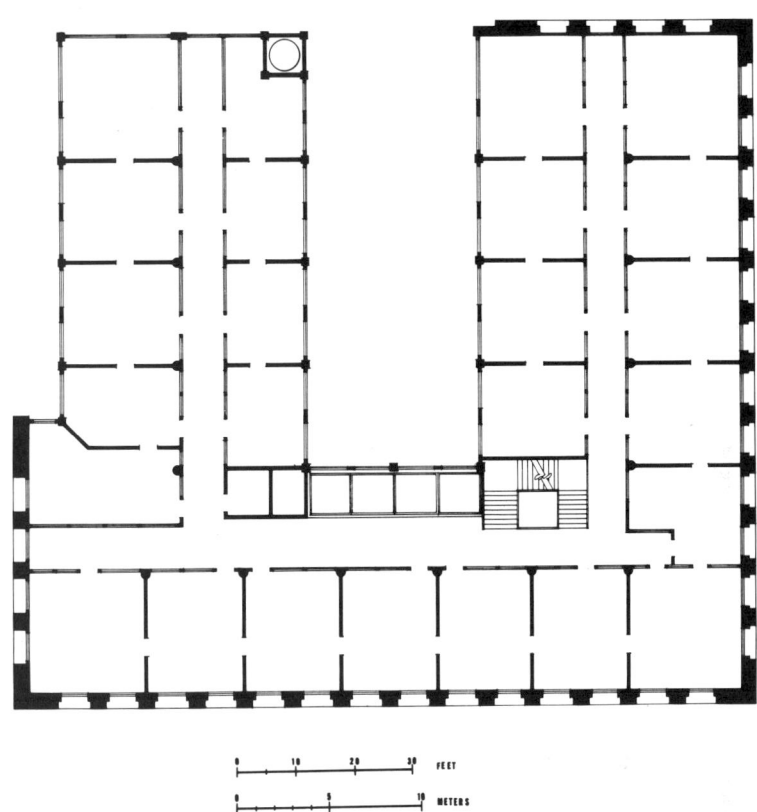

209
Guaranty Building (Prudential Building), Buffalo, New York. Adler and Sullivan, 1895. Exterior.

trained professor Eugène Letang, and an inconclusive year at the Ecole itself. Conservative compositional principles underlie Sullivan's designs although he detested the tyranny of the Ecole des Beaux-Arts and its pervasive influence in the official world of architecture. For him eclecticism was futile; a renewal of the creative process was imperative for salvation. Sullivan was given to philosophizing on these matters, sometimes abstrusely, always emotionally. "Form must ever follow Function," he demanded, but he himself understood that without the subjective element there can be no great architecture. Later modernists reared on such slogans equated functionalism with bald, utilitarian design. Nothing was further from Sullivan's intent.

Variety and richness characterize Sullivan's long series of multistory designs. His Gage Building in Chicago (1899) is an intimately scaled building, graced with two fluted, stalklike piers and an excrescence of crisp, stylized foliage breaking out at the top (210). Sullivan never designed a building that did not bear the stamp of his personality. The adjacent two structures to the south, also part of the Gage group, were designed by Holabird and Roche and contrast with Sullivan's in their leaner lines; they exemplify the more objective and programmatic approach that dominated the Chicago School.[7]

The Carson Pirie Scott & Co. store (originally Schlesinger and Mayer), built in 1899–1904, was a commission intended for the Adler and Sullivan firm but executed by Sullivan alone, with the assistance of George Grant Elmslie after the partnership with Adler had been dissolved. Here the facade is markedly horizontal and at first glance reminiscent of the European International Style of the 1920s (211). The banded rhythms of the horizontal windows are the expression of a department store's need for continuous, loftlike spaces. The treatment of the lower floors is rich in contrast with the simplicity above. Serving as a frame for merchandise in show windows, these wall surfaces are sheathed in decorative cast-iron ornament, energetic and fluid in character. This reaches a crescendo at the rounded corner entrance. Originally the top story was recessed as a shadowed loggia under a flat roof plane.

Sullivan's most dramatic skyscraper design, the Fraternity Temple (1891), intended for Chicago, was never executed (212). A signal departure from prevailing block forms, its composition was based on the setback principle, resulting in a pyramidal clustering with a central tower rising to thirty-five stories. The tower rather than the block became the characteristic form of later skyscrapers, especially in New York, where a fondness for towers was apparent early. Chicago faded as a center of interesting work when, in the last years

210
*Buildings of the Gage
Group, Chicago, Illinois.
Holabird and Roche (left),
Louis Sullivan (right),
1898–99. Exterior.*

211
*Carson Pirie Scott & Co.,
Chicago, Illinois. Louis
Sullivan, 1899–1904.
Exterior detail.*

212
*Project for Fraternity
Temple, Chicago, Illinois.
Adler and Sullivan, 1891.*

of the nineteenth century and the first of the twentieth, New York became the focus of skyscraper building. Adopting Chicago construction but not Chicago esthetics, New York architects created a commercial eclecticism based on book-learning rather than on imagination.[8] Sullivan's message was ignored.

*New York Skyscrapers*

The designing of skyscrapers in New York in the 1890s was accompanied by much talk concerning their proper form. Most architects held to the column analogy. This was convenient and popular because it allowed the bewildered architect to compose in a traditional manner at the bottom and top of his elevations, although at a dislocated scale, and released him from the obligation to be inventive in the middle. Bruce Price's proposal for the Sun Building (1890) was a "prototypical demonstration of the Beaux-Arts justification of the 'column analogy' for the composition of tall buildings." It was a picturesque version of the campanile in the Piazza San Marco in Venice; the middle portion, between the three-story decorated base and the pyramidal termination that began at the seventeenth floor, was treated with absolute uniformity. Price's American Surety Building of 1895 (now Bank of Tokyo), the most discussed and most influential skyscraper of the decade, was even more columnar; Price himself called it a "rusticated pillar." (213). Of white granite and handsomely finished off on all four sides, the American Surety Building rose conspicuously twenty-one stories without a setback, surpassing the 284-foot spire of Upjohn's Trinity Church across the street. The visual displacement of religion by commerce had begun; no longer would Manhattan's skyline be dominated by spires.

The wonder of skyscrapers may have impressed country cousins and European visitors, but concentrations of them caused serious urban problems. Antiskyscraper sentiments began to be heard when twenty-storied giants became common. Demands were made for regulating the skyscraper, even for outright abolition. Clustered skyscrapers vied for light and air, caused street congestion, and created a fire hazard—three disadvantages exacerbated in lower Manhattan with its narrow streets inherited from the Dutch-English village of the seventeenth century. In 1908 the architect Ernest Flagg proposed that street facades should be limited to 100 feet and towers should be permitted to rise to an unlimited height above them so long as they occupied no more than twenty-five percent of the site, a provision that was eventually adopted by the city code. Flagg wanted to "Parisianize" New York with even cornice lines yet allow for a "diadem of towers"; his own Singer Building (1908) shows what he meant.

213
*American Surety Build-
ing, New York City.
Bruce Price, 1895.
Exterior.*

214
Woolworth Building, New
York City. Cass Gilbert,
1910–13. Exterior.

Similar experiences with overcrowding in other cities led to controls long before New York enacted its 1916 regulation providing for height limitations and setbacks.[9] Meanwhile New York went its anarchical way with skyscraper building, made more intense by the threat of impending legislation. The worst offender was perhaps the Second Equitable Building of 1915 by Ernest R. Graham; at the winter solstice its thirty-seven stories rising without a setback cast a shadow of seven and a half acres.

The unruly skyscraper may have been curbed by municipal laws but no consensus as to its proper esthetic was ever reached. In the great majority of cases architects resorted to historical eclecticism, however incongruous the result. (The Mausoleum of Halicarnassos was a particular favorite as an apex.) Flagg's Singer Building was richly clothed in a modified French Second Empire Style. In the glazed terra-cotta crest of the Woolworth Building, Cass Gilbert mixed French and English Gothic (214). The client, Frank W. Woolworth, was aware of the fame of the Singer tower and deliberately went out for a building that would be even more striking and thus advertise the Woolworth five-and-ten-cent stores all over the world. Preliminary schemes were for a smaller site and smaller building, but the Gothic theme was fixed from the beginning, when Woolworth had shown Gilbert a photograph of the Victoria Tower of the Houses of Parliament. Gilbert had already proved his skill in adapting Gothic in the nearby West Street Building (1905); his first design for this building included a fanciful clock tower above the ridge of a steeply pitched roof. In its colored terra-cotta and other details the West Street Building was a preparation for the Woolworth commission. When completed the Woolworth Building was called "The Cathedral of Commerce." The general opinion was that it would be New York's true fane, despite St. John the Divine, then slowly rising in northern Manhattan, and that Gilbert had not only given commerce its most notable monument but had removed forever the slur on skyscrapers.

*Ecole des Beaux-Arts*          In the 1880s the two preceding decades, with their strongly held convictions about decoration, structure, and morality, came to be regarded as an age of architectural darkness. What emerged in this decade, for all its Renaissance leanings and emphasis on scholarship, was not merely an academic reaction, as it has been called, but rather a return to discipline and an interest in form, unity, and sobriety in reaction to the vagaries, picturesqueness, and willful exhibitionism of the High Victorian period.

The basics of discipline, as well as its niceties, could be best learned in Paris. The famous architectural school there, the history of which went back to Colbert's founding of the Royal Academy of Architecture in 1671, had been reorganized in 1819 as the Ecole des Beaux-Arts. This governmental school had always favored reason and correctness and discouraged eccentricity. Its logic of planning composition was one of the lasting lessons impressed upon its pupils, among whom were foreigners drawn by the acknowledged artistic supremacy of France.

It could be said that Jefferson was the first Paris-trained American architect; the first American to enroll in the Ecole des Beaux-Arts was Richard Morris Hunt, in 1846. His compatriots who followed him there much later did surprisingly well in competition with their French classmates, perhaps because they were usually older, often graduates of an American school, and sometimes had office experience; as foreigners, though, they could not compete for the coveted Grand Prix de Rome. Back home, their allegiance to French principles was clearly demonstrated in many monumental public and private buildings between 1885 and the First World War. These were the years when American attendance at the Ecole was at its peak. Even the student who could not travel to Paris learned at home in one of the newly founded schools of architecture from a French Ecole graduate, without whom no faculty could be considered complete.

The Ecole des Beaux-Arts stressed the working plan of a building. The student was taught—or, more properly, learned by experience through competition—quickly to analyze the essential parts of a plan and distribute them logically along a circulation spine, aided by crossing points and turnings. The facade was developed as a corollary of a successful plan. An appropriate setting contributed much to the final effect of the lavish, colored presentation drawings that were in themselves minor works of art. The Ecole was indifferent to structural theories and paid little attention to transitory fashions in decoration. "Her atmosphere," reported a recent alumnus, Ernest Flagg, in 1894, "is not congenial to the growth of sentimentality; one hears little about the picturesque . . . ."

*McKim, Mead and White*

More than twelve years lapsed between the completion of the Beaux-Arts training of the architect who became the leader in the renewal of classicism in America and his assumption of that historic role. On his return to New York from Paris in mid-1870, Charles Follen McKim joined the firm of Gambrill and Richardson. He withdrew in 1872, leaving unfinished drawings for Boston's Trinity Church for the new draftsman, Stanford White, who seven years later became his partner. McKim worked independently until 1878, when he formed a partnership with William R. Mead and William B. Bigelow. The latter resigned in 1879 and was replaced in the firm by Stanford White. All four shared a curiosity about Colonial architecture, then wholly neglected, and together, in 1877, went on a walking tour through the coastal towns north of Boston. Mead thought that the partiality of the office toward classical forms dated from this trip. Indeed, their memories prompted the two earliest essays in Colonial Revivalism: a house fot the Misses Appleton at Lenox, Massachusetts (1883–85), and one for H. A. C. Taylor in Newport, Rhode Island (1885–86). But the classical idiom with which McKim, Mead and

*215*
*Villard Houses, New York City. McKim, Mead and White, 1883–85. Exterior.*

White made their great reputation, that of the Italian Renaissance, was crystallized by an office draftsman named Joseph Morrill Wells.[1]

The firm's first work in Italian Renaissance was a group of six residences in New York City, built in 1883–85 and commissioned by Henry Villard, a friend of the McKim family and former Civil War correspondent and president of the Northern Pacific Railroad (215). The preliminary design for the U-shaped block was done by Stanford White; the exterior detailing was the work of Wells. However much the Villard group may recall Notman's Philadelphia Athenaeum of forty years earlier, Wells's inspiration was the Cancelleria palace in Rome, then thought to be by Bramante. Wells's passionate concern for finish and craftsmanship complemented the high design standards of the firm. The Renaissance ideal suggests a cultivated society, one of patronage and understanding of the arts; this was implied when the metropolitan leaders of financial and social life embraced it as patrons of architecture. It was a case of clients accommodating the taste of their architects.

McKim, Mead and White's conclusive statement in the language of the Renaissance was made with the Boston Public Library, built in 1887–95 (216). The high-minded patience and artistic conviction of Charles McKim over many years gave America one of its finest buildings, admired even by those doubtful of the validity of the revival of a dead language. The library's subdued white granite facade above a severe base—in the manner of Alberti, said McKim—contrasting with Richardson's Romanesque across Copley Square, proclaimed that a literate humanism best expressed America's culture. It put McKim, Mead and White indisputably at the head of the profession. Their Italian translation of Beaux-Arts French was soon imitated. Young men eagerly gained experience in their office and established competitive practices on their own.

In general form the Boston Public Library follows the hollow square of the Italian palace. A monumental staircase, a feature never found in Renaissance models but often in Baroque, is given a central position to reinforce the triple-portal entrance, preventing a direct view of the *cortile* beyond. The staircase leads to a high, barrel-vaulted reading room that stretches across the length of the facade. Book stacks on several levels are neatly compacted in the rear half of the overall square plan. The criticism sometimes levelled at the work of McKim, Mead and White, that content is suppressed in favor of external effect, with fitness giving place to show, may have some justification here. Yet the facade is superlative; it bears comparison with Richardson's Marshall Field Store and closely resembles Henri Labrouste's Néo-Grec Bibliothèque Sainte-Geneviève of

*216*
*Boston Public Library,*
*Boston, Massachusetts.*
*McKim, Mead and White,*
*1887–95. Exterior.*

1844–50 in overall arrangement and in detail, but it has its own special kind of civic dignity and patrician assurance. Furthermore, by its very reticence, it complemented the diverse structures facing the square, which then included the Ruskinian Museum of Fine Arts. It thus showed a sensitivity to ensemble, cultivated by the Beaux-Arts training, that is rarely in evidence today.

Praiseworthy too was the involvement of painters and sculptors. In the Boston Library are murals by Puvis de Chavannes, John Singer Sargent, and Edwin Austin Abbey, and sculpture by Augustus Saint-Gaudens and Daniel Chester French; Whistler was to have decorated the reading room. McKim's personal contribution was a naked bacchante by Frederick MacMonnies for the courtyard fountain. Prim Boston would have none of her, and she was banished.

The assured Renaissance manner of the Boston Public Library reflected the personality of its architect; in life as in art McKim avoided extremes. Outwardly deferential, he was as persistent in coaxing his clients to overspend as he was in seeking quality and refinement in his buildings, which never came cheap. J. Pierpont Morgan's request for a small private library to contain his collection of rare books and manuscripts proved to be a fortunate commission, although the client was a testy one (217). Built adjacent to Morgan's New York town house, the library was completed in 1906, inspired by a segment of Ammanati's Nymphaeum of the Villa Giulia in Rome. Like the stones of the Parthenon, its marble blocks were carefully honed to be laid without a mortar bed; thin strips of lead

217
*Morgan Library, New York City. McKim, Mead and White, 1906. Exterior.*

separate their vertical joints. The understated exterior conceals three diverse, lavishly decorated spaces: the lofty, galleried library, Morgan's red-damasked study, and a central marbled entrance hall, interiors that express a "covert love of picturesque variety persisting beneath the decorous austerity of academicism."

The unexpected opulence of period-decorated rooms that often occurs in McKim, Mead and White's buildings reveals the hand of Stanford White. White, who had considered becoming a painter before he decided on architecture, had a versatility and flair that greatly appealed to certain clients. Most of the exceptions to the Italian Renaissance mode, which had become an office habit by the early 1890s, were his, as were many of the charming interiors in the firm's numerous shingled summer houses of the eighties. White's personal version of the Romanesque is seen in a family town house in New York, designed in 1882 for Charles L. Tiffany, founder of the famous silver and jewelry store. For this he introduced a special brick, elongated in shape, tawny in color, and slightly glazed. Tiffany brick, set with bands of molded ornament, was repeated for the Judson Memorial Baptist Church in Washington Square (1891–92) with brilliant effect. Here White adopted an early Italian Romanesque style with a tiered campanile. A polychromed portal White had designed in 1902 for St. Bartholomew's Church in New York was so admired by its congregation that they reused it in their new church designed by Bertram Goodhue in 1919. Paying a tactful compliment to Hunt, in 1905 White designed a town house for W. K. Vanderbilt, Jr., in a château style similar to that of his father's next door.

New York was liberally embellished by McKim, Mead and White. With each new gentlemen's club in midtown came another *palazzo*. The University Club (1897–99), in stern Florentine *quattrocento*, shows McKim's predisposition to severity, a trait he finally succumbed to by adopting a Roman Neo-Classicism. The contrast of artistic temperaments in the firm is made clear by comparing it with Stanford White's Century Association (1889–91), an ingratiating variation on the *cinquecento*, with a recessed Palladian loggia and ornamental terra-cotta combined with brick. One of White's most lavish designs, possibly suggested by the firm's restoration of Jefferson's library at the University of Virginia after the fire of 1895, was Madison Square Presbyterian Church, also a domed rotunda. Jefferson, however, would not have condoned White's polychromed Pantheon: its walls were of yellow brick, its columns of polished green marble, its dome of glazed green tile. Completed in 1906—the year White was shot to death in his own Madison Square Garden nearby—the church survived only to 1919, to be replaced by a skyscraper.

*World's Columbian Exposition*

The return to classical discipline was initially an East Coast phenomenon. Chicago and the Midwest were strongholds of Richardsonian architecture, but they soon surrendered after what has been variously regarded as a salutary or pernicious event, the 1893 World's Columbian Exposition held in Chicago. The grandiloquent scenery of its aligned facades projected classicism and the fair's principal adviser, Daniel H. Burnham, onto the national scene.

Despite congressional approval of Chicago over rival cities, participation in this provincial event did not immediately appeal to the Eastern establishment, which had been invited by Burnham in December of 1890 to design its central buildings. Hunt, McKim, Mead and White, Post, and Peabody and Stearns had to be persuaded; Van Brunt and Howe of Kansas City accepted immediately. Because Chicago was paying for the fair, five local firms, Adler and Sullivan among them, were chosen to balance the five outsiders. The participating architects were presented with a planning decision made by Burnham and Frederick Law Olmsted for an architectural court around a water basin, with additional waterways throughout the site to be reclaimed from the marshy edge of Lake Michigan. Beaux-Arts principles of axis and cross-axis dominated the site planning, relieved by a picturesque wooded island, where only the Japanese government pavilion was allowed.

The splendor of the completed ensemble, with its sculptured fountains, its electrically lighted buildings reflected in lagoons, was a novel visual experience for the admiring crowds. Harmony was particularly evident in the Court of Honor portion, where it was agreed to design in a classical style, conform to a sixty-five foot cornice line, and paint all the plaster facades white (218). Five of the six Court of Honor buildings were assigned to the visiting team. Because those done by Chicago architects were scattered and more individual in style (especially Adler and Sullivan's Transportation Building and Henry Ives Cobb's Fisheries Building), they made a less emphatic statement. The iconoclastic Sullivan painted his in vivid colors. Much irritated by the invasion of Eastern taste, he regarded the fair as a setback of the progressive ideals of the Midwest.

The architecture of the Columbian Exposition dramatized the swift esthetic change of recent years toward classical order. As the spectacle of the "White City" was to be temporary, its designers felt free to indulge in pomp and architectural license. Surprisingly, Hunt's domed Administration Building at the end of the Court of Honor was a notably audacious combination of forms and details from different sources. The most disciplined classical design was the Fine Arts Building, intended to be the only permanent structure (219). (It was rebuilt in 1932.) This was designed by Charles B. Atwood, who had recently joined Burnham's office. An 1867 winning Prix de Rome project for a palace of fine arts for an exhibition by Emile Bénard conveniently provided Atwood with his inspiration.[2]

*The City Beautiful*

With the aftermath of the Chicago exposition came the impulse for urban planning in the United States, the "City Beautiful Movement," as it was called. Now more planner than architect, Burnham was called upon to serve on the McMillan Park Commission to rehabilitate L'Enfant's violated and neglected city plan for Washington. An enlargement of L'Enfant's original scheme proposed by Cass Gilbert in 1900 antedated the similar plan by McKim and Burnham that was accepted in 1901. The most dramatic accomplishment was the clearing of L'Enfant's Mall of all encroachments—no small matter because these included the station and train tracks of a line controlled by the Pennsylvania Railroad. The marshes of the Potomac were reclaimed, as those by Lake Michigan had been, and mirrored images of classical temples appeared. The main axis of the Mall was extended westward with a reflecting pool and the Lincoln Memorial (220) by Henry Bacon (1922), and an extended axis to the south terminated in the Jefferson Memorial by John Russell Pope (1943).

218
Court of Honor, World's
Columbian Exposition,
Chicago, Illinois. Daniel
H. Burnham and Freder-
ick Law Olmsted, 1893.

219
Palace of Fine Arts,
World's Columbian Expo-
sition, Chicago, Illinois.
Charles B. Atwood, 1893.
Exterior.

220
*Lincoln Monument, The Mall, Washington, District of Columbia. Henry Bacon, 1922. Exterior.*

After further experience as consultant for Cleveland, San Francisco, and Manila, Burnham turned his planning experience to his own city. In 1909 he and Edward H. Bennett presented their comprehensive and grandiose scheme for Chicago and the suburbs. "Make no little plans, they have no magic to stir men's blood. . . ." Burnham's advice was an echo of a Beaux-Arts professor's to the students in his *atelier*.

Such comprehensive master plans achieved unity and monumentality at the risk of the loss of vitality in individual buildings. Two examples are McKim's 1894 plan for Columbia University in New York and Cass Gilbert's for the University of Minnesota in Minneapolis. McKim's plan of 1894 had as its central focus a domed library flanked by symmetrical groupings of separate classroom buildings. The grassy mall included in the campus extension of 1903 made its symmetry more monumental. This wish for outward-ordered uniformity was shared by Cass Gilbert. His University of Minnesota plan of 1908 followed Jefferson's University of Virginia, but without its intimate scale and variety in buildings. Like McKim's Columbia buildings, Gilbert's are competent rather than memorable; yet his plan included both practical suggestion and heroic measure. Major automobile traffic through the campus was to be subterranean, and a terraced amphitheater was to carry the main axis down the bluffs to the Mississippi below. Later generations were too timid to follow Gilbert's suggestions.

*Railroad Stations*

The Pennsylvania and Grand Central stations in New York were of an unprecedented boldness, whether considered as architecture or as engineering. Their architects, Charles McKim and Whitney Warren, respectively, realized in them ideals and dreams of their Beaux-Arts training: clarity of circulation and spatial grandeur. The urbanistic scale and complexity of these railway terminals made them mega-structures long before the word was coined.

The muted Roman classicism of the Pennsylvania Station was a natural choice for McKim with his austere and correct taste. The president of the railroad, Alexander J. Cassatt—who earlier had magnanimously relinquished his claim on the Washington Mall—wanted a Manhattan terminal to eliminate the train shed in Jersey City and the ferry ride across the Hudson and to link the Pennsylvania Railroad with his newly purchased Long Island Railroad. The train tunnel was completed in 1906 and the station in 1910. The ancient Romans would surely have appreciated the ingenuity and heroic scale of this undertaking. Pennsylvania Station was McKim, Mead and White's largest work and the last project in which McKim participated before he died in 1909. The *parti* is simple but grand: a rectangle with an 800-foot axis transversed by two minor ones, which form the major axes of the waiting room and the train concourse (221). Six pedestrian entrances are located at the ends of these axes. Uniform screen facades of granite columns and pilasters recall Bernini's restrained colonnades before St. Peter's. Taxicabs swerve between Doric columns, down flanking ramps, to exit on side streets. Above the level attic story rise the eight lunette windows of the vast waiting room, McKim's translation of the tepidarium of the Baths of Caracalla, but exceeding the length of the original. The interior was of travertine, the first use of that "Roman marble" in America. From giant Corinthian columns, camouflaging steel supports, rose coffered groin vaults to a height of 150 feet. The spatial extravagance of this room (foretold by Hunt's pendentive-domed great hall at the Metropolitan Museum) was justified by the monumental character befitting a gateway to the metropolis (222).

Leading from the imitative Roman classicism of the waiting room toward the subterranean train tracks was the impressive concourse, as spacious as the waiting room (223). Built of unsheathed steel and glass, it was altogether modern in its transparency and lightness, even though these qualities were achieved in the traditional forms of groin and barrel vaulting. The destruction of the Pennsylvania Station in 1964 was an irreparable loss.

The ambitious circulation pattern of Grand Central is more complex, more compact, and more successful in a fully urban sense than

*221*
*Pennsylvania Station,*
*New York City. McKim,*
*Mead and White, 1910.*
*Plan.*

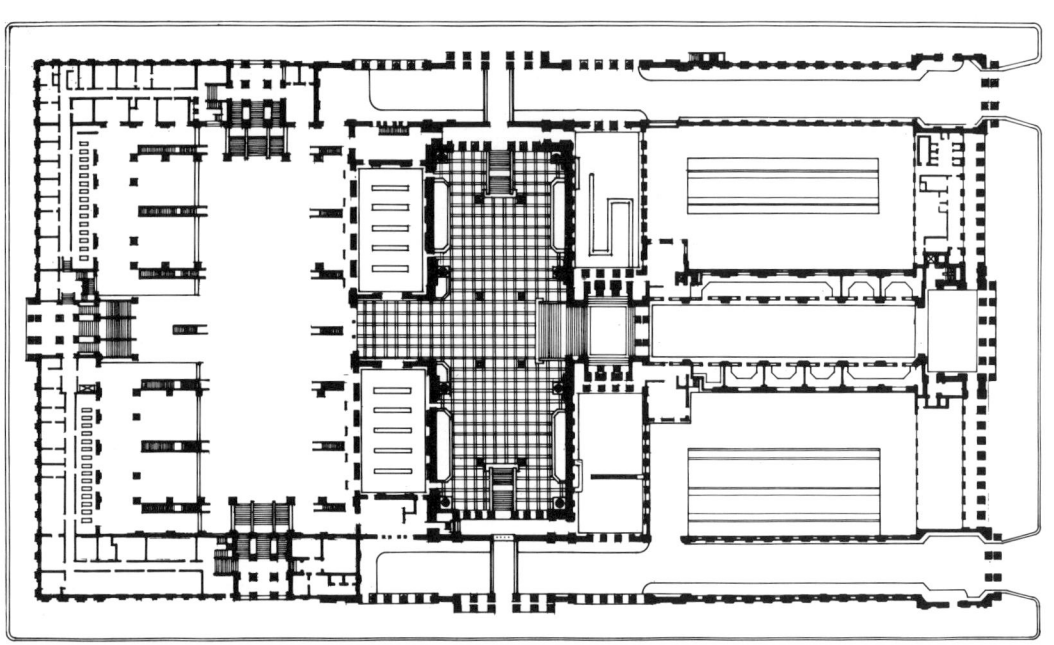

222
*Pennsylvania Station,
New York City. Waiting
room.*

223
*Pennsylvania Station,
New York City.
Concourse.*

224
*Grand Central Terminal,
New York City. Reed and
Stem; Warren and Wet-
more, 1907–13. Exterior.*

Pennsylvania Station. In the movement of people and machines, its designers attempted far more than what had been seen in any imaginary Beaux-Arts project, and they succeeded. There had always been a Grand Central Station straddling Park Avenue; its tracks originally lay in an open tunnel to the north. The third and present station, built 1907–13, was first planned in 1903 by Reed and Stem of St. Paul, Minnesota, specialists in railroad station design. In 1904 Warren and Wetmore were brought in as associate architects. It is fair to say that the planning concepts were Charles Reed's and the architectural expression Whitney Warren's. Credit should also be given to William J. Wilgus, chief engineer of the New York Central and Hudson River Railroad, for the initial suggestion of a multilevel terminal, using electric trains to eliminate smoke. By lowering the whole train yard and leasing air rights above, blocks of Manhattan were reclaimed for real estate. Pedestrian ramps and labyrinthine passages to adjacent buildings and city subway trains were part of Reed's initial plan; he also proposed the elevated roadway divided around the station to connect lower Park Avenue with the newly created northern extension. The reunited avenue exits through a pair of arches in the base of the thirty-four-storied New York Central (now Helmsley) Building, designed by Warren and built in 1929. (In 1963 the Pan American Building, fifty-nine stories tall, by Emery Roth and Sons, with Gropius and Belluschi as consultants, was built between it and the station to the south.)

The main concourse of Grand Central Terminal is comparable to McKim's tepidarium but of broader, lower proportions. Whitney Warren did not follow any specific historical model. The elliptical barrel vault, which appears to rest on simple, giant piers, is actually suspended from steel trusses; the lesser areas are vaulted in Guastavino tile.[3] Compared to the facades, which are derived from eighteenth-century France, these interiors are unexpectedly spare in detail (224).

Pennsylvania and Grand Central stations were the prodigies of the genre, but other stations in which Beaux-Arts ideals were realized on a more modest scale were no less effective: Union Station in Washington, D.C., (1908) by Daniel H. Burnham; Broad Street Station in Richmond, Virginia, (1919) by John Russell Pope; and Union Station in Chicago (1925) by Graham, Anderson, Probst and White, successors to Burnham's practice. All were in the restrained Roman manner initiated by McKim.

*Civic Architecture*

The Beaux-Arts decades, so to call them, were a time of much public building activity. Between 1886 and 1936 no less than twenty-four state capitols were built. The centers of American cities were defined by Beaux-Arts "palaces," which still serve as libraries, museums, city halls, and courthouses. Architects and laymen alike believed that some variation of the formal, classical facade expressed civic virtue, but this in no way circumscribed the actual results. The choice had widened. To the Italian model the French Renaissance was added. The plaster architecture of various expositions—St. Louis in 1904 and San Francisco in 1915 among them—encouraged a kind of baroque classicism: lavish decoration applied to an orderly arrangement of forms. Eventually a revival of the Georgian Style, again initiated by McKim, became an alternative, although one less often embraced in civic buildings than in schools, hospitals, and residences.

The City Beautiful Movement favored major buildings related to civic squares, public parks, or tree-lined boulevards. In Philadelphia the new Benjamin Franklin Parkway (1917–19) overlaid its baroque diagonal on William Penn's gridiron plan, terminating in Fairmount Park and the raised site of the Philadelphia Museum of Art. Horace Trumbauer's museum (1919–28) presented an acropolis grouping that centered on a temple front intended to be viewed from afar. (In his Hellenistic Widener Memorial Library of 1915, however, Trumbauer completely ignored the scale of its setting in Harvard Yard.) San Francisco's rebuilding after the earthquake included a civic center based on the French eighteenth century, in particular the work of Gabriel. The ensemble includes the Civic Auditorium (1913) by John Galen Howard and the Public Library (1916) by George W. Kelham. Its centerpiece is the domed City Hall (1916) by Bakewell and Brown, whose competition design of 1912 initiated this development (225).

225
*City Hall, San Francisco,*
*California. Bakewell and*
*Brown, 1916. Interior.*

*226*
*New York Public Library,*
*Carrère and Hastings,*
*1897–1911. Exterior.*

Bakewell and Brown were not alone in expressing admiration for St. Peter's dome; Cass Gilbert copied it too in his Minnesota State Capitol in St. Paul (1893–1904).

A specifically French character was favored by the younger generation of Beaux-Arts–trained architects, such as Carrère and Hastings, whose former employers, McKim, Mead and White, were never partial to French styles. Carrère and Hastings's preference is expressed in their masterpiece, the New York Public Library, a commission won in open competition in 1897 that took fourteen years to complete (226). Here all ceremonial approaches, axes, and turnings eventually lead to the grand reading rooms at the top. One of Horace Trumbauer's twin buildings on Franklin Parkway serving as the Philadelphia Free Library (1927) is also French, but is wholly plagiarized from Gabriel's facades in the Place de la Concorde. This was a departure from the principles of the Ecole, where direct copying was never approved.

*Residential Architecture*

A demand for houses of comparable academic character led some architects, including a number whose training at the Ecole des Beaux-Arts could hardly be considered appropriate preparation for it, to specialize in domestic work. Mansions, perhaps less grand than the Newport palaces but ample by any standard, appeared in the countryside and suburbs of major cities, such as Long Island, Chicago's North Shore, and Philadelphia's Main Line. An interest in authenticity, particularly in interior decoration, was stimulated and nurtured by Stanford White, who imported mantels and other architectural accessories—even panelling and ceilings of whole rooms—for his clients. Most popular was eighteenth-century Colo-

227
*Castle Hill, Crane Estate,
Ipswich, Massachusetts.
David Adler, 1927.
Exterior.*

228
*Vizcaya, Deering Estate,
Miami, Florida. F. Burrall
Hoffmann, Jr., 1914–19.
Exterior.*

nial, from Georgian to Adamesque, a taste that grew out of an awareness of the national heritage and advancing architectural scholarship and was epitomized in the Rockefeller restoration of Williamsburg, begun in 1927.

Prominent architects of domestic buildings in the East were William Adams Delano, his partner Chester Holmes Aldrich, Aymar Embury II, and Charles A. Platt. Their large houses, characteristically symmetrical in massing, were complemented by symmetrical settings. Platt is credited with the introduction of the formal Italian garden, which was sometimes attached incongruously to Georgian Style houses. His gardens were furnished with pergolas and balustrades as well as terraces whenever the site permitted. In Chicago distinguished work was done by David Adler, whose practice was solely residential. Most of his houses are on Lake Michigan's North Shore, but his largest is on the Atlantic coast, namely Castle Hill at Ipswich, Massachusetts (1927), built for Richard T. Crane, Jr. (227). Adler imitated the manner of Christopher Wren, using a pink Holland brick with limestone quoins; the roof balustrade and cupola formed a Baroque "widow's walk." In Atlanta, Georgia, Adler had a counterpart in Philip Trammell Shutze, whose Swan House for Edward Inman (1926–28) was English Georgian in design, though its placement on a terraced hill enlivened with cascades but bare of flowers recalled Italy rather than England. More idiosyncratic was the Norman farmhouse style of Mellor, Meigs and Howe of Philadelphia. Spanish models were usually restricted to Florida and California. Carrère and Hastings had much earlier, in 1887, introduced a free interpretation of the Spanish Renaissance to Florida in their Ponce de Leon Hotel in St. Augustine for Henry Flagler, the developer of Florida as a winter resort. Palm Beach became America's Riviera when the First World War prevented the very rich from travelling abroad. Addison Mizner was its leading architect. Of the many Florida houses of this period, Vizcaya, the Deering estate in Miami (1914–16), designed by F. Burrell Hoffmann, Jr., to take full advantage of its watery setting, is one of the more imaginative (228).

To the dismay of committed classicists, who constituted the great majority of the profession, the winning entry of the 1902 competition for the Military Academy at West Point was a Gothic design. The award brought national fame to its Boston architects, Cram, Goodhue and Ferguson, and initiated a popular modern Gothic style, which had a discipline of its own and proved a hardy rival of the prevailing classicism. Ralph Adams Cram was its leading practitioner.

From the beginning of his practice, Cram consciously chose to specialize in Gothic. His philosophy, embodied in his books as well as in his buildings, had little to do with the romanticism or the rationalism of the earlier Gothic Revival but much to do with ritual and a personal belief that art and religion were inseparable. Converted to Anglo-Catholicism at the age of twenty-three, Cram absorbed the liturgical and architectural teachings of the Oxford Movement; another influence was the architect Henry Vaughan, an English disciple of George F. Bodley, who was dispatched to Boston in 1882 on a High Church assignment.[4] Cram believed that the Reformation had destroyed art and that his duty was to return to the point reached in Tudor England in the early 1500s and continue the development by working creatively in the Gothic style. He aimed for re-creation, not archaeological imitation—in this like McKim, although the esthetic sympathies of the two were poles apart.

With All Saints', Ashmont (1891), Cram demonstrated his theory of creative development from an English Gothic base (229). A resolute, four-square entrance tower merges with the broad nave of this Boston church, which is built of uncoursed brown granite; the window tracery and a carved reredos supply the only relief from the general austerity.

The stubbiness of the Ashmont tower reappears in the stern silhouette of the firm's various West Point buildings, including the Cadet Chapel (1910) (230). The buttressed gray granite walls of the Post Headquarters (1904), rising from the ramparts of the Hudson, show the same respect for topography as Mont-Saint-Michel. The architectural heritage of West Point—Gothic buildings from the mid-nineteenth century, designed by one of its superintendents, Colonel Delafield—made Cram, Goodhue and Ferguson's choice of Gothic a reasonable one; McKim, Mead and White, in their Cullum Memorial Hall of 1899, a white, colonnaded form perched on the outer edge of the acropolis, had ignored such considerations.

Bertram Grosvenor Goodhue's association with Cram, which began in 1891 and lasted nearly a quarter of a century, is not unlike White's with McKim. Once a draftsman with Renwick, Goodhue

229
*All Saints' Church, Ash-
mont, Boston, Massachu-
setts. Ralph Adams
Cram, 1891. Exterior.*

230
*Cadet Chapel, United
States Military Academy,
West Point, New York.
Cram, Goodhue and Fer-
guson, 1910. Exterior.*

231
*St. Thomas's Church,*
*New York City. Cram,*
*Goodhue and Ferguson,*
*1906–13. Exterior.*

brought to the partnership a talent for rich architectural detail that complemented Cram's interest in plan and composition. St. Thomas's in New York City (1906–13), which replaced an Upjohn church destroyed by fire, points up their respective abilities (231). A freely conceived design, it mixes French and English sources and nicely balances simplicity and richness. The architects well understood that fine craftsmanship and embellishments of sculpture and stained glass were essential to the success of their modern Gothic. The reredos of St. Thomas's, designed by Goodhue and carved by Lee Lawrie, extends the full height and breadth of the chancel wall with dramatic effect, fulfilling the expectation set by the church's fine exterior. St. Thomas's is certainly Cram and Goodhue's joint masterpiece.

Cram's proclaimed disdain of copybook Gothic and pretensions to progressive developments are contradicted by his late work. Listless elegance replaced the vigor of the Ashmont church. His refectory for the Graduate College at Princeton, completed in 1913, while spatially magnificent, merely reproduces at a larger scale the dining halls of Oxford and Cambridge.[5] His University Chapel at Princeton (1925–28) likewise revives rather than revivifies Gothic.

The ultimate commission for a medievalist, a major cathedral, came to Cram in 1911 when he was asked to redesign the unfinished St. John the Divine Episcopal Cathedral in New York City. The choir had recently been completed according to Heins and La Farge's Romanesque scheme of 1889. But the Romanesque Revival had long since passed, and the trustees suggested a change of style; they now wanted Gothic, the current ecclesiastical fashion for which Cram was largely responsible. Cram obliged with a Gothic nave whose aisles are vaulted at the same height, approximately 124 feet, creating the spaciousness of a hall church and recalling the cathedral of Palma de Mallorca, an island where Cram had vacationed. Before his death in 1942, Cram was privileged, as no medieval master mason was, to walk the full length of his completed cathedral nave.

The momentum of the medievalism originated by Cram in Boston carried it nationwide. Cram's own firm accepted commissions in Houston and Los Angeles, and his example provoked architectural reassessment within American Roman Catholicism. Distinguished churches by Maginnis and Walsh can be counted among the results: St. John's in Cambridge, Massachusetts (1906), and St. Catherine's in nearby Somerville (1904–20), which was in an erudite Italian Romanesque (232).[6] Collegiate Gothic was built everywhere. Its most famous and costly example is James Gamble Rogers's Harkness Memorial Tower at Yale (1917–21), in French Gothic rather than the

*232
St. Catherine's Church,
Somerville, Massachu-
setts. Maginnis and
Walsh, 1904–20. Exterior.*

English Gothic usually favored by universities. Yale's adjacent dormitory quadrangle recalls the ambitious master plan, with four linked
quadrangles, for Trinity College in Hartford, Connecticut, which
was submitted by the English architect, William Burges, in 1874,
but of which little was ever executed.

**Goodhue and Cret**

In 1913 Bertram Goodhue expressed his growing dissatisfaction with
modern medievalism by his amicable departure from the Cram partnership. The final period of his career began with a shifting interest
in other architectures—ancient Egyptian, Persian, Byzantine, and
Spanish Baroque—some of which were expressed directly in his
work, such as the 1915 Panama-California Exposition in San Diego
with its Spanish theme. Goodhue ended his years with an inconclusive search for a modern style independent of historical precedents.
Oddly enough, Beaux-Arts classicism, with its system of sequential
spaces and the symmetrical resolution of ordered masses, captured
this once devoted medievalist. Its influence is unmistakable in Goodhue's last works, completed after his death in 1924: the Nebraska
State Capitol in Lincoln (1916–28) and the Los Angeles Public Library

(1922–26) (233, 234). What Goodhue thought was a move toward modernism was in reality a move towards classicism. His use of axis and cross-axis, his flat wall surfaces and simplified massing, the smoothly vaulted forms, are no more than the dry bones of Beaux-Arts classicism.

Perhaps because he risked less, Paul Philippe Cret of Philadelphia achieved a more successful modernism with a Beaux-Arts base. A French graduate of the Ecole, he was invited to teach at the University of Pennsylvania in 1903. Without struggle, yet without abandoning principles, Cret simplified the classical language of form, reducing the number and smoothing the profiles of mouldings and turning columns into rectangular piers. Outwardly his public buildings are stiffly heroic, marked by flat surfaces and set off by thin lines or edges of shadow, which create simultaneously massive and dainty effects. Inside, they are enduring examples of the straightforward, functional planning advocated by the Ecole. Cret's Indianapolis Public Library (1914) in its stripped classicism is a case in point (235).

For some architects the 1920s were a decade of lessened confidence and self-questioning, as they had been for Goodhue; others, Cret among them, believed that the times called for a move toward greater abstraction to be made without relinquishing the satisfactions of classicism. Cret's Folger Shakespeare Library in Washington (1930–32) shows the result of such thinking; here the engaged Doric colonnade of his Indianapolis Library becomes a wall of abstracted fluted piers. Cret's evolution toward modernism had its earlier parallels in Europe in Auguste Perret's and Joseph Hoffman's; unlike theirs, Cret's failed to provoke radical change. Yet liberal and individualistic spirits, not to be contained within an academic discipline of design, medieval or classic, were astir. Revolutionary rather than evolutionary changes lay ahead.

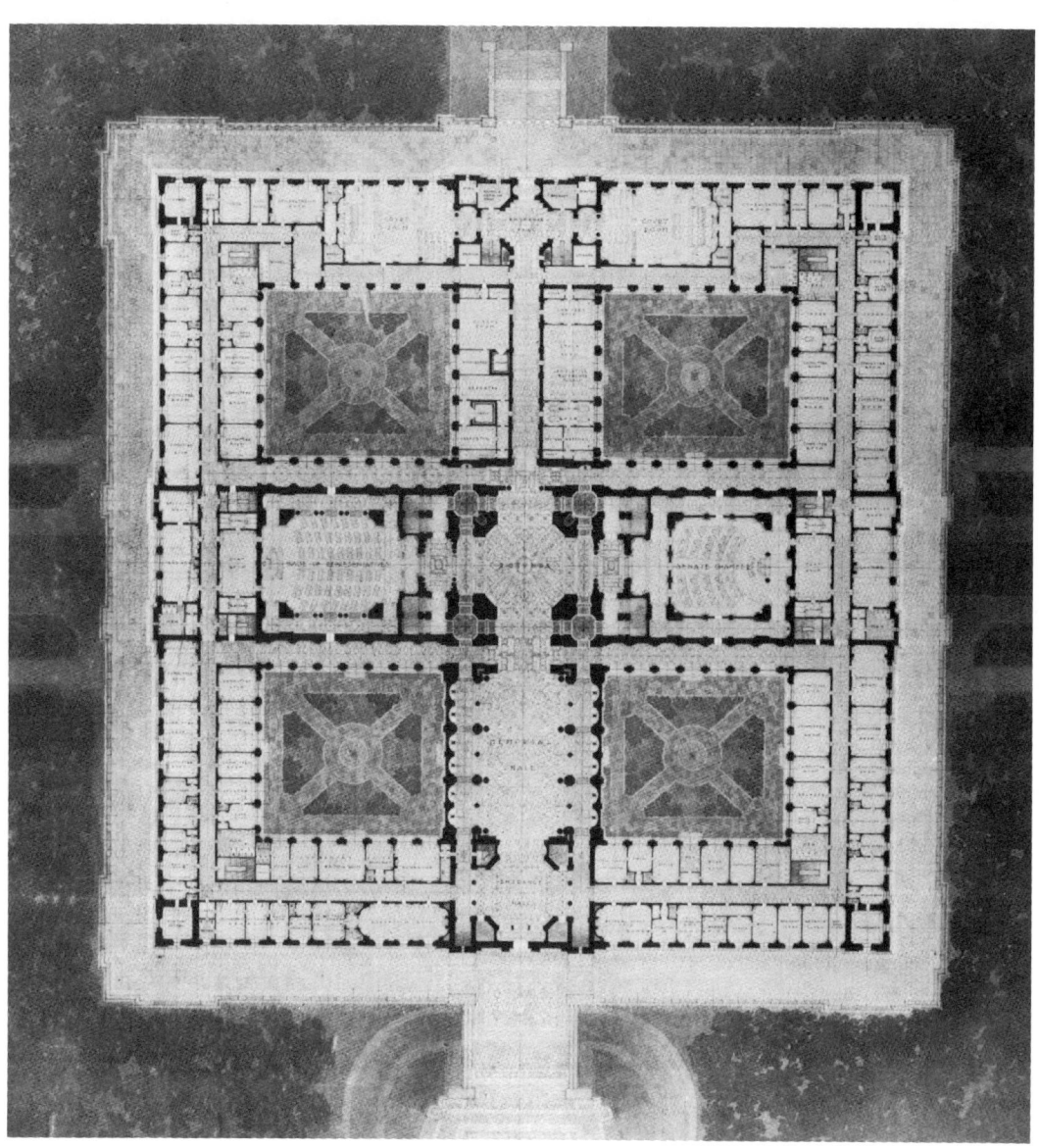

233
*Competition Drawing:*
*Nebraska State Capitol.*
*Bertram Grosvenor*
*Goodhue.*

234
*Nebraska State Capitol, Lincoln, Nebraska. Bertram Grosvenor Goodhue, 1916–24. Exterior.*

235
*Indianapolis Public Library, Indianapolis, Indiana. Paul Cret, 1914. Exterior.*

The 1876 Centennial Exposition in Philadelphia gave a new direction to the development of the American house. It was in the pavilion erected by Japan that Americans saw Oriental architecture for the first time. The entire pavilion was authentically Japanese; its cedar timbers, black roofing tiles, and other materials were imported from Japan and assembled by native workmen, "as nicely put together as a piece of cabinet work," remarked a contemporary observer. Although it was two stories, the building was emphatically horizontal, with continuous latticework below, sliding wood panels above, and a low-hipped roof.

The Japanese pavilion in Philadelphia helped to stimulate a popular craze for things Japanese. At a deeper level its influence soon appeared in the American house in a predilection for the open plan, latticework, extended eaves, a craftsmanlike assembly of parts, and the integration of the building with its landscaped setting. In 1886 Edward S. Morse's comprehensive illustrated book, *Japanese Houses and Their Surroundings,* appeared in Boston. Then in 1893 the Columbian Exposition in Chicago produced a second pavilion erected by the Japanese government. Called the Ho-O-Den, it also was imported and assembled by Japanese workmen. In the following year in San Francisco a Japanese village was erected for the Midwinter International Exposition. These recurring oriental stimuli influenced American design well into the early years of the twentieth century.

America was predisposed to accept the constructivist esthetic of Japanese building. Beginning in 1840, aided by pattern books and the popularity of Andrew Jackson Downing's views, a skeletal Stick Style emerged, far more declaratory of wood structure than the board-and-batten-clad mode of Davis and Upjohn. Its most conspicuous feature was trim in the form of diagonal and cross bracing, whose patterns enlivened the sides of suburban villas. The Griswold House at Newport of 1863, designed by Hunt, is a well-developed example; another is the Cram House at nearby Middletown, designed in 1871 by Dudley Newton. And at the Centennial several of the state pavilions, enlargements of domestic prototypes, proclaimed the cresting of the Stick Style.

It was also at the Philadelphia exposition that the American public had its first glimpse of the so-called "Queen Anne" Style, in two houses built by the English government for its officials and staff. Both buildings (in reality modest versions of Elizabethan-style manor houses made popular by Richard Norman Shaw in the late sixties in England) were two-storied, half-timbered, stucco panelled, and surmounted by steep roofs with cross gables and prominent chimneys. They presented a seductive image for American domestic architecture, justifiable on practical grounds and serving as mythic symbols of shelter and ancestry. Professional critics were enthusiastic on both counts about these "specimens of modern cottage architecture in England" and urged immediate adoption. The informality of the Queen Anne Style suggested the wholesome countryside rather than the wicked city, which Americans have always shunned, and the style was soon assimilated into the stream of American development.

One particular feature of Shaw's Queen Anne was the combination of a central hall with a stairway and a fireplace, a feature that was freely adapted in American practice in the simplified shingled houses which soon replaced the Shavian model. Commonly the largest room in the house, this stair-and-living hall was joined to adjacent rooms by large openings made possible, in part, by frame construction and, in part, by the advantages of central heating in winter and the need for breezes in summer. Thus began the development of the open plan, which culminated in the houses of Frank Lloyd Wright in which his aim was, as he expressed it, "to eliminate the room as a box and the house as another by making all walls enclosing screens— the ceiling and floors and enclosing screens to flow into each other as one large enclosure of space . . . ."

*Queen Anne to Shingle Style*

All the early Queen Anne characteristics appeared a year before the Centennial in Richardson's Watts Sherman House at Newport, the first example of the style in America (236). Its assorted textures of materials and picturesque roof lines were set out to please and may well have been the work of his assistant Stanford White. (The later interior embellishments are definitely White's). The living hall, extending the full depth of the plan, predicted the openness to follow. Although terraces partially encircle the house, it is without the covered porches which soon became standard and, when provided with French doors, continued the flow of interior space into the garden. Another imminent modification, first seen in a house at Mount Desert, Maine, designed in 1879 by William Ralph Emerson, was the use of shingles to cover the walls as well as the roof. Shedding its overt historical detail and becoming uniform in surface and more open in plan, the Queen Anne was transformed into the Shingle Style.

Wholly different in character from the firm's later work but equal to it in quality are the Shingle Style buildings done by McKim, Mead and White at Newport in the 1880s. Their Isaac Bell House of 1883, an informal house with a bell-roofed turret and a corner bay window, is a fine example of the simplifications and pleasantries that connote this style (237, 238). Its plan is particularly successful. The

236
*Watts Sherman House,*
*Newport, Rhode Island.*
*H. H. Richardson, 1874–*
*75. Exterior. (Service*
*wing addition by Dudley*
*Newton.)*

extended fireplace alcove of the hall with a lowered ceiling and the elaborately carved and screened stairway next to it subdivide and furnish the room architecturally. All openings to adjacent rooms are generous, and the largest is provided with a pair of sliding doors in the manner of a Japanese house. The Orient is also suggested by the frequent use of latticed or spindled screens to modulate space. The Casino at Newport (1879–81), one of the firm's most original buildings, combines a row of Queen Anne shops along the street and a private tennis club behind, also with a bell-roofed turret. Its extensive porches (piazzas as they were then called) are screened by a haremlike fantasy of wooden grillwork just short of frivolous.

A measure of the unorthodoxy of the Shingle Style is the frequent casually angular treatment of plan, including irregularly shaped porches. The Casino at Narragansett Pier, Rhode Island (1881–84), by McKim, Mead and White, follows an extended Z-shaped plan. Linear arrangements were favored by Wilson Eyre in his suburban Philadelphia houses, such as the Richard Ashurst House at Overbrook (ca. 1885), with its meandering sequence of connected spaces that were one-room deep, affording cross-ventilation and light (239). Eyre complemented the contour of the ridge into which his stone-based house is set by the extended length and lowness of the structure and by a linear porch across the rear. Indeed, the asymmetrical massing of such designs are as much a part of their potent charm as the varied textures and ornamental profiles. Symmetry was rare.

237
*Isaac Bell House, New-
port, Rhode Island.
McKim, Mead and White,
1883. Exterior.*

238
*Isaac Bell House, New-
port, Rhode Island. Plan.*

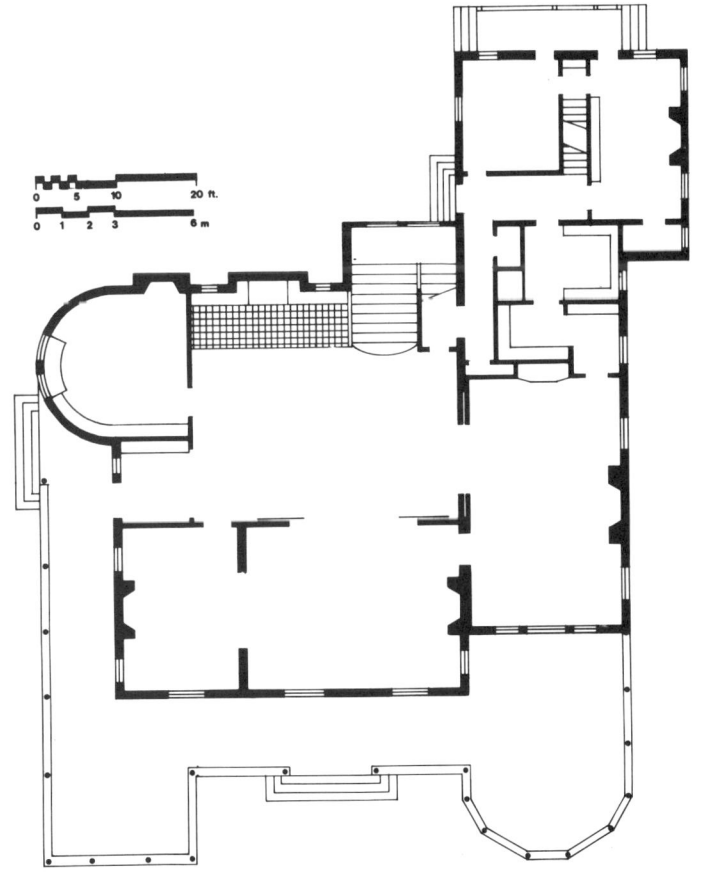

239
*Richard Ashurst House,*
*Overbook, Pennsylvania.*
*Wilson Eyre, circa 1885.*
*Exterior.*

240
*William Kent House,*
*Tuxedo Park, New York.*
*Bruce Price, 1885.*
*Exterior.*

241
*Mrs. F. M. Stoughton
House, Cambridge, Massachusetts. H. H. Richardson, 1882–83.
Exterior.*

Several houses by Bruce Price at Tuxedo Park, New York, such as the one for William Kent of 1885, are exceptions; their cruciform plans hint at Wright's later development of this idea (240).

The Shingle Style was the spiritual heir of the seventeenth-century New England house, and it was in New England, from Maine to Rhode Island, that its purest examples were raised. Several seaside houses by John Calvin Stevens in Maine revive the gambrel roof, a feature never seen in the Queen Anne. The sharp edges of these colonial houses were carried over into the Shingle Style to give a similar emphasis on volumetric enclosure, a quality that Vincent Scully has observed to be germane to twentieth-century modernism. The dominance of the roof in vernacular medieval building (which is what American building of the 1600s was) was strikingly translated by McKim, Mead and White in the William Low House of 1887 at Bristol, Rhode Island, where a single, unbroken gabled roof encompasses the entire house, including its porches. Richardson, too, simplified his designs; in the few years that separate the Sherman House and the Stoughton House in Cambridge, Massachusetts (1882–83), one observes the change to a lower, simpler massing and the uniformity of the shingle skin for wall and roof (241).

The 1880s witnessed a revived interest in the American past. Some architects, Robert Peabody of Boston for one, regarded current trends as a legitimate development of colonial architecture, and this view found support in the designs of Arthur Little and in some of those of McKim, who as early as 1872 had done a "Colonial" interior for an eighteenth-century Newport house. But the results of these antiquarian tendencies were quite free from pedantry; at most a classicized wooden support might faintly resemble a column or a spindle a Georgian baluster. This later Queen Anne, widely popular across America—as the Shingle Style was not—was deplored by the critic Montgomery Schuyler, who viewed its "emancipation from all restraints" as corrupting. The most audacious specimens, mixing mansarded and Victorian Gothic strains with "free classic," were the work of the prolific Newsom brothers, Samuel and Joseph, in California. Their wholly original detailing—"bizzare" was Charles Locke Eastlake's word for the style named after (and disavowed by) him—is epitomized in the Carson House at Eureka (1884–86). In southern California the Reid brothers, James and Merritt, concocted, with only slightly less exuberance, a giant Queen Anne gazebo for the Hotel del Coronado (1886–88) across the bay from San Diego.

**Wright and the Prairie House**

In the spring of 1887 a youth of nineteen left Madison, Wisconsin, for Chicago, determined to become an architect; his name was Frank Lloyd Wright.[1] His first job was as apprentice draftsman to Joseph Lyman Silsbee, who had recently arrived from Syracuse, bringing the Shingle Style to the Midwest with him. Before the year's end Wright had left Silsbee for Adler and Sullivan, a momentous move because the following years were to give him the only architectural education he ever had, with Louis Sullivan acting as his informal teacher.[2] Then in 1893 Wright was dismissed by Sullivan for doing outside work, his "bootlegged" houses as he called them.

Two of Wright's early houses, his own house in Oak Park, Illinois (1889), and the W. H. Winslow House in River Forest (1893), illustrate the influence of Silsbee and Sullivan, respectively. His own house, with its open plan and inglenook, its steeply gabled roof and row of casements, recalls the Eastern Shingle Style. Wright added a studio in 1895, a remarkable design wholly different from the house to which it is attached. One sees Wright forging a personal style, favoring a lower profile, deeply shadowed elements, and blocky geometry, a contrast to the taut and angular house that rises above it.

In the Winslow House there is much that came from Sullivan. Its facade is a symmetrical boxlike enclosure of orange glazed brick. The effect is monumental and massive and utterly unlike the asymmetrical domesticity of the Shingle Style (242). Above the brick runs a deeply molded dark brown terra-cotta frieze, setting the height of the second-story windows. The low-hipped roof is capped by the horizontal mass of the chimney, reinforcing the multiple horizontals that begin with the water-table base. The white limestone panel framing the doorway and adjacent windows is bordered with an

242
*W. H. Winslow House,*
*River Forest, Illinois.*
*Frank Lloyd Wright,*
*1893. Exterior.*

intaglio band repeating the motif (perhaps designed by Wright himself) of Sullivan's 1892 Wainwright tomb in St. Louis.

The entrance hall of the Winslow House continues the symmetry of the facade with a formal fireplace and inglenook, screened from the passage by a Sullivanesque arcade in wood. Though reminiscent of earlier stair-living halls, the effect is far more ceremonial, and Wright has hidden the stair from view, attaching it to one side of the chimney mass. The central chimney acts as a pivot for the encircling elements of the plan in much the same way as the chimney of the seventeenth-century New England house did. In the rear the boxlike form is broken open by the dining room bay that projects boldly beyond it, a screened service porch that juts from one corner, and a side terrace that is subtracted from the implied rectangular form; adding to these disruptions, which suggest an unfolding from within and an incipient dynamism in Wright's approach, is a polygonal stair-tower.

In 1900 Wright produced four designs that established the principles of the Prairie house, which gave its name to Wright's first mature period. Two of the designs, never executed, were commissioned by the *Ladies' Home Journal* and published the following year; the first was entitled "A Home in a Prairie Town." The Bradley and the Hickox houses are in Kankakee, Illinois. All four are decisively cruciform in plan, and major first-floor rooms are interconnected spatially but not in the loose manner of Shingle Style houses. The house for Warren Hickox exemplifies the principles of the Prairie house (243). The short axis is fixed by the masonry core of the fireplace and extends outside to an ample terrace as wide as the

243
*Warren Hickox House,
Kankakee, Illinois. Frank
Lloyd Wright, 1900.
Exterior.*

length of the living room. A long axis is formed by the polygonal alcoves for a dining room and a library, which project from the short ends of the living room. The alcoves are separated from the living room by spur walls, embryonic piers that were to become basic to Wright's structural rhythms. Both the dining room and library are banded with a continuous row of leaded casement windows, which act as "light screens" and reinforce the horizontal motifs of the exterior. The combination of dark wood trim with light-colored stucco suggests the Japanese post-and-panel module, although it may be seen as a variant of Queen Anne half-timbering or even a residual feature of the Stick Style. The gabled roofs likewise suggest Japanese, medieval, or American prototypes. Whatever his sources (and he usually denied all and any), Wright established his own esthetic. More significantly, he introduced a dual theme of continuous space and integrated structure, to be developed further in the following years.

With his engaging manner and articulate convictions, Wright found it easy to secure clients for his radical houses, most of them of modest scale but having a compactness and deceptive simplicity that affords a sense of generous space in a limited area. Clarity and consistency are ensured by Wright's innate sense of order. Exteriors are reduced essentially to one material, and ornament—with the exception of the decorative leading of the windows, which takes the place of curtains—is rare. Simple banding is often used inside and out. Wright extolled the beauty of machine-made materials, and his use of them recalls the Japanese "severe simplicity of form and beautiful materials left clean for their own sake." Notwithstanding his admitted admiration for Japanese domestic architecture, Wright

cautioned C. R. Ashbee, whom he had asked to write the introduction
to an edition of his work, that it would be wrong to say that he had
adopted Japanese forms.[3] This volume, published by the German
Wasmuth Press in 1911, had been preceded the year before by
another Wasmuth publication of Wright's work, a sumptuous folio
of one hundred plates of drawings. These two publications accorded
Wright his first formal recognition. They also influenced a generation
of European architects.

The evaluation of Wright's position in the history of architecture
was not left by him entirely to others; Wright participated to the
full in this self-satisfying task. He saw Richardson, Root, and Sullivan as his predecessors in the search for an "organic architecture."
This concept, first presented in 1908, was defined in a later essay of
1914 as "an architecture that *develops* from within outward in harmony with the conditions of its being as distinguished from one that
is *applied* from without." Relations of form and function, which
Wright saw as one, were to be learned from Nature's pertinent object
lessons, the basis for design. This method did not ensure a beautiful
building, Wright admitted, but it did have an integrity that the
architecture of taste and erudition, namely that of the Renaissance
and Baroque, wholly lacked. Thus he conceived his Prairie houses as
metaphors for moral goodness and honesty—precisely those ethical
qualities sought by Pugin and Morris.

The Prairie houses show no consistent development as a series. A
late example, the J. K. Ingalls House in Oak Park of 1909, is as
resolutely symmetrical as the facade of the Winslow House of 1893.
Wright interchanged three roof types in the Prairie houses: the
gabled roof was used in the Kankakee houses; the low-pitched, hipped
roof, presenting an even ridge against the sky or assembled in pyramidal group, was used in the Winslow stable; and the flat roof was
proposed in his third design for the *Ladies' Home Journal* in 1906
and used in the Mrs. Thomas Gale House in Oak Park (1909), the
most cubistic of all his early designs.

The compact, elementary cruciform plan of the Hickox House was
succeeded in 1901 by the extended cruciform of the Ward Willits
House in Highland Park (244, 245). Here the forward, two-story
pavilion for the living room (with its own high-waisted terrace) on
the first story and the master bedroom on the second is flanked by
the movement and tension of the cross-axis, whose comparatively
open wings of one story stretch out for more than a hundred feet.
The plan is an enlargement of Wright's second *Ladies' Home Journal*
design. Especially effective is the pinwheel motif of the rotated fireplaces with their space-modulating screens.

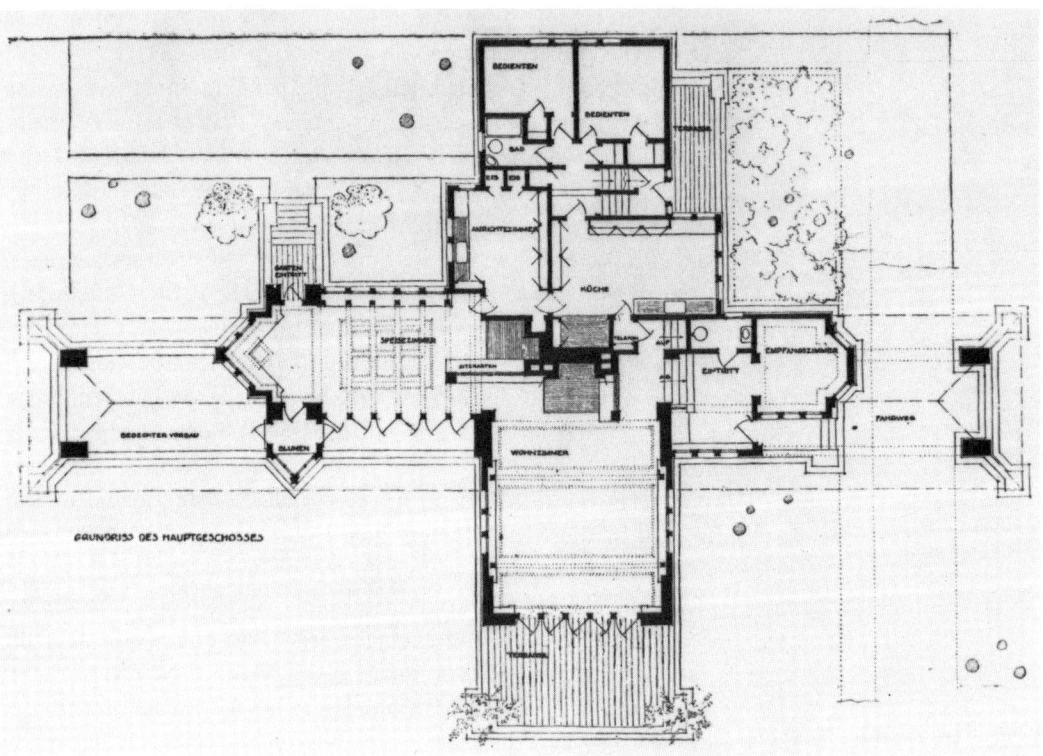

244
*Ward Willits House,
Highland Park, Illinois.
Frank Lloyd Wright,
1901. Exterior.*

245
*Ward Willits House,
Highland Park, Illinois.
Plan.*

246
*Darwin D. Martin House,
Buffalo, New York. Frank
Lloyd Wright, 1904. Plan.*

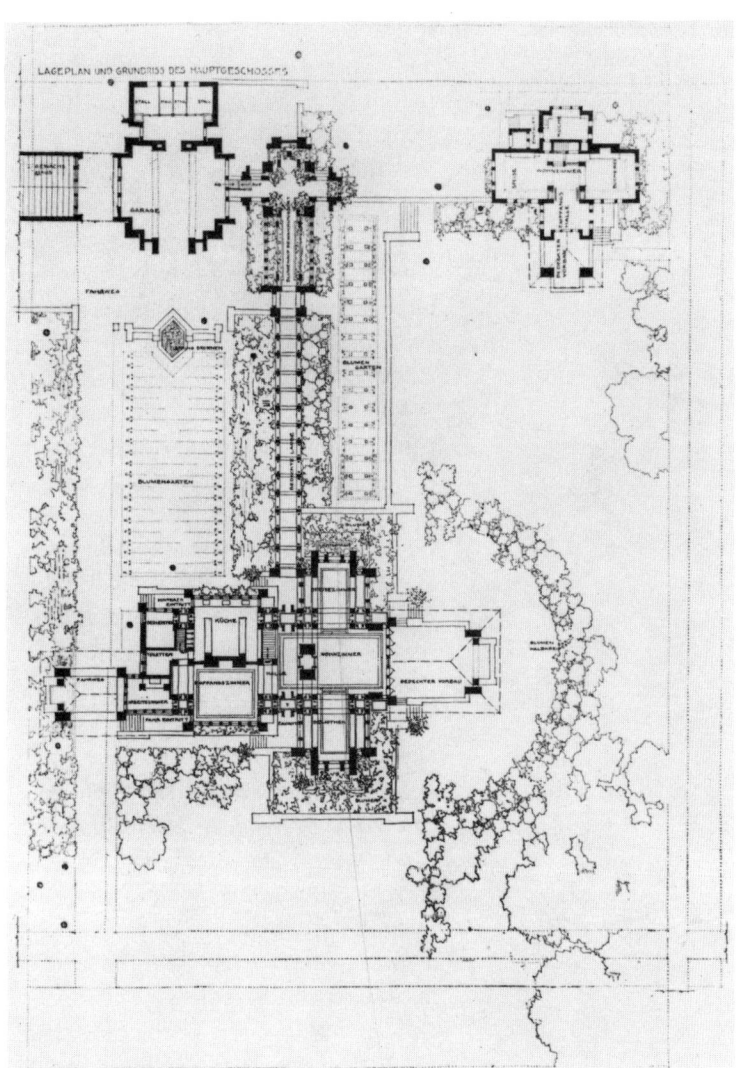

The Darwin D. Martin House in Buffalo of 1904 is similarly open and expansive (246). It is also the most ceremonial and the most radical of all Wright's houses: here there are no walls, only piers. Wright arranged them on the flat site to define spatial boundaries and the several axes of the composition, in a way reminiscent of Stonehenge. Space became fluid, and yet the design reveals restraint and geometry as well. Wright captured that "fragrance of rhythm" which eluded Sullivan, who had a relatively inert conception of the pier. Even the heating system is incorporated into the sets of quadruple piers that also serve to frame the bookcases. Form, space, function, and structure have merged into one.

The Chicago suburb of Riverside, laid out by Olmsted in 1869, contains the most extensive of Wright's Prairie houses and, in his opinion, the most successful: the Avery Coonley House of 1908 (247). Its plan is an elaboration of the centrifugal design for the Hillside School of 1902 at Spring Green, Wisconsin. All major rooms are on a second level above grade to provide a balconylike perspective of the surrounding gardens and a river beyond. The house and its setting became one. Jens Jensen, whose insistence on using native plants of the prairie complemented Wright's thoughts about the self-sufficiency of the Midwest, was responsible for the landscaping. To experience the grandeur of this villa by encircling its fretted periphery may suggest that Wright consciously sought picturesque effects. But the impression is false; rather he conceived the Coonley design as an intense, sculptured order of volumes whose various axes project strongly outward, relating to the flat site. A service road skirting the major block of the house passes underneath two projecting wings. This conscious threading of the warp and woof of the plan is restated in the rectilinear stucco decoration of the upper story, which is enlivened with insets of colored square tile.[4]

Equal to the Coonley House but of completely different character—blunt rather than gracious—is the house built for Frederick C. Robie in Chicago in 1909 (248). Perhaps the intensity of the city and the marginal site conspired to shape its aggressive, overscaled forms. Wright, curbed from developing a cruciform scheme, arranged two parallel but dislocated masses, one for living and dining, the other for kitchen and servant quarters. He emphasized the primary axis by stressing horizontal layers in the elevation: the parapets of red brick with their stone copings, the extended series of windows, and the dramatic cantilevers of the low-hipped roof, which reach far beyond the central chimney mass from which they seemingly originate. In its fortresslike security, the Robie House is a miniature

247
*Avery Coonley House,*
*Riverside, Illinois. Frank*
*Lloyd Wright, 1908.*
*Exterior.*

248
*Frederick C. Robie House,*
*Chicago, Illinois. Frank*
*Lloyd Wright, 1909.*
*Exterior.*

Mycenae, to be breached only by discovering the hidden, shadowed entrance located at the rear. The circuitous path with triple turns leads across the entrance hall and up a folded stair to the living room hearth in the very center of the house. Living room and dining room are brought into one flowing space by a continuous ceiling passing through the separate fireplace flues and by a dozen French windows arrayed like an extended Japanese screen across the entire front of the house.

Both poet and pragmatist shaped the interiors of the Robie House. Wright's concern for practicality is apparent. Heating is provided by recessed radiators under every window and hot water pipes set into the floor beneath the row of window-doorways leading to the south balcony. Electric lights, controlled by dimmers, are concealed behind oak grilles and frosted glass in the ceiling strips. Fresh air is brought through the eaves to ventilate the low attic and then exhausted through an adjacent chimney. And the provision of the first attached garage, here an ample three-car one, makes the Robie House a landmark in the history of the American house.

Not the least of Wright's concerns was the furnishing of his houses. Disdainful of miscellaneous possessions and crude, mission-style furniture, he was pleased when clients allowed him to design appropriate furniture, which was almost always severe and angular with few concessions to comfort. Wright was at his best in dining rooms, where the ceremony of the family meal and the opportunity for a built-in sideboard could reinforce his architectonic scheme. The Robie House dining room is a prime example: Six high-backed chairs are placed around a thick slab of oak supported by four miniature plinths, each topped by a fragile lantern shading an electric light (249).

Wright's concepts of space and structure were applied to buildings other than houses with equal success; for example, the Larkin Company Administration Building in Buffalo (1903) and Unity Temple in Oak Park (1906) (250, 251). These differ significantly from the Prairie houses because they are rigidly symmetrical in plan and largely opaque in exterior form; consequently interior spaces are more static. Yet, despite that, they are no less open. The dissimilar problems of an office building and a church have been solved in similar ways: both have introverted, skylit interiors with peripheral balconies served by enclosed stairs within opaque pylons at the outer corners of the composition. The result is an intense focus within to the exclusion of the outside world, a sense of concentration and mysterious power. The Larkin Building is as much a sanctuary for work as Unity Temple is for worship.

249
Frederick C. Robie House,
Chicago, Illinois. Dining
room.

250
*Larkin Building, Buffalo,*
*New York. Frank Lloyd*
*Wright, 1903. Interior.*

251
*Unity Temple, Oak Park,*
*Illinois. Frank Lloyd*
*Wright, 1906. Exterior.*

*Wright's Followers*

Among the assistants in Wright's studio who subsequently became independent architects were Walter Burley Griffin, Marion Mahony (later Griffin's wife), and William E. Drummond. All three copied their master's manner with personal variations instead of developing their own formal language from his principles as he would have wished. Other Midwest architects who were never Wright's employees but shared the progressive ambience of Chicago, such as George Maher, William Gray Purcell, and George Grant Elmslie, drew heavily on Wrightian models as well as on those of Sullivan, who had been on his own since the end of his partnership with Adler in 1895. Sullivan continued to practice, but at a drastically lessened pace. His work also contributed to what Wright labelled in 1908 a "New School of the Middle West." Sullivan's few house designs are overshadowed by several elegant, highly decorative banks in small Midwestern towns. Wright, however, remained the fountainhead of the Prairie School. After 1909, when Wright closed his Oak Park studio and left for Europe, the Prairie School group, released from his dominating presence, had its most flourishing years.[5] Then it went down before the demand for revivalism. Ironically, the change of taste was abetted by those very women's magazines that had earlier supported the Arts and Crafts Movement and the Prairie house.

*Bay Area Architects*

The years 1890 through 1915 saw a similar burst of creative activity in domestic architecture on the West Coast. In Northern California this was the result of the arrival of four architects in the Bay Area: Ernest Coxhead, Bernard Maybeck, Willis Polk, and John Galen Howard. These men were not amateurs. Maybeck and Howard had attended the Ecole des Beaux-Arts, and Howard had experience in the offices of Richardson and McKim, Mead and White. Coxhead, an Englishman, had been well trained in London. Polk had worked for Van Brunt and Howe in Kansas City and for A. Page Brown in New York; he came to San Francisco with Brown, who moved his office there in 1889.

The informality of California and its climate combined with an aspiring but undogmatic clientele to produce a distinctive Bay Area tradition, with strains of the imported Queen Anne and Shingle styles modified by local materials and craftsmanship. The engaging work of the Bay Area, however, was neither centered on any intellectual position nor articulated by any single spokesman.[6]

The work of Coxhead, although overshadowed by Maybeck's reputation, is of substantial interest. His commissions were divided between Anglican churches and residences, and in both he used his favorite siding material, shingles. The rounded shapes of St. John's

252
*Porter House and Waybur House, San Francisco, California. Ernest Coxhead, 1904 and 1902. Exterior. © Morley Baer, from* Bay Area Houses.

Episcopal Church in Monterey (1891) suggest an Expressionist design, in contrast to his residential work, which commonly exhibits knowledge of English manor houses and historical detail. In San Francisco the Waybur House of 1902 and the adjacent Porter House of 1904 suggest Norman Shaw's London town houses on the Chelsea embankment and his turn toward Neo-Georgian (252).

Simplicity and sophistication, juxtaposed in Coxhead's designs, are more likely to be found separately in Maybeck's. His capability in the grand manner is evident in his Neo-Baroque Palace of Fine Arts for the Panama-Pacific International Exposition held in San Francisco in 1915, which contrasts with his numerous informal redwood houses in Berkeley across the bay. In the construction of Maybeck's houses, corbels, struts, and trusses common in medieval timberwork are reduced to domestic scale and are poised on posts evenly distributed on a modular plan. The effect is at times astonishingly Japanese. The early Laura Hall House in Berkeley (1896), Alpine Gothic in its exterior silhouette with a sensitively constructed and exposed redwood frame inside, is a good example of his work. Other houses of similar size and construction are the Boke (1902), the Flagg-Ransome (1912), and the Mathewson (1916), all in Berkeley (253). Alcoves and window bays and sometimes sliding doors assist in dividing a basically open plan into one of diverse spatial character, often augmented by enclosed gardens and pergola-covered terraces.

253
George H. Boke House,
Berkeley, California. Ber-
nard Maybeck, 1902.
Exterior.

254
First Church of Christ,
Scientist, Berkeley, California. Bernard Maybeck,
1910. Exterior.

Maybeck's architecture was at ease in the suburban hills of Berkeley, but less so in San Francisco. Whether to assert itself in a competitive urban setting or to indulge a wealthy client, the Leon Roos town house (1909, additions 1926) is aggressively stylistic; it displays Maybeck's romantic medievalism almost to excess. Tudor motifs, notably the bold half-timbered effect of dark painted wood and light stucco panels, are heightened by the heavily scaled, vaguely Gothic carving of the balustrade and roof brackets. Maybeck's personalized historicism, not to say eccentricity, is more fully expressed in what many consider his masterpiece, the First Church of Christ, Scientist, in Berkeley (1910, enlarged 1928). Here his uninhibited use of exposed concrete, asbestos siding, and factory windows, his free mixture of Oriental, classical, Romanesque, and Gothic motifs all combine to produce one of the most unusual monuments in America (254). That it defies the historian's classification would delight the mischievous Maybeck.

Willis Polk's sympathies were attuned more to cosmopolitan life than to suburbia and the moral values of the simple house. An early example of his work is the Batten House in San Francisco (1891), a mixture of Queen Anne and Colonial Revival with charming irregularities of plan and facade. His Bourn mansion in the same city (1894) is handsomely Georgian but hardly academic. Polk's urbanity was continued in suburban Belvedere in the Rey House (1893), which states his version of the Monterey Peninsula Style with arched stucco walls, cantilevered wooden balconies, and red-tiled roof. Polk was versatile, stylish, and unpredictable—a verdict he would readily endorse. As further proof of his unpredictability there is that remarkable forerunner of the glass curtain wall, the Hallidie Building in San Francisco (1917).

The opportunity to design buildings for the University of California brought John Galen Howard to Berkeley. The Hearst Mines Building of 1907 illustrates his eclectic approach; it was imaginatively Mediterranean Renaissance with a metal-framed interior court with skylight domes. One of Howard's employees—and Maybeck's too—was Julia Morgan, an engineering graduate of the university who went on to Paris to study at the Ecole, the first woman to do so. Like Howard, her loyalties were divided between the local tradition in wood, as seen in her residentially scaled St. John's Presbyterian Church in Berkeley (1910), and a free eclecticism, as seen in W. R. Hearst's San Simeon (begun in 1919), her most well-known (if not her best) work.

*The Bungalows of*
*Greene and Greene*

The term bungalow, a corruption of a Hindustani word meaning "of Bengal," came to be applied in the early twentieth century to almost any kind of single-story house with a low sloping roof, which, more often than not, extended to form a porch or veranda. According to a popular book on the subject, however, a house of more than one story could not be a true bungalow but might be "built along bungalow lines." The bungalow was valued for its suitability in a warm climate and also for its creative possibilities. Divisions between inside and out could be minimized, rooms could open freely into one another, generous eaves would protect against the sun, and natural materials and colors would blend into the landscape—advantages not so very different from those possessed by the shingled houses of New England or the cottages advocated by Andrew Jackson Downing. Although they were built from coast to coast, bungalows were identified particularly with southern California. Some Los Angeles firms offered sets of working drawings for as little as five dollars, but at the other end of the scale were the bungalows of the brothers Charles Sumner and Henry Mather Greene. Their most famous bungalow in its day—it has been much altered—was the Bandini bungalow of 1903 at Pasadena. Built around a court, it was the first of the so-called patio bungalows.

All the houses of the Greene brothers are "built along bungalow lines." As open in plan as any, they are remarkable for their gentleness and elegance and extraordinary craftsmanship and sensitive use of materials—in the cobblestones and native plants of their settings no less than the wood of their structures. Two Pasadena houses, those for Robert C. Blacker (1907) and David B. Gamble (1909), and one at Ojai for Charles M. Pratt (1909), with their ample budgets and sites, stand out as *chefs-d'oeuvres* (255, 256). More modest commissions, however, such as the Crow House at Pasadena of 1909, are equally successful; perhaps their scale and modesty are more in keeping with the craftsman esthetic.

Without question, the monuments of the Arts and Crafts Movement in the United States were built by Greene and Greene. They conceived their houses as pieces of cabinetwork, extensions of the furniture they often designed. C. R. Ashbee, that most cosmopolitan follower of William Morris, recognized their genius; on one of his American visits he expressed greater sympathy for the Greenes' work than for Wright's. Like Wright, they came under the spell of Japan, most obviously in the Adelaide Tichenor House of 1904 in Long Beach. Japan was the land where carpentry was transformed into art. The articulated trellises and porches that embellish Greene and Greene houses can be seen as transformations of temple architecture.

255
*David B. Gamble House,*
*Pasadena, California.*
*Greene and Greene, 1909.*
*Exterior from garden.*

256
*David B. Gamble House,*
*Pasadena, California.*
*Plan.*

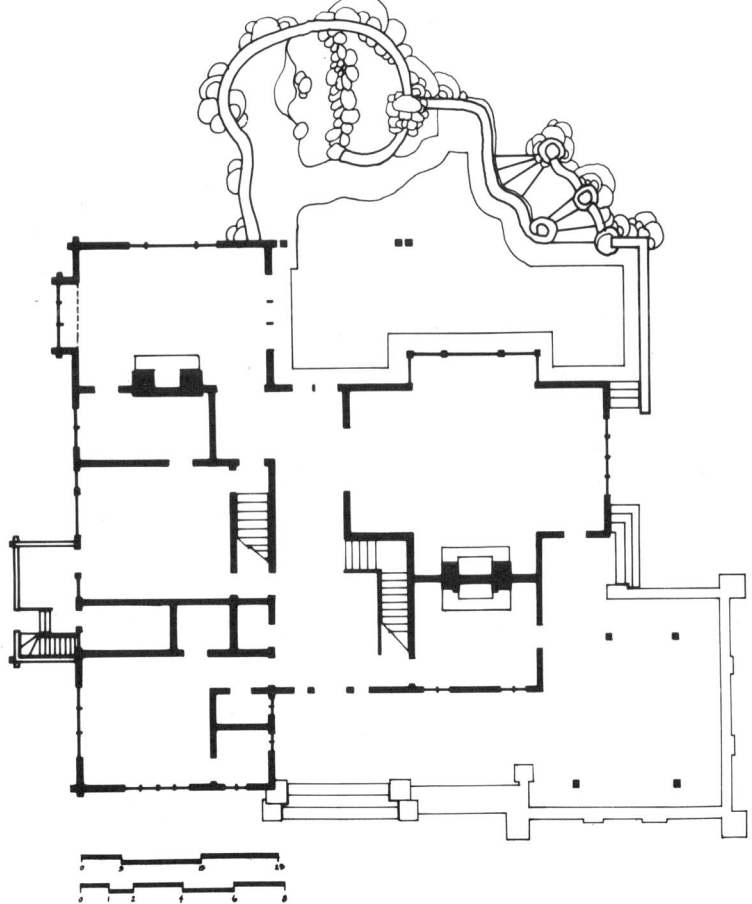

Comparison with Maybeck is inevitable. The Greenes' work, although perhaps intrinsically finer, is more limited in its range of expression and lacks the provocative quality of Maybeck's. But no greater serenity can be found in any other houses in the Western world.

*Irving Gill*

The houses of Irving Gill are very different in appearance from those of Greene and Greene and his Bay Area contemporaries. Abstractions of the California missions, their blocklike massing suggests the even earlier pueblos of the Southwest Indians, such as those at Taos, which he had visited and admired. Purity of shape and the reduction of every detail to its least obtrusive form make Gill America's first minimalist architect. This is somewhat unexpected. His limited apprenticeships prior to his arrival in San Diego in 1893 included a year or so with Adler and Sullivan in Chicago. His early work gave little hint of the novel simplicity that surfaced in 1907 in two works, the Homer Laughlin House in Los Angeles and the Melville Klauber House in San Diego. This abrupt change in style came with his use of a structural system of concrete and hollow tile and appropriately simple details both outside and in, the latter from a conscious desire for a sanitary, labor-saving house. Gill's wide range of practical devices—built-in storage walls, skylighted bathrooms, a central vacuum-cleaning system, even an automatic car-washing device in the garage—would appeal to the American consumer today. By comparison Le Corbusier's house as a machine-for-living-in is a tardy concept. Gill's concern for structural economy and functional efficiency, his interest in low-cost housing, and his belief in the social responsibility of the architect make him akin to the German avant-garde of the 1920s. Even more striking is the similarity of his stark facades to Adolf Loos's Steiner House of 1910 in Vienna. It was Loos who, in a famous pamphlet written in 1908, proclaimed that "the evolution of culture marches with the elimination of ornament from useful objects." Although he was not given to declamatory statement, Gill's work was no less prophetic.

The Walter L. Dodge House in Los Angeles (1914–16) was Gill's masterpiece (257). Its extended shape, related to its generous site by balconies, terraces, and garden walks, suggests a parallel with Wright's Coonley House, although Gill's interior spatial planning was never as dynamic as Wright's. The basic rectangular form was hollowed out on the southeast by a court open to the sky but walled with arched openings as a room, foretelling the similar feature in Le Corbusier's Villa Savoye of 1929. These "green rooms," as Gill

257
*Walter L. Dodge House,*
*Los Angeles, California.*
*Irving Gill, 1914–16.*
*Garden facade.*

called them, often with pergolas supported by Tuscan columns, are frequent in his work. The garden facade of the Dodge House, with its seamless unity of creamy white walls yielding to an asymmetrical arrangement of frameless windows but betraying no sign of the hidden roof, conveyed a tranquil but not solemn classicism. Gill should have had more influence on twentieth-century architecture, but his productive years, like those of other progressive architects in California, and many in the Midwest as well, were ended by the First World War.

The conception of the skyscraper, wholly American bred, fascinated the avant-garde architects of Europe. To them it symbolized the modern world of the machine. Auguste Perret conceived a visionary city of towers linked by a ten-story-high roadway. The Italian Futurists, Antonio Sant'Elia and Mario Chiattone, sketched designs that suggested giant pieces of machinery. Equally dramatic are the designs of the Russian Constructivists, particularly Eliezer Lissitzky, whose daringly cantilevered skyscrapers still belong to future worlds. In his Expressionist phase Mies van der Rohe made two designs for all-glass skyscrapers with irregular plans but absolute uniformity in elevation. And the archpropagandist Le Corbusier shocked Parisians with his Plan Voisin of 1925, which replaced the venerable Marais quarter with a marching rhythm of sixty-storied towers openly spaced in a parklike landscape. Successive books by architects of the twenties, Eric Mendelsohn (1926), Richard Neutra (1927), and Bruno Taut (1929), gave a prominent place to the American skyscraper, its form and construction, and extolled it as an image of the future.

It is therefore not surprising that of the 260 designs submitted in the competition for a tall office building for the *Chicago Tribune* held in 1922 no less than 100 should have come from Europe. The entries from Germany and Holland were particularly numerous and, when compared with the American submissions, proved the advanced esthetics of these two countries, where tall buildings had never been built. But it was the half-modern entry of the Finn Eliel Saarinen, which placed second, that earned the greatest praise from American critics and architects, including Louis Sullivan, who wrote an article on it (258).[1] Eliel Saarinen's design influenced American skyscrapers of the twenties and thirties, and the generally more radical character found in other foreign architects' submissions had its belated impact in succeeding decades. It is not too much to say that it was Europe that supplied answers to the esthetic problem of the American skyscraper.

In contrast to the Neo-Gothic design (259) by Howells and Hood that took first prize and was executed as the Tribune Tower, Saarinen's proposal was not overtly based on any recognizable historical style. What made it immediately appealing were its fluent vertical lines, its rhythmic setbacks faintly suggestive of a medieval tower, and the softening effect of its ornament and sculpture. Both of the winning architects paid tribute to Saarinen's design by adapting it in later works: Raymond Hood in his American Radiator Building (1924) and John Mead Howells in his Panhellenic Hotel (1927–30), both in New York.

258
*Competition Drawing,*
*Chicago Tribune Tower.*
*Eliel Saarinen, 1922.*

*259*
*Tribune Tower, Chicago,*
*Illinois. Howells and*
*Hood, 1922. Exterior.*

260
*Christ Lutheran Church,
Minneapolis, Minnesota.
Eliel Saarinen, 1949–50.
Interior.*

261
*Crow Island School, Win-
netka, Illinois. Eliel Saarinen, 1939–40. Exterior.*

Saarinen's near-success in the *Chicago Tribune* competition led to his settlement in America. In 1924 he was appointed visiting professor of architecture at the University of Michigan, where one of his students was a son of George G. Booth, publisher of the *Detroit News*. The young Booth introduced him to his father, who commissioned Saarinen to design a series of educational buildings. The first was a boys' school in 1925, and the last was a museum and library in 1940 on the Booth estate, called Cranbrook, in Bloomfield Hills, Michigan. From 1932 until his death in 1950, Saarinen was president of the Cranbrook Academy of Art, for which the museum and library were built. Saarinen's philosophy of design was craft oriented—he admired the traditional materials of wood, brick, and stone and the craftsmanship they demand—and his Cranbrook buildings are eclectic in style, recalling the early twentieth-century work of such architects as Berlage, Olbrich, Hoffmann, and Behrens, as well as the Scandinavian cultural renaissance in which he himself participated during his earlier years in Finland.

Admittedly derivative, Saarinen's work is always sensitive. His Tabernacle Church in Columbus, Indiana (1940), and Christ Lutheran Church in Minneapolis, Minnesota (1949–50), are among the handsomest American churches of the century (260). However, the elementary school in Winnetka, Illinois, Crow Island School, which he designed in 1939, is his most significant work, even though it lacks his usual decorative details; its scale and the individualized learning spaces attest to his human approach to design (261). A very different commission was the Smithsonian Gallery of Art, to face the Mall in Washington, D.C. This unexecuted project of 1939, designed in collaboration with his son Eero, is monumental, as was required, yet still poetic. That its sculptural massing should recall Willem Dudok's buildings in Holland or Gropius's proposed Academy of Philosophy in Erlangen of 1924 shows how lasting was the effect that the Dutch de Stijl esthetic had on architecture.

*Art Deco*

The influence of Joseph Hoffmann and the Wiener Werkstätte, which he founded in 1903, was very potent in the twenties. The Wiener Werkstätte is the primary source of the so-called Art Deco Style. Other Viennese architects, Otto Wagner and Joseph Maria Olbrich, had prepared the way in their Secessionist Movement, a revolt against the Academy and a turning away from Art Nouveau as well. Hoffman's work marked an important step forward in twentieth-century art. He may have lamented the use of the machine, but his furniture and other designs produced by traditional handicraft methods were startlingly geometric in form; they combined simplicity

*262*
*New York Telephone*
*(Barclay-Vesey) Building,*
*New York City. Mc-*
*Kenzie, Voorhees and*
*Gmelin, 1923–26. Exte-*
*rior detail.*

with low-relief or linear ornament and were frankly decorative and modish as well as expensive. New Yorkers came to know the Wiener Werkstätte at firsthand when it opened a showroom there in 1919 under the management of Austrian-born Joseph Urban, who was later an architect of Art Deco buildings in Manhattan. The most telling instances of its wide influence were the decorative exhibits and pavilions of the Paris Exposition Internationale des Arts Décoratifs et Industriels Modernes of 1925, from which the popular style of the twenties took its name.

Paris, which initiated the department store in the nineteenth century, lent its new style to the 1928 Bullock's Wilshire Store in Los Angeles by John and Donald B. Parkinson. The exterior, sheathed in tan terra-cotta with decorative spandrels in copper, is marked by a distinguished tower intended to cap a ten-story block that was never completed. The store's elegant interiors, enhanced by the work of several muralists and designers, bear witness to the contribution of the artist and craftsman to Art Deco's success.

Curiously and not altogether appropriately, this style of surface ornament and rich materials, so effective in interior design and objects of luxury, was applied to the outside of giant skyscrapers. The small scale characteristic of Art Deco was hardly suited to the bulk and economic purpose of the skyscraper; yet Art Deco ornament satisfied a certain self-conscious urban taste for modernity, albeit much of it is lost to the distant eye. On close inspection decorative spandrels and other embellishments come into view. Two New York examples are the exotic animals and plants carved on the New York Telephone (Barclay-Vesey) Building (262) by McKenzie, Voorhees and Gmelin (1923–26) and a lively cubist pattern of red and black bricks on the spandrels of the Daily News Building by Raymond Hood (1929–30). Art Deco ornament was more appropriate in entrance portals and elevator lobbies, where the display of fancy metalwork, colored marbles, and contrasting wood veneers could be fully appreciated. Curvilinear patterns appear alongside zigzag motifs derived in part from the Expressionistic architecture of Holland and Germany and sometimes even from Mayan or Egyptian sources. Certainly the most exuberant Art Deco concoction is William Van Alen's crown for the Chrysler Building in New York (1928–30), which terminates in a needlelike spire rising from diminishing semicircles, each set with a radiating zigzag rhythm of triangular windows (263). Recognizing that it was the design of its apex that gave a skyscraper a distinctive identity, Van Alen seized an opportunity that was resolutely ignored by the architects of the flat-topped office buildings of the succeeding decades.

263
*Chrysler Building, New
York City. William Van
Alen, 1928–30. Exterior.*

264
Zoning Envelope Diagrams, Hugh Ferriss.

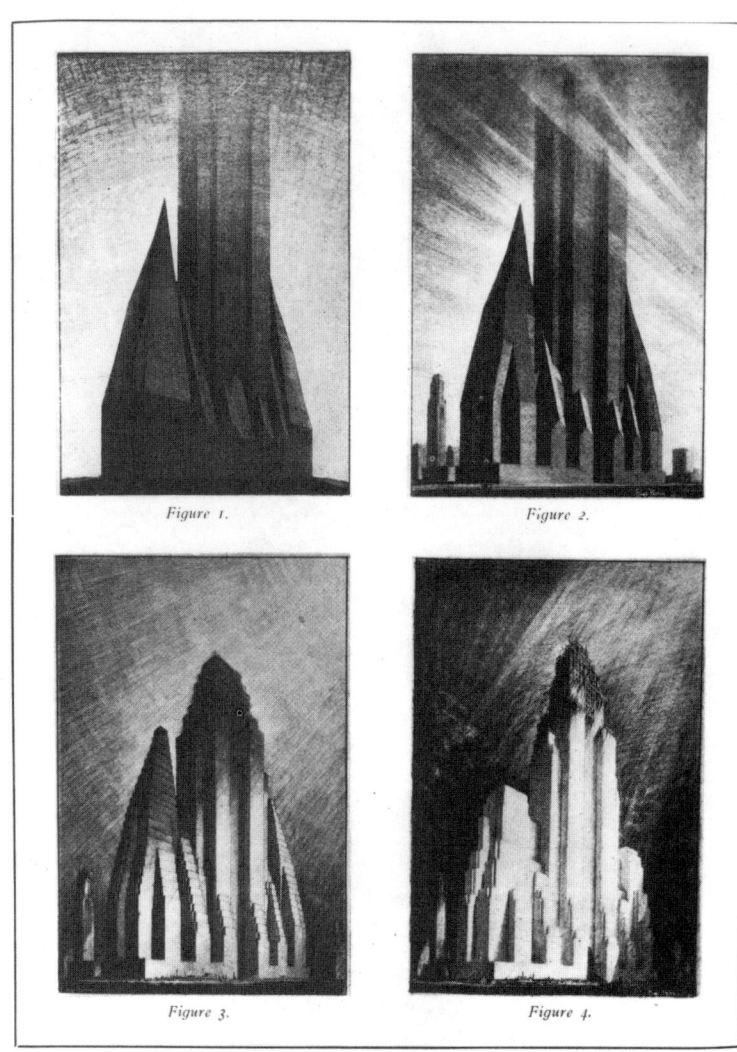

Figure 1.

Figure 2.

Figure 3.

Figure 4.

329

265
*Daily News Building,
New York City. Raymond
Hood, 1929–30. Exterior.*

*266*
*Rockefeller Center, New*
*York City. Raymond*
*Hood and others, 1932–*
*40. Aerial view.*

A far more important consideration in the design of the New York skyscraper than its decorative treatment was the necessity of conforming to the 1916 zoning regulations. Such a law need not have inhibited creativity. In a series of convincing renderings published in 1923, Hugh Ferriss showed how, starting with the overall zoning envelope, an evolving sequence of setbacks could result in a dramatic composition (264). A zigguratlike base and a lofty tower, as seen in the Barclay-Vesey Building and the Chrysler Building, became the usual formula.

In the Daily News Building, Raymond Hood chose a rectangular plan for the tower, giving it a slablike effect suggestive of Le Corbusier's skyscraper designs (265). A more emphatic slab is seen in the seventy-story RCA Building, which is the centerpiece of several skyscrapers constituting Rockefeller Center in New York City (266). This complex project (1928–34 and later) extending over three whole city blocks was fundamentally shaped by the city Zoning Resolution of 1916 and its amendments. With its generous provision of services and the amenities of urban life as well as light and air (and a high financial return), the RCA Building answered the vexing questions posed by the skyscraper at the beginning of the century. Perhaps a clue to its enduring success is to be found in the fact that lawyers and businessmen (including John D. Rockefeller, Jr.) sat with the architects and engineers on the design committee.

The essential form of the RCA Building was proposed by Raymond Hood. Its layered and staggered blanks reflect the interior plan and function; in particular, the terminations of certain elevator banks leave a constant usable floor area and standard distance from inner office wall to outside windows. Unfortunately the lithe vertical rhythms of Hood's Daily News Building were not carried over into the RCA Building, but the latter is far more dramatic in its chiseled, slender mass and also benefits from its calculated placement in relation to other buildings in the ensemble.

### Streamline Moderne

Around 1930 the Art Deco was replaced by a simpler and more economical style, which has been named Streamline Moderne. In contrast to the exclusive Art Deco Style, which had relied on custom handicraft, Streamline Moderne was stripped of ornament and easily adapted to mass duplication. Furthermore, it was thought to be symbolic of the dynamic twentieth century, of speed and machines, fast motor cars, railway trains, and steamships. It penetrated deep into the vernacular of American building and appeared in small towns everywhere, in the modest WPA post office as well as the roadside diner. Its popularity was promoted by a new professional, the industrial designer, who eagerly gave streamlined shapes to every implausible object, from pencil sharpeners to fountain pens.[2]

Like Art Deco, Streamline Moderne had European origins. Two architects in particular had experimented with curved forms: the Belgian Henri van de Velde in a theater built for the 1914 Deutscher Werkbund Exhibition in Cologne, and the German Eric Mendelsohn in three department stores, in Stuttgart, Chemnitz, and Breslau, in the late twenties. In its American adaptation, sleek, mechanically perfect curves appeared everywhere—at the corners of buildings, in cylindrical helix stairs, circular windows, and spherical knobs. It became a largely autonomous style for commercial commissions, especially office buildings and movie theaters; Radio City Music Hall in Rockefeller Center is its most distinguished interior. Many of the sensitive designs were often private residences, notably those designed by Edward Durell Stone, George Fred Keck, and the Swiss-born William Lescaze. In its usual manifestations, Streamline Moderne shunned the color experiments and expensive materials of Art Deco and happily relied on synthetics—plastics, plywood, ivory-colored formica, black glass, and chrome strips.

An American architect who avowedly rejected all forms of modernism from Europe nonetheless produced a classic monument of Streamline Moderne while avoiding its clichés. In his Johnson Wax Company Administration Building in Racine, Wisconsin (1936–39), Frank Lloyd Wright used streamlined massing rather than material or color to convey the spirit of the thirties (267, 268). Like the Larkin Building and Unity Temple, Wright's Racine Building is internalized, sealed behind rhythmic curved bands of brick walls and glass-tube glazing that make an outside view from within impossible. To achieve this effect Wright used his favorite constructive principle, the cantilever. The focus of the plan is a lofty columnar hall for clerks and typists. Its fifty-four white concrete supports, reinforced with metal mesh, taper downward to a nine-inch-diameter base. The large concrete discs they carry form the roof, with the spaces between filled with more tubular glazing. The effect is as ceremonial and awesome as the hypostyle hall at Karnak or the mosque at Cordoba. Wright believed it to be "as inspiring a place to work as any cathedral was in which to worship" and immodestly proclaimed it "one of the world's most remarkable structures."

267
*Johnson Wax Administration Building, Racine, Wisconsin. Frank Lloyd Wright, 1936–39. Exterior.*

268
*Johnson Wax Administration Building, Racine, Wisconsin. Interior.*

*Schindler and Neutra*     In Europe, meanwhile, a new and fundamentally different architecture had established itself. Inspired by the precepts and practice of such pre-First World War pioneers as Auguste Perret of France, Peter Behrens of Germany, and Adolph Loos of Austria, its advocates insisted that viable architecture must employ the new materials and methods of construction introduced in the nineteenth century, welcome the contributions of the engineer, and satisfy the special functional needs of the day; only thus could it become (as Sullivan had demanded) a true expression of its age. They had no use at all for ornament, so much a part, and indeed sometimes the whole, of Art Deco.

Three of the leaders of the movement, Walter Gropius, Ludwig Mies van der Rohe, and Eric Mendelsohn, left Europe to settle in the United States in the late thirties and early forties. They were preceded by three younger men with a commitment to and first-hand knowledge of the new architecture: Rudolph Schindler as early as 1914, William Lescaze in 1920, and Richard Neutra in 1923. Each of the latter three arrived soon after completing his architectural studies, and their work in the twenties was comparable to the best in Europe.

Chicago was a magnet for European architects; it was where Schindler, like Neutra later, first worked in the United States. When America entered the war in 1917, Schindler, an enemy alien, became a grateful employee of Wright. Through the Aline Barnsdall (Hollyhock House) commission, which Schindler supervised while Wright was in Tokyo busy with the Imperial Hotel, he came to know Los Angeles, where he was to live and practice independently.

In 1921 Schindler began building his own house, a double one shared with the family of a contractor named Clyde Chase (269). His astonishing originality is immediately apparent in the cunningly arranged pinwheel plan, which provides a private patio garden for each unit of the design, and in the economical yet vigorous construction, with tilt-slab concrete walls, sandblasted redwood timbers, and canvas sliding doors, all on a four-foot module. Schindler's concrete technology was a distinct advance over that of Irving Gill's, whose Dodge House stood immediately across the street. Wright's influence may be detected in the plan and in the pervasive tactile quality, but everywhere Schindler's independence, as well as his special buoyant, primitive qualities, shines through. The sliding movement of planes—with walls of clipped shrubbery as well as actual walls—extends outward, defining spatial areas, with little distinction between indoors and out. (Mies van der Rohe's 1923 project for a brick country house proposes a similar if more abstract spatial conception.)

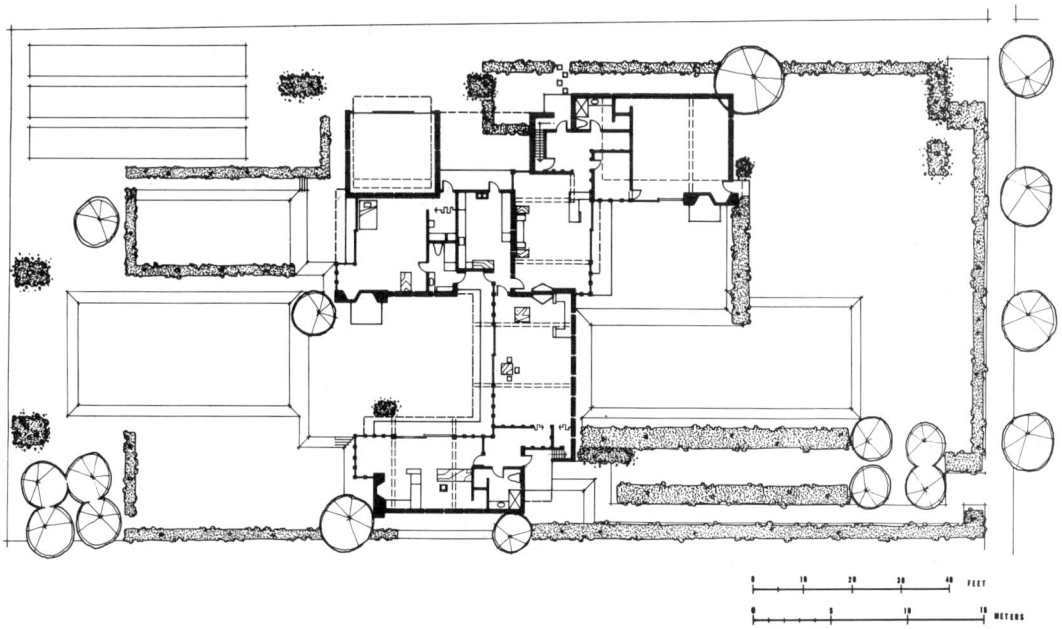

269
*Schindler-Chase House,
Los Angeles, California.
R. M. Schindler, 1921--
22. Plan.*

270
*Philip Lovell Beach
House, Newport Beach,
California. R. M. Schind-
ler, 1925–26. Exterior.*

271
*Philip Lovell House, Los Angeles, California. Richard Neutra, 1928.*

As early as 1912, while still in Vienna, Schindler's manifesto declared that "the architect has finally discovered the medium of his art: SPACE." His double house was little noticed when new; today one admires it as an experimental design wholly at ease in all its parts, doctrinaire perhaps, yet nevertheless gratifyingly habitable.

Even more astonishing is Schindler's design for Dr. Philip Lovell's Newport Beach house, conceived in 1922 and built in 1925–26 (270). It may be baffling for the historian who sees tantalizing parallels with Russian Constructivism and projects by Le Corbusier, yet nothing quite like the Lovell House was ever built again, even by Schindler. An assertive structural skeleton composed of five parallel open concrete frames, unmasked and evenly spaced, carries two upper floors, leaving the sandy ground free except for a garage. An open sleeping balcony juts beyond the line of supports, and within the house a gallery giving access to the bedrooms overlooks the two-story living room. The Wrightian patterns of the sash bars do not compromise the building's unique character as a powerful, open sculpture that receives and directs a flow of ambient space. Subsequently Schindler yielded to more conventional structural methods and in his later (mostly residential) work employed interlocking forms like those of the Dutch de Stijl artists.

Schindler and Neutra had much in common: both were born and educated in Vienna; both admired the progressive architecture of the Midwest and worked briefly for Wright; both did their most significant work in the twenties while struggling with lean Los Angeles practices. Jointly they submitted a scheme for the 1926 competition for the Geneva Palace of the League of Nations that was honored by being chosen for exhibition by the Deutscher Werkbund. And the same Dr. Lovell, a health faddist by profession, became Neutra's client for another memorable house, one in the Hollywood hills of Los Angeles designed in 1928 (271). Concrete walls were sprayed against reinforcing mesh, and standard steel casement windows were fitted into the modular rhythm of the skeleton. Neutra's details here are more impressive than his interior planning. Sharp edges and the thin planes of wall and window suggest enclosed volumes rather than mass: the house looks like a giant paper kite tethered for the moment to the hillside. The similarity of the second Lovell House to European work, its precision and its visual weightlessness—together with Neutra's writings and flair for publicity—brought the house wide recognition abroad, whereas Schindler's rugged experiments and spatially more active designs were ignored. Neutra's theoretical projects for Rush City Reformed (1923–30) show the range of his abilities. Limited in quantity though it was, the work of Schindler and Neutra in the Los Angeles area was the most progressive in America in the 1920s. It suggests an intriguing hypothesis: a modern architecture might have matured in the United States without the aid of the celebrated architect-immigrants who arrived in the late thirties.

*Howe and Lescaze*

While Neutra's Lovell House was under construction on the West Coast, an American-born East Coast architect, George Howe, who trained at Harvard and at the Ecole des Beaux-Arts, courageously abandoned a successful practice as an eclectic and enrolled full time in the modern movement. Commissioned to design a new office building for the Philadelphia Saving Fund Society (PSFS), Howe collaborated with William Lescaze, ten years his junior, who had studied in Zurich under Karl Moser. Lescaze's intuitive and visual approach to design complemented Howe's intellectual and rational convictions. What each partner actually contributed may be debated, but no one contests that the PSFS Building was the most advanced skyscraper of its time. Even more significant, it was as skillful and complete a summation of European modernism as could be found in Europe; it was comparable to Walter Gropius's Bauhaus at Dessau, even if without its seminal importance.[3]

The PSFS Building consists of a tower, T-shaped on plan, rising from a base containing shops at street level and a banking hall above, with elevators grouped at the rear (272). A canonical requirement of the new architecture was expression of the structural rhythms, here supplied by the continuous projected verticals of the flanks, which, incidentally, were insisted upon by the client, who vetoed the uniformly layered design proposed by the architects because he thought it looked like a warehouse. Banded horizontals with continuous win-

272
PSFS Building, Philadel-
phia, Pennsylvania. Howe
and Lescaze, 1929–32.
Floor plans.

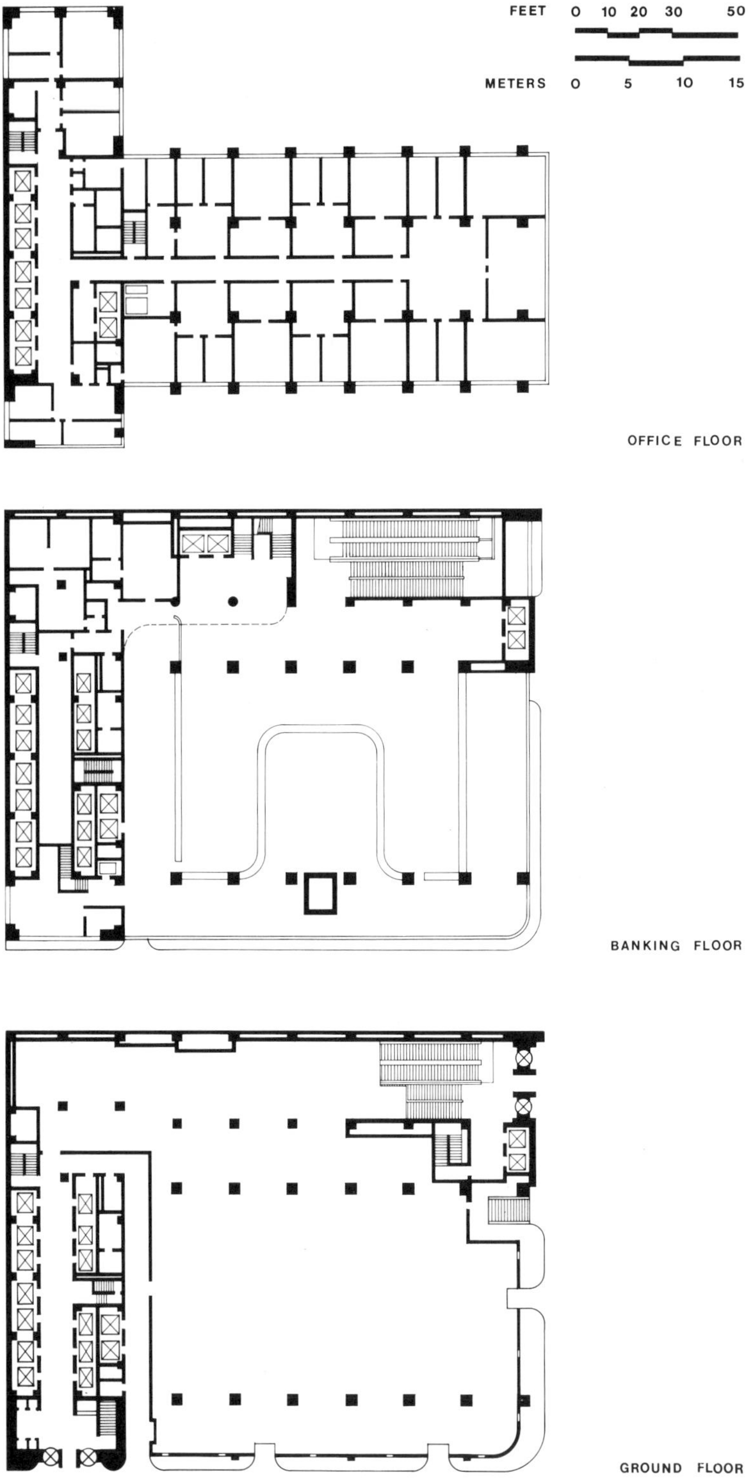

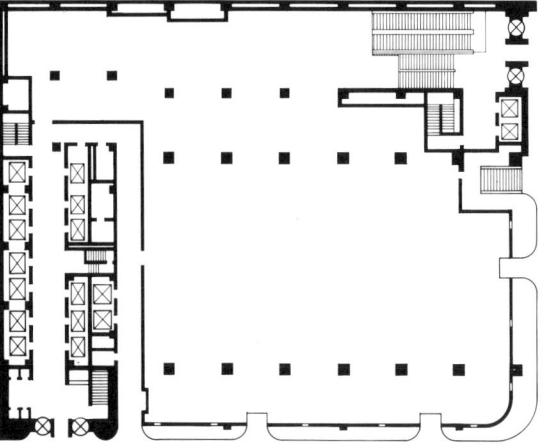

FEET    0  10 20  30        50

METERS   0     5     10    15

OFFICE FLOOR

BANKING FLOOR

GROUND FLOOR

273
*PSFS Building, Philadel-*
*phia, Pennsylvania.*
*Exterior.*

dows set flush and placed forward of the structural skeleton empha-size volumetric enclosure rather than mass—another canonical requirement (273). Mendelsohn and Le Corbusier had earlier ex-ploited the ribbon window, which became a cliché, and Hood followed suit with mixed success in his sixty-story McGraw-Hill Building of 1931 in New York. The conflicting obligations to express structure and volume are nicely balanced in the PSFS Building by retaining the banded windows folded around the corners of the cantilevered face of the building. The PSFS was also obedient to the demand for purity of surface. By means of sharp and thin detailing, the masonry veneer of polished granite, limestone, and smooth brick is made to appear as a continuous skin; nowhere is there any applied ornament, a feature of the new style that was most difficult for the layman to accept.

*The International Style*

In 1932, the year in which the PSFS was completed, the architecture it represented was christened "The International Style" by Henry-Russell Hitchcock and Philip Johnson in a book with that title. The book was written on the occasion of a retrospective exhibition held by the Museum of Modern Art in New York, which they had organized. Although it was primarily European in coverage, the exhibition gave some recognition to American architects, namely Wright, Hood, Neutra, and Howe and Lescaze, on the insistence of the museum trustees; Schindler offered work, but it was rejected.[4] In the book, from which Wright was excluded, Hitchcock and John-son adopted a critical and didactic tone; not content to summarize and draw objective conclusions, they wrote what is in effect a primer, giving explicit instructions about such matters as how to maximize the effect of volume, what materials to use, and how to arrange lettering on a building. With its first exhibition of architecture, the Museum of Modern Art made history. It soon became the tastemaker for design in the United States, which, for the next two decades, was dominated by the principles of the International Style as set forth by Hitchcock and Johnson.

*Gropius, Breuer, and Aalto*

Another event that helped establish the International Style in the United States was the arrival of Walter Gropius, in 1937, after two years in England. Heir to the lessons of Peter Behrens, for whom he had worked early in the century, and the principles of the Deutscher Werkbund, Gropius was exemplary of the tough-minded Germanic approach to the new architecture, but with his visionary yet analy-tical powers he was remarkably successful in presenting his ideas. From 1919 to 1928 he had been the director of the school of design

274
*Walter Gropius House,
Lincoln, Massachusetts.
Gropius and Breuer,
1937. Exterior.*

called the Bauhaus, which was virtually his own creation, first in Weimar and then in Dessau; in 1937 he became chairman of the Department of Architecture at Harvard. In this manner the United States was formally introduced to a radical German educational program, which, as it spread from school to school, overturned the doctrines and methods of the Ecole des Beaux-Arts. The Bauhaus curriculum, as rerun in the United States, was inevitably tempered by the passage of years. An academic edifice was built to house memories of its lively, polemical youth, and year after year young graduates, indoctrinated with the convictions of an older generation, went forth as zealous emmissaries to fight the battle of progress.[5] Modern architecture, particularly in the view of its German adherents, was not only to fulfill the functional needs of the new century but assume an ethical and social role and bring about a reformed and collective society.

Gropius's first American works were detached houses, mostly in New England, done in collaboration with Marcel Breuer, who had been a student at the Weimar Bauhaus, later an instructor in charge of woodworking, and who was Gropius's partner from 1938 to 1943. The houses they designed were quite unlike the work either had done in Germany or in England (where Breuer also had practiced briefly). Gropius's own house in Lincoln, Massachusetts (1937), illustrates an immediate and sympathetic response to the vernacular New England

275
*Robinson House, Williamstown, Massachusetts. Marcel Breuer, 1947. Exterior.*

276
*Robinson House, Williamstown, Massachusetts. Plan.*

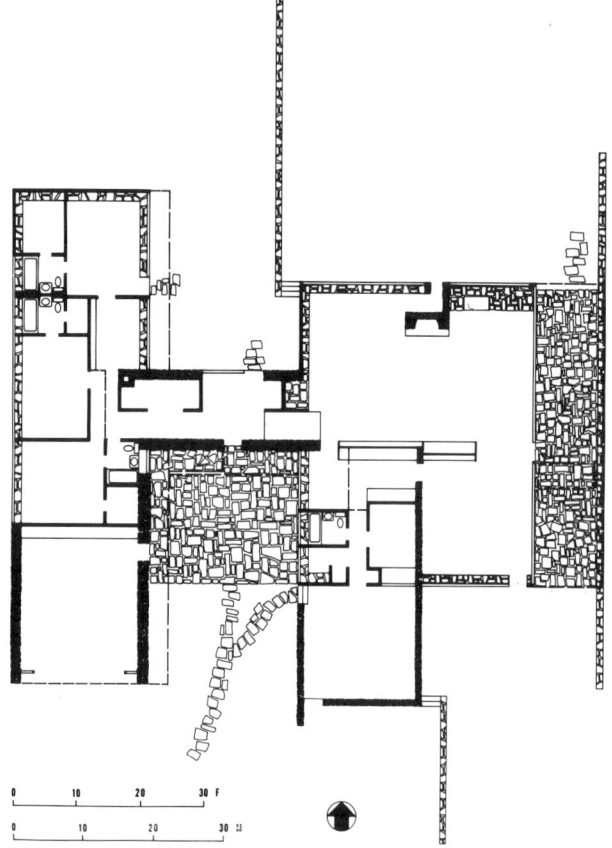

building tradition (274). Interest in joinery and tactile surfaces contrasts with the impersonality of Gropius's 1925–26 houses for the Bauhaus faculty at Dessau, including his own. The Lincoln house is constructed of a wood frame with vertical board siding, painted brick, steel Lally columns, glass block, paving and low walls of irregular stones, and a prefabricated cast-iron spiral stair—a mixture hardly intellectually or esthetically consistent, yet one which supports Gropius's belief in architecture as an ever-changing search. To have defined the movement as a "style," as Hitchcock and Johnson did, was in his opinion harmful and misleading.

The houses designed independently by Marcel Breuer were more agreeable and also more influential than the work he did as Gropius's partner. Bauhaus-trained though he was, Breuer was unafraid of frankly pictorial elements. His designs have substance and visual weight. He was partial to fieldstone walls and natural siding and, even when he sensibly adjusted his interior planning to the disciplines of timber framing, he never denied spatial richness. In the Geller House of 1945 in Lawrence, Long Island, he reintroduced the sloping roof and initiated a binuclear type of plan that separated active from passive functions, which he repeated in the Robinson House of 1947 in Williamstown, Massachusetts (275, 276). Breuer influenced many architects of the first Bauhaus-guided generation in America, among them Carl Koch and Hugh Stubbins.

Breuer's career became identified with a personal style, whereas Gropius, however prominent as spokesman, favored anonymity. Always a believer in teamwork, in 1946 Gropius and seven young architects established a group practice called The Architects Collaborative (TAC), which still exists today. An early commission in which he had a leading hand is the Harvard University Graduate Center, designed in 1949 (277). Elements of Gropius's pioneer work in mass housing, such as his Siemensstadt Siedlung in Berlin, reappear in the Harvard project, though treated with less rigidity. The site plan intentionally recalls Harvard Yard nearby with loose, courtyardlike spaces defined by separate dormitory units. An ambitious effort was made to integrate the arts, an old Bauhaus ideal, by commissioning works by Jean Arp, Joseph Albers, Richard Lippold, and others.

The Harvard Graduate Center is to be honored more for its intentions than for its achievement. Much more forward-looking, forecasting the experiments of the sixties, is another building for student housing by a European architect (though not an immigrant) in the same city, namely the Baker House dormitory at MIT, designed by Alvar Aalto in 1948 (278). Aalto dared to replace the smooth recti-

277
*Harvard Graduate Center,
Cambridge, Massachu-
setts. The Architects Col-
laborative, 1949–50.
Exterior.*

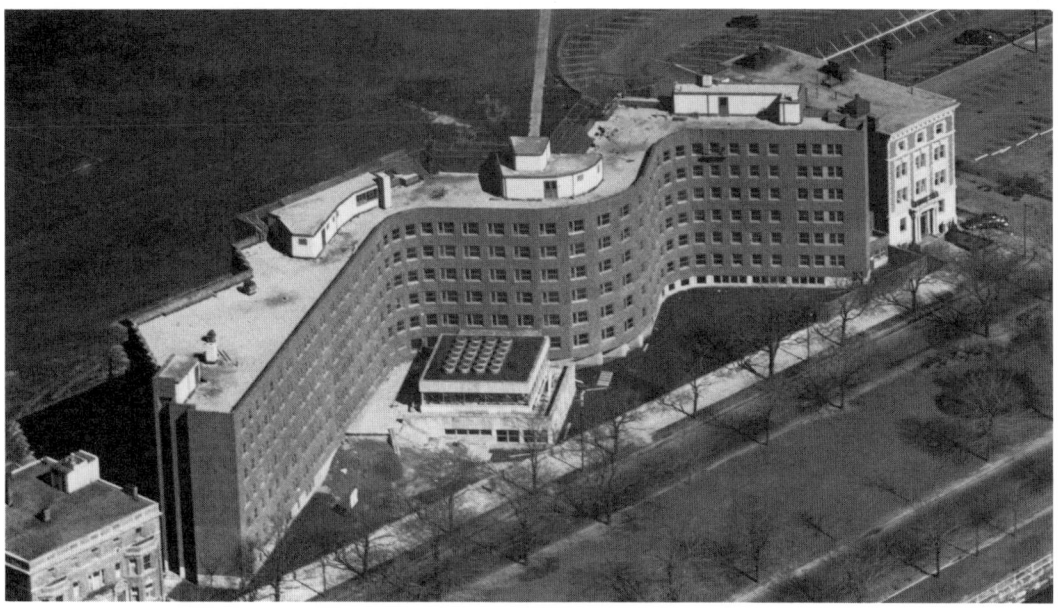

278
*Baker House, Massachusetts Institute of Technology, Cambridge, Massachusetts. Alvar Aalto, 1948. Aerial view.*

linear slab of the International Style with a six-story serpentine one, aggressively textured in red brick. The building curves along the Charles River embankment in order to obtain views up and down the river, and nestled in one of its bends is the angled square block containing the student lounge and dining hall. The entrance elevation, completely different from the river front and far more complex, is centered on a conspicuous pair of cantilevered stairways, originally detailed for light metal. The building had no immediate influence on American work; indeed its enigmatic character puzzled many who were just learning the rules of the International Style.

**The Acceptance of Modernism**

The lingering years of the Depression and the entry of the United States into the war in 1941 were not propitious for the new architecture. The influence of Gropius and the other immigrants was muted until after the war. Yet several federally sponsored low-cost housing projects demonstrated, with modular framing, prefabrication, and simple, functional planning, the very qualities that modern architecture espoused. Among them were Channel Heights in San Pedro, California (1943), by Richard Neutra, and Aluminum City Terrace housing at New Kensington, Pennsylvania (1941), by Gropius and Breuer; another project of the same class, the Agricultural Workers' Community at Chandler, Arizona (1936), by Burton D. Cairns and Vernon DeMars, was built of adobe. Stringent cost limits proved beneficial in these spartan but distinguished examples of bureaucratic architecture. Baldwin Hills in the Los Angeles area, dating from 1942, is another excellent example of housing integrated with community facilities and shared open space.

The full tide of the new architecture came in the late 1940s with the accumulated needs of building in the postwar years and the rush of veteran enrollments in schools of architecture infiltrated by European modernism. Gropius at Harvard and Saarinen at Cranbrook were not the only European educator-architects. Laszlo Moholy-Nagy, a Dessau colleague of Gropius, had founded a new Bauhaus, the Institute of Design, in Chicago in 1937. A year later Mies van der Rohe had been invited to teach at Illinois Institute of Technology, then still the Armour Institute. In 1940 Alvar Aalto had become a part-time professor at MIT while retaining his practice in Helsinki. Eric Mendelsohn taught a graduate class at Berkeley starting in 1945. Konrad Wachsmann, a former associate of Gropius, gave courses on prefabricated structures at the University of Southern California. With one accord the educational establishment gave way to expatriate leadership, and in one school after another curricula based on Beaux-Arts theory and practice were dealt the coup de grâce.

Of all the proponents of European modernism of the 1940s only one pressed on to achieve a new synthesis: Ludwig Mies van der Rohe. In this country and abroad his reflected images are everywhere, so that we speak of Miesian architecture; only once before in history has an architect's name, that of Palladio, become synonymous with a unity of theory and style.

What identifies Mies van der Rohe's architecture is his singular concern with structure. He viewed architecture as an expression of the order and reason that are embodied in structure, which in turn is dependent on science and the technology of the time. In this he shows himself an intellectual heir of Eugène Emmanuel Viollet-le-Duc, who, in his *Entretiens sur l'architecture* (1863, 1872), cited structure as the cultural expression of an age. Viollet-le-Duc saw Gothic cathedrals not as symbols of Christianity but as logically constructed cages of cut stone wherein every part—pier, rib, and buttress—was necessary for the stability of the whole. For him medieval architecture was the quintessence of stone construction. He admonished his contemporaries: "All forms not dictated by structure should be suppressed." This principle of structural rationalism using the new material of iron, he was convinced, should be the basis for a monumental and significant architecture of the nineteenth century.

This recurrent French view of the interaction of architecture and technology, expressed earlier by Henri Labrouste and later by Auguste Perret, was central in Mies's philosophy. "Whenever technology reaches its true fulfillment, it transcends into architecture." Mies saw two driving and sustaining forces in the twentieth century: economics and technology. Only if architecture was fully responsive to such forces could it hope to give expression to an epoch. For Mies, this was architecture's ultimate goal.

Structure was inseparable from materials to Mies, who often spoke of the healthy beauty of timber and of well-laid masonry walls. In his veneration of materials, steel and concrete among them, he understood, more than any other modern architect, their distinctive characteristics, individual capacity, and the discipline of design appropriate to each. For Mies the lowliest brick had a no less hallowed place in building than a bronze mullion.

The arrival of Mies van der Rohe in Chicago in 1938 was an historically appropriate event in the city that half a century earlier had surprised the world with its first steel-framed skyscrapers. "The most important idea in modern architecture is the skeletal idea developed right here in Chicago," said Mies of his adopted city and spiritual home. His designs for tall buildings have been accepted as the most complete embodiment of that idea.

Mies did not come unprepared for the task fate had in store for him. In Germany, beginning in 1919, he had worked out various solutions for the skyscraper, none of which was ever built. Given the skeletal frame and the enclosing skin, future architecture would no longer be one of shades and shadows but of reflective glass surfaces. Accordingly, his proposals are for all-glass skyscrapers, crystalline and transparent. Mies disliked the interior light courts common in rectangular office buildings and suggested irregular, indented peripheries and later, starting in 1926, more disciplined, thin rectangular forms. Often he placed the glass curtain wall in front of the line of supports, which were revealed only at street level as a colonnade in front of a recessed entrance. We recognize these designs of the twenties as already mature prototypes for his American buildings.

Mies van der Rohe's first executed tall building was the Promontory Apartments in Chicago (1948–49).[1] Studies began in 1946 with two preliminary steel versions before the final version was built in reinforced concrete (279). At first glance it appears elementary, even prosaic, with the regular grid of its structural frame evident in all elevations. As the building rises, one notices subtle variations, such as the reduced beam depths on the flanks and the reduced cross section of the vertical supports across the front and back. Also, incised pouring joints are carefully considered. Such concern for details is typical of Mies's approach, even with the ordinary materials of this building, which uses exposed concrete, buff-colored common brick, and aluminum-framed windows. Mies's architecture does not depend on expensive, elegant materials, as is often supposed, although he was always willing to consider these when the budget allowed. In terms of Mies's precision and care, one can understand a bricklayer's son's definition of architecture as "one brick . . . laid upon another brick, *carefully.*"

How to treat the enclosure of a skeletal building is a major theme in Mies's American work—a seemingly narrow problem, but for Mies a justifiable obsession. The classic example is the pair of apartment towers for 860–880 Lake Shore Drive in Chicago (1948–51). Mies's details for the identical elevations are as direct and expressive of their steel frames as the Promontory Apartments is of its reinforced concrete frame (280, 281). The fireproofed columns and edge beams are encased with black-painted steel plates. Each bay is subdivided into four window units by three wide-flange steel mullions needed for stiffening; a supplementary mullion is welded to the face

279
*Promontory Apartments,*
*Chicago, Illinois. Ludwig*
*Mies van der Rohe, 1948–*
*49. Exterior.*

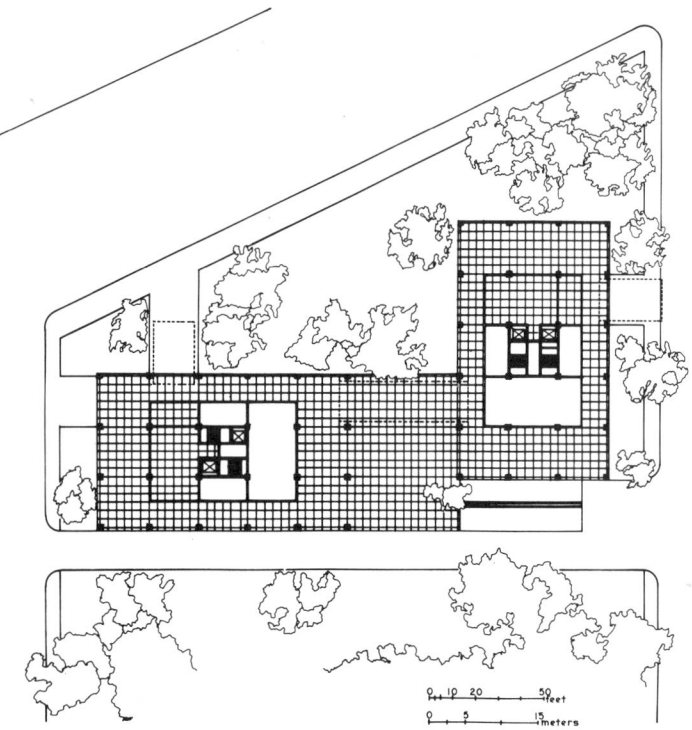

280
*860–880 Lake Shore Drive Apartments, Chicago, Illinois. Ludwig Mies van der Rohe, 1948–51. Lobby and exterior.*

281
*860–880 Lake Shore Drive Apartments, Chicago, Illinois. Plan.*

of each exterior column to sustain the rhythm set by the others. Placed within these divisions are aluminum-framed floor-to-ceiling windows with a lower transom whose horizontal bar acts as an enclosing rail. Each element has its place in a structural hierarchy. Later buildings by Mies have more uniform and more efficient curtain-wall treatments, but none more fully satisfies the eye and mind than that of 860–880 Lake Shore Drive.

The manner in which these twin towers are placed on the trapezoidal site is also effective. The open colonnade on ground level creates a ceremonial welcome, an unexpectedly expansive horizontal movement given the limited site, while continuous travertine paving, suggesting the stylobate of a classical temple, links the two buildings. A connecting canopy also links the buildings, and two additional canopies cantilevered over the separate entrances invite exploration of the space, besides providing psychological cover from street to lobby. Such deceptive simplicity, purged of dross, is the end result of exhaustive study and revision and is confirmation of the dictum, "Less is more" (attributed to Mies, though in fact it originated with his early employer, Peter Behrens).

In successive apartment buildings Mies developed a curtain wall placed in front of the structural frame to accommodate vertical heating and cooling ducts, resulting in an unbroken array of wide-flange mullions running the full height of the building. This solution, which appeared a decade earlier in a steel version for the Promontory Apartments, was followed for the Esplanade and Commonwealth Apartments in Chicago (both 1953–56), where tinted glass was introduced.

Because the technology and spatial requirements of an office building are similar to those of an apartment tower, Mies did not alter his factual approach in designing his first commercial building to be constructed, the Seagram Building, built in 1954–58 in New York (with Philip Johnson as associate architect) (282). He also satisfied the client's wish for a building of fine quality by the use of bronze and an indented plaza on Park Avenue. Dark, amber-tinted glass reinforces its warm and sensuous color, unifying a surface already made more dense by a greater number of bronze mullions per bay. The rich materials, however, do not lessen the somber mien of the building. The wide, granited-paved plaza is treated simply, a space relieved only by flanking pools and a discreet planting of trees. The effect is urbane, impersonal, and classical. Commerce assumes a noble presence usually reserved for religion and government.

282
*Seagram Building, New York City. Ludwig Mies van der Rohe, 1954–58. Exterior.*

*Design of Low Buildings*     The low buildings of Mies form a separate category and, though varied requirements make their solutions more varied, they are also governed by structure. But because fireproofing of the steel was not always necessary, structure is often expressed more directly and more eloquently.

It was on the campus of the Illinois Institute of Technology, for which he designed the master plan (1939–41) as well as the buildings, that Mies's distinctive structural language was first spoken (283). A 24-by-24-foot grid laid over the entire site determined the placement and shape of the buildings, and a 12-foot module controlled their height. Mies chose very simple materials: black-painted steel, buff-colored brick, and aluminum-framed windows. The product of these self-imposed restraints is a campus of great spatial diversity and buildings with surprisingly varied elevations. The austere rectangles delineated by dark frames suggest a Mondrian painting, although Mies said he was not influenced by de Stijl art. The welded assembly of wide-flange, channel, and angle sections in these steel-framed buildings and the nonstructural infilling of brick and glass received the same minute attention of Mies's exacting eye for detail. In particular it is the structurally descriptive corner detail that elucidates the steel skeleton. Mies made every architect corner-conscious; talent became equated with ability to turn a corner—a problem as ancient as the Greek Doric order.

The IIT project, together with Mies's curtain wall, became the origin of a generic style of the forties. However intrinsically aristocratic or demanding his approach, Mies's precedent provided a workable vernacular for modern American architecture for more than two decades. To adapt Mies was the best most architects could do.

Mies's series of clear-span structures, which began in 1945–46, are a dramatic demonstration of the passage of engineering into the realm of pure art. They also point up, even if they do not explain, the anomaly of discipline interlocked with spiritual content. The first two designs of the series were for all-glass buildings without interior support, the Cantor Drive-In Restaurant in Indianapolis and the Edith Farnsworth House at Plano, Illinois; only the latter was built, and not until 1950 (284). These designs share the concept of a single, universal space with free-standing partitions and a fixed service core. Historically they are progressive extensions of his 1929 Barcelona Pavilion, itself an extension of the "decellularization" of space that began with Wright's flowing Prairie house plans. Crown Hall (1950–56), which houses the department of architecture at IIT (and was Mies's favorite building), is similar to the Drive-In Restaurant: major spanning elements of structure are visible above a flat roof plane

283
*Illinois Institute of Technology, Chicago, Illinois.
Ludwig Mies van der
Rohe, 1939–41 and later.
View of campus.*

284
*Edith Farnsworth House,
Plano, Illinois. Ludwig
Mies van der Rohe, 1946–
50. Exterior.*

285
*Crown Hall, Illinois Institute of Technology, Chicago, Illinois. Ludwig Mies van der Rohe, 1950–56. Exterior.*

suspended from their underside (285). For the restaurant Mies used two open-work trusses placed longitudinally and supported on four columns; for Crown Hall he used four plate girders placed transversely on eight columns; in both, the roof plane is cantilevered outward, exploiting the tension, elasticity, and strength of steel.

The sensation of lift—almost the denial of gravity—is intensified in the final development of Mies's clear-span series: the two-way stressed roof structure. It first appeared in a design made in 1950–51 for a 50-foot square house. Here welded steel plates form a rigid egg-crate roof that is supported by a single exterior column at the center of each side. With enclosing walls entirely of glass, the double cantilever frees the corners, opening up the interior to the surrounding landscape. This project became the basis for the Bacardi Office Building in Cuba (1957), designed for reinforced concrete but never built, and the National Gallery in Berlin (1962–68), designed in steel and measuring 214 feet square. Completed thirty years after Mies left that city for Chicago and one year before his death, the Berlin Museum is the only executed example of his two-way structures.

Mies's achievement cannot be properly assessed without taking his unexecuted projects into account. One of these is an enduring challenge to the timidity of twentieth-century architecture as a whole. For the Chicago Convention Center (1953–54) Mies proposed a huge multipurpose hall seating fifty thousand persons within a 750-foot square clear-span structure (286). Its latticework steel roof was to be formed by 30-foot deep two-way trusses carried by 60-foot deep outer wall trusses that were to rest on six tapered concrete supports on each side. All unnecessary weight was to be removed. Gigantic scale and structural vigor were to be projected without ambiguity or

*286*
*Project for Convention
Center, Chicago, Illinois.
Ludwig Mies van der
Rohe, 1953–54. Model.*

disguise in the lively triangular pattern of its exterior. It would have
been the largest uninterrupted enclosed space in the world.

In the context of the modern movement Mies van der Rohe is
atypical in many respects: in his interest in traditional values, symmetry, structure, and craftsmanship, in his self-imposed restrictions,
his distrust of propaganda and the role of architecture in social
reform. He himself was temperate, fastidious, and philosophical. The
future may well see his buildings as a tranquil and coherent episode
in a century as stylistically diverse as the preceding one.

**Followers of Mies**

It was always Mies's intent that his approach and vocabulary be put
to wider use. The most ambitious examples of Miesian architecture
came from large firms staffed with devoted and knowledgeable designers, some of them former pupils from IIT, where he headed the
architecture faculty from 1938 to 1958. Curiously, while a former
generation of rebellious architects renounced authority and precedent, the postwar generation willingly accepted the preeminence of
Mies. They put aside the pursuit of novelty and concentrated on
clarifying formal relationships and perfecting details of construction,
at times overlooking Mies's own caution that a mechanistic principle
of order fails to satisfy our feelings.

The curtain-wall grid became the outward and visible sign of
Miesian convictions and a popular expression of a technological culture. A remarkably early example appeared in Portland, Oregon, in
1948, the Equitable Savings and Loan Building by Pietro Belluschi.
Even though it is a tall building, it draws upon the IIT project. A
polished sheet aluminum skin covers its reinforced concrete frame,
and darker, cast-aluminum spandrels and tinted glass are set within

an inch of their covering so that the effect is that of a single, smooth reflective plane—more machinelike than any building by Mies.

The firm of Skidmore, Owings & Merrill, with major offices in New York and Chicago, early identified itself with the Miesian esthetic and, in turn, with its prestige commissions for corporate business headquarters, made Miesian architecture a symbol of financial probity. Its first such commission was Lever House in New York (1952), designed by Gordon Bunshaft (287). Ironically this building, with its elegant curtain wall of stainless steel, opaque blue glass, and tinted windows, became more influential than any single building by Mies; for instance, similar curtain-wall effects were soon made easy by catalog components. Lever House was also praised for creating pedestrian open space in the city—Rockefeller Center had more successfully achieved this earlier—and for breaking the linear uniformity of Park Avenue with its vertical slab perpendicular to the street—which some critics now regard as unfortunate.

For the Inland Steel Building in Chicago (1954) Walter A. Netsch, also of Skidmore, Owings & Merrill, put aside the usual cellular structural frame and adapted the Miesian concept of universal space for commercial use. Each floor of the Inland Steel Building resembles a Farnsworth House, a totally column-free space, with vertical supports confined to the outside flanks. The elevators and other services are contained in an opaque tower attached to one side of the building.

Eero Saarinen's early works acknowledge the precedent of Mies van der Rohe. Mies's IIT campus plan clearly provided the model for Saarinen's General Motors Technical Center in Warren, Michigan (1948–65), which serves as a research branch of the company (288). Saarinen designed six major buildings around a huge artificial lake, but they are so widely spaced that no interrelationship between them is possible. The IIT campus concept, based on pedestrian scale, is disconcerting when enlarged to that of the automobile. Saarinen was more successful with his study of details; for example, his technical advance in the curtain wall, adapting a rubber gasket seal similar to that of an automobile windshield, and the introduction of color, red, blue, or yellow, in panels of glazed brick, heightening the suggestion of a Mondrian painting. Saarinen's role in developing Miesian architecture was that of an intermediary. With his special ability to present a building as a visual package acceptable to American taste, he filled his role as an interpreter extremely well.

Philip Johnson was a quite different interpreter of Mies. First, as an architectural historian, he presented Mies in a fine monograph appearing in 1947. Second, as an architect, he restated Mies's idea of an all-glass house in his own residence in New Canaan, Connect-

287
*Lever House, New York City. Skidmore, Owings & Merrill, 1952. Exterior.*

288
*General Motors Technical Center, Warren, Michigan. Saarinen and Saarinen Associates, 1948–65. General view.*

289
*Johnson House, New Ca-
naan, Connecticut. Philip
Johnson, 1949. Interior.*

icut, built in 1949 (289). Like Lever House, Johnson's glass house became more famous than its prototype, the Farnsworth House (not yet built but known to Johnson from the plans). But for all its fame and refinement, the Johnson House as a bachelor's country retreat was of limited value as a model and was not directly emulated. Its similarity to the Farnsworth House lies in the visible steel framing and the open plan, where living and dining areas, bedroom, and kitchen are implied by partial partitions or the placement of furniture; only the bath is enclosed, in a brick cylinder that projects slightly above the roof. As historian turned architect, Johnson has said of his own house that far stronger influences than Mies are at work and he knew them all.[2] Certainly in the Johnson House, as the visitor experiences it, structure is the least insistent element, whereas in the Farnsworth House it is the dominant one. Mies's house is rigorous and demanding; Johnson's is sybaritic and subordinate to the landscape.

More valuable as models were Johnson's versions of those unbuilt atrium-house projects Mies designed in Germany between 1931–35. Johnson reinterpreted their simple brick planes and wide expanses of glass in a series of houses of intentionally formal character. The Davis House of 1954 in Wayzata, Minnesota, is an example: its flowing interiors, its exacting craftsmanship in brick, and its podium setting are unmistakably the result of lessons learned from Mies, lessons well learned and sensitively applied. (On the opposite coast, another disciple, Craig Ellwood, adapted light-weight steel framing for a number of elegant yet simple houses in Southern California.)

More often than not what passes for Miesian architecture is Miesian in outward appearance only, resulting in bland uniformity. Most of the exceptions are works by the small circle of architects who studied under Mies at ITT and remained loyal to his doctrine of structure. In the Civic Center (1963–68) by Jacques Brownson, a former pupil of Mies, Chicago honors Mies with its municipal offices and courts housed in skyscraper form, a building that is at once fellow to the commercial skyscrapers of the Loop and yet is quickly perceived as civic, not by any superficial pomp or symbol but by its visual weight and heroic measure of proportion. The eighty-seven-foot length of the bays, requiring Warren trusses, was unprecedented in high-rise construction at the time the Civic Center was built. Mies's fondness for the immediacy of construction—one of the things the nineteenth century called "reality"—is expressed with an alloy of steel called Cor-Ten, whose rusted surface is self-healing and darkens with age. As an unofficial memorial to Mies, leader of the

*290*
*McCormick Place, Chi-*
*cago, Illinois. C. F. Mur-*
*phy Associates, 1968–71.*
*Exterior.*

so-called "Second Chicago School of Architecture," the Civic Center appropriately shares Dearborn Street with buildings by Jenney, Burnham and Root, Holabird and Roche, and the Federal Center (1956–65) by Mies himself.

Another reflection of Mies's late preoccupation with large scale—most obvious in his Convention Hall project—is a similar building, McCormick Place in Chicago (1968–71), designed by another pupil, Gene Summers, while he was working in the office of C. F. Murphy Associates (290). McCormick Place consists of an exhibition hall and an auditorium. Both are sheltered by the same lofty, flat roof composed of 15 foot deep trusses, all exposed and painted black, spanning 150 feet in each direction and cantilevered half as much on all sides. As Mies would have conceded and Viollet-le-Duc might have approved, McCormick Place can claim a more distant antecedent than the nearby Crown Hall: the train sheds and exhibition halls of nineteenth-century Europe.

### Wright's Second Career

In 1940 Mies van der Rohe recalled how thirty years earlier he and other young modernists in Europe had been stirred by the "clarity of language and disconcerting richness of form" in the work of Frank Lloyd Wright as revealed to them by the exhibition of his work in Berlin and the Wasmuth portfolio. "So after this first encounter," he wrote, "we followed the development of this rare man with wakeful hearts. We watched with astonishment the exuberant unfolding of [his] gifts. . . . In his undiminishing power he resembles a giant tree in a wide landscape, which year after year, attains a more noble crown."[3] What Mies could not have known was that the giant tree—one of the two giant trees in the wide landscape of

American twentieth-century architecture—still had nearly two decades in which to put out new growth.

The 1920s and the early 1930s were personally difficult and architecturally unproductive for Wright. In the midst of the Depression Wright despaired of ever seeing another project built and resigned himself to rural life at Taliesin, his ancestral farm near Spring Green, Wisconsin. In 1932 he established the Taliesin Fellowship for young people who wished to study architecture informally, to live and work as part of Wright's extended family. He saw his remaining years as a philosopher-architect inculcating his apprentices with his oblique wisdom and prejudices. His recovery and his second career began in 1934 with the unexpected but welcome commission for a modest house for the Malcolm Willeys of Minneapolis. Two years after the Willey House, even more unexpectedly, came two unique commissions within months of each other, the Kaufmann House called "Fallingwater" and the Johnson Wax Building. The year 1940 began two more decades sustained by continued opportunities and a bold display of his incomparable talent, fully justifying Mies van der Rohe's tribute.

*Baroque Interlude*

Between Wright's first mature period, ending with his departure for Europe in 1909, and his second career, beginning in the mid-1930s, is work of a wholly different character. Some have called it his Baroque phase, for it is characterized by very complex forms and florid decoration. Wright's new fascination with the triangle and the circle is also evident during these years. He subsequently withdrew from Baroque exuberance, but triangular and circular motifs became the basis for many of his late works.

Two examples illustrate Wright's Baroque interlude, one very large and one very small. Midway Gardens occupied a full city block in Chicago, comprising a restaurant and a large outdoor cafe with a bandstand (291). Built in 1914, its short life ended sadly with Prohibition. The extensive base was overwhelmed by patterned concrete block, cubist figure sculpture cast in concrete, and fanciful towers in which sculptural and architectural forms were interwoven.[4] This decorative treatment was appropriately festive and not wholly unexpected in view of Wright's earlier use of pattern, as in the stucco and tile panels of the Coonley House. But in the earlier work decoration is fully controlled by architectonic effects; in Midway Gardens it is the other way about. Wright's Imperial Hotel in Tokyo (1918–22) is even more flamboyant, with its decorative details in lava stone instead of concrete.

291
*Midway Gardens, Chicago, Illinois. Frank Lloyd Wright, 1914. Exterior.*

Pleased with his transformation of the lowly concrete block into a decorative as well as structural material, Wright called it "textile block" because he threaded its joints with strands of reinforcing steel. He used this technique for a small house in Pasadena, California, for Mrs. George Millard (1923), illustrating as well his continued interest in decoration. Restrained only in silhouette, the exterior is entirely of patterned concrete block, some of it pierced for a trellised effect. The identical block appears inside, where its scale is perhaps less appropriate. Yet in total effect "La Miniatura," as the Millard House is called, enchants us with an almost Venetian sensuality, veiled by eucalyptus and reflected in a pool in the hollow of its ravine site. Wright continued to use decorative concrete block through the twenties in a number of buildings, including several houses in Los Angeles, none as satisfying as that in Pasadena.

**Usonian Houses**

During the idle years of the early thirties Wright created his imaginary Broadacre City, which illustrates "Usonia," Wright's 1927 coinage for an idealized America.[5] Beginning in 1936 he applied the term to a series of small houses that realized the impossible: distinctive architecture and privacy at a modest price. The first Herbert Jacobs House in Madison, Wisconsin (1937), is the complete Usonian prototype, although many elements of Usonian planning were anticipated in the Willey design. Wright began with an advantageous

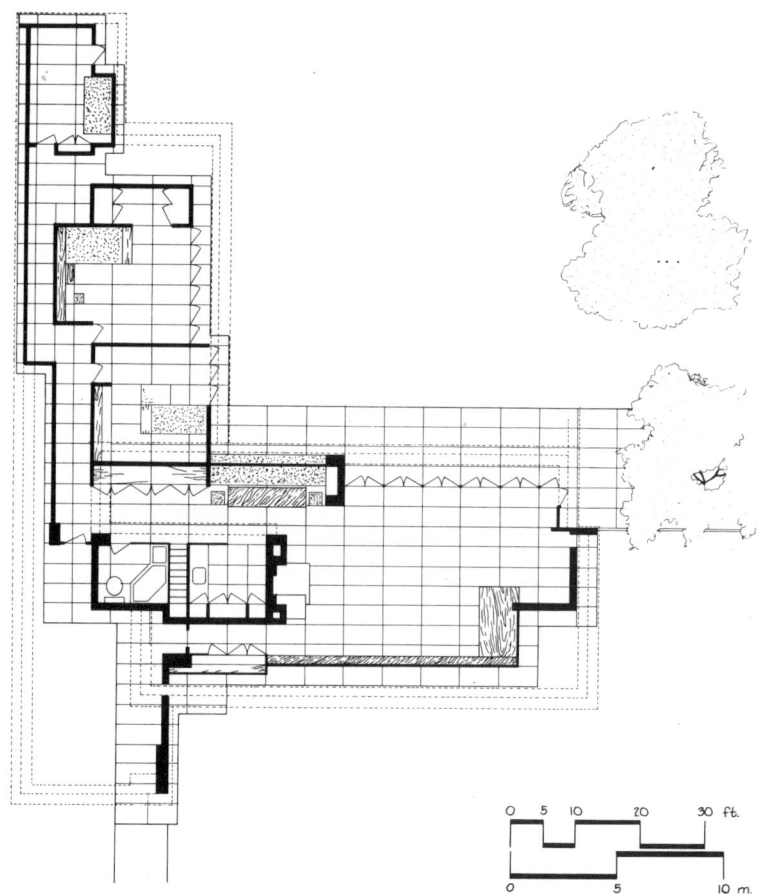

292
*Herbert Jacobs House,*
*Madison, Wisconsin.*
*Frank Lloyd Wright,*
*1937. Plan.*

293
*Goetsch-Winkler House,*
*Okemos, Michigan. Frank*
*Lloyd Wright, 1939.*
*Exterior.*

off-center placement of the house on its site; there is no useless front yard; a carport near the street supersedes the driveway; and all major rooms look out on a generous garden (292). Anticipating prefabrication, he simplified construction by replacing the conventional stud wall with a triple-layered board sandwich separated by insulating paper, standardizing construction details, and basing the whole plan on a modular grid, usually two feet by four. Heating is by the gravity system, with hot water or steam circulating in coils embedded in a concrete slab poured on grade. The kitchen, which Wright called the workspace, together with the bath, utility room, and often the fireplace, are located at a central point in these houses— at the elbow in L-shaped plans such as that of the Jacobs House. Spaciousness is achieved by combining the dining room with the living area and linking it to the nearby workspace, more an alcove than a separate kitchen. This openness differs from the bedroom wing, where the chambers are minimal and the corridor is often as narrow as that of a Pullman car. The cost of the Jacobs House, including the architect's fee, was only $5,500.

With his Usonian series Wright confirmed that he was by temperament primarily a designer of houses. The sensitivity and variety seen in it is remarkable. Even in conventional flat locations Wright's layered horizontal roofs, on occasion visually reinforced by banked earth berms, make a perfect marriage of house and site. The most lyrical of all Usonian examples is the Goetsch-Winkler House in Okemos, Michigan (1939), with its arrested movement of shifted planes both in plan and elevation (293). As we turn from the nearly thirty-foot sweep of windows and French doors to the seclusion of the fireplace alcove, we become fully aware of an interior integral with the exterior and the supporting role of built-in tables and seating. What is overwhelming is the poetry of space and structure that Wright shrugged off as "natural simplicity." To live in a Wright house, as owners have happily confessed, is to acquiesce in Wright's values and way of life.

*Square, Triangle, and Circle*

The idea of a weekend house set deep in the woods does not conjure up the high drama of "Fallingwater," one of the two or three most famous houses of the twentieth century (294). Here is not a timid act of deference to the wilderness but an exaltation of man-made geometry. However unprecedented in being poised over a rocky stream, Fallingwater is esthetically familiar: here is the same play of intersecting and projected planes in space that appears in the Prairie houses, most emphatically in the Mrs. Thomas Gale House of 1909. But in Fallingwater Wright assembled his supporting piers

294
*Fallingwater, Kaufmann
House, Bear Run, Penn-
sylvania. Frank Lloyd
Wright, 1936. Exterior.*

all to one side, on one bank of the stream. This cluster acts as a dislocated pivot for a triple tier of rooms with extended terracelike balconies in three directions. Fallingwater suggests spontaneity; in fact, those working with Wright at the time have said that the design was conceived almost instantaneously. Certainly its intensity is appropriate for intermittent rather than continuous occupancy. The Kaufmann weekend retreat remains the freshest monument of modern architecture.

In his long lifetime of triumphs and disappointments, Wright could never have forgotten the significance of the year 1936: the start of his Usonian cycle of houses, the Johnson Wax commission, and the popular success of Fallingwater. At the age of sixty-nine he surprised the world, if not himself, with his seemingly inexhaustible lode of talent. He continued to flout the architectural establishment and scorn the advancing modernism from Europe.[6] The work that followed was increasingly subjective, willfully assertive, daring, even improbable, such as his fantasy proposal for a mile-high skyscraper for Chicago (1956). Wright had no patience for the tabulation of requirements, budgets and bureaucracy, or design by committee. The diversity of his last works resists stylistic analysis. The individual artist simply yielded "to the fascination of creation."

To comprehend Wright's diversity it is perhaps useful to return to his theory of organic architecture. For example, the botanical analogy of a plant stem suggested the design of a wooden windmill called "Romeo and Juliet," which he built for his aunts at Spring Green in 1897. This organic concept of growth and the relatedness of parts was elaborated for several skyscraper designs using the cantilever principle, the structure analogous to the supporting trunk of a tree, its branches, and the outer enclosure of leaves. One of these was the St. Mark's Tower project of 1929 for New York City, abandoned on account of the Depression. Here Wright devised an ingenious pinwheel plan of four duplex apartments on each floor with an intermediate bedroom level rotated 30° so that it formed a balcony overlooking the living room; one bedroom was to have an outside balcony as well. The exterior form expresses every interior condition. Years later, in 1956, the design was executed in modified form as the H. C. Price Tower in Bartlesville, Oklahoma (295). Three of the quadrant tiers are standard office floors, but the fourth tier is retained as duplex apartments almost identical to those of the 1929 prototype. The Price Tower and the earlier Johnson Wax Research Tower (1950) at Racine are Wright's only executed tall buildings. Overlooking his own anti-urban prejudices—Wright could

295
Price Tower, Bartlesville,
Oklahoma. Frank Lloyd
Wright, 1953–56.
Exterior.

never live or work in a skyscraper—his proposals give us a personal view of an assignment that Mies saw as a generic one.

On numerous other occasions Wright recycled his unexecuted ideas in part or in whole. A recurrent motif is the prow-shaped terrace that first appeared in projects of the early twenties, among them the Doheny Ranch for the Sierra Madre mountains and summer cabins for Lake Tahoe. It is reused in the Willey House, Taliesin West, and the First Unitarian Church in Madison, Wisconsin. In the church, completed in 1950, Wright heightened the prow effect with a copper-sheathed, pointed roof above a triangular plan, a roof he likened to folded hands in prayer, even though the form appears earlier in the Lake Tahoe Summer Colony project and elsewhere. Symbolism aside, the Madison church is one of Wright's most disarmingly simple compositions with many subtleties of plan and siting. His most dramatic sloping roofs, however, were those that combined wall and roof, such as in his tentlike, steel-and-glass cathedral for a million people proposed for New York in 1926. Changing his cluster plan to a more simple tripartite one and substituting corrugated plastic for glass, Wright finally, in 1959, realized his interfaith cathedral design in the Philadelphia suburb of Elkins Park, the Beth Sholem Synagogue.

That the circle is far more difficult to adjust in plan than the square or triangle or that its corollary forms—arc, spiral, and dome—are difficult to construct was hardly a limitation for Wright. He understood the circle as a readily identifiable and satisfying form and used it in both large and small projects. His two most interesting houses based on the circle are the Ralph Jester House (1938) and the second Herbert Jacobs House (1948–49). In the Jester project, planned for a hillside at Palos Verdes, California, the rooms are separate circles loosely connected by a partially roofed rectangular terrace whose edge borders a huge, circular swimming pool.[7] The Jacobs House in Middleton, Wisconsin, is set at the edge of prairie farmland. In this 1943 design Wright used a hollow ring, part house, part earth berm, to enclose a circular, sunken garden, viewed through a crescent of tall windows.

The venerable shadow of the Pantheon, with its countless copies, conditions us to accept the circle and dome as appropriate to monumental buildings. Yet Wright was able to reinterpret these motifs as if he were using them for the first time in history. That is the thought when viewing his Annunciation Greek Orthodox Church in Wauwatosa, outside Milwaukee, Wisconsin (1956), or the Guggenheim Museum in New York (1956–59). Both illustrate the plastic shaping made possible with concrete. The form of the church

296
*Guggenheim Museum,
New York City. Frank
Lloyd Wright, 1956–59.
Interior.*

suggests two cupped saucers, separated by a decorative ring of windows, the whole cradled by four supports; it could possibly be an abstraction of a raised chalice. It is a spectacular image in ivory-colored concrete, accented by a dazzling blue dome and girdled with gold anodized aluminum—the same colors are used inside—an effect that to some may evoke the Arabian nights rather than the traditions of the Greek Orthodox Church.

The Guggenheim Museum project, begun in 1943, suffered many changes and delays (296). Over more than a decade before construction, Wright struggled with his concept of a circular, spiral-ramped interior, even at one time proposing a hexagonal version. A commission that came to him during this period, the V. C. Morris Store in San Francisco of 1948, gave Wright the chance to experiment with this concept in a limited way, remodelling an existing building into a miniature Guggenheim and giving it a handsome flat facade recalling both Richardson and Sullivan. An open spiral is an unorthodox solution for either a gift shop or a museum. It suggests an automobile ramp, which is exactly the function it had in Wright's Maryland planetarium project of 1925 and a Pittsburgh self-service garage scheme of 1947. For all that, the ramp concept affords a clear circulation path for museum visitors: one takes an elevator to the top level and then strolls downward past the exhibits, although

297
*Taliesin West, Scottsdale,*
*Arizona. Frank Lloyd*
*Wright, begun in 1938.*
*Exterior.*

everything is admittedly viewed on a slant. The dynamic interior of the Guggenheim is, for some, too competitive for the display of art, but no one disputes that it is one of the memorable spaces in all architecture.

The city was not Wright's milieu, as the anomalous character of the Guggenheim Museum in its New York setting proves. His own choice, in 1938, was the then lonely Arizona desert north of Phoenix as the site for a permanent encampment to serve as winter home for himself and his Fellowship. Wright's Taliesin West was a low, extended arrangement of primitive desert stone and poured concrete with a superstructure of spaced redwood frames fitted with taut, white canvas (now replaced with plastic) (297). This brooding, introspective monastery, modified by Wright over the years, is still inhabited by his disciples, who work under the name of Taliesin Associated Architects and the leadership of William Wesley Peters, the first Fellowship apprentice in 1932. After Wright's death they completed his largest commission, the Marin County Civic Center at San Rafael, California.

*Inspiration from Wright*     Under his enormous shade few of Wright's students were able to summon up the self-confidence necessary for independent, creative work. Among those who did are Alden Dow and John Lautner. Lloyd Wright (Frank Lloyd Wright, Jr.), one of two sons who became architects, was never formally his father's pupil, but he did supervise the building of Wright's Los Angeles houses in the twenties. It is instantly recognizable that Lloyd Wright's work was inspired by his father's, even if it is always more agitated. This is immediately apparent when one compares the redwood framing of Taliesin West with that of the Wayfarers' (Swedenborg Memorial) Chapel (298). Designed in 1946 and built in 1951 with later additions, this chapel at Palos Verdes, California, suggests prisms of glass, which are combined with triangles set with blue tile; both are held in a structural web that itself suggests the armature of vaulting. The chapel complements its dramatic setting amid redwoods on a promontory overlooking the Pacific where architectural reticence would have been inappropriate.

Among those who savored life in Wright's Oak Park studio at the turn of the century was Francis Barry Byrne; an assistant for seven years, he left in 1908. Byrne was always loyal to the progressive stance of Sullivan and Wright, but his curiosity and open-mindedness allowed him to absorb such divergent viewpoints as the abstractions of Irving Gill and (notably in the Church of St. Thomas the Apostle in Chicago built in 1922) the Expressionism of Hans Poelzig, both of whose works he knew firsthand. He was favored by the Roman Catholic hierarchy in the Midwest with several churches in the twenties that demonstrate a mature and original style. The sculptor of Midway Gardens, Alfonso Iannelli, assisted him on several projects. One of Byrne's later buildings, the Church of St. Francis Xavier (1949) in Kansas City, Missouri, with a fish-shaped plan and smoothly curved brick walls, is his best-known work.

Wright's precedent guided many young architects other than those who had worked under him. Bruce Goff is doubtless the most conspicuous, though not for his Wrightian forms. (As a curious boy, Goff wrote to Wright asking for information about his work and Wright replied by sending him gift copies of the Wasmuth volumes.) Goff made Wright's stand for individuality, respect for site, and use of materials points of departure for his own career and work. Starting at the age of twelve, Goff learned architecture in the Tulsa office of Rush, Endacott and Rush; by fifteen he had designed his first building, a creditable Prairie Style house near Los Angeles (1919). Sullivan influenced him in his Boston Avenue Methodist-Episcopal Church (1925–28) in Tulsa, Oklahoma, which he designed

298
*Wayfarers' Chapel, Palos
Verdes, California. Lloyd
Wright, 1951. Interior.*

299
Gene Bavinger House,
Norman, Oklahoma.
Bruce Goff, 1950–55.
Exterior.

while working for the same firm. Goff's first independent commission, the Unseth House in Park Ridge, Illinois (1934–41), began a series of radical and entertaining houses that have been the despair of critics and the joy of their owners. His architecture is literally inimitable, and only his pupil Herb Greene has worked in the same spirit. The Bavinger House near Norman, Oklahoma (1950–55), is based on a seashell curve in stone, which rises to support a mast from which tension cables descend to support "floating" bedrooms as well as a roof and stairs (299). Goff's maverick architecture is very different from Wright's, yet by reason of that difference the more impressive as testimony of the fructifying power of Wright's example.

The doctrines of the International Style were not accepted everywhere. All through the 1940s and beyond the architects of the San Francisco Bay region and the Pacific Northwest resisted them, despite the presence of Mendelsohn at Berkeley. This resistance was rooted in the self-conscious regionalism that Maybeck and his circle had originated in the early years of the century. An architect who continued this trend in his residential work in the late twenties and thirties was William W. Wurster. Wurster respected tradition but did not regard it as sacrosanct. His houses were modest yet precisely built; one of the best (and earliest) is the Gregory farmhouse in Santa Cruz (1927), which follows the courtyard plan of Anglo-Spanish ranch houses. Although in the forties the geometrical clarity and modular rhythms of the International Style could be detected in Wurster's designs, his buildings remained unobtrusive, their scale small, and their material often wood; an example is the rural office building for the Schukl Canning Company in Sunnyvale (1942).

Following Wurster's lead in the forties were John Funk, Gardner Dailey, Joseph Esherick, and Harwell Hamilton Harris. Further north, in Oregon, the domestic work of Pietro Belluschi is similarly sensitive and regional in feeling, unassuming yet personal. Belluschi's churches, for example the redwood Central Lutheran Church in Portland (1948), are reminiscent of the wooden churches of Richard Upjohn and they are equally fine.

In 1947 the critic Lewis Mumford, calling into question the deficiencies of the International Style in domestic architecture, praised the houses of Maybeck and Wurster for their "native and humane form of modernism." [1] "They took good care," he wrote, "that their houses did not resemble factories or museums." Thus the Bay Region Style, as the manner of the West Coast architects came to be called, was recognized as another modernism—and a native one—at a time when modernism from Europe in the form of the International Style was beginning to come under fire from former adherents as well as architects and critics who had never accepted its claim to be the style of the twentieth century.

By the mid-1950s the International Style was being attacked from all sides, the motivation of its assailants ranging from dissatisfaction with its narrow esthetic to disappointment with its diversion from lofty goals. Many were openly critical of the very premises of the twentieth-century modern movement, although their own objectives were diffuse, their vision clouded, and their criteria subjective. Some proposed an existentialist architecture to express the uncertainties of the age; others advocated a return to neglected symbols to increase communication in an architecture that had become too abstract; yet others, restless from the inhibiting limitations of the International Style, were for deserting the Phileban forms of solid geometry for freer shapes. Uniformity and dogma were replaced by diversity and experiment.

It must be acknowledged that the products of the International Style in the thirties and forties had their weaknesses; however, these were only the delayed effect of what occurred earlier when modern architecture withdrew from the rigorous structural, technological, and functional objectivity that it originally espoused to compromise with an easier, more painterly manipulation of visual forms and surfaces. For example, the early resolve to employ the industrial process and materials was followed up to a point only. Experiments with mass-produced, prefabricated houses were limited; never did a satisfactory solution sustain itself in the marketplace. It was Buckminster Fuller, more inventor than architect, who in 1927 designed the truly original Dymaxion House, with its hexagonal form suspended from a central mast anchored in the ground (300). Totally uninterested in conventional visual solutions, even of the modern sort, Fuller had as his goal maximum performance with maximum economy. His second version of the Dymaxion principle, a house built in Wichita, Kansas, in 1946, resembled a sheet-metal igloo. Fuller's challenge to live in a metal capsule was not taken up, and architects were reluctant to follow his lead for fear of abandoning their traditional role as visual designers. In 1949 Charles Eames designed a much admired semiprefabricated house for himself in Pacific Palisades, California (301). Assorted standard sections of factory glazing and opaque panels were fitted between a light steel skeleton. The two-story living room with bedroom balcony derives from LeCorbusier's series of artists' houses; its esthetic ancestor is the post-beam-panel Japanese teahouse. But much of the appeal of the house came from the juxtaposition of its terse form with the surrounding trees and the flair with which the designer furnished it. Although traditional by comparison with Fuller's inventions, the Eames House did not, despite its popularity, provoke much direct imitation.[2]

Nor was the ideal of reuniting engineering with architecture realized. The space-frame constructions of Konrad Wachsmann and the Geodesic domes of Fuller were employed only in limited ways. One exceptional structure was the State Fair Arena at Raleigh, North Carolina, completed in 1953, which the Polish-born Matthew Nowicki designed before his death in 1950. It was the first major suspension-roof structure. two giant arches are positioned to form

300
Dymaxion House. Buck-
minster Fuller, 1927.
Model.

301
Charles Eames House,
Pacific Palisades, Califor-
nia. Charles Eames, 1949.
Exterior.

a cradlelike structure from which suspension cables span a distance of 325 feet. Secondary cables placed at right angles to the primary cables form a net to support the roof.

*Expressionism Revived*

Even those who believed that the cycles of art history ensure a return to individualism after the impersonality of a classic period must have found it surprising that the change should first appear in the work of an architect who had been a tasteful interpreter of Mies. Eero Saarinen's later buildings, those designed between 1956 and 1961, revived the assertive forms of German Expressionism of the early 1920s, particularly those of Mendelsohn. The streamlined shapes used have analogies in automobile styling, which considers visual identity above all else. Saarinen was, without a doubt, also affected by the bold concrete structures of Nervi and Candela, but his interest was more visual than technical. The Kresge Auditorium at MIT built in 1955, is a concrete shell—one-eighth of a sphere resting on three points—with neither the inevitable logic nor the soaring grace of the engineer's art; it contains an inner acoustic shell of different profile, a spherical segment being exactly the shape to be avoided for the acoustics of an auditorium. Unsuitability aside, Saarinen created an image that is instantly recognizable though not really expressive of anything but its own geometry (302).

Saarinen's Expressionist period began in 1956 with the Ingalls Hockey Rink at Yale University, which was completed in 1958, and the Trans World Airline Terminal at Kennedy Airport in New York, completed in 1962 (303, 304). These buildings flaunt Saarinen's then unorthodox view of choosing "the style for the job"; he sought to express in them the excitement of ice hockey and air travel, creating a vessel for sport and a winged canopy for flight. The Yale rink is spanned lengthwise by a center parabolic supporting arch in reinforced concrete; tension cables are suspended from the arch and are anchored laterally in low concrete walls, which enclose the building and are of similar curvature on plan. At each end the arched spine is extended outward in a reverse curve to form a cantilevered beam supporting entrance canopies. Once a student of sculpture, Saarinen contrasted curves with countercurves, concave with convex.

The TWA Terminal, developed from a more complex program than the Yale rink, achieved a similar visual drama. That its arching roofs looked like a bird in flight was coincidental, according to the architect, though he had long felt that the "urge to soar great distances . . . to reach upward and outward [is] man's desire to conquer gravity." The building consists of a reinforced concrete roof

with four curved segments supported by four Y-shaped buttresses, all of which shelters a central waiting room. The thickness of the concrete shell varies from seven to forty inches. Pier Luigi Nervi said that it was too heavy and the design too elaborate for the problem it seeks to solve. But Saarinen was a sculptor-architect, not an engineer. Inside the terminal, one inhabits a piece of sculpture. A search for precedents uncovers a Naum Gabo project of 1931 for a double auditorium in Moscow, the twisted forms of sculpture by Gabo's brother Antoine Pevsner, and the cavelike spaces of Antonio Gaudi.[3]

For the Dulles International Airport (1958–62), which serves Washington, D.C., Saarinen reverted to a rectangular plan but maintained a sculptured effect (305). The mobile lounges that shuttle passengers between the terminal and the planes simplified the plan and made for compactness. Three terraced levels, serving as access ways for automobiles, provide a visual platform for a series of monumental concrete piers across the front. Between these and a lower row of piers across the back is hung a cable roof, infilled with precast panels where wood had been used at Yale. The piers lean dramatically outward to counteract the pull of the cables, and the projection of the roof resulting from this serves as a bold canopy for the 600-foot length of the structure. The building was designed to be easily extended at either end. In the Dulles Airport, his last Expressionist work, Saarinen balanced, in nearly equal measure, utility, structure, esthetics, and symbolism. At a time of widespread questioning about architectural directions, Saarinen's answer was that public architecture should express the nature of its special purpose in our lives.

Saarinen's work aside, most Neo-Expressionist buildings are churches. Three examples illustrate their range: the First Presbyterian Church in Stamford, Connecticut (1958), by Harrison and Abramovitz; the Chapel of the United States Air Force Academy at

303
*Ingalls Hockey Rink, Yale University, New Haven, Connecticut. Eero Saarinen & Associates, 1956–58. Exterior.*

304
*Trans World Airlines Terminal, New York City. Eero Saarinen & Associates, 1956–62. Interior.*

305
*Dulles International Airport, Chantilly, Virginia. Eero Saarinen & Associates, 1958–62. Exterior.*

306
*Chapel, United States Air Force Academy, Colorado Springs, Colorado. Skidmore, Owings & Merrill, 1956–62. Exterior.*

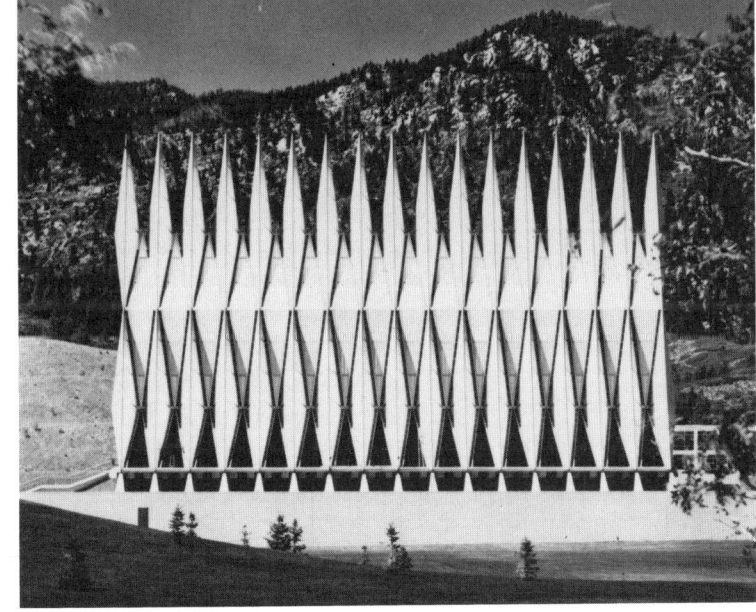

Colorado Springs (1956–62) by Walter Netsch of Skidmore, Owings & Merrill; and St. Mary's Cathedral in San Francisco (1971) by Pietro Belluschi and Pier Luigi Nervi. The radical appearance of the Stamford church is due in large part to its fish-shaped plan, employed for reasons of acoustics as well as symbolism. The structure is a jigsaw assembly of one hundred fifty-two precast-concrete panels, slanting inward to form a crimped skin. Quadrangular panels are covered with slate, and triangular ones contain tracery fitted with colored glass; the effect is so striking as to deny attention to the chancel. The Air Force Academy Chapel, which is also triangular in cross section, is more restless in form despite its precision (306). One hundred prefabricated tetrahedrons of welded steel pipe were assembled on a rectangular plan and the resultant cage was sheathed in silvery aluminum and set with strips of colored glass. But the effect remains intellectual; it is a chapel without ceremonial space and unresponsive to its mountainous setting.[4]

In contrast to this fragile geometry, the 190-foot-high sweeping roof of St. Mary's Cathedral, formed by four hyperbolic paraboloids in concrete, seems exactly suited to its hilltop site (307). The interior is equally dramatic. A wire sculpture by Richard Lippold serves as a baldacchino for the altar, which is placed off-center instead of, as one might have expected, at the crossing of the bisymmetrical structure, itself a giant canopy over the entire volume of space.

Large dimensions are usually demanded to sustain the unique shapes of Neo-Expressionism; there are few Neo-Expressionist houses and very few successful ones. The most memorable was built in Lincoln, Massachusetts, in 1965, by Thomas McNulty and his architect-wife. Simply constructed of plain concrete exposed inside and out, it is given life by its plan, comprising a single continuous space, 150 feet long, shaped by segments of curved walls. With each alternating enclosure and release come changing patterns of light across pale gray, textured walls (308).

Related to Expressionism in its outward form but evolved from a rational, sociotechnological system is the extraordinary project called Arcosanti, under construction in central Arizona. Designed as a small (3,000 inhabitants) prototype for a city of the future, Arcosanti is a demonstration of "Arcology," a concept of Italian-born Paolo Soleri, who was briefly a student-apprentice of Wright. The antithesis of Wright's Broadacre City, Soleri's ideal city is an extremely compact one because compactness in his view is necessary to offset the increased complexity of modern life. Although Arcosanti is a laboratory for studying environmental problems, the individual structures that have appeared on the barren landscape are sculptured designs in

*307*
*St. Mary's Cathedral,*
*San Francisco, California.*
*Pietro Belluschi and Pier*
*Luigi Nervi, 1971.*
*Exterior.*

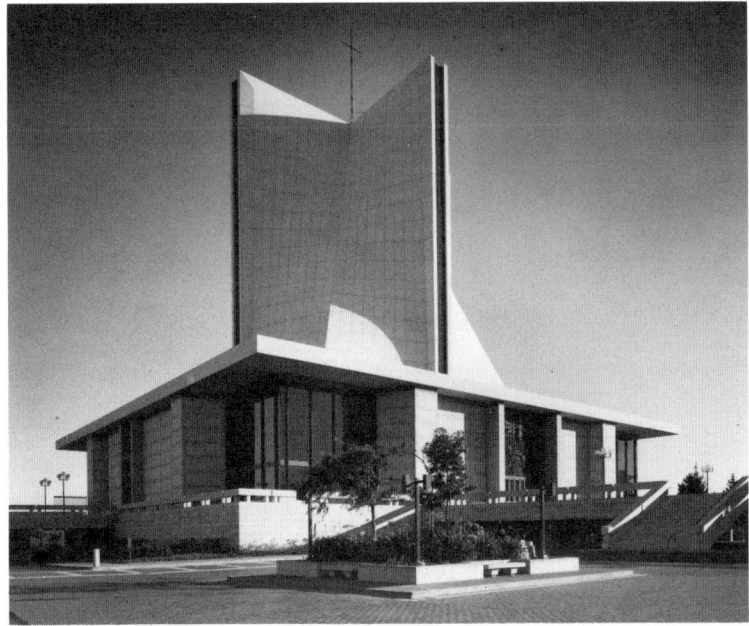

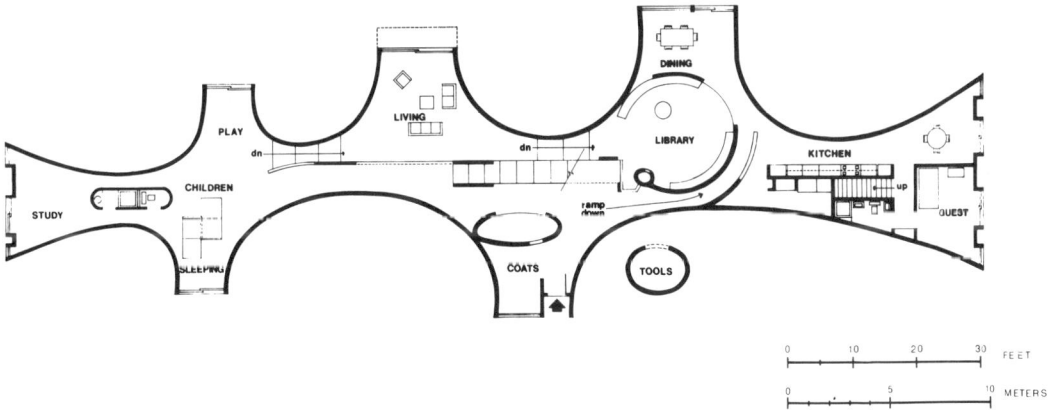

*308*
*Thomas McNulty House,*
*Lincoln, Massachusetts.*
*Thomas McNulty and*
*Mary Harkness, 1965.*
*Plan.*

concrete with segmental forms, reminiscent of those used by Soleri earlier in his Cosanti Foundation near Phoenix (begun in 1955). As the latter was, Arcosanti is being built by mostly unskilled, young apprentices who form Soleri's following.

*The New Formalism*

The movement variously called Neo-neo-Classicism or New Formalism had many more adherents than Neo-Expressionism ever did. Conspicuous among them were Edward Durell Stone, Minoru Yamasaki, Philip Johnson, Wallace Harrison, and Max Abramovitz; even Walter Gropius in his designs with TAC for Athens and Baghdad succumbed to its power of attraction. The respectable and perhaps bland presence that could be given to buildings of skeletal frame construction, whether of steel or reinforced concrete, was in its favor. Clients readily accepted the superficial elegance of the New Formalism as an artistic achievement and a worthy symbol of their culture, government, or business enterprise. Some architects were quick to flatter themselves that they had restored long-exiled beauty to architecture. In fact the New Formalism lacked vigor and had little real importance; it was a minor episode in the reaction against the programmed severities of the International Style.

The classical attributes of symmetry, enclosed form, and regular structure were never wholly absent from modern architecture. It is possible to regard Mies's Seagram Building as a pointer of the New Formalism, but the building in which all the salient characteristics of the movement were first manifested was Edward Stone's American Embassy at New Delhi (1954). Here was the temple reclaimed: a suave pavilion with gilded steel supports in front of a seductive screen of openwork terrazzo blocks to filter out sunlight. (Wright used similar block in the Millard House of 1923.) Stone reused the formula of the New Delhi embassy in the Stuart Pharmaceutical Company in Pasadena (1956), the Stanford University Hospital (1959), and the Kennedy Center for Performing Arts in Washington (1959) (309). He himself lived in a remodelled New York brownstone (1956) whose facade was replaced by a screen of concrete blocks.[5]

Yamasaki joined in the pursuit of delight after a visit to New Delhi. His neoformalist designs are more lively in their detail than Stone's and often contain a suggestion of Gothic mixed with classicism. In the McGregor Memorial Conference Center for Wayne State University in Detroit (1958) Yamasaki bisected the length of a rectangular building with a two-story lobby recalling a Victorian conservatory. Its faceted glass reflects the bevelled motif of triangular concrete box-beams. This formal yet delicate building, set among water gardens such as Stone had used at New Delhi, was hailed as

309
*Stuart Pharmaceutical
Company, Pasadena, Cal-
ifornia. Edward D. Stone,
1956. Exterior.*

310
*McGregor Memorial Con-
ference Center, Wayne
State University, Detroit,
Michigan. Minoru Yama-
saki and Associates, 1958.
Exterior.*

311
*Sheldon Memorial Art
Gallery, University of
Nebraska, Lincoln, Ne-
braska. Philip Johnson,
1963. Exterior.*

312
*Lincoln Center for the
Performing Arts, New
York City. Harrison and
Abramovitz and Philip
Johnson, 1962–68. View.*

a timely loosening of esthetic strictures (310). Yamasaki followed the conference center with the Reynolds Aluminum Building of 1959, also in Detroit. This is basically a Miesian structure of three stories with a skylit interior court and the upper stories fitted with exterior screens of gold-anodized aluminum, a metallic version of Stone's openwork concrete block. Miesian austerity was apparent at a distance, but close at hand was the sensuous sight of a golden veil over a water-lilied moat and a plush purple carpet overlaid on an expanse of polished white terrazzo. Yamasaki took the final step toward the temple form in the Northwestern Life Insurance Company in Minneapolis (1962–64). A six-story office building inset with dark-green marble and gray glass to minimize floor levels, it is wrapped in an ethereal screen of tall, slender white concrete arches, reflected in pools of water.

Philip Johnson's formalist buildings are distinguished from those of Yamasaki and Stone by a more intellectual monumentality both within and without. With his scholarly mind, especially open to the influence of Schinkel and Soane, Johnson was an anomaly among the rank-and-file architects who viewed themselves as futurists or at least fully contemporary practitioners and him as a dilettante, although his sizable commissions soon led them to revise this opinion. In particular, Johnson's sympathy with the Beaux-Arts and his awareness of the processional element in design and siting gave his work an altogether more serious character.

Once a self-proclaimed disciple of Mies, Johnson turned from his Lieber Meister's principles in 1956, ironically the very year he was asked to associate with Mies on the Seagram Building. The Kneses Tifereth Israel Synagogue at Port Chester, New York, a steel-framed box enclosed with white concrete panels with only staggered slits of colored glass in between, was the first work of his apostasy. Although largely opaque, it has a sense of airiness and unreality, an illusion sustained within by a scalloped canopy suspended underneath the length of the structural ceiling.

Such delicate effects do not appear in Johnson's later formalist buildings: the Amon Carter Museum in Fort Worth, Texas (1961), and the Sheldon Memorial Art Gallery for the University of Nebraska at Lincoln (1963) (311). Both museums are arcaded in sculptured stone; their unbroken curves and tapered lines suggest a giant frame molded in one piece. Juxtaposed with these arcades are Miesian elements of curtain wall and, in the Sheldon Art Gallery, a Miesian stairway. The small and shallow plan of the Carter Museum behind the presumptuous facade is further dwarfed by Johnson's conception of the building as a viewing platform for the axial sequence of descending terraces and the skyline beyond. In both the museum and the art gallery a new visual vocabulary was being tested without abandoning the proven usefulness of the old.

That America never regained the ease with monumentality of the McKim years is proved by the assortment of auditoriums in New York called the Lincoln Center for the Performing Arts, completed in 1968 (312). The Campidoglio-like plan is focused on Wallace Harrison's Metropolitan Opera House (1966), flanked by Max Abramovitz's Philharmonic (now Avery Fisher) Hall (1962), and Philip Johnson's New York State Theater (1964), each with a variation on the theme of the monumental colonnade. The various provincial culture centers that Lincoln Center spawned, with their plazas and colonnades, did not improve upon the center's quality, and before the end of the sixties enthusiasm for the New Formalism ran out.

*The Influence of*
*Le Corbusier*

Simultaneously with the rise of the New Formalism another generation, disenchanted with Mies and Gropius, was turning to the third patriarch of the International Style, Le Corbusier (Charles-Edouard Jeanneret). Unlike the two emigrés Le Corbusier was never favorably disposed to American values or opportunities. But the intensity and primitivism of his postwar buildings, notably the Unité d'Habitation in Marseilles, the Maisons Jaoul at Neuilly, and the Monastery of La Tourette, had a strong appeal for architects to whom the quite different qualities of his earlier works had become insufficient. The feature common to all the three buildings is the exposed concrete with the imprint of the wooden forms left upon it—"béton brut," as Le Corbusier called it, supplying a convenient derivation for the term Brutalism, commonly used to designate the work of his followers, even if it originated in another context.[6]

The only building by Le Corbusier in the United States is the Carpenter Visual Arts Center (1961–64) at Harvard University (313). An iconoclastic building of raw concrete snugly inserted between Neo-Georgian buildings of fastidious brick, the Carpenter Center would at first seem to represent an outright rejection of the kind of respect for locale shown by Richardson's Sever Hall across the street. But Le Corbusier provided connective tissue with the campus by means of an oblique pathway through the building, a pathway that begins with entrance ramps at street level, front and back, and rises to the third level within. On each side the ballooning shapes of studios, in which light is monitored by the deep reveals of brise-soleils, cushion the genteel neighbors. It is a building that engages the emotions; one cannot remain indifferent to it. Unfortunately, Le Corbusier never saw the center.

313
*Carpenter Visual Arts Center, Harvard University, Cambridge, Massachusetts. Le Corbusier, 1961–64. Exterior.*

314
Boston City Hall, Boston,
Massachusetts. Kallmann,
McKinnell and Knowles,
1963–68. Exterior.

José Luis Sert, a follower of Le Corbusier since the thirties, was dean of the Harvard Graduate School of Design when the Carpenter Visual Arts Center was built and supervised its construction. In his own work for Harvard, Married Student Housing (1964) and Holyoke Center (1965), Sert remained loyal to Le Corbusier's philosophy, balancing a modular rationale with visual diversity and maintaining a high density of occupation to secure the amenities of urban life.

The year the Carpenter Center was designed a competition for a new city hall for Boston was announced. It drew 256 entries. A much publicized event in professional circles, it brought recognition to a trio of architects who had never built a major building, Kallmann, McKinnell and Knowles. Their winning design, executed in 1963–68, is the closest emulation of Le Corbusier's late style in the United States (314). Besides repeating the free-standing, slablike supports and cellular divisions of the upper floors of La Tourette, the architects have, more importantly, followed Le Corbusier's thinking. They have conceived their city hall not as a static, isolated monument but as an active form embedded in the matrix of the city, drawing upon the movement of people across the square, into and through the building. The red brick paving is a traditional Bostonian feature; it is used here not only for that reason but also as a means of uniting building and square and of symbolizing the breaking down of barriers between the people and their city government, which was the central philosophical aim of the architects. The council chamber, with a large window directly over the main entrance, is linked with the square by a stair tower faced with the same red brick.

## Rudolph and Breuer

The movement away from linear order and transparency was joined by some who had only recently completed their Bauhaus-oriented training. The best-known of these apostates is Paul Rudolph, former pupil of Walter Gropius. In the Sarasota Senior High School in Florida (1960) Rudolph turned to the spatial complexities possible with reinforced concrete, yet the essentials of his design forms were based on the integration of structural and mechanical systems. Here, and in most of his other works, Rudolph avoids direct borrowings from Le Corbusier; an exception is the Married Student Housing for Yale University (1961), with its obvious debts to the Maisons Jaoul.

The Art and Architecture Building at Yale, begun in 1958 and completed in 1964 (years when Rudolph was chairman of the department), was perhaps the most provocative American building of the decade (315, 316). Free of any Bauhaus constraints, Rudolph caused a collision of forms and interlocking spaces with cavernous

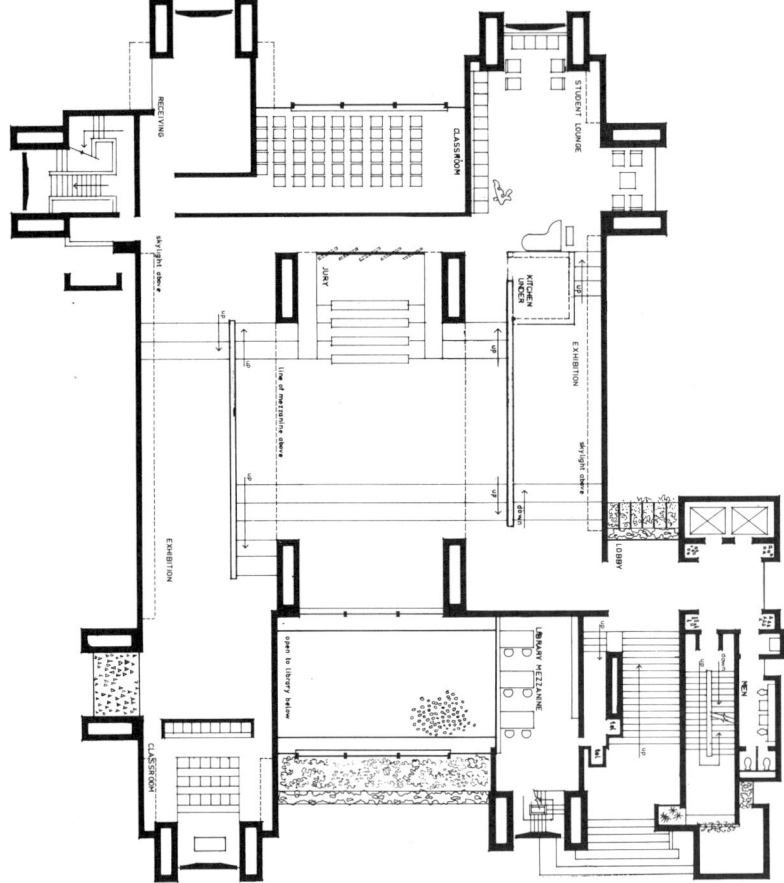

shadows, imparting a Piranesian element of mystery. The opaque, hollow piers for services, the windmill positioning of stairways, and a central skylighted space take us back to Wright's Larkin Building and Unity Temple. The sliding movement of horizontal beams past vertical supports, however inefficient structurally, recall Rietveld's de Stijl esthetics. The building is of a fascinating complexity. It contains a multiplicity of levels (thirty-seven in all) with crossing bridges and traylike spaces that may disorient the visitor but are arranged to separate various functions; there is even a penthouse suite for visiting critics. The contrived texture of the building stirred as much argument as more basic considerations. The vertical corrugations of concrete were the result of special formwork and were later hand-hammered to expose the inner aggregate and achieve an instant patina of age. Thus came the passing of an architectural ideal: a perpetual shining newness gave way to the weathered look.

Paul Rudolph survived the celebrity of the Yale building. Subsequent commissions of larger scale and with more demanding requirements tested his abilities, and the results enhanced his reputation. Characteristic of his work is a sense of onward rush, a compulsive drive toward a crescendo—exhausting to those who prefer architecture of a more tranquil tempo. Yet by virtue of its intrinsic principle, it is never merely exhibitionistic. Rudolph could produce architecture of distinction even within the stringent cost limits of public housing. Crawford Manor in New Haven (1962–66), consisting of high-rise apartments for the aged, is a case in point. Here the deeply fluted shadows created by the indented plan of the tower are repeated in more delicate fashion in the ribbing of the specially molded concrete block that covers the entire surface, including the cylindrically curved balconies.

Rudolph's Government Center in Boston (1962–68) is an urban complex of considerable size, executed with the cooperation of four other architectural firms. The splayed arrangement and stepped forms of the buildings on their triangular site suggest the influence of Alvar Aalto but are more declamatory in expression. In other urban projects Rudolph welcomed the difficult problem of combining pedestrian use with automobile access by devising buildings that are virtually miniature cities, or megastructures. The unexecuted Graphic Arts Center (1967), to be built over the West Side Drive in Manhattan, is an example. Here offices and apartments were to be combined with other services, including schools and a marina. Believing that the trailer-home is "the brick of twentieth-century technology," Rudolph stacked prefabricated apartment units in a manner similar to Moshe Safdie's Habitat housing built for the Montreal Exposition of the same year.

The qualities of design provided by Rudolph would have been totally incomprehensible had they appeared a decade earlier: walled forms, harsh textures, inward orientations, and a directional quality of space, not to mention an interest in monumentality and ceremony. These qualities, while conspicuous in Rudolph, were not his sole possession. In the unmistakable shifting of values in the mid-1950s others embraced them too, including a European expatriate, who, second to Mies, had the most illustrious and patronized career as a practicing architect in America: Marcel Breuer. Breuer, who came to the Bauhaus as an eighteen-year-old student in 1920, later to be an instructor, had been an intimate and constituent figure in German architectural development of the twenties and early thirties. Yet his innately pliable approach to design enabled him, as early as 1936, to temper the asceticism of the Bauhaus style, as seen in an exhibition pavilion in Bristol, England (designed in association with F. R. S. Yorke). The Gane's Pavilion was Breuer's turning point toward a more weighty and variable esthetic: uncoursed masonry wall-planes contrasted with large sheets of glass. Breuer was seemingly without the latent guilt about individuality common to many German modernists. From the very beginning his American work showed an open sympathy toward the visual craftsmanship of construction, toward a tactile language of building that reminds us of the muscularity of early Schindler. Furthermore, Breuer is the one German-trained architect who benefited from Le Corbusier, following his sense of individuality and primitiveness as well as adapting his planning and architectural motifs, particularly the pilotis and the brise-soleil.

Breuer's design for St. John's Monastery and College in Minnesota shows how he acknowledged the necessity for a broader esthetic and a considerably enlarged vocabulary of architecture (317). The Benedictines of St. John's, aware of their historic tradition of artistic patronage, interviewed five architects, including Gropius, Byrne, and Neutra—Belluschi and Saarinen declined—before choosing Breuer as their master architect for a comprehensive plan for a century of building. First constructed were a monastic wing and the great abbey church (1953–61). Breuer had never before built a ceremonial building of any kind, although he was working concurrently on the UNESCO Headquarters in Paris. For both projects he enlisted the talents of the Italian engineer-architect, Pier Luigi Nervi. It was Nervi who provided the folded-plate concrete shell design for the roof and walls of the church, similar to that of the UNESCO conference hall. As in the Romanesque and Gothic styles, one feels the

317
*St. John's Abbey Church,*
*Collegeville, Minnesota.*
*Marcel Breuer, 1953–61.*
*Exterior.*

flow of stresses through the structure; the structure itself becomes the architecture. And for the equivalent of the skyward thrust of medieval towers, Breuer conceived a free-standing bell banner, a pierced trapezoidal slab of raw concrete whose base supports also serve as an archway entrance to the church. Individuality and discipline, once opposites in Bauhaus doctrine, were united.

In Breuer's subsequent deflections from European modernism it became evident that the oldest of materials, wood and masonry, rather than the newest, steel and plate glass, held greater fascination for him. Breuer preferred the walled effects of masonry—in reinforced concrete, to be sure—over the skeletal frame. The lecture hall at New York University, one of a group of four buildings for University Heights in New York City (1956–61), is lifted above the ground by three supports. The textured patterns of formwork left in the concrete are contrived in trapezoidal areas to dramatize further the oblique angles of its side elevations.

Given the great number and variety of museums built in the third quarter of the century, one could easily write a synoptic architectural history of these years based on this single building type. Included would be the Whitney Museum in New York (1963–66) where Breuer, as in the NYU lecture hall, formed the building as a sculpture—one with serious functional requirements, said Breuer, as if to defend his design. The cantilevered, inverted stepped form of the lecture hall is repeated at the Whitney Museum with perhaps more reason because an entrance and a sunken sculpture court are provided on the small site. Although the inversion suggests the Guggenheim Museum, the Whitney is without Wright's dramatic interior, but in compensation it satisfies the more conventional requirements of flexible exhibition space. In the Whitney Museum and in all his commissions from the mid-1950s and beyond, in both the United States and Europe—his practice was a markedly international one—Breuer sought an enrichment of architectural forms rather than a substantial redirection in point of view. He might well be labelled a moderate iconoclast.

*Radical Proposals*

A far more radical architecture of dissent than any we have considered hitherto was proposed by the English Archigram group in the late sixties. It challenged all fixed assumptions, proposed expendability and change, and favored designs of seemingly random assemblies of parts arranged solely for flow and movement. Le Corbusier's thinking was revived with the forecast of a wholly machine-made architecture, not the hand-made one, which, despite superficially radical appearances, all so-called modern architecture continued to

be. Engineering and the mechanical services were no longer to be the "shameful secret of the architectural family" but a visible and expressive part of the whole. Theoretically, components as large as a room or a house could be plugged in, moved to another location, or exchanged for an updated model.

While no Archigram building ever materialized in England, one that could be accepted as such appeared in Oklahoma, in the Mummers Theater in Oklahoma City (318). It was designed in 1966 by John Johansen, who, like Rudolph, was a student of Gropius. The building comprises three separate theaters of different types in raw concrete, loosely tied together by brightly painted, lightweight metal stairs and walkways. A conspicuous feature is the exposed air-conditioning tower, which rises above a central courtyard space, sprouting visible ducts leading to the various components of the design. No attempt was made to adjust disparate elements into the patterned logic of conventional design or a preconceived form. Instead, the architect took pride in creating a nonarchitecture of pure content. For him this visually chaotic design, a literal translation, so to speak, of the functional program, expressed honesty and "reality."

A similar approach was taken by the architects of Hardy Holzman Pfeiffer Associates, for example, in the Occupational Health Center in Columbus, Indiana (1969–73). The program was analyzed without preconceptions, and the result is very different from the stereotypical clinic: an openly planned and unregimented interior, decidedly provisional to the traditional eye, is decorated with structural steelwork

319
*Guild House, Philadel-
phia, Pennsylvania. Ven-
turi and Rauch, 1960–63.
Exterior.*

320
*Sea Ranch Condominium,
Sea Ranch, California.
Moore, Lyndon, Turnbull,
Whitaker, 1964–66.
Exterior.* © *Morley Baer,
from* Bay Area Houses.

painted in bright green and exposed ducts in blue, all inside an exterior envelope of silver and black glass.

The indirect influence of Archigram and similar groups sustains the pattern of the European avant-garde in providing the ideas and archetypes needed to nourish the mainstream of American architectural development. The basic conservatism of America over the years—and centuries—has resulted in a lack of generative ideas but not of technology or desire to carry them out.

Another expression of iconoclasm, this time American-generated, was contained in a manifesto entitled *Complexity and Contradiction in Architecture*, written in 1962, published in 1966. The author was the practicing Philadelphia architect Robert Venturi, who formulated his argument in the late fifties. Claiming to be writing from the personal view of an architect rather than that of a theoretician or objective critic, Venturi stated his preference for "messy vitality" over imposed visual order, for "the difficult unity of inclusion" over "the easy unity of exclusion." He also stated that the International Style had failed because of its cool disregard of those hybrid impurities of the real world. In Venturi's view this was not the age for grand architecture; his "reality" lay in the images of everyday America, of Main Street and the highway strip.

Of Venturi's limited number of executed works, Guild House in Philadelphia (1960–63) may stand as a representative (319). By no means as radical as one might expect from his dicta, this intelligently planned housing for the elderly, with its unassuming brick walls and functional window pattern, could not express its purpose more directly or fit its neighborhood better. Guild House is quite without rhetoric, save a nonfunctioning replica of a television antenna ceremonially placed on top as an ironic symbol of the lives of its inhabitants. Yet in the understatement of his designs Venturi, who claims to appreciate popular taste, surely ignores what the public really likes, for example, the Fontainebleau Hotel in Miami Beach (1952), designed by the master of modern kitsch, Morris Lapidus.

The ordinariness of vernacular building advocated by Venturi was artfully transposed at Sea Ranch, a development of second homes in Sonoma County north of San Francisco, built in 1964–66 (320). Designed by Moore, Lyndon, Turnbull, Whitaker (MLTW) in association with the landscape architect Lawrence Halprin, the condominium cluster of ten units could be mistaken for abandoned mine buildings in Utah if it were not for the rugged coastal cliff that forms its perch. The units are assembled to minimize their similarity, although each has a shed roof and unpainted vertical siding. The serious unpretentiousness of the Sea Ranch Condominium—once

321
*Kresge College, University of California, Santa Cruz, California. MLTW (Charles Moore and William Turnbull), 1972–74. Exterior.*

fresh, now cloying—suggests a twentieth-century *hameau*, a rustic weekend retreat for city folk. Even if Sea Ranch Condominium provided no answer to pressing problems of architecture, its stark and irregular silhouette supplied a memorable image that has filtered down into housing tracts and shopping centers—a very different vernacular from the one from which Sea Ranch sprang.[7]

In the course of time the work of MLTW became freer and more imaginative, with conscious attempts to incorporate historical and cultural symbolism. Two commissions for the University of California, the Faculty Club on the Santa Barbara campus (1966–68) and Kresge College for the Santa Cruz campus (1972–74) illustrate this trend (321). Everyone, including the architects (Charles Moore and William Turnbull in these two cases), acknowledged theatrical and irreverent qualities in these designs. There was much dispute as to whether such qualities were appropriate in buildings that were to serve the serious purposes of university life. In the Santa Barbara Faculty Club baronial allusions in the whimsical furnishings are mocked by banners made of neon tubing; at Santa Cruz a noninstitutional character was obtained by erecting a cardboardlike village street set in a redwood forest. In both projects the ephemeral nature of stage scenery is suggested by angled plans, paint, and layered effects obtained by superimposing cut-out screen walls. (The last device was first used by Ralph Rapson in the Tyrone Guthrie Theater in Minneapolis in 1963.)

*Influences of History*

The dissenters and apostates of the fifties and sixties adopted a range of attitudes too multifarious to be identified by a common title. The once accepted values of modern architecture, anonymity and conformity, a commitment to structure, and a spartan view of function, no longer provided common ground. Sensibilities shifted. In ascendancy were allusion and symbolism, cultivation of a personal style and a more sensory involvement, and respect for vernacular architecture and the past. The value of modernity itself was challenged by the rise of the historical preservation movement. That the old could be beautiful, relevant, and still useful was acknowledged by the annual awards (starting in 1976) given by the American Institute of Architects for the adaptive reuse of buildings.

Acceptance of historical preservation, a cause originating with the public rather than with architects, produced still another response: a revived eclecticism founded on tradition and regionalism and regard for the genius loci. Years earlier, when it was completed in 1958, Rudolph's Jewett Arts Center for Wellesley College in Massachusetts perplexed a wary profession with its echoes of the pseudo-Gothic of adjacent campus buildings. Rudolph dared to relate his design not only by extending the crescentlike siting of James Gamble Rogers's work but by evoking Gothic forms with concrete columns of quatrefoil section and a spiky rhythm of pointed skylights.[8] Again flirting with history, Rudolph recalled the Greek Revival plantation houses of the South for the Wallace House in Athens, Alabama (1961–64), with a grid of stately columnar supports in white-painted brick. Although more interesting for their intent than for absolute achievement, such examples nonetheless indicate a substantial reevaluation of and a willingness to reconsider the past. One of the most discussed projects now is Philip Johnson's design for the American Telephone and Telegraph Building in New York (1978), which deliberately recalls the McKim, Mead and White era of the 1890s. Johnson has adopted the column formula of skyscraper design so popular in that decade; the base of his skyscraper was suggested by Brunelleschi's Pazzi Chapel; and a giant broken pediment adorns its top. Once again history has infiltrated the practice of architecture.

"Architecture is the masterly, correct and magnificent play of volumes brought together in light." Not only was Le Corbusier's post-World War II work the inspiration of the Brutalists, the classic definition in his book of 1923 describes a concept of architecture embodied in many of the most notable American buildings of the sixties and seventies. In these decades a growing number of American architects became absorbed with the arrangement of geometrical forms and patterns and the exploration of the possibilities of light and reflecting surfaces, and precisely curved shapes and oblique, faceted planes, often suggesting the structure of crystals, turned buildings into geometrical sculpture.

Europe anticipated this development. Two skyscrapers, one in Milan and the other in Dusseldorf, built after the Second World War when skyscrapers appeared for the first time abroad, demonstrated that the high-rise office block could be shaped and treated as a piece of sculpture. The Pirelli Tower, Gio Ponti's slender prism rising 400 feet above the skyline of Milan, is a reinforced concrete structure based on a lenticular plan, subtly bevelled so that its bulk is disguised by tapered ends. A sculptured effect of a different sort was obtained by Hentrich and Petschnigg in the Phoenix-Rheinrohr Building. Its composite form is of three layered, staggered slabs, the center one higher by three floors. These two buildings, both completed by 1960, caught the restless eyes of American architects seeking a release from the rectangular parallelepiped, and once again, as in the *Chicago Tribune* competition, Europe set a new course for the American skyscraper.

Thus it came about that in the sixties and seventies skyscrapers were designed for effects of sculptural form, and the expression of structure and function, once held to be accountable values, were subordinated. This new architecture of appearances gave license to arbitrary design. To obtain the unbroken and scaleless unity of form, entrances, floor levels, and individual windows were suppressed, often with a loss of convenience. Rather than communicating living functions within, such buildings celebrate an abstract ideal. Eero Saarinen was a master of this kind of simplification, as he proved in the CBS Building in New York, completed in 1965 after his death. The closely spaced supports of the square plan are seen as dark granite piers, which are triangular in section; between them are recessed windows of dark glass. When viewed at an angle, the windows become invisible and the flank appears as a monolithic wall of stone. The effect is one of great density, unity, and sobriety. The same brooding quality pervades Philip Johnson's Kline Biology Tower at Yale (1966), where round piers in brick replace the angular granite ones of the CBS Building.

Saarinen's granite stela marked the waning of the Miesian tradition: in the CBS Building the primary motivation was not to express the structure but to dramatize the surface with accordionlike facets, emphasizing the skin rather than the bones of the building. Saarinen's Law Library for the University of Chicago (1960) was similarly faceted, but with blue-green glass. Tinted glass was soon exchanged for mirrored glass in gold, silver, and copper tones, which has improved solar properties and allows one to see out but not to see in. The latter advantage permitted the architect to extend the glass over the solid walls and relieved him of the necessity of acknowledging interior relationships, which were only revealed when lights were turned on at dusk. By day such buildings were giant mirrored images of the immediate environment; chameleonlike, they changed color with the sky and weather. As mullions became more slender, almost pencil-thin—in some cases, butt-jointed glass sealed with epoxy glue or vinyl tubing dispensed with mullions altogether—all sense of architectonic construction was dispelled.[1]

The dematerialization of mass achieved with even grids of panes of mirrored glass became the prevailing characteristic of the new vernacular for office buildings; a random example is the Equitable Building in St. Louis (1971) by Hellmuth, Obata and Kassabaum. In such a design all edges, corners, top, and bottom are given no greater weight than the narrow mullions that elsewhere divide the sheets of mirrored glass, so one can only guess how many stories high the building is. The same is true of the reflective glass cube that contains offices for the Blue Cross-Blue Shield of Maryland (1970–72) in Towson, Maryland (322). The architects Peterson and Brickbauer have retained its purity of form by placing the entrance and parking below a grass-covered platform; for the sake of contrast, mechanical equipment is placed within a separate, smaller cube covered in bright red glazed brick. In Atlanta John C. Portman, Jr.'s, Peachtree Center Plaza Hotel, completed in 1976 as the tallest reinforced concrete structure in the world, is a seventy-story cylinder sheathed in bronze reflective glass, sending forth in all directions fractured images of the city. In Los Angeles the Great Western Savings Center (1972) by William L. Pereira & Associates is wrapped in a more conventional curtain wall; it is unusual for its elliptical plan, a shape antithetical to a rectangular structural grid. Seen in the light of history, these experiments represent a return to earlier proposals that emphasize the glass skin, for example, Mies van der Rohe's two projects for all-glass skyscrapers of 1919–22. Indeed, the latter one was the direct

322
*Blue Cross-Blue Shield of*
*Maryland, Towson,*
*Maryland. Peterson and*
*Brickbauer, 1970–72.*
*Exterior.*

inspiration for the curvilinear plan of Lake Point Tower (1968), a Chicago apartment building designed by two of his former pupils, George Schipporeit and John Heinrich.

The merging of architecture and sculpture was reciprocated by contemporary minimalist sculptors, such as Donald Judd and Larry Bell, whose purely geometrical works could well serve as model projects for buildings. The monotonous, boxlike skyline that threatened larger cities was averted by the rise of elegant prisms in taut, shiny skins, such as I. M. Pei's Hancock Building in Boston (1972), which stands across from Richardson's Trinity Church. The attenuated trapezoidal plan of the Hancock Building is notched at its narrow end to emphasize its slenderness. The device of offsetting various planes was often used to accelerate the vertical rhythms of a tall building, and with striking success. This staggered treatment benefited the interior plan of the recent Minneapolis landmark, the Investors Diversified Services Building (1968–73) by Philip Johnson and John Burgee, where the serrated ends of the lozenge plan provide multiple corner offices (always considered the most desirable) instead of only four (323). Both the Boston and Minneapolis buildings are glazed with mirrored glass.

How to design the enclosure of a skeletal building had long been a major problem of modern architecture. Certainly an all-glass exterior expressed perfectly the nonstructural character of a skin; yet it might be undesirable for practical or esthetic reasons. An unusual experiment of 1952 is the Alcoa Building in Pittsburgh by Harrison and Abramovitz, which is sheathed in thin sheet aluminum, formed in 6-by-12-foot prefabricated panels incorporating both window and spandrel. The precision of factory parts, the sensibly rounded corners of the windows, and the rapidity of installation demonstrated the advantages of a fully technological curtain wall. This bold example was neglected for two decades until the idea reappeared, with equally convincing results, in the Bronx Developmental Center in New York, designed by Richard Meier & Associates and completed in 1976 (324). Without the crimped pattern of the Alcoa Building, its reflective aluminum panels have a smooth, machined appearance. A very different effect is achieved by the curtain walls of the Beinecke Rare Book Library at Yale (1964) (325). These are constructed of translucent marble slabs, one and one-quarter inches thick, set in huge Vierendeel trusses. Gordon Bunshaft of Skidmore, Owings & Merrill was the designer. Different again is the envelope of opaque blue glass of the Pacific Design Center in Los Angeles (1971–76), designed by Cesar Pelli for Gruen Associates. Nicknamed the "blue

323
*Investors Diversified
Services Building, Minne-
apolis, Minnesota.
Johnson/Burgee, 1968–73.
Exterior.*

324
*Bronx Developmental
Center, New York City.
Richard Meier & Associ-
ates, 1970–76. Exterior
detail.*

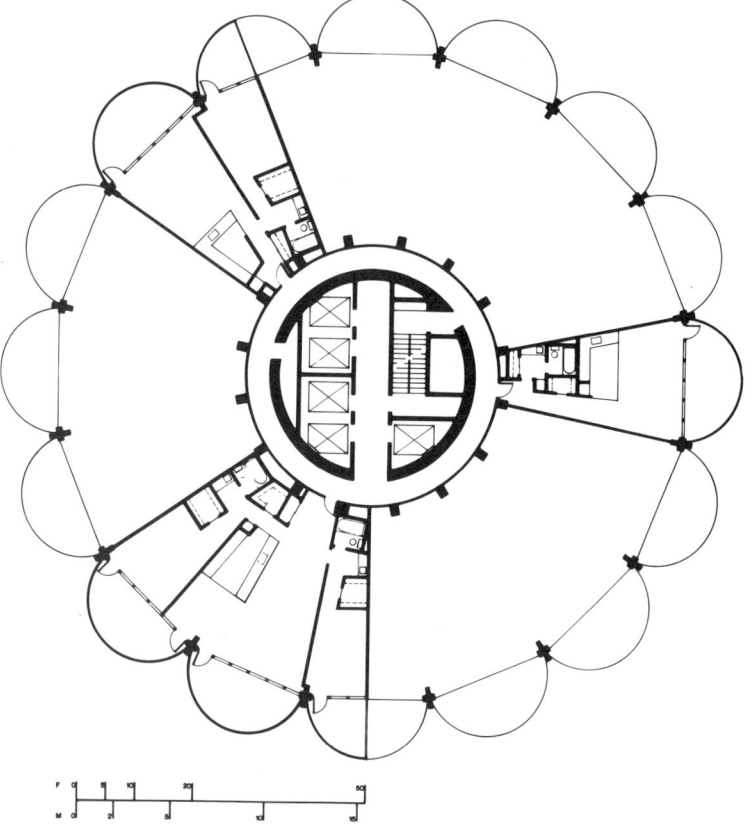

325
Beinecke Rare Book Library, Yale University, New Haven, Connecticut. Skidmore, Owings & Merrill, 1964. Exterior.

326
Marina City, Chicago, Illinois. Bertram Goldberg Associates, 1961–63. Plan.

whale," this swollen building, practically windowless although it is completely sheathed in glass, brings the development of the curtain wall full circle.

**Chicago after Mies**

It is not surprising that Chicago should have been the source of the new geometries that evolved primarily from structural rather than esthetic considerations. It was, after all, the city that gave birth to skyscraper construction and became the adopted home of Mies van der Rohe. Chicago architects in general were uncomfortable with the permissive fashions that engaged the attention of much of the country during these decades, and the presence of Bertram Goldberg, Fazlur Kahn, Myron Goldsmith, and other disciples of Mies was insurance against the Chicago tradition being overturned by any merely cosmetic style.

Faithfulness to structural ethics yielded several remarkable buildings by Bertram Goldberg. Once a student of Mies, in practice Goldberg found both more freedom and more logic in reinforced concrete than in steel. However outwardly rhapsodic, his designs are in essence rigorously controlled by engineering and cost factors. In Chicago three of the most important designs employ curved forms in concrete: Marina City (1961–63), the Raymond Hilliard Housing (1964–66), and the Prentice Women's Hospital (1970–75).

The Marina City complex is dominated by twin sixty-story cylindrical towers. The lower third of each contains helical parking ramps, and the upper two-thirds consists of forty floors of apartments, divided on plan into sixteen petallike segments (326). The ramp and apartment floors are cantilevered from a central core with an outer ring of secondary supports; on the apartment floors curved balconies project from each segment. The splayed walls of the apartments are unconventional but suggest a joyous outward release of space. The use of formwork of molded plastic left the concrete surfaces smooth, requiring only a coat of paint. Goldberg made intensive use of the three-and-a-half-acre site: in addition to the apartment towers there are a ten-story office block and a theater (of markedly sculptural form) as well as a public skating rink, restaurant, and shops at a lower level and boat-docking facilities at the water's edge. It was no small achievement to have dramatized a neglected river, realized an intensely urban design, and demonstrated a viable alternative to the steel frame of Chicago tradition.

What might at first sight seem arbitrary in the Hilliard Housing is justified by economical structural forms that have the advantage of creating interior spaces as well (327). The curved segments of the bearing walls of these four high-rise apartment buildings—two cir-

327
*Raymond Hilliard Housing, Chicago, Illinois. Bertram Goldberg Associates, 1964–66. Exterior.*

cular towers for the elderly and two crescent-shaped ones for families—were chosen for their strength and the oval windows for minimum stress in puncturing the walls. With the use of slip forms, concrete was poured at the rate of one vertical foot an hour. Technology and economics, Mies's determinants, set the design for the un-Miesian end result. Washington officials initially objected to Goldberg's proposal as being too good for the poor; bleak and regimented designs had become the accepted standard in public housing.

The Prentice Women's Hospital, with its giant quatrefoil of nursing wards billowing out nearly fifty feet beyond a central mastlike support, is equally vulnerable to misjudgment as a mere tour de force, but it too demonstrates Goldberg's belief in the efficiency of the circle. Liberation from the right angle came as a corollary of Goldberg's search for optimal structure and useful space in one form.

An upswing in the construction of tall buildings starting in the sixties produced skyscrapers rising well beyond the thirty- to forty-story height set as the economical limit for the rigid frame, a basic idea initiated by William LeBaron Jenney. A jump to sixty to a hundred stories was facilitated by certain technological advances, and made the added stories economically feasible. The Chicago office of Skidmore, Owings & Merrill developed new structural systems for very tall buildings by using the tubular concept, applicable to reinforced concrete as well as steel. Recognizing that the horizontal stress caused by wind is the decisive factor rather than the vertical load, this concept regards the tall building as a cantilevered tube anchored in the ground. By allocating the major structural role to the periphery, interiors could be free of columns and transverse shear walls, with substantial cost savings. Often the inner service core is treated as a structural tube as well so that the whole building becomes a tube within a tube. Early examples of this, both in reinforced concrete, are Saarinen's CBS Building and the Brunswick Building in Chicago (1966) by the local office of Skidmore, Owings & Merrill, with Myron Goldsmith in charge. In both, the closely spaced mullions are structural; the visual result is a dense surface grid rather than a linear framework merely holding the glass in place.

This transfer of the structure to the surface of the building is obvious in the John Hancock Center in Chicago with its huge X-pattern of bracing, recalling the wall trusses of Mies van der Rohe's Chicago Convention Center project (328). In the age of Jenney, skyscrapers had been stiffened with knee bracing and cross bracing, but these were always hidden from view. In the Hancock Center the diagonal geometry essential to stability forms a rigid tube structure to resist the wind. The tapering profile resulted from a program requiring a lesser volume of apartments above a greater volume of offices, shops and parking. Like Marina City, the multiple-function Hancock Center is in effect a small town, a place to live and work, with commercial and recreational facilities within the city. Completed in 1968, it was designed by Bruce Graham of Skidmore, Owings & Merrill, with Fazlur Kahn as the structural engineer.

The same designers were responsible for the Sears Tower in Chicago, completed in 1976 (329). Rising 1,450 feet, this is the world's tallest structure, 100 feet taller than the twin towers of the World Trade Center in New York by Minoru Yamasaki and Associates and more than 300 feet higher than the Hancock Center. The tubular concept was repeated: nine structural tubes, each 75 feet square in plan, are bundled together and terminate at various levels; only two rise to the building's full height. The staggered silhouette recalls Adler and Sullivan's proposal for the Fraternity Temple; the building as a whole bears a striking resemblance to a visionary skyscraper for Moscow projected by the Russian Constructivist architect Lopatin in 1923.

Meanwhile the Chicago office of Skidmore, Owings & Merrill was experimenting with the suspension principle. The central building for Baxter Laboratories in Deerfield, Illinois (1976), was the result. The designers, again Graham and Kahn, suspended the entire roof of a double-square building (144 by 288 feet) with cables hung from two masts, one in the center of each square. Additional cables placed inside the building and along the periphery prevent any twisting or

328
*John Hancock Center,*
*Chicago, Illinois. Skid-*
*more, Owings & Merrill,*
*1966–68. Exterior.*

329
*Sears Tower, Chicago, Illinois. Skidmore, Owings & Merrill, 1974–76. Aerial view.*

330
*Federal Reserve Bank
Building, Minneapolis,
Minnesota. Gunnar Birk-
erts, 1968–72. Exterior.*

deflection of the roof—a crucial consideration because excessive movement would crack the aluminum and glass curtain wall.

The suspension principle, common in long-span bridges, was rarely justified in architecture but on occasion was used for a theatrical effect, as the Minneapolis Federal Reserve Bank Building (1968–72) shows (330). To meet the requirement of a column-free basement, Gunnar Birkerts suspended the ten-story office building from two inverted catenary arches, constructed of cables and welded steel plates. The arches drop downward from a pair of concrete towers spaced 275 feet apart and braced from toppling inward by a deep truss at roof level. The complicated structural relationships are summarized on the facade, with the mirrored glass set on the inner face of the mullion within the curve and on the outer face elsewhere. The play of light and shadow on this detail makes for a facade that is photogenic, certainly, but its self-consciousness and scale prevent it from harmonizing with its neighbors.

*Glazed Atriums*

In the standard histories of modern architecture, Peter Behrens and his German factory buildings are credited with advancing straightforward design, and emphasizing structural clarity and spacious, transparent enclosures. Behrens's American counterpart in this respect is Albert Kahn. Kahn's factories, such as the much admired Dodge Half-Ton Truck Plant in Detroit (1938), however, were regarded as having a special drama too categorical to be assimilated into architecture proper. But this changed. Starting rather timidly in the early work of Yamasaki, skylighted spaces were revived when the client's program allowed for such extravagances. These spaces recalled not only the factory esthetic but also light courts in office buildings before the days of electricity and Victorian greenhouses. Architects had long admired Paxton's Crystal Palace, and the sheltered *gallerie* of Italy still proved their worth as urban amenities; the Providence Arcade Building (1828) and the Cleveland Arcade (1890) are surviving American examples of the latter. In this spirit Johnson and Burgee attached a skylighted concourse to their IDS Tower in Minneapolis, linking shops and a hotel and thereby providing an impressive retreat from Minnesota winters. Earlier, in 1967, John Portman revolutionized hotel design by providing the Hyatt Regency Hotel in Atlanta with an immensely high skylighted lobby or atrium with shops and restaurants, which, though completely enclosed and air-conditioned, suggests an open-air plaza. Portman successfully followed the same formula in his other Hyatt hotels, one at the Chicago O'Hare Airport (1971) and another in San Francisco (1974). In Harvard's Gund Hall by John Andrews (1968–

*331*
*Gund Hall, Harvard University, Cambridge, Massachusetts. John Andrews, 1968–72. Exterior.*

72), a saw-tooth, factory-type roof is carried by deep tubular trusses to shelter four hundred design students (331). Ten times as many people will congregate in the star-shaped Crystal Cathedral for the Garden Grove Community Church in California (1978–80), by Philip Johnson and John Burgee. This space-frame structure entirely enclosed with glass recalls the proposals of another German pioneer, Bruno Taut.

A revival of the Victorian obsession with horticulture made its contribution. The Ford Foundation in New York (1963) is an L-shaped building fitted to a vertical greenhouse planted with tall trees around a tiny pool, which most of the offices overlook. Roche and Dinkeloo were the architects, Dan Kiley the landscape architect. With more commercial interests in mind, Cesar Pelli's Rainbow Center Mall and Winter Garden in Niagara Falls, New York (1976–78), successfully combines shopping with botanical pleasures. An earlier design, the Commons-Courthouse Center for Columbus, Indiana (1974), also by Cesar Pelli for Gruen Associates, prepared the way.[2]

**The Le Corbusier Revival**

The evidence of geometry is everywhere in Le Corbusier's work, in plans and elevations, in the composition of forms and the spaces within. The late sixties saw the beginning of what amounted to a revival of the earlier *style Corbu*, inspired by his poetic handling of space in his two masterpieces of the late twenties, the Stein House at Garches and the Villa Savoye at Poissy. At the center of this revival was a mandarin group of young, New York-based architects, which included Peter Eisenman, Charles Gwathmey, and Richard

*332*
*House in Old Westbury,*
*Long Island, New York.*
*Richard Meier & Associ-*
*ates, 1971. Exterior.*

Meier. Of these Eisenman was the most provocative, independent, and theoretical; Gwathmey was the most ingratiating and the least theoretical; Meier's work came closest to the spirit of Le Corbusier's buildings of the twenties. Meier consciously repeated the master with his white-painted geometrical forms poignantly contrasting with the green surroundings, his grid system of columns that freely interrupted the open plan or sometimes raised the house above the ground, and his two-story living space with interior balconies. In a house by Meier at Old Westbury, Long Island (1971), the nautical forms, the ramps, and the circular stair of the Villa Savoye all reappear, together with a comparable serenity and precision (332). The absence of domesticity is compensated by the satisfactions of a distilled, pure-white construction, meticulously executed, forming an abstract sculpture of space.

Similar sharp edges and unbroken planes characterize the houses of Charles Gwathmey, but his designs are less indebted to Le Corbusier. His use of an oblique plane set at a 45-degree angle and a half-circle are more likely to establish spatial measure than a grid of structural supports. Gwathmey's frequent use of natural cedar siding and slate floor paving recalls Breuer's similar choice of materials in the late forties. Yet Gwathmey's way of cutting into an overall geometrical form to create space, as seen in his residence and nearby studio built at Amagansett, New York (1965–68), is clearly derived from Le Corbusier.

The minimalist tendencies in Meier and Gwathmey are more pronounced in Eisenman. More important, the theoretical character of his work, mostly small houses, results from a proportional system that in application severely limits the functional ordering of spaces. Instead of comfort or convenience, Eisenman offers delight in a cerebral esthetic order; unlike Palladio, he disdains to reconcile geometry and proportion with human needs.

## Netsch and Pei

The most ambitious combination of theory and geometry ever attempted by a modern architect was proposed by Walter Netsch of the Chicago office of Skidmore, Owings & Merrill. He called it "field theory." Its objective was an arrangement of spaces more varied than those obtained with a conventional grid pattern, yet still compact. Characteristic of field-theory plans is the unit of a square rotated 45 degrees to form a star-shaped module. A repetition of such modules, each with its own subdivisions, yields designs of intense formal complexity, as seen in the Behavioral Science Center (1968–70) and other buildings on the Chicago Circle Campus of the University of Illinois (333). Outwardly these designs retain the fascination of snowflake patterns; indoors, for all the claims of efficiency and flexibility made for the field-theory system, substantial problems of orientation arise from introverted mazes of angular rooms and oblique corridor intersections. Netsch's field theory, with its controlled system of spaces, was one of the results of a widespread quest for a more emphatic and permanent shaping of space, a quest begun in the fifties by Louis Kahn.

The triangulations, knife edges, and opaque, skylighted forms of the Chicago Circle Campus buildings were found elsewhere in the designs of others, though without Netsch's rigorous geometry. An example is the East Building of the National Gallery of Art in Washington, D.C. (1974–78), by I. M. Pei who, in the balance between intellect and imagination ever present in architecture, leaned towards the latter (334). Pei elaborated on the trapezoidal site set by L'Enfant's city plan by designing a fluid and poetic geometry of pale pink marble triangles to counterpoint the static, classical form of John Russell Pope's building. The result displays all the reserve and urbanity that had long been characteristic of Pei's work, heeding as he does the caution that "strength is born of restraint and dies in freedom"; yet the central, three-story triangular lobby achieves a spatial animation that is rare in his work. Outside, as well as within, the building is sheathed in marble, fastidiously detailed, to achieve some degree of harmony with its neighbors on the Mall, although its success in this regard is counterbalanced by a sculptural assertiveness that—as in Wright's Guggenheim—is something of a threat to the modern art it was designed to contain.

419

333
*Behavioral Science Center, Circle Campus, University of Illinois, Chicago, Illinois. Skidmore, Owings & Merrill, 1968–70. Aerial view.*

334
*East Building, National Gallery of Art, Washington, District of Columbia. I. M. Pei and Partners, 1974–78. Exterior.*

335
*Christian Science Center,*
*Boston, Massachusetts.*
*I. M. Pei and Partners,*
*1968–74. Exterior.*

Much of Pei's success derives from his ability to design in the urban context and within limits of economic investment. Many of his earlier large schemes were done in association with William Zeckendorf, president of the real estate firm of Webb and Knapp. Among them are Mile High Center in Denver (1955), Place Ville Marie in Montreal (completed 1961), Kips Bay Plaza in New York City (1960), and Society Hill Towers in Philadelphia (1964). In all of these Pei adopted the clear forms and site planning of Mies van der Rohe and applied the lessons of Rockefeller Center. For apartment buildings he developed a reinforced concrete exterior wall with relatively narrow window openings that eliminate the need for sub-mullions. The most ceremonial of all his designs is the Christian Science Center, completed in 1974, a major urban renewal project for Back Bay in Boston (335). Here Pei turned from the reductionism of Mies to the massive, sculptural presence of Le Corbusier's late buildings, the High Courts Building at Chandigarh in particular. The colonnaded structure connecting the Mother Church (1894 and 1904) with new administrative buildings forms an architectural boundary to a vast, rectangular reflecting pool that terminates in a giant circular fountain. The controlled bravura of Pei's conception injects an alien character into the Boston cityscape, unexpected but welcome.

Pei's work, like Johnson's, cannot be identified by a single stylistic label: it is neither avant-garde in a doctrinaire manner nor impulsive in a personal one. He has advanced with measured and adroitly placed steps, making intelligent use of others' work, not only of Mies but also, in the National Center for Atmospheric Research near Boulder, Colorado (1964–66), of Kahn's.

*Post-Modern Architecture*

Time will tell whether the architecture of the sixties and seventies is a transformation of the themes of the twenties or whether entirely new developments have supplanted a moribund International Style. Certainly post-modern architecture, as it has been called, is diverse; it ranges from reactionary, which includes an extraordinary reappearance of the arbitrary geometry of Beaux-Arts composition, once the *bête noire* of modernists, to radical.

Clarity of an overall *parti* and firmness of volumes are Beaux-Arts qualities well suited to large-scale commissions and bring focus to diverse requirements. In the work of Saarinen's former associates, Kevin Roche and John Dinkeloo, these qualities were joined with regularity of structure. An example is the Richard C. Lee High School in New Haven (1967). Conceptually it is the exact opposite of the dispersed, fingerlike school plans first seen in the forties, such as those by Ernest Kump in California, in which the various functions were clearly articulated. Roche and Dinkeloo's school is compact and formal, with four large square modules of classroom clusters separated by Greek-cross corridors and an entrance in the center of each side of the overall square plan. Ceremonial axes and powerful shadows created by overhangs, together with rough concrete surfaces, contribute to an intensely formidable character. Although the school has the diagrammatic clarity of a Beaux-Arts solution, there is none of the use of appropriate detail to give it scale that Beaux-Arts theory required.

The effect is livelier in Roche and Dinkeloo's Knights of Columbus Building and Veterans Memorial Coliseum in New Haven, designed as a complementary pair and begun in 1965. In both, structure is paraded in a self-conscious way. (In Goldberg's buildings the outward appearance of the structure, however flamboyant, is a byproduct of economy and efficiency). It is apparent that in designing the twenty-three-story Knights of Columbus tower Roche and Dinkeloo had more of an eye than a mind for structure, which can be taken in a glance by the speeding motorist on the highway: four cylindrical corner legs of concrete sheathed in purplish-brown tile support visible girders of Cor-Ten steel, which darkens to a similar color (336).[3] The corner "silos" contain stairs and toilets and function as supports; the center elevator core is also structural. The adjacent Coliseum is more successful because, by its very complication, the structure enriches the design. Eighteen 70-foot-high rectangular concrete piers are arranged in a double row to support four levels of parking constructed of open-work trusses, also in Cor-Ten steel (337). This parking element forms a giant roof over the arena and the services below. Two circular auto ramps provide access to the parking levels. The greater forcefulness of the Coliseum points up the affected simplicity of the Knights of Columbus Building. In both buildings there is something that reminds us of Mies's last designs as well as his practice of arranging buildings in groups.

Roche and Dinkeloo's tendency toward the ostentatiously dramatic was reinforced by the search for a distinctive corporate image for the headquarters of the College Life Insurance Company in Indianapolis, Indiana (1967–71). Like their Knights of Columbus Building in New Haven, it seems to be designed for the passing motorist (338). Three identical office buildings, each square in plan and ten stories high, are formed by two adjacent vertical stone walls and two sloping greenhouse walls of blue reflecting glass. These deformed pyramids, half glass, half wall, linked by bridges and underground passages, are aligned on a skew and will eventually be complemented by six

336
*Knights of Columbus,*
*New Haven, Connecticut.*
*Kevin Roche, John Dinke-*
*loo & Associates, 1965–*
*69. Exterior.*

*337*
*Veterans Memorial Coliseum, New Haven, Connecticut. Kevin Roche, John Dinkeloo & Associates, 1965–72. Exterior detail.*

*338
College Life Insurance
Company, Indianapolis,
Indiana. Kevin Roche,
John Dinkeloo & Associ-
ates, 1967–71. Exterior.*

others to form a three-by-three grid. Such mute and wholly abstract geometry, with the highest refinement in detail and execution although uncommunicative and seemingly uninhabited, has been a major theme in Roche and Dinkeloo's architecture.

*Louis Kahn*

The greatest architect to appear since the mid-1900s was Louis I. Kahn. Already fifty when he was given the commission for his first major building, the Yale University Art Gallery (1951–63), he soon became a hero to a younger generation of architects, many still in school.[4] Curiously, his views were conservative. Believing that architecture was an art—a sore point with the Bauhaus-trained generation—he impressed upon his work strong, essential forms, arranged in an almost Renaissance manner but more vigorously rhythmical in the final result. He presented anew the timeless architectural elements of column, wall, beam, and truss. Most of Kahn's conceptions were expansive in nature. He was as eager to design cities as buildings, as his inventive redesign of historic Philadelphia, his home city, shows. But to see Kahn's largest and most awesome works one must travel abroad: to Bangladesh for his government buildings in the capital city of Dacca and to India for those at Ahmedabad.

Kahn's major buildings, crowded into scarcely more than a dozen years—he died in 1974—form a lucid and complete statement of his architectural theory, which is remarkable because of his apparent lack of a consistent approach to design before 1950. He had been both a student and employee of Paul Cret and, by temperament, was unsympathetic to the tenets of the International Style. The open, flowing plan did not interest him. Instead he sought well-ordered and defined spaces, proposing containment and separation of volumes and reasserting the wall and pier to achieve these ends. He favored definition and weight over fluidity and transparency. His plans, always more expressive than his elevations—as were those of the Beaux-Arts architects—were composed of additive spatial units, often axially arranged. Although he was not committed to axiality as such, every building of Kahn's is rooted in axis and geometrical form. Although he did not attend the Ecole, his work is in the tradition of Durand, Choisy, and Guadet, whose expository treatises guided an earlier age of discipline.

Kahn swept aside the accretions of modernism and asked simply: What does the building want to be? His design for the Richards Medical Research and Biology Buildings at the University of Pennsylvania (1957–61) was his answer to this basic question (339, 340). The building consists of six separate but linked towers, each floor limited to a 47-foot square to retain the intimacy of a laboratory workspace. Dominating the composition are windowless brick towers, some of them nostrils for the intake and exhaust of air and others for stairways, which cluster around the sides of the laboratories and rise above their roofline. They look like supports, but in reality the structure is a less obvious precast concrete skeleton with complicated Vierendeel trusses, arranged so that the corners are open and without support. Kahn called his giant brick tubes "servant spaces." In his wish to separate and articulate function he necessarily discarded the simple envelope and surface unity. Paradoxically his elementary question produced answers that were, esthetically, visually assertive rather than minimal. Although picturesque effect was not what he sought, the Richards Medical Research and Biology Buildings present an animated group of towers on the skyline. For those ready for a change, this richness of form articulated with such authority was particularly welcome. Kahn's work, as this building predicted, was to be quite different in kind from what all others had done before, despite his conservative bias.

At the Salk Institute of Biological Studies at La Jolla, California (1959–65), Kahn had an opportunity to express his ceremonial predilections, which had been inhibited by the limited site on the Philadelphia campus (341). Again he chose differentiated architectural forms to express different functions: access, research work, and study. The parallel pair of large laboratory buildings is augmented by a bold file of projecting stair towers on the outer flanks and a rhythmic series of individual studies for scientists on the courtyard side. Kahn repeated the reinforced concrete frame and Vierendeel truss of his Philadelphia laboratory—August Komendant was the structural engineer for both buildings—but here the long-span and thus story-high trusses more easily accommodate the numerous ducts and services in their ample openings. (Kahn preferred concrete and after 1950 never used a steel frame.) For all the openness that the site on a bluff overlooking the Pacific allowed, he kept the plan symmetrical. The wide, travertine-paved courtyard between the laboratories suggests the nave of a roofless church: serene, ceremonial, and timeless. Its axis is marked by a slot of water in the paving, streaming towards a magnificently simple fountain at the seaward end.

A laboratory, however, did not lend itself to the full realization of the poetic quality that Kahn could achieve in interior spaces, interweaving elements of structure and light; Kahn believed that "structure is the maker of light." This special quality can be seen in the First Unitarian Church in Rochester, New York (1956–64), and

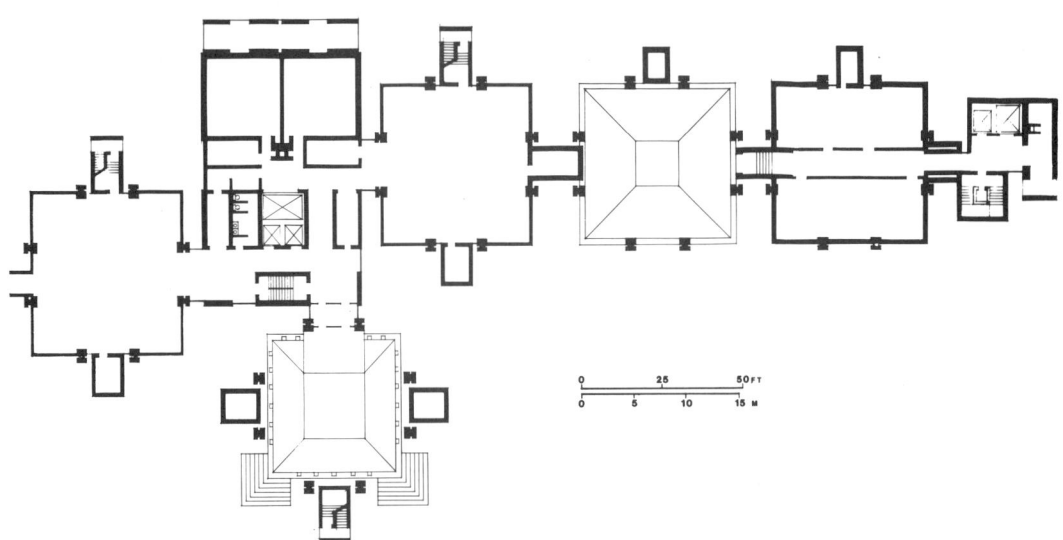

339
*Richards Medical Re-
search and Biology Build-
ings, University of
Pennsylvania, Philadel-
phia, Pennsylvania. Louis
I. Kahn, 1957–61.
Exterior.*

340
*Richards Medical Re-
search and Biology Build-
ings, Philadelphia,
Pennsylvania. Plan.*

341
*Salk Institute of Biological
Studies, La Jolla, California. Louis I. Kahn, 1959–
65. Central courtyard.*

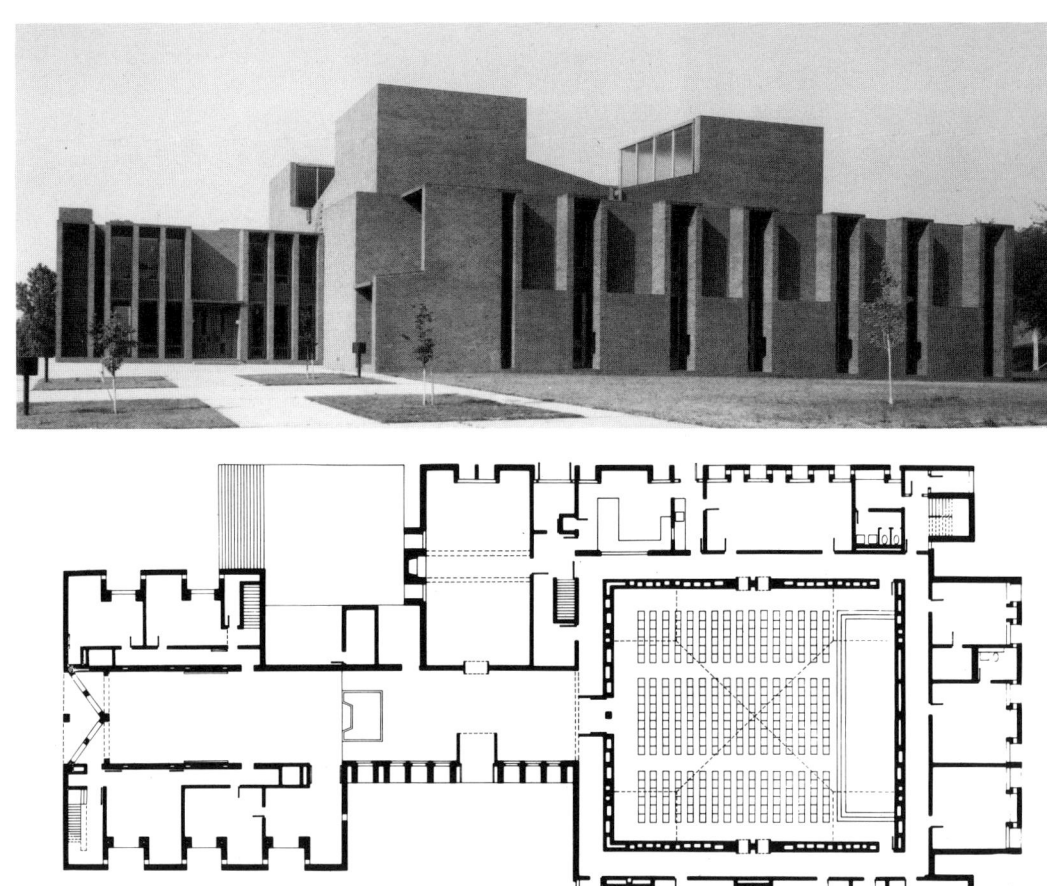

342
*First Unitarian Church,
Rochester, New York.
Louis I. Kahn, 1959–64.
Exterior.*

343
*First Unitarian Church,
Rochester, New York.
Plan.*

the Kimbell Art Museum in Fort Worth, Texas (1967–72). The meeting room of the church is a stern and frugal cubelike space that would satisfy any Gothic revivalist's call for "truth" (342, 343). Devoid of trivia and any kind of distracting element, meticulously detailed though never sleek, its space extends upward in the corners, in which partially concealed clerestories provide the only source of light. The inverted, keellike ceiling of concrete, a cross in plan, is supported by a concrete column at the center of each side. The meeting room is double-walled by cinder block with discrete slots to provide for the circulation of air; its cool gray interior suggests a Cistercian rigor or the spirit of the American Quakers. Around it Kahn has placed the "servant spaces" of classrooms, offices, and a library, with outer walls folded inward at intervals to sustain the introverted nature of the design.

Kahn's art is infused with a meditative quality that is an extension of his own introspective personality. His buildings are tranquil and resolute. They often unexpectedly mix traditional compliance with radical assertiveness. The library of Phillips Exeter Academy in New Hampshire (1967–72) is a case in point. Without esthetic injury to older campus buildings, Kahn designed a well-mannered cubic form with chamfered edges and identical elevations. The library's outer structure, simple but handsome red brick bearing walls with piers that grow progressively narrower as they rise and windows spanned by flat voussoired arches that grow progressively wider (recalling the identical structural logic of Richardson's Marshall Field Wholesale Store), is married to an inner structure of bare reinforced concrete. The central court, skylighted and six levels high, is framed by four walls, each pierced with a single, huge circular opening revealing bookstacks behind (344). The usual bland and bureaucratic quality of libraries is not evident here, and one instinctively grasps Kahn's purpose: to express the stimulation and intimacy of learning from books. Ascending the levels one discovers study spaces arranged around the periphery, with a coziness reminiscent of window seats in Shingle Style houses, and an inner ring of bookstacks conveniently near. Kahn's combination of the heroic and the humane is a rare achievement.

A measure of the admiration so quickly accorded Kahn by his peers is his influence on their work. The Boston Public Library Annex designed by Johnson and Burgee (1965–73) derives its plan and forms from Kahn. The bisymmetrical plan of nine equal squares divided by squared clusters of supports enlarges upon Kahn's Bath House for the Jewish Community Center at Trenton, New Jersey (1956), in which Kahn first effected the separation between the served

*344*
*Library, Phillips Exeter*
*Academy, Exeter, New*
*Hampshire. Louis I.*
*Kahn, 1967–72. Interior.*

345
*Kimbell Art Museum,
Fort Worth, Texas. Louis
I. Kahn, 1967–72.
Interior.*

and servant spaces. The segmental arched forms of Johnson's elevations, sheathed in granite, recall Kahn's governmental buildings in Ahmedabad, which are in structural brick.

Kahn's warmth and reverence toward culture—he had once considered becoming a concert violinist—is nowhere more strongly sensed than in the Kimbell Art Museum in Fort Worth, Texas (345). Here Kahn was inspired by Roman vaulting to use a vaultlike reinforced concrete beam, which needed support only at the ends of its 100-foot length. These cycloid-curved vaults are arranged in parallel rows in sets of three and form the entire structure of the building. Each vault section is slotted to admit natural light, which then is evenly distributed by reflective baffles. The visual harmony of light and structure combined with a sense of permanence appropriate to its function makes the Kimbell Art Museum perhaps the most quietly satisfying museum ever built.

Kahn's buildings epitomize the major shift in contemporary architecture toward geometrical order and the celebration of the wall after many decades of ascendancy of the metal skeleton. Even more important, he reaffirmed the architect as an artist—a position taken by Richardson, Sullivan, Wright, and Mies van der Rohe. Kahn recognized that "the architect builds primarily not for need but for Art. Art is the only language of Man."

## Notes

**Foreword**   1. W. F. Deknatel, quoted by B. Zevi, *Towards an Organic Architecture* (London: Faber & Faber, 1950), p. 126.

**1**   1. Forman, *The Architecture of the Old South*, p. 28.

2. In the English colonies piazza (Italian for an open space or square in a town) was the common designation of any kind of porch—in the South it still is. This was a result of Inigo Jones's giving to the great square he planned for the Earl of Bedford in 1631 the name of Covent Garden Piazza. Londoners transferred the outlandish new term from the square to what was for them the most novel feature of the development, the arcaded walks under the houses bounding it on two sides.

3. The *galerie* seems to have come into general use in the 1740s. In 1751 the plantation owner Jean de Pradel wrote to his brothers in France of his new house, Monplaisir: "It will be one hundred and sixteen feet in length by forty-eight in width, including the galleries which will surround the house. What a great convenience these galleries are in this country!"

4. See J. Evans, *Monastic Architecture in France from the Renaissance to the Revolution* (Cambridge: Cambridge University Press, 1964), figs. 388, 390, 541. The resemblance between the stair at New Orleans and the one at Auberive is striking but can only be coincidental, since the former was retained from the building of 1727–34 and Auberive was not built until circa 1750.

5. The resemblance was more marked before 1847, when the balustrades over the cornices of the Cabildo and Presbytère were removed and mansard roofs added.

**2**   1. J. A. Baird, Jr., *The Churches of Mexico 1530–1810* (Berkeley and Los Angeles: University of California Press, 1962), p. 5.

2. The present woodwork of the *portal* dates from a restoration in 1909.

3. When the friar's house was in the usual position its flat roof could be used as a halfway platform for hoisting the materials for the roof of the church.

4. In 1776, when Fray Dominguez visited and reported on the church, there were three windows in the south wall.

5. Today the effect can still be experienced at Isleta, Trampas, and Ranchos de Taos. Most transverse clerestories have been blocked up at one time or another because of their tendency to leak.

6. The *presidio* church of San Miguel, Santa Fe, is one of the few with eastern sanctuaries; the church at Pecos was another.

7. The *retablo* is dated 1780 in an inscription on the back; the decoration of the walls of the sanctuary is presumably coeval. The murals in the nave must be much later. Similar but less extensive paintings in the nave at Acoma were whitewashed over circa 1970.

8. H. de la Croix, *Military Considerations in City Planning: Fortifications* (New York: Braziller, 1972), p. 44.

9. The churches of the other two missions near San Antonio, San Francisco de la Espada and San Juan Capistrano, have been too thoroughly reconstructed to count as eighteenth-century buildings. The Moorish arch of the

doorway of San Francisco is not without interest, although its voussoirs were "incorrectly reassembled in a restoration." P. Goeldner, *Texas Catalog: Historic American Buildings Survey* (San Antonio: Trinity University Press, 1976), p. 193.

10. For example, the *portadas* of La Valenciana near Guanajuato and of the parish church of Lagos de Moreno in Jalisco; see Baird, *The Churches of Mexico 1530–1810*, plates 153 and 146.

11. It was rebuilt once before, incorrectly, in 1884.

3   1. The best brief account of these books is in R. Wittkower, *Palladio and Palladianism* (New York: George Braziller, 1974), chapter 7.

2. The area had been settled in the seventeenth century by planters from Barbados.

3. For what it really was, see Wittkower, *Palladio and Palladianism*, pp. 79–85.

4. The plan of Coleshill must have crossed the Atlantic be some other means than a book, for it was not published in one until 1771, when it appeared in the continuation of *Vitruvius Britannicus* by J. Woolfe and J. Gandon.

4   1. The portico was not built until 1785–87, and then of wood instead of stone; Harrison's design is said to have been followed faithfully. The balustrade was originally continued around the roof of the nave.

2. The Swanenburch House, Halfweg.

3. "The Capitol is a light and airy structure, with a portico in front of two orders, the lower of which, being Doric, is tolerably just in its proportions and ornaments, save only that the intercolonnations are too large. The upper is Ionic, much too small for that on which it is mounted, its ornaments not proper to the order, nor proportioned within themselves. It is crowned with a pediment, which is too high for its span." (*Notes on the State of Virginia*, p. 152).

4. A "penitentiary house" containing sixteen cells for solitary confinement was built to the rear of Smith's building in 1791

5. Mount Airy was gutted by fire in 1844.

6. The craftsmen who did the decorations in the dining room at Mount Vernon were Lamphier and Sears; they were probably from Philadelphia.

5   1. The detailed treatment of Monticello I was Palladian. The uninterrupted templelike roof between the pediments, its most Neo-Classical feature, had Anglo-Palladian precedent in Colen Campbell's Wanstead, built in 1715–20.

2. Jefferson may also have been influenced by seeing a painting by Hubert Robert ("Robert des Ruines"), *La Réunion des Plus Célèbres Monuments Antiques de la France*, with the Maison Carrée in the foreground, which was exhibited in the Salon du Louvre when he was in Paris in 1785.

3. In 1807 Bulfinch had rebuilt the spire of Old North, blown down in a gale three years before, reducing the total height of the steeple from 191 feet to 175 feet.

4. So called because the first operation with ether used as an anaesthetic was performed in it on October 6, 1846.

**6**  1. He won the Gold Medal at the Royal Academy Schools in 1781 and in 1790 received the first Travelling Scholarship in Architecture awarded by the Academy.

2. As in the Walnut Street Prison, Philadelphia.

3. When it was dedicated in 1821, Baltimore Cathedral lacked its portico, and its east end terminated in an apse, flanked by square rooms, abutting the piers under the dome. The present portico was completed in 1865 by Latrobe's son, John H. B. Latrobe, and the domed choir was added in 1890, in accordance with Latrobe's plan, which had been truncated for reasons of economy. (The choir being equal in length to the nave is one of the clearest evidences of the relationship to Wren's St. Paul's.) The onion domes on the belfries date from 1832 and were not designed by Latrobe.

4. H.-R. Hitchcock, *Architecture: Nineteenth and Twentieth Centuries*, p. 7.

5. The interior was altered radically in 1893.

6. He went first to London, where he spent seven years; his only building there, as well as another in which elements of a competition design by him were incorporated, has been destroyed. In 1827 he returned to France, where he ended his career as Architect of the Department of Mayenne.

7. Mills already had independent commissions when he joined Latrobe, and it was in connection with one of them that Latrobe wrote him a letter which contains a classic description of the situation of the professional architect in America at the time: "The profession of architecture has been hitherto in the hands of two sorts of men. The first, of those, who from travelling or from books have acquired some knowledge of the theory of the art, but know nothing of its practice; the second, of those who know nothing but the practice, and whose early life being spent in labor, and in the habits of a laborious life, have had no opportunity of acquiring the theory. The complaisance of these two sets of men to each other, renders it difficult for the Architect to get in between them, for the building mechanic finds his account in the ignorance of the *Gentleman-architect*, as the latter does in the submissive deportment which interest dictates to the former" (T. F. Hamlin, *Benjamin Henry Latrobe*, p. 586).

**7**  1. Under the head of curvature, only the entasis of the columns of the Parthenon had yet been observed, for the first time in 1810; their inclination—inward, so that their vertical axes meet about a mile above the earth's surface—went unnoticed until 1829, and the curvature of the stylobate and entablature until 1837.

2. An explanation is offered by R. G. Carrott, *The Egyptian Revival*, pp. 120–21.

**8**  1. Assuming that the traditional but apparently undocumented attribution is correct.

2. In the history of architecture as an art, that is. Upjohn also has an important place in the history of the architectural profession. In his office on February 23, 1857, the meeting that led to the founding of The American Institute of Architects was held. Including Upjohn and his son Richard M. Upjohn, fourteen architects were present; twelve more were invited to subsequent meetings, and the institute was incorporated two months later. Upjohn was President of the AIA for its first eighteen years.

3. The most important nineteenth-century technical innovation in building in wood, the balloon frame, was first used for St. Mary's Church, Chicago, by the Connecticut architect and builder A. D. Taylor in 1833. It was unknown in the East until the end of the fifties, when it was described first in a New York newspaper in 1857 and then, with illustrations, in *Carpentry Made Easy* by William Bell (Philadelphia, 1858). In the sixties it was called "Chicago construction." It would be hard to exaggerate the importance of the part that the balloon frame, which required only know-how (as distinct from skill) and lent itself to the prefabrication of buildings, played in the westward movement and the urbanization of the Middle West. But its effect on architectural design was negligible.

4. The first iron-fronted building in America was erected on Washington Street, Boston, in 1842 by Daniel Badger. The Miners' Bank at Pottsville, Pennsylvania, built in 1829 to Haviland's design, was a masonry structure faced with iron plates, like the Narva Triumphal Arch in St. Petersburg, which was completed in 1816, the year in which Haviland left Russia for America. Russia was a leader in iron technology; there was an all-iron house in St. Petersburg by 1765, when it was visited by Casanova (Giacomo Casanova, *History of My Life*, translated and edited by W. R. Trask (New York: Harcourt, Brace & World, 1966–71), X, p. 132). The earliest known iron columns in America are (as already noted) in Christ Church, Washington, completed to Latrobe's design in 1808; in 1820 Strickland used iron columns in the Chestnut Street Theatre, Philadelphia. The first iron roof was also, it would seem, due to Latrobe, who covered Nassau Hall, Princeton, with one in 1803 when he renovated the building after a fire. Iron was also used for fire-proofing. A building in which it proved its worth for this purpose was Mills's Record Office in Charleston, whose window frames, sashes, and shutters of iron, combined with the brick vaults supporting the floors and the copper sheathing of the wooden roof structure, enabled it to survive the fire at the beginning of the Civil War.

**9**    1. Owen Jones published two volumes on the Alhambra (1842 and 1845) before his *Grammar of Ornament* (1856). In 1850–51 he served as color consultant for Paxton's Crystal Palace, whose supports and girders were painted red, yellow, and pale blue.

2. Ruskin's architectural Lamp of Truth did "not admit iron as a constructive material," although, like other mid-Victorians, Ruskin vaguely prophesied "the time is probably near when a new system of architectural laws will be developed, adapted entirely to metallic construction."

3. Charles Eliot Norton, a key member of the building committee, was the first professor of fine art at Harvard (1875–98), just as Ruskin, whom Norton knew well, had been at Oxford. Norton's belief in the idea of collegiate architecture as an influence on youth has its parallel in Jefferson's thoughts in designing the University of Virginia. Despite the enduring effects of architecture, the selected competitors for Memorial Hall were given only twenty-five days in which to prepare their designs. Norton, without giving specific reasons, did not like the final building. Wight and Russell Sturgis would have been more sympathetic architects, but then they were not graduates of Harvard College.

4. Later, in 1864, William Robert Ware opened an *atelier* of his own in Boston. The following year he was asked to form an architectural department at MIT. Actual instruction did not begin until 1868, in Rogers Hall in Boston. The second school of architecture was founded at the University of Illinois in 1867. Subsequently schools were established at Cornell in 1871, Syracuse in 1873, Michigan in 1876, and Columbia in 1880, the last also under Ware.

5. Durand, professor of architecture at the Paris Ecole Polytechnique, published two volumes summarizing French theory and practice (1802–1805). His emphasis on repetition of elements forced a joint clarity of plans and elevations.

**10**   1. The term skyscraper first appeared in print in 1890: "A new system has found much favor here, and is being generally followed now in the construction of mammoth buildings known as 'Sky-scrapers,' which has given Chicago a new celebrity." John J. Flinn, *Chicago: A History, an Encyclopedia and a Guide*, p. 129.

2. The firm name Burnham and Root was not changed until 1894 when it became D. H. Burnham and Co., which it remained until Burnham's death in 1912. In his *Autobiography* Wright tells of Burnham's offer to him of an expense-paid Beaux-Arts training, which Wright refused.

3. Raft foundations proved unreliable. Portions of the Monadnock have settled more than twenty inches. Today's practice is to sink concrete caissons down to bedrock, which in Chicago lies more than 100 feet below ground level. The first use of caissons in Chicago building was under the west party wall of the Chicago Stock Exchange, completed in 1894. William Sooy Smith was the engineer; Adler and Sullivan were the architects. Pneumatic caissons were first developed by English and French engineers in the mid-nineteenth century.

4. The first use of terra-cotta for sheathing a facade was in 1889–90 in Burnham and Root's second Rand McNally Building. It soon became popular for tall buildings everywhere, the Woolworth Building in New York being the largest example.

5. Interior courts were frequent delights in nineteenth-century buildings of all sorts. Some examples are the Palace Hotel in San Francisco (1874–75), the second John Shillito Store in Cincinnati (1878), the Old Pension Building in Washington, D.C. (1883), the thirteen-story Chamber of Commerce Building in Chicago (1888–89), the Brown Palace Hotel in Denver (1892), and the Bradbury Building in Los Angeles (1893).

6. Even before the building was completed Adler and Sullivan moved into the tower, the loftiest office suite in Chicago at that time. Here Frank Lloyd Wright assisted Sullivan on the final decorative details of the Auditorium Building.

7. Holabird and Roche received the 1898 Gage commission for a trio of buildings on South Michigan Avenue, of eight, seven, and six stories. For the tallest, at the north, a millinery establishment, Sullivan was asked to design the facade, which included a four-foot band of translucent glass above the clear glass windows of each grouping to diffuse the glare for the benefit of close needlework. Sullivan's facade was increased in 1902 by the addition of four stories, which were according to the same design as the lower stories.

8. The first use of Chicago construction in New York was in the Tower Building by Bradford Gilbert (1888–89).

9. Prior to 1916 the building code of New York City merely limited the weight of a building on rock foundation to fifteen tons per square foot. On this basis it would have been theoretically possible to erect on a 200-foot square plot an office building 2,000 feet high.

**11**   1. To Wells it was "inconceivable . . . how any civilized architect [could] design in the Romanesque or Gothic styles." The story goes that Wells declined a partnership in the firm saying, with sly humor, that he could not with self-respect sign his name to such mediocre work. Wells served as a draftsman in the firm for ten years. He died in 1889.

2. The French educational model was so highly esteemed that in the following year McKim instigated plans for an architectural study center in Rome. After a trial, the American Academy was founded in 1898 to provide a graduate experience for architects, sculptors, and painters.

3. This vaulting method was introduced to America in 1881 with the arrival of the Spaniard Rafael Guastavino. He had perfected the traditional Catalan tile vault with an improved mortar, essential because the principle of adhesion rather than compression is the source of its strength. Tiles are laid in horizontal layers; centering is not required. McKim, Mead and White used Guastavino vaulting in the Boston Public Library, Madison Square Presbyterian Church, and the rebuilding of Jefferson's library at the University of Virginia.

4. Vaughan never returned to England. From his Boston base he continued to receive commissions for ecclesiastical work, notably St. Paul's School Chapel in Concord, New Hampshire, completed in 1888 (except for the tower), and the Cathedral Church of St. Peter and St. Paul in Washington, D.C., a joint commission received with Bodley in 1907. The cathedral was incomplete at the time of Vaughn's death in 1917 and remains so.

5. Cram was perhaps more the antiquarian than the modern medievalist he claimed to be. He was quite proud that the hammer-beam trusses of his Princeton dining hall had no hidden steel. He advocated, to no avail, Latin for the services in the Princeton chapel and boasted that on his estate he built a chapel first, a garage second.

6. Although never enunciated, there seems to have been an understood apportionment of styles to various sects. Gothic and Colonial were acceptable for Protestants of all types; earlier medieval styles, both Lombard and Tuscan, with a permitted touch of Byzantine, were principally for Roman Catholics; synagogues opted for Moorish and Byzantine combinations. Newer, freer cults were a problem. The Christian Scientists seemed to find most inspiration under a Pantheon-like dome.

**12**   1. Wright was born in 1867 but claimed 1869 in *An Autobiography*, published in 1943. The willful error is perpetuated on his grave marker at Spring Green, Wisconsin.

2. Wright had equal admiration for Dankmar Adler and went out of his way to make known the injustice of underrating Adler's contribution to the firm. (See "Recollections," 10 July 1940, letter from Wright to The Art Institute

of Chicago. Burnham Library, The Art Institute of Chicago.) Wright believed that Adler, not Sullivan, deserved the credit for the dictum form follows function.

3. Wright to Ashbee, 26 September 1910: "Do not say that I deny my love for Japanese art has influenced me—I admit that it has but claim to have digested it—"

4. The discipline of Wright's interlocking forms and geometrical massing has been traced to the Froebel "gifts." These were constructive games of maple blocks and colored papers to be arranged against a linear grid that encouraged an instinctive order in the creative act. See Grant Manson, "Wright in the Nursery: The Influence of Froebel Education on the Work of Frank Lloyd Wright," *Architectural Review* CXIII (June 1953): 114–123.

5. When Wright returned to the United States in 1911, he established himself at Spring Green and began to build Taliesin. He revived his architectural practice using a downtown Chicago office but this ended when he sailed for Japan in the winter of 1915–16 to begin work on the Imperial Hotel.

6. The West Coast, unlike the Midwest, was not given to pronouncements on architecture or essays in print. An exception is the modest book by Charles A. Keeler, *The Simple Home*, San Francisco, 1904. Illustrated were various Berkeley houses, including his own by Maybeck.

**13**  1. Louis Sullivan, "The Chicago Tribune Competition," *Architectural Record* LIII (February 1923): 151–157. Saarinen's proposal was not wholly new; his Helsinki Railroad Station, designed in 1904, incorporated a tower of similar design.

2. In the midst of the Depression most Americans could not afford a Streamline Moderne house, but they might content themselves with household items designed by Raymond Loewy, Russel Wright, Donald Deskey, and Henry Dreyfus.

3. A likely source for the PSFS Building is the Tagblatt Turm in Stuttgart (1927–28) by E. Otto Osswald, which was published in the February 1929 issue of *Architectural Record*.

4. The exhibition and the accompanying catalog did include Wright's work and that of other Americans because a numerical balance between Europeans and Americans was a condition of the museum trustees' approval.

5. A symptom of an impending academic phase of the modern movement was the founding in 1928 of the Congrès Internationaux d'Architecture Moderne (CIAM). Through its meetings and publications it began to codify the loose theories of the twenties.

**14**  1. Promontory Apartments was the first of numerous projects done in association with the developer Herbert Greenwald, whose dedication to Mies places him among the important patrons of modern architecture. He died in 1959 in a plane crash.

2. At a time when temperate glances backward were inadmissible, Johnson freely confessed in print a number of historical sources of inspiration for his glass house. See "House at New Canaan . . ." *Architectural Review* CVIII (September 1950): 152–160.

3. Mies van der Rohe, "Frank Lloyd Wright," 1940. An appreciation written for the unpublished catalog of the Frank Lloyd Wright Exhibition held at the Museum of Modern Art, New York. Reprinted in P. Johnson, *Mies van der Rohe* (New York, 1947): 195–196.

4. In 1913 Wright's son John recommended the sculptor Alfonso Iannelli as an assistant for the Midway Gardens project. Iannelli accepted Wright's offer, leaving San Diego, where he had been working with John Wright, and spent eight months in Chicago alongside of Richard W. Bock, who had previously done sculpture for Wright's Oak Park studio. Together they executed Wright's designs for sculptured figures and four large stair towers for Midway Gardens. Iannelli later regretted that he did not accept Wright's offer to continue with the Imperial Hotel project in Japan, but he did return to the Midwest to collaborate with Purcell and Elmslie and also with Barry Byrne.

5. Wright's solution for urban problems was to eliminate the city altogether by substituting a decentralized, agrarian society. His answer, Broadacre City, was first outlined in his book, *The Disappearing City* (William Farquhar Payson, 1932). A model of Broadacre City was exhibited at Rockefeller Center in New York in April 1935.

6. Knowing Wright's animosity and fearful of his wit, the American Institute of Architects, which Wright had dubbed the "Arbitrary Institute of Appearances," delayed awarding its Gold Medal to him until 1949.

7. The Ralph Jester House design was built in Arizona at Taliesin West in 1972 as a residence for Bruce Pfeiffer, archivist for the Frank Lloyd Wright Foundation. Concrete was substituted for the intended curved plywood walls.

**15**   1. "The Skyline," *New Yorker*, XXIII, October 11, 1947. Mumford's recognition of a Bay Region style was reinforced by a 1949 exhibition entitled "Domestic Architecture of the San Francisco Bay Region," held at the San Francisco Museum of Art.

2. The Eames House is one of a series that constituted the Case Study House program organized by John Entenza, editor of the Los Angeles-based *Arts and Architecture*. Between 1945 and 1962 the magazine acted as client in commissioning houses by such Californians as Pierre Koenig; Craig Ellwood; Buff, Straub and Hensman; and Killingsworth, Brady and Smith.

3. Saarinen was one of four jury members for the international competition of 1956 for the Sydney Opera House. Jorn Utzon's winning entry, while impractical structurally and functionally, was nonetheless chosen for its evocative image of billowing, saillike forms. Utzon's scheme may have influenced Saarinen, who was at work on the TWA design at the time. Yet Saarinen had long been interested in curvilinear shapes, as seen in his plastic shell chair of 1948, the Aspen music tent of 1949, and the St. Louis Jefferson Memorial Arch, designed in 1948 and completed in 1964.

4. Netsch's chapel is the exception to his Miesian architecture at the Air Force Academy. For the chapel at the Illinois Institute of Technology Mies chose to differentiate the design in a comparatively subtle way, substituting brick bearing walls for the steel frame he used elsewhere.

5. Edward Stone began his career in the thirties as an advocate of the International Style. A testimonial example of this is the Museum of Modern

Art in New York of 1939, for which Stone was associated with Philip L. Goodwin.

6. The phrase New Brutalism first appeared in print in December 1953. The first building to which it was applied was the Hunstanton School in England by Peter and Alison Smithson, designed in 1949 and completed in 1954. However, the Hunstanton School is a studiously crude version of Mies van der Rohe's work and is visually unrelated to the raw concrete and exposed brickwork of Le Corbusier's Maisons Jaoul, which became the basis of Brutalism as a style despite its proponents' regard of Brutalism as an ethic rather than an esthetic of building.

7. The beauty of primitive and vernacular buildings, particularly in their village context, was being rediscovered in the late forties and fifties. It was formally acknowledged by an exhibition sponsored by the Museum of Modern Art, the substance of which is contained in *Architecture without Architects* by Bernard Rudofsky (1964). Sympathy for nonpedigreed architecture was indicative of dissatisfaction with formal architecture. Some architects, John Johansen and Frederick Kiesler among them, proposed a revival of the primitive experience by returning to cavelike forms of shelter.

8. Rogers was a consultant and supervising architect for Wellesley College for many years. Day and Klauder were the architects of adjacent Founders and Green Hall.

**16**   1. The slenderizing of curtain-wall mullions together with minimized detailing of the corners and roof lines began in Denmark in two works of Arne Jacobsen: the offices for Jespersen and Sons in Copenhagen and the town hall at Rødovre, both completed in 1956.

2. The city of Columbus, Indiana, is a microcosm of recent architecture. Largely through the patronage of J. Irwin Miller, president of Cummins Engine Company, the Cummins Engine Foundation has paid architectural fees for new schools and other buildings by distinguished architects. The diversity of the sixties and seventies is illustrated by a church by Harry Weese, a library by I. M. Pei, and a school by Mitchell-Giurgola Associates.

3. Because it is largely visible, the steel structure is carefully designed. The major girder, spanning 80 feet between the "silo" supports, is five feet from the recessed glass walls. Secondary beams welded to this girder at 10-foot intervals are exposed inside as well as out. The suggestion of a trellis that shades the glass comes from the Deere and Company Administrative Center at Moline, Illinois (1962–64), designed by Saarinen and executed by Roche and Dinkeloo.

4. The Yale Art Gallery commission was secured by George Howe, who was then chairman of the Department of Architecture, for his former Philadelphia associate. Kahn first came to Yale in 1947 as a visiting critic and remained ten years before returning to Philadelphia to resume practice and hold a professorship at the University of Pennsylvania.

# Sources of Illustrations

*1*  1. Adam Thoroughgood House, Princess Anne County, Virginia. Virginia State Library.

2. Boardman House, Saugus, Massachusetts. Marcus Whiffen.

3. Boardman House, Saugus, Massachusetts. Historical American Building Survey (HABS), Library of Congress. Redrawn by Cynthia Cobb.

4. John Ward House, Salem, Massachusetts. Sandak, Inc.

5. Bacon's Castle, Surry County, Virginia. HABS, Library of Congress.

6. Bacon's Castle, Surry County, Virginia. HABS, Library of Congress. Redrawn by Cynthia Cobb.

7. McIntire Garrison House, Scotland, Maine. HABS, Library of Congress.

8. McIntire Garrison House, Scotland, Maine. HABS, Library of Congress. Redrawn by Cynthia Cobb.

9. Second Meeting House, Sudbury, Massachusetts. Wesleyan University Press.

10. Old Ship Meeting House, Hingham, Massachusetts. Wesleyan University Press.

11. Old Brick Church (St. Luke's), Isle of Wight County, Virginia. Marcus Whiffen.

12. Old Brick Church (St. Luke's), Isle of Wight County, Virginia. HABS, Library of Congress. Redrawn by Cynthia Cobb.

13. Capitol, Williamsburg, Virginia. Colonial Williamsburg Foundation.

14. Stadthuys (City Tavern), New Amsterdam. New-York Historical Society.

15. Dyckman House, New York City. HABS, Library of Congress.

16. Dyckman House, New York City. HABS, Library of Congress. Redrawn by Cynthia Cobb.

17. The Cloister (Klosters), Ephrata, Pennsylvania. HABS, Library of Congress.

18. Cahokia Courthouse, Cahokia, Illinois. HABS, Library of Congress.

19. Parlange, Pointe Coupée Parish, Louisiana. HABS, Library of Congress.

20. Parlange, Pointe Coupée Parish, Louisiana. HABS, Library of Congress. Redrawn by Cynthia Cobb.

21. St. Louis Cathedral, New Orleans, Louisiana. Maryland Historical Society.

22. Cabildo, New Orleans, Louisiana. Marcus Whiffen.

*2*  23. Palace of the Governors, Santa Fe, New Mexico. Marcus Whiffen.

24. San Estevan, Acoma, New Mexico. HABS, Library of Congress.

25. San Estevan, Acoma, New Mexico. HABS, Library of Congress. Redrawn by Cynthia Cobb.

26. Santo Tomás, Trampas, New Mexico. Marcus Whiffen.

27. San Francisco, Ranchos de Taos, New Mexico. Marcus Whiffen.

28. San Francisco, Ranchos de Taos, New Mexico. HABS, Library of Congress. Redrawn by Cynthia Cobb.

29. San José, Laguna, New Mexico. Marcus Whiffen.

30. San José, Laguna, New Mexico. Marcus Whiffen.

31. Castillo de San Marcos (Fort Marion), St. Augustine, Florida. HABS, Library of Congress.

32. Castillo de San Marcos (Fort Marion), St. Augustine, Florida. HABS, Library of Congress. Redrawn by Cynthia Cobb.

33. Nuestra Señora de la Purisima Concepcion de Acuna, San Antonio, Texas. Marcus Whiffen.

34. Nuestra Señora de la Purisima Concepcion de Acuna, San Antonio, Texas. HABS, Library of Congress. Redrawn by Cynthia Cobb.

35. San Antonio de Valero (The Alamo), San Antonio, Texas. HABS, Library of Congress.

36. San José y San Miguel de Aguayo, San Antonio, Texas. Marcus Whiffen.

37. San Xavier del Bac, near Tucson, Arizona. Marcus Whiffen.

38. San Xavier del Bac, near Tucson, Arizona. HABS, Library of Congress. Redrawn by Cynthia Cobb.

39. San Xavier del Bac, near Tucson, Arizona. HABS, Library of Congress.

40. San Carlos Borromeo, Carmel, California. G. E. Kidder Smith, *A Pictorial History of Architecture in America.*

41. San Luis Rey de Francia, near Oceanside, California. Marcus Whiffen.

42. San Luis Rey de Francia, near Oceanside, California. HABS, Library of Congress. Redrawn by Cynthia Cobb.

43. Santa Barbara, Santa Barbara, California. HABS, Library of Congress.

44. Governor's Palace, Williamsburg, Virginia. Colonial Williamsburg Foundation.

45. McPhedris-Warner House, Portsmouth, New Hampshire. Detroit Photographic Company Collection, Library of Congress.

46. College of William and Mary, Williamsburg, Virginia. Colonial Williamsburg Foundation.

47. President's House, College of William and Mary, Williamsburg, Virginia. Colonial Williamsburg Foundation. Redrawn by Cynthia Cobb.

48. Westover, Charles City County, Virginia. Marcus Whiffen.

49. St. James's, Goose Creek, South Carolina. Marcus Whiffen.

50. Christ Church, Lancaster County, Virginia. Marcus Whiffen.

51. St. Philip's, Charleston, South Carolina. Courtesy of The Henry Francis du Pont Winterthur Museum.

52. Old North Church (Christ Church), Boston, Massachusetts. Courtesy of The Society for the Preservation of New England Antiquities.

53. Old North Church (Christ Church), Boston, Massachusetts. G. E. Kidder Smith, *A Pictorial History of Architecture in America.*

54. Old South Meeting House, Boston, Massachusetts. Courtesy of The Society for the Preservation of New England Antiquities.

55. Stratford Hall, Westmoreland County, Virginia. Courtesy of The Robert E. Lee Memorial Association.

56. Stratford Hall, Westmoreland County, Virginia. HABS, Library of Congress. Redrawn by Cynthia Cobb.

57. Whitehall, Newport, Rhode Island. Courtesy of The Preservation Society of Newport County.

58. Westover, Charles City County, Virginia. Marcus Whiffen.

59. Mulberry, St. John's Parish, South Carolina. Carnegie Survey of the Architecture of the South by Frances Benjamin Johnston, Library of Congress.

60. Drayton Hall, Charleston, South Carolina. G. E. Kidder Smith, *A Pictorial History of Architecture in America.*

61. Drayton Hall, Charleston, South Carolina. Carnegie Survey of the Architecture of the South by Frances Benjamin Johnston, Library of Congress.

62. Drayton Hall, Charleston, South Carolina. HABS, Library of Congress. Redrawn by Cynthia Cobb.

63. Old Colony House, Newport, Rhode Island. John Hopf.

64. Christ Church, Philadelphia, Pennsylvania. G. E. Kidder Smith, *A Pictorial History of Architecture in America.*

65. Christ Church, Philadelphia, Pennsylvania. G. E. Kidder Smith, *A Pictorial History of Architecture in America.*

**4** 66. Redwood Library, Newport, Rhode Island. Courtesy of The Preservation Society of Newport County.

67. King's Chapel, Boston, Massachusetts. Sandak, Inc.

68. Brick Market, Newport, Rhode Island. John Hopf.

69. Christ Church, Cambridge, Massachusetts. HABS, Library of Congress.

70. St. Michael's, Charleston, South Carolina. Courtesy of William H. Pierson, Jr.

71. St. Michael's, Charleston, South Carolina. HABS, Library of Congress. Redrawn by Cynthia Cobb.

72. First Baptist Meeting House, Providence, Rhode Island. Sandak, Inc.

73. Shirley Place, Roxbury, Massachusetts. *Old-Time New England.*

74. Shirley Place, Roxbury, Massachusetts. *Old-Time New England.*

75. Carter's Grove, James City County, Virginia. HABS, Library of Congress. Redrawn by Cynthia Cobb.

76. Carter's Grove, James City County, Virginia. Colonial Williamsburg Foundation.

77. Gunston Hall, Fairfax County, Virginia. Courtesy of The Board of Regents, Gunston Hall.

78. Mount Airy, Richmond County, Virginia. Marcus Whiffen.

79. Vassall-Longfellow House, Cambridge, Massachusetts. 1759. HABS, Library of Congress.

80. Whitehall, Anne Arundel County, Maryland. Sandak, Inc.

81. Miles Brewton House, Charleston, South Carolina. Marcus Whiffen.

82. Cliveden, Germantown, Pennsylvania. HABS, Library of Congress.

83. Cliveden, Germantown, Pennsylvania. J. P. Sims and C. Willing, *Old Philadelphia Colonial Details.* Redrawn by Cynthia Cobb.

84. Chase-Lloyd House, Annapolis, Maryland. HABS, Library of Congress.

85. Hammond-Harwood House, Annapolis, Maryland. HABS, Library of Congress.

86. Brandon, Prince George County, Virginia. Marcus Whiffen.

87. Mount Vernon, Fairfax County, Virginia. Courtesy of The Mount Vernon Ladies Association of the Union.

5     88. Monticello I, Albemarle County, Virginia. Courtesy of The Massachusetts Historical Society.

89. Virginia State Capitol, Richmond, Virginia. Virginia State Library.

90. Monticello II, Albemarle County, Virginia. Virginia State Library.

91. University of Virginia, Charlottesville, Virginia. Thomas Jefferson Papers, University of Virginia Library.

92. University of Virginia, Charlottesville, Virginia. Pat Tomich.

93. University of Virginia, Charlottesville, Virginia. Marcus Whiffen.

94. Bremo, Fluvanna County, Virginia. HABS, Library of Congress.

95. Massachusetts State House, Boston, Massachusetts. G. E. Kidder Smith, *A Pictorial History of Architecture in America*.

96. Massachusetts State House, Boston, Massachusetts. Sandak, Inc.

97. New South Church, Boston, Massachusetts. Courtesy of The Society for the Preservation of New England Antiquities.

98. Meeting House, Lancaster, Massachusetts. Marcus Whiffen.

99. Unitarian Church, Wayland, Massachusetts. Marcus Whiffen.

100. The Woodlands, Philadelphia, Pennsylvania. Sandak, Inc.

101. The Woodlands, Philadelphia, Pennsylvania. HABS, Library of Congress. Redrawn by Cynthia Cobb.

102. Gore Place, Waltham, Massachusetts. G. E. Kidder Smith, *A Pictorial History of Architecture in America*.

103. Gore Place, Waltham, Massachusetts. HABS, Library of Congress. Redrawn by Cynthia Cobb.

104. Homewood, Baltimore, Maryland. HABS, Library of Congress.

105. Gardner-Pingree House (Essex Institute), Salem, Massachusetts. Detroit Photographic Company Collection, Library of Congress.

106. Nathaniel Russell House, Charleston, South Carolina. Sandak, Inc.

6     107. United States Capitol, Washington, District of Columbia. Library of Congress.

108. United States Capitol, Washington, District of Columbia. G. Brown, *History of the United States Capitol*. Redrawn by Cynthia Cobb.

109. United States Capitol, Washington, District of Columbia. G. Brown, *History of the United States Capitol*.

110. The Octagon (American Institute of Architects), Washington, District of Columbia. HABS, Library of Congress.

111. Tudor Place, Georgetown, District of Columbia. HABS, Library of Congress.

112. Virginia Penitentiary, Richmond, Virginia. Virginia State Library.

113. Bank of Pennsylvania, Philadelphia, Pennsylvania. Maryland Historical Society.

114. Bank of Pennsylvania, Philadelphia, Pennsylvania. Courtesy of William H. Pierson, Jr. Redrawn by Cynthia Cobb.

115. St. Mary's Cathedral, Baltimore, Maryland. Sandak, Inc.

116. St. Mary's Cathedral, Baltimore, Maryland. Courtesy of William H. Pierson, Jr. Redrawn by Cynthia Cobb.

117. St. Mary's Cathedral, Baltimore, Maryland. Courtesy of William H. Pierson, Jr.

118. State Bank of Louisiana, New Orleans, Louisiana. HABS, Library of Congress.

119. State Bank of Louisiana, New Orleans, Louisiana. HABS, Library of Congress. Redrawn by Cynthia Cobb.

120. New York City Hall, New York. Detroit Photographic Company Collection, Library of Congress.

121. New York City Hall, New York. Sandak, Inc.

122. Unitarian Church, Baltimore, Maryland. Marcus Whiffen.

123. Unitarian Church, Baltimore, Maryland. Engraving by W. Goodacre, Maryland Historical Society.

124. Union College, Schenectady, New York. Courtesy of Union College.

125. Scarborough House, Savannah, Georgia. Carnegie Survey of the Architecture of the South by Frances Benjamin Johnston, Library of Congress.

126. Monumental Church, Richmond, Virginia. Courtesy of William H. Pierson, Jr.

7    127. Second Bank of the United States (Customs House), Philadelphia, Pennsylvania. Marcus Whiffen.

128. Second Bank of the United States (Customs House), Philadelphia, Pennsylvania. HABS, Library of Congress. Redrawn by Cynthia Cobb.

129. Second Bank of the United States (Customs House), Philadelphia, Pennsylvania. Sandak, Inc.

130. Customs House (Federal Hall National Memorial), New York City. National Park Service.

131. Customs House (Federal Hall National Memorial), New York City. HABS, Library of Congress. Redrawn by Cynthia Cobb.

132. Ohio State Capitol, Columbus, Ohio. Wayne Andrews.

133. Tennessee State Capitol, Nashville, Tennessee. G. E. Kidder Smith, *A Pictorial History of Architecture in America.*

134. Tennessee State Capitol, Nashville, Tennessee. HABS, Library of Congress. Redrawn by Cynthia Cobb.

135. St. Paul's, Richmond, Virginia. Marcus Whiffen.

136. Unitarian Church (Stone Temple), Quincy, Massachusetts. Wayne Andrews.

137. Hustings Courthouse, Petersburg, Virginia. Marcus Whiffen.

138. Girard College, Philadelphia, Pennsylvania. Sandak, Inc.

139. Patent Office (National Portrait Gallery), Washington, District of Columbia. HABS, Library of Congress.

140. Providence Arcade, Providence, Rhode Island. Marcus Whiffen.

141. Tremont House, Boston, Massachusetts. W. H. Eliot, *A Description of Tremont House.*

142. Tremont House, Boston, Massachusetts. W. H. Eliot, *A Description of Tremont House.*

143. Lee Mansion, Arlington, Virginia. Virginia State Library.

144. Judge Wilson House, Ann Arbor, Michigan. 1843. Hedrich-Blessing.

145. Judge Wilson House, Ann Arbor, Michigan. HABS, Library of Congress. Redrawn by Cynthia Cobb.

146. Uncle Sam Plantation, St. James Parish, Louisiana. Carnegie Survey of the Architecture of the South by Frances Benjamin Johnston, Library of Congress.

147. Uncle Sam Plantation, St. James Parish, Louisiana. HABS, Library of Congress. Redrawn by Cynthia Cobb.

148. New York City Halls of Justice and House of Detention (The Tombs), New York City. Metropolitan Museum of Art.

8   149. St. Mary's Chapel, Baltimore, Maryland. HABS, Library of Congress.

150. Eastern State Penitentiary, Philadelphia, Pennsylvania. Historical Society of Pennsylvania.

151. Lyndhurst, Tarrytown, New York. G. E. Kidder Smith, *A Pictorial History of Architecture in America.*

152. Lyndhurst, Tarrytown, New York. Metropolitan Museum of Art.

153. Kingscote, Newport, Rhode Island. Courtesy of The Preservation Society of Newport County.

154. Kingscote, Newport, Rhode Island. Upjohn Collection, Avery Architectural Library, Columbia University.

155. Kingscote, Newport, Rhode Island. Courtesy of The Preservation Society of Newport County.

156. Edward King House, Newport, Rhode Island. Courtesy of The Preservation Society of Newport County.

157. Edward King House, Newport, Rhode Island. A. J. Downing, *The Architecture of County Houses.*

158. Morse-Libby House, Portland, Maine. HABS, Library of Congress.

159. Trinity Church, New York City. Municipal Art Society of New York.

160. St. Mary's, Burlington, New Jersey. HABS, Library of Congress.

161. St. James the Less, Philadelphia, Pennsylvania. Courtesy of Phoebe B. Stanton.

162. Emmanuel Church, Cumberland, Maryland. Courtesy of Phoebe B. Stanton.

163. St. John Chrysostom's, Delafield, Wisconsin. HABS, Library of Congress.

164. The Chalet, Newport, Rhode Island. Courtesy of The Preservation Society of Newport County.

165. Old Stone Church, Cleveland, Ohio. HABS, Library of Congress.

166. Smithsonian Institution, Washington, District of Columbia. Detroit Photographic Company Collection, Library of Congress.

167. Athenaeum of Philadelphia, Philadelphia, Pennsylvania. HABS, Library of Congress.

168. Haughwout Store, New York City. Cervin Robinson.

169. Customs House (Post Office), Georgetown, District of Columbia. HABS, Library of Congress.

170. United States Capitol, Washington, District of Columbia. Sandak, Inc.

**9** 171. Boston City Hall, Boston, Massachusetts. HABS, Library of Congress.

172. State, War and Navy Building (Executive Office Building), Washington, District of Columbia. HABS, Library of Congress.

173. All Souls' Unitarian Church, New York City. New-York Historical Society.

174. National Academy of Design, New York City. Museum of the City of New York.

175. Museum of Fine Arts, Boston, Massachusetts. *American Architect and Building News.*

176. Nott Memorial Library (Alumni Hall), Union College, Schenectady, New York. Courtesy of Union College.

177. Church of the Holy Trinity, New York City. The Huntington Library, San Marino, California.

178. Memorial Hall, Harvard University, Cambridge, Massachusetts. Western Reserve Historical Society.

179. Pennsylvania Academy of the Fine Arts, Philadelphia, Pennsylvania. HABS, Library of Congress.

180. Provident Life and Trust Company, Philadelphia, Pennsylvania. Historical Society of Philadelphia.

181. Trinity Church, Boston, Massachusetts. G. E. Kidder Smith, *A Pictorial History of Architecture in America.*

182. Trinity Church, Boston, Massachusetts. Mrs. Schuyler Van Rensselaer, *Henry Hobson Richardson and His Works.*

183. Crane Memorial Library, Quincy, Massachusetts. Sandak, Inc.

184. Crane Memorial Library, Quincy, Massachusetts. Redrawn by Michael Riley.

185. Sever Hall, Harvard University, Cambridge, Massachusetts. The Museum of Modern Art, New York.

186. Allegheny County Court House, Pittsburgh, Pennsylvania. The Museum of Modern Art, New York.

187. Allegheny County Court House, Pittsburgh, Pennsylvania. Redrawn by Pamela Meyer.

188. Marshall Field Wholesale Store, Chicago, Illinois. Chicago Historical Society.

189. Stanford University, Palo Alto, California. Stanford University Archives.

190. Lenox Library, New York City. Museum of the City of New York.

191. W. K. Vanderbilt House, New York City. Brown Brothers.

192. Biltmore, Asheville, North Carolina. HABS, Library of Congress.

**10** 193. Western Union Building, New York City. New-York Historical Society.

194. Tribune Building, New York City. Museum of the City of New York.

195. New York Produce Exchange, New York City. New-York Historical Society.

196. First Leiter Building, Chicago, Illinois. Art Institute of Chicago.

197. Home Insurance Company Building, Chicago, Illinois. Chicago Historical Society.

198. The Rookery, Chicago, Illinois. Author's collection.

199. The Rookery, Chicago, Illinois. Chicago Historical Society.

200. Monadnock Building, Chicago, Illinois. HABS, Library of Congress. Photograph by Jack E. Boucher.

201. Monadnock Building, Chicago, Illinois. Redrawn by Donald L. Looney.

202. Tacoma Building, Chicago, Illinois. Chicago Historical Society.

203. Reliance Building, Chicago, Illinois. Chicago Historical Society.

204. Guaranty Loan Building (New York Metropolitan Life Building), Minneapolis, Minnesota. *Minneapolis Tribune.*

205. Proposal for a twenty-eight-story building. Northwest Architectural Archive, University of Minnesota.

206. Auditorium Theater and Hotel Building, Chicago, Illinois. The Museum of Modern Art, New York.

207. Wainwright Building, St. Louis, Missouri. Hedrich-Blessing.

208. Wainwright Building, St. Louis, Missouri. Redrawn by Gregory Hankins.

209. Guaranty Building (Prudential Building), Buffalo, New York. HABS, Library of Congress.

210. Buildings of the Gage Group, Chicago, Illinois. Chicago Municipal Library.

211. Carson Pirie Scott & Co., Chicago, Illinois. G. E. Kidder Smith, *A Pictorial History of Architecture in America.*

212. Project for Fraternity Temple, Chicago, Illinois. The Museum of Modern Art, New York.

213. American Surety Building, New York City. Museum of the City of New York.

214. Woolworth Building, New York City. G. E. Kidder Smith, *A Pictorial History of Architecture in America.*

*11*    215. Villard Houses, New York City. Museum of the City of New York.

216. Boston Public Library, Boston, Massachusetts. HABS, Library of Congress.

217. Morgan Library, New York City. *A Monograph of the Work of McKim, Mead and White, 1879–1915.*

218. Court of Honor, World's Columbian Exposition, Chicago, Illinois. Chicago Historical Society.

219. Palace of Fine Arts, World's Columbian Exposition, Chicago, Illinois. Philip Turner.

220. Lincoln Monument, Washington, District of Columbia. Library of Congress.

221. Pennsylvania Station, New York City. Redrawn by Gerald Leco, Graciela Lopez, and Stanford Smith.

248. Frederick C. Robie House, Chicago, Illinois. HABS, Library of Congress.

249. Frederick C. Robie House, Chicago, Illinois. *Frank Lloyd Wright: Ausgeführte Bauten.*

250. Larkin Building, Buffalo, New York. *Frank Lloyd Wright: Ausgeführte Bauten.*

251. Unity Temple, Oak Park, Illinois. *Frank Lloyd Wright: Ausgeführte Bauten.*

252. Porter House and Waybur House, San Francisco, California. © Morley Baer, from *Bay Area Houses.*

253. George H. Boke House, Berkeley, California. Charles Keeler, *The Simple Home.*

254. First Church of Christ, Scientist, Berkeley, California. College of Environmental Design, University of California, Berkeley.

255. David B. Gamble House, Pasadena, California. Marvin Rand.

256. David B. Gamble House, Pasadena, California. Redrawn by Georgia Kajer.

257. Walter L. Dodge House, Los Angeles, California. Marvin Rand.

*13*    258. Competition Drawing, Chicago Tribune Tower. *The International Competition for a New Administration Building for the Chicago Tribune MCMXXII.*

259. Tribune Tower, Chicago, Illinois. Hedrich-Blessing.

260. Christ Lutheran Church, Minneapolis, Minnesota. G. E. Kidder Smith, *A Pictorial History of Architecture in America.*

261. Crow Island School, Winnetka, Illinois. Hedrich-Blessing.

262. New York Telephone (Barclay-Vesey) Building, New York City. Cervin Robinson.

263. Chrysler Building, New York City. G. E. Kidder Smith, *A Pictorial History of Architecture in America.*

264. Zoning Envelope Diagrams. Hugh Ferriss, *Pencil Points.*

265. Daily News Building, New York City. Cervin Robinson.

266. Rockefeller Center, New York City. Thomas Airviews, Courtesy of Rockefeller Center, Inc.

267. Johnson Wax Administration Building, Racine, Wisconsin. Marcus Whiffen.

268. Johnson Wax Administration Building, Racine, Wisconsin. Courtesy of Johnson Wax.

269. Schindler-Chase House, Los Angeles, California. Redrawn by Jerome Stastny.

270. Philip Lovell Beach House, Newport Beach, California. Architectural Archives UCSB Art Museum, University of California, Santa Barbara.

271. Philip Lovell House, Los Angeles, California. Julius Shulman.

272. PSFS Building, Philadelphia, Pennsylvania. Redrawn by Ronald James Bartlo.

273. PSFS Building, Philadelphia, Pennsylvania. Courtesy PSFS, Philadelphia.

305. Dulles International Airport, Chantilly, Virginia. Courtesy Revere Copper and Brass.

306. Chapel, United States Air Force Academy, Colorado Springs, Colorado. Courtesy Skidmore, Owings & Merrill.

307. St. Mary's Cathedral, San Francisco, California. Gabriel Moulin Studios.

308. Thomas McNulty House, Lincoln, Massachusetts. Redrawn by Oscar Burgueno.

309. Stuart Pharmaceutical Company, Pasadena, California. Julius Shulman.

310. McGregor Memorial Conference Center, Wayne State University, Detroit, Michigan. Courtesy of Wayne State University.

311. Sheldon Memorial Art Gallery, University of Nebraska, Lincoln, Nebraska. Esto, Ezra Stoller.

312. Lincoln Center for the Performing Arts, New York City. Courtesy of Lincoln Center for the Performing Arts, Inc. Photograph by Bob Serating.

313. Carpenter Visual Arts Center, Harvard University, Cambridge, Massachusetts. Julius Shulman.

314. Boston City Hall, Boston, Massachusetts. G. E. Kidder Smith, *A Pictorial History of Architecture in America.*

315. Art and Architecture Building, Yale University, New Haven, Connecticut. Julius Shulman.

316. Art and Architecture Building, Yale University, New Haven, Connecticut. Courtesy Paul Rudolph.

317. St. John's Abbey Church, Collegeville, Minnesota. Hedrich-Blessing. Courtesy of Marcel Breuer Associates.

318. Mummers Theater, Oklahoma City, Oklahoma. Balthazar Korab.

319. Guild House, Philadelphia, Pennsylvania. Courtesy Venturi and Rauch.

320. Sea Ranch Condominium, Sea Ranch, California. © Morley Baer, from *Bay Area Houses.*

321. Kresge College, University of California, Santa Cruz, G. E. Kidder Smith, *A Pictorial History of Architecture in America.*

**16**   322. Blue Cross-Blue Shield of Maryland, Towson, Maryland. G. E. Kidder Smith, *A Pictorial History of Architecture in America.*

323. Investors Diversified Services Building, Minneapolis, Minnesota. Courtesy Johnson and Burgee, Photograph by Richard W. Payne.

324. Bronx Developmental Center, New York City. Esto, Ezra Stoller.

325. Beinecke Rare Book Library, Yale University, New Haven, Connecticut. G. E. Kidder Smith, *A Pictorial History of Architecture in America.*

326. Marina City, Chicago, Illinois. Redrawn by Alan Maglaughlin.

327. Raymond Hilliard Housing, Chicago, Illinois. Orlando Cabanban.

328. John Hancock Center, Chicago, Illinois. Hedrich-Blessing.

329. Sears Tower, Chicago, Illinois. Orlando Cabanban.

330. Federal Reserve Bank Building, Minneapolis, Minnesota. Balthazar Korab.

331. Gund Hall, Harvard University, Cambridge, Massachusetts. Steve Rosenthal.

332. House in Old Westbury, Long Island, New York. Retoria, Y. Futagawa.

333. Behavioral Science Center, Circle Campus, University of Illinois, Chicago, Illinois. Orlando Cabanban.

334. East Building, National Gallery of Art, Washington, District of Columbia. National Gallery of Art.

335. Christian Science Center, Boston, Massachusetts. G. E. Kidder Smith, *A Pictorial History of Architecture in America.*

336. Knights of Columbus, New Haven, Connecticut, New Haven. G. E. Kidder Smith, *A Pictorial History of Architecture in America.*

337. Veterans Memorial Coliseum, New Haven, Connecticut. G. E. Kidder Smith, *A Pictorial History of Architecture in America.*

338. College Life Insurance Company, Indianapolis, Indiana. Retoria, Y. Futagawa.

339. Richards Medical Research and Biology Buildings, University of Pennsylvania, Philadelphia, Pennsylvania, John Lautman.

340. Richards Medical Research and Biology Buildings, University of Pennsylvania, Philadelphia, Pennsylvania. Redrawn by Henry C. Mahlstedt.

341. Salk Institute of Biological Studies, La Jolla, California. Jim Cox.

342. First Unitarian Church, Rochester, New York. John Ebstel.

343. First Unitarian Church, Rochester, New York. Redrawn by Jeffrey Sessions.

344. Library, Phillips Exeter Academy, Exeter, New Hampshire. Photograph by Herndon Associates with permission of the Trustees of Phillips Exeter Academy.

345. Kimbell Art Museum, Fort Worth, Texas. Courtesy of Kimbell Art Museum. Photograph by Bob Wharton.

# Select Bibliography

Books published before 1895 are not included in this bibliography. Refer to H.-R. Hitchcock, *American Architectural Books: A List of Books, Portfolios and Pamphlets Published in America before 1895 on Architecture and Related Subjects* for a complete bibliographical listing of these books. A comprehensive bibliography of writings on the period covered in part I is F. J. Roos, Jr., *Bibliography of Early American Architecture: Writings on Architecture Constructed Before 1860 in Eastern and Central United States* (Urbana: University of Illinois Press, 1968). For part II there are the guides to information sources by L. Wodehouse, *American Architects from the Civil War to the First World War* (Detroit: Gale Research Company, 1976) and *American Architects from the First World War to Present* (Detroit: Gale Research Company, 1977).

Adams, E. B., and Chavez, F. A., editors. *The Missions of New Mexico, 1776: A Description by Fray Francisco Atanasio Dominguez with Other Contemporary Documents.* Albuquerque: University of New Mexico Press, 1956. Reprinted in 1975.

Adams, W. H., editor. *Jefferson and the Arts: An Extended View.* Washington, D.C.: National Gallery of Art, 1976.

Alexander, R. *The Architecture of Maximilian Godefroy.* Baltimore: Johns Hopkins University Press, 1975.

American Philosophical Society. *Historic Philadelphia from the Founding until the Early Nineteenth Century.* Issued as Vol. XLIII, Part 1, of the *Transactions* of the American Philosophical Society, 1953.

Andrews, W. "Alexander Jackson Davis." *Architectural Review* CIX (May 1951): 307–312.

Andrews, W. *Architecture, Ambition, and Americans.* New York: Free Press, 1947. Revised edition, 1978.

Architectural Book Publishing Company. *A Monograph of the Work of McKim, Mead and White.* 4 vols. New York, 1915–25.

Baigell, M. "James Hoban and the First Bank of the United States." *Journal of the Society of Architectural Historians [JSAH]* XXVIII (May 1969): 135–136.

Baigell, M. "John Haviland in Philadelphia 1818–1826." *JSAH* XXV (October 1966): 197–208.

Baldwin, C. C. *Stanford White.* New York, 1931. Reprinted by Da Capo Press, New York, 1971.

Banham, R. *The Architecture of the Well-Tempered Environment.* Chicago: University of Chicago Press, 1973.

Beirne, R. R., and Scarff, J. H. *William Buckland, 1734–1774, Architect of Virginia and Maryland.* Annapolis: Maryland Historical Society, 1958.

Bridenbaugh, C. *Peter Harrison: First American Architect.* Chapel Hill: University of North Carolina Press, 1949.

Briggs, M. S. *The Homes of the Pilgrim Fathers in England and America.* London and New York: Oxford University Press, 1932.

Brooks, H. A. *The Prairie School: Frank Lloyd Wright and His Midwest Contemporaries.* Toronto: University of Toronto Press, 1972.

Brown, G. *History of the United States Capitol.* 2 volumes. Washington: Government Printing Office, 1900, 1902.

Burchard, J., and Bush-Brown, A. *The Architecture of America: A Social and Cultural History.* Boston: Little, Brown and Co., 1961.

Burnham, A. "The New York Architecture of Richard Morris Hunt." *JSAH* XI (May 1952): 9–14.

Cardwell, K. H. *Bernard Maybeck: Artisan, Architect, Artist.* Santa Barbara and Salt Lake City: Peregrine Smith, 1977.

Carrott, R. G. *The Egyptian Revival: Its Sources, Monuments, and Meaning.* Berkeley: University of California Press, 1978.

Carter, P. *Mies van der Rohe at Work.* New York: Praeger, 1974.

*Chicago Tribune. The International Competition for a New Administration Building for the Chicago Tribune MCMXXII.* Chicago, 1923.

Christ-Janer, A. *Eliel Saarinen.* Chicago: University of Chicago Press, 1948. Reprinted in 1979.

Condit, C. W. *American Building: Materials and Techniques from the Beginning of the Colonial Settlements to the Present.* Chicago: University of Chicago Press, 1969.

Condit, C. W. *The Chicago School of Architecture.* Chicago: University of Chicago Press, 1964.

Cook, J. *The Architecture of Bruce Goff.* New York: Harper and Row, 1978.

Cook, J. W., and Klotz, H. *Conversations with Architects.* New York: Praeger, 1973.

Coolidge, J. *Mill and Mansion: A Study of Architecture and Society in Lowell, Massachusetts, 1820–1865.* New York: Russell and Russell, 1942.

Coolidge, J. "Peter Harrison's First Design for King's Chapel, Boston." In *De Artibus Opuscula XL: Essays in Honor of Erwin Panofsky,* edited by M. Meiss, pp. 64–75. New York: New York University Press, 1961.

Cortissoz, R. *Monograph of the Work of Charles A. Platt.* New York: Architectural Book Publishing Company, 1913.

Cummings, A. L. "The Foster-Hutchinson House." *Old-Time New England* LIV (January–March 1964): 59–76.

Cummings, A. L. *The Framed Houses of Massachusetts Bay, 1625–1725.* Cambridge: Harvard University Press, 1979.

Danz, E. *Architecture of Skidmore, Owings & Merrill, 1950–1962.* New York: Praeger, 1963.

Donnelly, M. C. *The New England Meeting House of the Seventeenth Century.* Middletown, Conn.: Wesleyan University Press, 1968.

Dorsey, S. P. *Early English Churches in America 1607–1807.* New York: Oxford University Press, 1952.

Downing, A., and Scully, V. J., Jr. *The Architectural Heritage of Newport, Rhode Island.* Cambridge: Harvard University Press, 1952. Second edition published by Clarkson N. Potter, New York, 1970.

Drexler, A., editor. *The Architecture of the Ecole des Beaux-Arts.* New York: Museum of Modern Art, 1977.

Early, J. *Romanticism and American Architecture.* New York: A. S. Barnes, 1965.

Eaton, L. K. *Landscape Artist in America: the Life and Work of Jens Jensen.* Chicago: University of Chicago Press, 1964.

Edgell, G. H. *The American Architecture of Today.* New York: C. Scribner's Sons, 1928. Reprinted by AMS Press.

Ferriss, H. *The Metropolis of Tomorrow.* New York: I. Washburn, 1929.

Fitch, J. M. *American Building: The Historical Forces that Shaped It.* Boston: Houghton Mifflin Co., 1966. Second edition published by Schocken Books, New York, 1973.

Fitch, J. M. *Walter Gropius.* New York: George Braziller, 1960.

Floyd, M. H. "A Terra-Cotta Cornerstone for Copley Square: Museum of Fine Arts, Boston, 1870–1876, by Sturgis and Brigham." *JSAH* XXXII (May 1973): 83–103.

Forman, H. C. *The Architecture of the Old South.* Cambridge: Harvard University Press, 1948. Reprinted by Russell and Russell, 1969.

Frary, I. T. *Early Homes of Ohio.* Richmond: Garrett and Massie, 1936.

Frary, I. T. *Thomas Jefferson, Architect and Builder.* Richmond: Garrett and Massie, 1950.

Y. Futagawa, editor. *Kevin Roche, John Dinkeloo and Associates 1962–1975.* New York: Architectural Book Publishing Company, 1977.

Gallagher, H. M. P. *Robert Mills, Architect of the Washington Monument.* New York: Columbia University Press, 1935. Reprinted by AMS Press, 1975.

Garvan, A. N. B. *Architecture and Town Planning in Colonial Connecticut.* New Haven: Yale University Press, 1951.

Gebhard, D. *Schindler.* New York: Viking Press, 1971.

Giedion S. *Space, Time and Architecture.* Cambridge: Harvard University Press, 1946. Fifth revised and enlarged edition, 1979.

Gilchrist, A. A. "Additions to *William Strickland, Architect and Engineer, 1788–1854.* Supplement to *JSAH* XIII (October 1954).

Gilchrist, A. A. "John McComb, Sr. and Jr., in New York, 1784–1799." *JSAH* XXXI (March 1972): 10–21.

Gowans, A. *Images of American Living: Four Centuries of Architecture and Furniture as Cultural Expression.* Philadelphia: Lippincott, 1964.

Granger, A. H. *Charles Follen McKim: A Study of His Life and Work.* Boston: Houghton Mifflin Company, 1913.

Grube, O. W.; Pran, P. C.; and Schultz, F. *One Hundred Years of Architecture in Chicago.* Chicago: Follett, 1976.

Hamlin, T. F. *Benjamin Henry Latrobe.* New York: Oxford University Press, 1955.

Hamlin, T. F. *Greek Revival Architecture in America.* New York: Oxford University Press, 1944.

Heyer, P. *Architects on Architecture.* New York: Walker & Co., 1966.

Hines, T. S. *Burnham of Chicago: Architect and Planner.* New York: Oxford University Press, 1974.

Hitchcock, H.-R. *American Architectural Books: A List of Books, Portfolios and Pamphlets Published in America before 1895 on Architecture and Related Subjects.* Minneapolis: University of Minnesota, 1965.

Hitchcock, H.-R. *The Architecture of H. H. Richardson and His Times.* New York: Museum of Modern Art, 1936. Revised edition published by Anchor Books, Hamden, 1961.

Hitchcock, H.-R. *Architecture: Nineteenth and Twentieth Centuries.* London and Baltimore: Penguin Books, 1958. Fourth edition, 1977.

Hitchcock, H.-R. *Rhode Island Architecture.* Providence: Rhode Island Museum Press, 1939.

Hitchcock, H.-R. "Ruskin and American Architecture, or Regeneration Long Delayed." In *Concerning Architecture,* edited by J. Summerson, pp. 166–208. London and Baltimore: Allen Lane, 1968.

Hitchcock, H.-R., and Johnson, P. *The International Style: Architecture since 1922.* New York: W. W. Norton and Company, 1932.

Hitchcock, H.-R., and Seale, W. *Temples of Democracy: The State Capitols of the U.S.A.* New York: Harcourt Brace Jovanovich, 1976.

Hoffmann, D. *The Architecture of John Wellborn Root.* Baltimore: Johns Hopkins University Press, 1973.

Jacobus, J. *Twentieth-century Architecture: The Middle Years 1940–65.* New York: Praeger, 1966.

Jencks, C. A. *The Language of Post-Modern Architecture.* New York: Rizzoli, 1977.

Johnson, P. *Mies van der Rohe.* New York: Museum of Modern Art, 1947.

Johnson, P. *Writings.* New York: Oxford University Press, 1979.

Johnston, N. B. "John Haviland, Jailor to the World." *JSAH* XXIII (May 1964): 101–106.

Hunter, W. H., Jr., editor. *The Architecture of Baltimore: a Pictorial History.* Baltimore: Peale Museum, 1953.

Jordy, W. H. *American Buildings and Their Architects: The Impact of European Modernism in the Mid-Twentieth Century,* Vol. 4. Garden City, N.Y.: Doubleday & Co., 1976.

Jordy, W. H. *American Buildings and Their Architects: Progressive and Academic Ideals at the Turn of the Century,* Vol. 3. Garden City, N.Y.: Doubleday & Co., 1976.

Jordy, W. H. "Veterans Memorial Coliseum, New Haven, Connecticut." *Architectural Review* CLIII (April 1973): 228–232.

Kaufmann, E., Jr., editor. *The Rise of an American Architecture.* New York: Praeger in association with the Metropolitan Museum of Art, 1970.

Kelly, J. F. *Early Connecticut Meetinghouses.* New York: Columbia University Press, 1948.

Kelly, J. F. *The Early Domestic Architecture of Connecticut.* New Haven: Yale University Press, 1924.

Kimball, S. F. *American Architecture.* Indianapolis and New York, 1928.

Kimball, S. F. *Domestic Architecture of the American Colonies and of the Early Republic.* New York: C. Scribner's Sons, 1922. Reprinted by Dover Publications, 1966.

Kimball, S. F. "Gunston Hall." *JSAH* XIII (May 1954): 3–8.

Kimball, S. F. "Jefferson and the Public Buildings of Virginia: I—Williamsburg, 1770–1776." *Huntington Library Quarterly* XII (February 1949): 115–120.

Kimball, S. F. "Jefferson and the Public Buildings of Virginia: II—Richmond, 1779–1780." *Huntington Library Quarterly* XII (May 1949): 303–310.

Kimball, S. F. *Mr. Samuel McIntire, Carver, Architect of Salem.* Portland: The Southworth-Anthoensen Press, 1940.

Kimball, S. F. *Thomas Jefferson, Architect.* Boston: Riverside Press, 1916.

Kirker, H. *The Architecture of Charles Bulfinch.* Cambridge: Harvard University Press, 1977.

Komendant, A. E. *Eighteen Years with Architect Louis I. Kahn.* Englewood, N.J.: Aloray, 1975.

Kramer, E. W. "Detlef Lienau, An Architect of the Brown Decades." *JSAH* XIV (March 1955): 18–25.

Krinsky, C. H. *Rockefeller Center.* New York: Oxford University Press, 1978.

Kubler, G. *The Religious Architecture of New Mexico in the Colonial Period and Since the American Occupation.* Colorado Springs: Taylor Museum, 1940. Fourth edition published by the University of New Mexico Press, 1972.

Lancaster, C. *The Japanese Influence in America.* New York: W. H. Rawle, 1963.

Lancaster, C. "New York City Hall Stair Rotunda Reconsidered." *JSAH* XXIX (March 1970): 33–39.

Landy, J. *The Architecture of Minard Lafever.* New York: Columbia University Press, 1970.

Lehmann, K. *Thomas Jefferson, American Humanist.* New York: Macmillan Co., 1947.

Lockwood, C. "The Italianate Dwelling House in New York City." *JSAH* XXXI (May 1972): 141–151.

Maginnis, C. *The Work of Cram and Ferguson.* New York: Pencil Points Press, 1929.

Manson, G. C. *Frank Lloyd Wright to 1910: The First Golden Age.* New York: Reinhold, 1958.

Makinson, R. L. *Greene and Greene: Architecture as a Fine Art.* Salt Lake City and Santa Barbara: Peregrine Smith, 1977.

McCallum, I. R. M. *Architecture, U.S.A.* London: Architectural Press, 1959.

McCoy, E. *Five California Architects.* New York: Reinhold, 1960.

McCoy, E. *Richard Neutra.* New York: George Braziller, 1960.

McHale, J. *Buckminster Fuller.* New York: George Braziller, 1962.

McKee, H. J. "St. Michael's Church, Charleston, 1752–1762: Some Notes on Materials and Construction." *JSAH* XXIII (March 1964): 39–42.

Meeks, C. L. V. "Henry Austin and the Italian Villa." *Art Bulletin* (June 1948): 145–149.

Meeks, C. L. V. *The Railroad Station.* New Haven: Yale University Press, 1956.

Meeks, C. L. V. "Romanesque before Richardson in the United States." *Art Bulletin* XXXV (March 1953): 17–33.

Mendelsohn, E. *Amerika: Bilderbuch eines Architekten.* Berlin: R. Mosse, 1926.

Metcalf, P. "Boston Before Bulfinch: Harrison's King's Chapel." *JSAH* XIII (March 1954): 11–14.

Michels, E. "Late Nineteenth Century Published American Perspective Drawing." *JSAH* XXXI (December 1972): 291–308.

Middleton, W. D. *Grand Central . . . The World's Greatest Railway Terminal,* San Marino, Calif.: Golden West Book, 1977.

Miller, J., II. "The Designs for the Washington Monument in Baltimore." *JSAH* XXIII (March 1964): 19–28.

Moholy-Nagy, S. *The Architecture of Paul Rudolph.* New York: Praeger, 1970.

Moore, C. *The Life and Times of Charles Follen McKim.* Boston: Houghton Mifflin, 1929.

Moore, C.; Allen, G.; and Lyndon, D. *The Place of Houses.* New York: Holt, Rinehart & Winston, 1974.

Morrison, H. S. *Early American Architecture from the First Colonial Settlement to the National Period.* New York: Oxford University Press, 1952.

Morrison, H. S. *Louis Sullivan: Prophet of Modern Architecture.* New York: Museum of Modern Art, 1935. Reprinted by Greenwood Press, Westport, 1971.

Mujica, F. *History of the Skyscraper.* New York: Archaeology and Architecture Press, 1930.

Mumford, L. *The Brown Decades.* New York: Harcourt, Brace and Company, 1931. Second revised edition published by Dover Publications, New York, 1955.

Mumford, L. *Roots of Contemporary American Architecture.* New York: Reinhold, 1952. Second edition republished with updated biographical sketches by Dover Publications, New York, 1972.

Mumford, L. *The South in Architecture.* New York: Harcourt, Brace and Company, 1941.

Mumford, L. *Sticks and Stones.* New York: Boni and Liveright, 1924. Second revised edition published by Dover Publications, New York, 1955.

Museum of Modern Art. *Modern Architecture: International Exhibition.* New York, 1932.

Nelson, G. *The Industrial Architecture of Albert Kahn.* New York: Architectural Book Publishing Company, 1939.

Neutra, R. *Wie Baut Amerika.* Stuttgart: J. Hoffman, 1927.

Newcomb, R. *Architecture in Old Kentucky.* Urbana: University of Illinois Press, 1953.

Newcomb, R. *Architecture of the Old North-West Territory.* Chicago: University of Chicago Press, 1950.

Newcomb, R. *The Old Mission Churches and Historic Houses of California.* Philadelphia and London: J. B. Lippincott Company, 1925.

Newton, R. H. *Town & Davis, Architects.* New York: Columbia University Press, 1942.

Nichols, F. D. *The Early Architecture of Georgia.* Chapel Hill: University of North Carolina Press, 1957.

Noffsinger, J. P. *The Influence of the Ecole des Beaux-Arts on the Architects of the United States.* Washington: Catholic University of America Press, 1955.

Norton, P. F. *Latrobe, Jefferson, and the National Capitol.* New York: Garland Publishing, 1977.

O'Gorman, J. F. *The Architecture of Frank Furness.* Philadelphia: Philadelphia Museum of Art, 1973.

O'Gorman, J. F. *Henry Hobson Richardson and his Office.* Cambridge: MIT Press, 1974.

Orr, C. *Addison Mizner: Architect of Dreams and Realities.* Palm Beach: The Gallery, 1977.

Park, H. *A List of Architectural Books Available in America Before the Revolution.* Los Angeles: Hennessey & Ingalls, 1973.

Perrin, R. W. E. "'Fachwerkbau' Houses in Wisconsin." *JSAH* XVIII (March 1959): 29–33.

Peterson, C. E., editor. *Building Early America.* Radnor: Chilton Book Company, 1976.

Pickens, B. "Mr. Jefferson as a Revolutionary Architect." *JSAH* XXXIV (December 1975): 257–279.

Pickens, B. "Wyatt's Pantheon, the State House in Boston and a New View of Bulfinch." *JSAH* (May 1970): 124–131.

Pierson, W. H., Jr. *American Buildings and Their Architects: The Colonial and Neo-Classical Styles*, Vol. 1. Garden City, N.Y.: Doubleday & Co., 1970.

Pierson, W. H., Jr. *American Buildings and Their Architects: The Corporate and Early Gothic Styles*, Vol. 2. Garden City, N.Y.: Doubleday & Co., 1978.

Place, C. A. *Charles Bulfinch, Architect and Citizen.* Boston and New York: Houghton Mifflin, 1925.

Portman, J. C., Jr., and Barnett, J. *The Architect as Developer.* New York: McGraw-Hill Book Co., 1976.

Pratt, R. *David Adler: The Architect and his Work.* New York: M. Evans & Co., 1971.

Randall, F. A. *A History of the Development of Building Construction in Chicago.* Urbana: University of Illinois Press, 1949.

Robinson, C., and Bletter, R. H. *Skyscraper Style: Art Deco.* New York: Oxford University Press, 1975.

Roper, L. W. *FLO: A Biography of Frederick Law Olmsted.* Baltimore: Johns Hopkins University Press, 1974.

Rose, H. W. *The Colonial Houses of Worship in America.* New York: Hastings House, 1963.

Roth, L. M. *The Architecture of McKim, Mead and White, 1870–1920, A Building List.* New York: Garland Publishing, 1978.

Rutledge, A. W. "The Second St. Philip's, Charleston, 1710–1835." *JSAH* XVIII (October 1959): 112–114.

Saarinen, A. B., editor. *Eero Saarinen on His Work.* New Haven: Yale University Press, 1962.

Schless, N. H. "Dutch Influence on the Governor's Palace, Williamsburg." *JSAH* XXVIII (December 1969): 254–270.

Schless, N. H. "Peter Harrison, the Touro Synagogue, and the Wren City Church." *Winterthur Portfolio 8* (1973): 187–200.

Schuyler, M. *American Architecture and Other Writings.* W. H. Jordy and R. Coe, editors. 2 vols. Cambridge: Harvard University Press, 1961.

Scully, V. J., Jr. *American Architecture and Urbanism.* New York: Praeger, 1969.

Scully, V. J., Jr. *Frank Lloyd Wright.* New York: George Braziller, 1960.

Scully, V. J., Jr. *Louis I. Kahn.* New York: George Braziller, 1962.

Scully, V. J., Jr. *Modern Architecture: The Architecture of Democracy.* New York: George Braziller, 1961.

Scully, V. J., Jr. "Romantic Rationalism and the Expression of Structure in Wood: Downing, Wheeler, Gardner, and the 'Stick Style,' 1840–1876." *Art Bulletin* XXXV (June 1953): 121–142.

Scully, V. J., Jr. *The Shingle Style.* New Haven: Yale University Press, 1955.

Shurtleff, H. R. *The Log Cabin Myth.* Cambridge: Harvard University Press, 1939.

Smith, G. E. K. *A Pictorial History of Architecture in America.* 2 vols. New York: W. W. Norton & Co., 1976.

Smith, N. K. *Frank Lloyd Wright: A Study in Architectural Content.* Englewood Cliffs: Prentice-Hall, 1966.

Stanton, P. B. *The Gothic Revival and American Church Architecture.* Baltimore: Johns Hopkins University Press, 1968.

Stebbins, T. E., Jr. "Richardson and Trinity Church: The Evolution of a Building." *JSAH* XXVII (December 1968): 281–298.

Stern, R. A. M. *George Howe: Toward a Modern American Architecture.* New Haven: Yale University Press, 1975.

Stickley, G. *Craftsman Homes.* New York: The Craftsman Publishing Company, 1909.

Stillman, D. "New York City Hall: Competition and Execution." *JSAH* XXIII (October 1964): 129–142.

Stoddard, R. "A Reconstruction of Charles Bulfinch's First Federal Street Theater, Boston." *Winterthur Portfolio 6* (1970).

Stoney, S. G. *Plantations of the Carolina Low Country.* Charleston: The Carolina Art Association, 1938.

Sturges, W. K. "Arthur Little and the Colonial Revival." *JSAH* XXXII (May 1973): 147–163.

Sullivan, L. H. *The Autobiography of an Idea.* New York: W. W. Norton and Company, 1924. Reprinted by P. Smith, New York, 1949.

Sullivan, L. H. "The Chicago Tribune Competition." *Architectural Record* LIII (February 1923): 151–157.

Sullivan, L. H. *Kindergarten Chats and Other Writings.* New York: Wittenborn, Schultz, 1947.

Summerson, J. N. *Architecture in Britain 1530 to 1830.* London and Baltimore: Penguin Books, 1953. Sixth revised edition, 1977.

Sweeney, R. L. *Frank Lloyd Wright: An Annotated Bibliography.* Los Angeles: Hennessey & Ingalls, 1978.

Tallmadge, T. E. *Architecture in Old Chicago.* Chicago: University of Chicago Press, 1941.

Tallmadge, T. E. *The Story of Architecture in America.* New York: W. W. Norton and Company. Enlarged and revised edition, 1936.

Tatum, G. B. *Penn's Great Town: 250 Years of Philadelphia Architecture.* Philadelphia: University of Pennsylvania Press, 1961.

Taut, B. *Modern Architecture.* London: The Studio, 1929.

Torres, L. "Federal Hall Revisited." *JSAH* XXIX (December 1970): 327–338.

Torres, L. "John Frazee and the New York Custom House." *JSAH* XXII (October 1964): 143–150.

Tselos, D. "The Enigma of Buffington's Skyscraper." *Art Bulletin* XXVI (March 1944): 3–12.

Tselos, D. "Exotic Influences in the Architecture of Frank Lloyd Wright." *Magazine of Art* XLVI (April 1953): 160–169, 184.

Tunnard, C., and Reed, H. H. *American Skyline.* Boston: Houghton Mifflin, 1955.

Turner, P. V. *The Founders and the Architects: The Design of Stanford University.* Palo Alto: Department of Art, Stanford University, 1976.

Upjohn, E. M. *Richard Upjohn, Architect and Churchman.* New York: Columbia University Press, 1939.

Van Brunt, H. *Architecture and Society: Collected Essays of Henry Van Brunt.* Cambridge: Harvard University Press, 1969.

Van Derpool, J. G. "The Restoration of St. Luke's, Smithfield, Virginia." *JSAH* XVIII (March 1958): 12–18.

Van Zanten, D. T. "Jacob Wrey Mould: Echoes of Owen Jones and the High Victorian Styles in New York, 1853–1865." *JSAH* XXVIII (March 1969): 41–57.

Venturi, R. *Complexity and Contradiction in Architecture.* New York: Museum of Modern Art, 1966. Revised edition, 1977.

Waterman, T. T. *The Dwellings of Colonial America.* Chapel Hill: University of North Carolina Press, 1950.

Waterman, T. T. *The Mansions of Virginia.* Chapel Hill: University of North Carolina Press, 1946.

Waterman, T. T., and Barrows, J. A. *Domestic Colonial Architecture of Tidewater Virginia.* New York: C. Scribner's Sons, 1932.

Weisman, W. "The Commercial Architecture of George B. Post." *JSAH* XXXI (October 1972): 176–203.

Weisman, W. "Commercial Palaces of New York: 1845–1875." *Art Bulletin* XXXVI (December 1954): 285–302.

Weslager, C. A. *The Log Cabin in America: From Pioneer Days to the Present.* New Brunswick: Rutgers University Press, 1969.

Whiffen, M. *American Architecture Since 1780: A Guide to the Styles.* Cambridge: MIT Press, 1969.

Whiffen, M. "The Early County Courthouses of Virginia," *JSAH* XVIII (March 1959): 1–10.

Whiffen, M. *The Eighteenth-Century Houses of Williamsburg, Colonial Capital of Virginia.* Williamsburg: Colonial Williamsburg, 1960.

Whiffen, M. *The Public Buildings of Williamsburg, Colonial Capital of Virginia.* Williamsburg: Colonial Williamsburg, 1958.

Whiffen, M. "Some Virginia House Plans Reconsidered." *JSAH* XVI (May 1957): 17–19.

Whitaker, C. H., editor. *Bertram Grosvenor Goodhue, Architect and Master of Many Arts.* New York: Press of the American Institute of Architects, 1925.

White, T. B. *Paul Philippe Cret: Architect and Teacher.* Philadelphia: Art Alliance Press, 1974.

White, T. B., editor. *Philadelphia Architecture in the Nineteenth Century.* Philadelphia: University of Pennsylvania Press, 1953.

Wight, P. B. "Reminiscences of Russell Sturgis." *Architectural Record* XXVI (August 1909): 123–131.

Wilson, S., Jr. "Louisiana Drawings by Alexandre de Batz." *JSAH* XXII (May 1963): 75–89.

Wilson, S., Jr. "Religious Architecture in French Colonial Louisiana." *Winterthur Portfolio 8* (1973): 63–106.

Wilson, S., Jr., and Huber, L. V. *The Cabildo on Jackson Square.* New Orleans: Friends of the Cabildo, 1970.

Withey, H. F., and Rathburn, E. *Biographical Dictionary of American Architects (Deceased).* Los Angeles: New Age Publishing Company, 1956.

Wodehouse, L. "Alfred B. Mullett and his French Style Government Buildings." *JSAH* XXXI (March 1972): 22–37.

Wodehouse, L. "Ammi Burnham Young, 1798–1874." *JSAH* XXV (December 1966): 268–286.

Woodbridge, S., editor. *Bay Area Houses.* New York: Oxford University Press, 1976.

Wrenn, G. L. "'A Return to Solid and Classical Principles,' Arthur D. Gilman, 1859." *JSAH* XX (December 1961): 191–193.

Wright, F. L. *Ausgeführte Bauten und Entwürfe von Frank Lloyd Wright*. Berlin: Wasmuth, 1910. Reprinted as *Buildings, Plans and Designs*, Horizon Press, 1963. Also as *Studies and Executed Buildings by Frank Lloyd Wright*, Prairie School Press, 1975.

Wright, F. L. *An Autobiography*. London and New York: Longmans, Green and Company, 1932. Second edition published by Duell, Sloan and Pearce, New York, 1943.

Wright, F. L. *Frank Lloyd Wright: Ausgeführte Bauten*. Berlin: Wasmuth, 1911. Reprinted as *Frank Lloyd Wright: The Early Work*, Horizon Press, 1968.

# Index